SINICA LEIDENSIA

EDIDIT

INSTITUTUM SINOLOGICUM LUGDUNO BATAVUM

Vol. XVII

REMNANTS OF CH'IN LAW

REMNANTS OF CH'IN LAW

An annotated translation of the Ch'in legal and administrative rules of the 3rd century B.C. discovered in Yün-meng Prefecture, Hu-pei Province, in 1975

BY

A.F.P. HULSEWÉ

LEIDEN
E.J. BRILL
1985

Published with financial support from the Netherlands Organization for the Advancement of Pure Research (Z.W.O.)

ISBN 90 04 07103 2

PRINTED IN THE NETHERLANDS BY E. J. BRILL

CONTENTS

PREFACE

When, after having moved to Switzerland, I had at last again time to spend behind my desk, I started on preparatory work for a long neglected task: the writing of the second volume of the *Remnants of Han law*, published more than twenty years earlier. But when in the summer of 1976 the Ch'in laws and regulations were published I put the work on this second volume aside and began with the study of this new material; after all, the Han had taken over the Ch'in legislation, and in studying this, I would also be working on Han law. Since then, six years have gone by, and for the time being my work on the Ch'in laws in finished. For the time being, because studies concerning these laws continue to appear, throwing new light on obscure passages in these difficult texts, with the result that before long I may be obliged to publish a list of corrections.

It must be said that these texts are difficult. No legal text in any language is easy, but the Chinese technical jargon of the 3rd century B.C. is particularly hard to understand. My experience with Han law was of some help, but nevertheless, translating often remained a process of trial and error and a complete(?) understanding was only reached after considerable time. And still, lacunae are left; fortunately, not too many, and mostly, I believe, not of essential importance. Still, I cannot claim that my translation is definitive—as if one could ever make such a claim! Even the Chinese editors insist that their translation is tentative, stressing the difficulties presented by the lapidary style.[1]

Like all scholars interested in the history of China during the period of the Warring States, I owe a great debt of gratitude to the group of our Chinese colleagues who deciphered and published the Ch'in texts. It is only fair that their names[2] should be recorded here, on the very first page of a study that is wholly based on their labours. They are: Yü Hao-liang[3] 于豪亮, An Tso-chang 安作璋, Liu Hai-nien 劉海年, Chu Ssu-chung*[4] 朱思中, Li Hsüeh-ch'in 李學勤, Ch'en K'ang-sheng* 陳抗生, Chang Cheng-lang* 張政烺, Kao Heng 高恒, T'ang Tsan-kung 唐贊工, Tseng Hsien-t'ung* 曾憲通, Shu Chih-mei* 舒之梅, Ch'iu Hsi-kuei* 裘錫圭, and Miss Tou Ai-li 竇愛麗. The final editing was done by Professor Li Hsüeh-ch'in.

The present work also owes more than I can say to the compilers of several handbooks, like the indices to the *Shih-chi*, the *Han shu* and *the Hou-Han shu*, and the monumental glossary of the *Hou-Han shu* by Fujita Shizen[5]. In this respect my greatest debt, however, is to the author of the 12-volume Sino-

---

[1] See point 10 of the *fan-li* 凡例 in SS (for this abbreviation see p. 4 below).

[2] Listed on p. 5 of the introduction in SS.

[3] He died in the summer of 1982.

[4] The persons whose names are marked by an asterisk did no longer participate in preparing the third edition of these texts in SS.

[5] See the bibliography *s.v.* Fujita.

Japanese dictionary, the late Morohashi Tetsuji 諸橋轍次[6] and his collaborators. His work constantly adduced pertinent information from ancient texts outside my ken and helped me to solve numerous riddles; his *magnum opus* surely is the indispensable tool for all those students, of whom I am one, who do not possess the wide reading and the astonishing memory of the traditional Chinese scholar.

How much I owe to the editors of the Ch'in texts and to a host of Chinese and Japanese authors of books and learned articles devoted to these texts is clearly shown by the notes to my translation and by the bibliography. Without their labours, my work would have been so much the poorer.

It would have been also much poorer, if a number of friends and colleagues had not regularly sent me books as well as xerox-copies of Chinese and Japanese articles, all inaccessible to me in this rural retreat, far from well-equipped sinological libraries. I therefore gratefully remember the great help I received from

Mr. D. H. W. Allistone, until recently in Waseda University, Tokyo.
Dr. Emura Haruki 江村治樹 of Nagoya University, Nagoya.
Professor Hori Tsuyoshi 堀毅 of Waseda University, Tokyo.
Professor Huang Sheng-chang 黄盛璋 of the Academy of Social Sciences, Peking.
Dr. W.J.F. Jenner of the University of Leeds.
Professor Koga Noboru 古賀登 of Waseda University, Tokyo.
Dr. Kudō Moto-o 工藤元男 of Waseda University, Tokyo.
Professor Li Hsüeh-ch'in 李學勤 of the Academy of Social Sciences, Peking.
Mr. John T. Ma and the library staff of the Sinologisch Instituut, Leiden University, Leiden, Holland.
Mr. B. J. Mansvelt Beck of the Sinologisch Instituut, Leiden University, Leiden, Holland.
Professor Ōba Osamu 大庭脩 of Kansai University, Osaka.
Dr. R. D. S. Yates of Harvard University, Cambridge, U.S.A.

It is only right that I should single out my dear friend Dr. Michael Loewe, Lecturer in Chinese Studies in the University of Cambridge, for a separate expression of my profound gratitude. For he not only sent me books and papers, but he also undertook the ungrateful and time-consuming task of correcting my English, as well as offering many precious suggestions concerning the translation. If readers will still be shocked by an occasional stiffness of style or by irregularities of diction, these are to be imputed solely to me.

Finally, I wish to acknowledge the great obligation under which I stand to the Netherlands Organization for the Advancement of Pure Research for their generous grant, which made the publication of this work possible.

Romont, Switzerland, November 1982. A. F. P. Hulsewé.

[6] See the bibliography *s.v.* Morohashi.

INTRODUCTION[1]

The cruel laws of the cruel state of Ch'in are a byword in traditional Chinese historiography; the same accusation is sometimes even found in modern studies. But although the inquities of Ch'in have become proverbial, the factual grounds for this allegation are never given, except in the most general terms.[2] It is even more striking to observe that the Ch'in authors of the School of Law, Shang Yang and Han Fei, hardly ever adduce concrete examples of the legislation of this state. However, this silence ceases to be surprising when it is realized that these writers were not so much interested in the contents of the laws as in their use as a political tool. To them, the predominantly penal laws and a system of rewards, especially for deeds of military valour, were the two "handles" which the ruler was to manipulate in order to compel the population to do their utmost in two domains: agriculture and warfare. The silence of the Ch'in authors on the actual contents of the laws shows that they took their existence for granted. This shows, by the way, that the creation of codified law in Ch'in is to be placed considerably earlier than the middle of the 4th century—the time of Shang Yang—whereas in the eastern part of China codification will have started at an earlier date than is usually assumed, perhaps as early as the 8th century B.C.[3] As a result of this silence, we used to know far less about the actual laws of Ch'in than about the legislation of the following Han dynasty[4] (202 B.C.–220 A.D.), fragmentary as this knowledge is. At most, one could have assumed that, because the Han had adopted the laws of Ch'in from the outset, some known Han rules might have found their origin in Ch'in.

The recent discovery of a number of Ch'in laws and regulations has changed the situation significantly, but it should be stressed that we are still far from possessing the whole of the Ch'in code. It is quite clear that these new texts are only a selection from a much larger body of laws; they are a selection made for the use of a subordinate official in the local administration, who was eventually buried with the texts he had constantly used during his lifetime. It is practically certain that these texts belonged to a person called Hsi 喜; another document found in the tomb provides precious information on his life. Born in 262 B.C. he became a government scribe in 244 B.C., to be promoted Prefectural Clerk in 241 B.C.; in 235 B.C. he was charged with trying criminal suits.[5] This explains why the texts found in his tomb include both administrative rules and material on penal law.

This legal material, written on bamboo strips, forms part of a collection of 1155 strips, found in December 1975 in the coffin of tomb no. 11. This is one

---

1 This introduction partly repeats what I have written in "Ch'in documents", "Legalists" and "Economy".—For all abbreviated titles see the bibliography.

2 See e.g. *HSPC* 23.12a, *RHL*, p. 332.

3 See my "Ch'in documents", pp. 216–217, and "Legalists", pp. 3–4.

4 Partly collected in *RHL*.

5 See my "Ch'in documents", p. 177, and especially "Legalists", pp. 9–10.

of a group of graves, discovered during the digging of a drainage canal in the Shui-hu ti area 睡虎地 of the Hsiao-kan District 孝感區, Yün-meng Prefecture 雲夢, central Hu-pei Province.[6] The texts were written on bamboo strips, because bamboo and wooden strips of different sizes were the normal writing material before the invention of rag paper in the 2nd century of our era; even then they continued to be used for another three centuries.[7] Such strips usually contained one column of characters, written with a brush of rabbit hair and black ink made of pine soot; the strips were held together by several sets—usually three—of intertwined strings.[8]

The legal and administrative material occupies 612 strips and parts of another 13 strips. The remaining strips contain prose writings[9] and mantic texts.

The tomb in which this treasure was found can be dated c. 217 B.C., and it is beyond any doubt that the texts are Ch'in texts and that they belong to the 3rd century B.C. Incontrovertible proof is provided by the repeated mention of the Ch'in capital Hsien-yang, because already in the very first year of the Han ruler who was later canonized as Kao-tsu (i.e., 206 B.C.) Hsien-yang was renamed Hsin-ch'eng 新城, and after its destruction by Hsiang Yü later in the same year the place completely lost its importance.[10] Although it is difficult, if not impossible, to determine when the contents of the strips were copied from unknown prototypes, there are a few indications concerning the time when some of the texts were established. Some must have been written after named events, such as the battle of Hsing-ch'iu which was fought in 266 B.C.,[11] or the death of the Ch'in dukes Hsien and Hsiao, indicating a date after 338 B.C.[12] The term "sacrifices by the Royal House" shows that the article was written after 325 B.C., when the Ch'in ruler adopted the title of king.[13] Custom demanded that in writing the name of the ruler as well as some of its homophones, certain characters were avoided and replaced by synonyms. When we therefore observe that in some passages the Village Chief, normally called *li cheng* 里正, is called *li tien* 典[14] we know that these passages were copied, if not created, during the reign of the king of Ch'in who acceded as such in 246 B.C. and became the First Emperor in 221. As his personal name was Cheng 政, the documents in question may be dated after 246 B.C.[15] One article mentions the existence of twelve commanderies and several authors conclude from this figure that the article

---

[6] For further details see my "Ch'in documents", p. 175 f., and the articles quoted there, as well as CM.

[7] See Tsien, p. 90 f.

[8] See the description in *RHA* I, pp. 25–39.

[9] See "Ch'in documents", pp. 181–186.

[10] For further details and references see "Ch'in documents", p. 176 f.

[11] *SC* 5.75, *Mh* II, p. 90. The battle is mentioned in E 13 and E 15.

[12] D 169 mentions the funerary temples of these dukes. For the death of duke Hsiao see *SC* 6.108, *Mh* II, p. 239 f.

[13] The expression is found in D 23. For the date see *SC* 15.78, *Mh* III, p. 43.

[14] This substitution is found in A 7, D 177, E 19 and E 21.

[15] In one of the prose pieces, "Governor T'eng's written instruction", *cheng* 正 is substituted by *tuan* 端; see SS, pp. 15 and 19. The letter is dated "20th year", i.e. 227 B.C.

must date from the middle of the 3rd century B.C.[16] Without exception *tsui*, "crime", is written 辠, and one author therefore believes[17] that this indicates that the texts were written before 221 B.C., when king Cheng of Ch'in created the title *huang-ti* 皇帝, "emperor". This argument rests on the statement in the *Shuo-wen* dictionary of A.D. 100 that at that time 辠 was replaced by 罪, because the former resembled 皇.[18] However, this has been refuted by another scholar,[19] who shows that an inscription of the First Emperor of 215 B.C. contains 罪, whereas a later inscription, of 210 B.C., still has 辠![20] In other words, there is no doubt that the texts belong to the 3rd century B.C., at the latest.

The present arrangement of the material is chiefly the work of the editors, because the strings which had held the strips together had completely decayed. In this, they were guided by several external factors. Firstly by the place where the strips had been found inside the coffin; they were situated either beside the head or the chest of the corpse, or across the thighs, or at the feet.[21] Secondly, by the size of the strips, for some had a length of one Ch'in-Han foot of c. 23 cm., whereas others measured c. 27,5 cm. or 1 ft. 2 in. Thirdly, in some groups the strips were fully covered with writing, but in others only partly, leaving blank spaces. The strips which now have been assembled to form groups A, B and E bear titles of statutes, whereas others do not. The editors had to overcome these handicaps in order to arrive at a meaningful arrangement of the strips, and they deserve the highest praise for having successfully solved this forbidding puzzle, which was rendered all the more difficult because quite a number of strips had been broken into several fragments.[22] Unfortunately, the individual fragments are not indicated in the transcription in S III – VII; the photographs in S I and II are too fuzzy to allow distinguishing any clear breaks, whereas those in CM are too black. Still, the present arrangement seems to be quite acceptable, because the texts make sense; only a perfect facsimile edition will show, whether a different order would provide a better meaning for some passages.

The editors are to be complimented for their acumen in deciphering the crabbed handwriting[23]; they seem to have worked partly on enlarged photographs, such as those published in the popular illustrated journal *Renmin huabao*.[24] This handwriting sorely puzzles the outsider, who is therefore mostly constrained to accept the editors' transcription. I have tried to check the printed text against the photographs, but to my regret I have to acknowledge defeat.

So far, there exist four editions of the texts.

1. in the archaelogical journal *Wenwu* for 1976, issues 6, 7 and 8, entitled

---

[16] A 79, note 1.

[17] Shu Chih-mei, p. 6.

[18] *SWKL*, p. 6583b.

[19] Li Hsüeh-ch'in, "Ku wen", p. 338.

[20] The current text of *SC* 6.45 and 63 (*Mh* II, pp. 166 and 188), which records these inscriptions, writes 罪 in both cases.

[21] See the sketch in ill. 15 of CM, p. 13.

[22] See the list in CM, pp. 74–102.

[23] For the development of the forms of the characters during this period see Emura, "Sengoku".

Yün-meng Ch'in chien shih wen 雲夢秦簡釋文. The texts—without the mantic texts—are transcribed in modern, abbreviated characters; they are not numbered, nor annotated; there are no photographs.

2. in a folio slipcover, containing seven stitched fascicles, Chinese style, entitled *Shui-hu-ti Ch'in mu chu chien* 睡虎地秦墓竹簡 (Peking, Wen-wu ch'u-pan-she, 1977). This publication contains the full-size photographs of the legal and administrative texts and of the prose writings (but again without the mantic texts), their transcription into modern, abbreviated characters, and some brief annotations. This edition (as well as edition no. 4) indicates the division of the texts into strips, which are provided with numbers.

3. in a paper-back, small in-8° edition, published in 1978 under the same title and by the same publishers as edition no. 2. Thix edition contains only a few photographs of the strips by way of illustration, but, beside the transcription into modern, abbreviated characters, it has much fuller notes than edition no. 2, and it provides a full translation into modern Chinese. The mantic texts are again excluded; furthermore, in the transcription the division of the text into strips is not indicated.

4. in a large in-8° edition, where the strips form part of the archaeological report on the excavation of all the Ch'in tombs in the area, compiled under the auspices of the Hu-pei Provincial Museum, and entitled *Yün-meng Shui-hu-ti Ch'in mu* 雲夢睡虎地秦墓 (Peking, Wen-wu ch'u-pan-she, 1981). This publication includes photographs of all the texts, including the mantic ones, and their transcription into traditional characters, but no notes nor a translation. As mentioned above, this edition attaches numbers to the strips, but these are different from those in edition no. 2!

In the following translation, every article is headed by indications enabling the reader to find the Chinese text in the four editions listed above; abbreviations have been used as follows:

W 7 and W 8, followed by a number and the letter a or b, indicate *Wenwu* 1976/7 and 8, the page number, and the left or the right-hand column. W 7.1a therefore indicates page 1, the left-hand column, in *Wenwu* 1976/7.

S, followed by a Roman numeral, indicates the seven fascicles of the folio edition; the following figures, accompanied by a or b, indicate the page and its recto or verso. The fascicles I and II contain the photographs, whereas III – VII contain the transcription and the notes. S I.10a and S III.22a therefore indicate that the photograph is to be found on page 10 recto of fascicle I and the transcription on p. 22 recto of fascicle III.

SS followed by a figure indicates the in-8° paperback and its pages.

CM indicates the archaeological report of the Hu-pei Provincial Museum.

str. followed by a figure indicates the number of the strip—of which there are two: the first is the number assigned to the strips in the folio edition, the second, placed between brackets, is that provided by the archaeological report.

Because I expect that readers will have more easily access to the journal

---

[24] 人民畫報 1976/7, p. 42.

Wenwu than to the other publications, I have followed the order in which the laws and regulations have been published in that journal. This order differs sometimes from that in the other publications, but the references inserted in the heading of each article and the finding list should allow easy consultation of all editions.

The groups A – E into which the texts are divided, are divisions adopted by the editors, mainly based on the position of the strips in the coffin. The titles of these groups were partly invented by the editors (A, C and D), whereas those of B and E are original. To these five groups I have added groups F and G.

I have tried to make the translation correspond with the contents of each strip, and to be as literal as possible; whenever this leads to a certain stiffness, I hope that this will not be held against me. In this connection I should note that I have recently been told that my rendering of *tang* 當 by "warranted; warranting", is contrary to correct English usage. However, I have not corrected this. Perhaps this unidiomatic expression will remind the reader that *tang* basically means "to be equivalent; to outweigh; to counterbalance", in the sense that the negative effect of the crime is neutralized by the punishment. In theory, it is the crime which is *tang*. and not the criminal; this meaning would not come out clearly if *tang* had been rendered as "to deserve; to merit", both words with moral overtones which are wholly absent in the Chinese term.[25]

In my annotation I have tried to be as complete as possible. It goes without saying that the notes in the folio volume and especially the much richer remarks in the in-8° paperback have been of enormous help to me, but the editors often proved to have been too hasty and too easily satisfied with dictionary explanations. In many cases it was therefore necessary to go back *ad fontes* and this has inevitably led to long excursions, for which I again crave the reader's indulgence.

These texts contain a great many loan characters, as has been duly noted by the editors. However, they not unfrequently fail to produce convincing arguments to support their suggestions regarding the words actually intended. In order to uphold or to refute these suggestions I have constantly referred to Bernhard Karlgren's "Grammata serica recensa" and to his "Loan characters in Pre-Han Chinese texts", although I am well aware that his reconstructions of Archaic Chinese have been severely criticized. There was no other way, because so far no scholar—Chinese, Japanese or western—has been able to arrive at a consistent and complete reconstruction of the pronunciation of Han time Chinese.

As mentioned above,[26] the present collection is far from being the complete Ch'in code, being only a selection made for the day to day use of a subordinate official. This official's main tasks appear to have concerned labour, performed both by free labour-conscripts fulfilling their periodical turn of duty and by hard-labour convicts, the management and control of government granaries and the distribution of the grain stored there. The presence of the judicial

[25] See the discussion in *RHL*, p. 80 f.
[26] See p. 1.

material is explained by this official's duty of trying criminal suits,[27] but it is disappointing to observe that this material is far from presenting us with at least part of the penal legislation. For, whereas the nearly two hundred administrative rules are without exception complete articles from numerous statutes, mentioned by title, the judicial material, although as voluminous as the administrative rules, consists merely of explanations of terms and phrases, with only sometimes a quotation from a penal statute, of which the title is never indicated.

The administrative texts mention the titles of at least twenty-eight statutes, namely the eighteen statutes of group A and ten statutes recorded in group C. The former are listed in the table of contents, whereas the latter are found in C 1, 3, 4, 9, 10, 16, 20, 22, 24 and 25. To these should be added the titles of statutes referred to in passing: in A 16 the *fan-ling lü* 犯令律, in A 56 and 88 the *chi lu* 齎律, in A 87 the *p'ing tsui-jen lü* 平罪人律, in A 108 the *pi lü* 辟律. Curiously enough, hardly any of these titles agree with those of known Han statutes or ordinances.[28]

In many articles there are references to "the statutes" without further details about their contents, like e.g., in A 64, which lays down that Controllers of Works were "to be sentenced according to the Statutes" when submitting wrong estimates. The opposite phenomenon appears in the penal material assembled in group D, where complete stipulations as well as isolated terms or phrases are quoted without indicating the title of the statute to which they belonged. Perhaps this was the Statute on Robbery, *tao lu* 盜律, known in the Han period[29], but never mentioned in the present texts. However this may be, complete passages from the penal statutes are found in forty-one articles, namely D 1, 17–21, 25, 26, 41–43, 52, 56, (cf. 59), 58, 65, 75, 79, 80, 87, 88, 91, 92, 96, 101, 105, 108, 118, 126, 136, 139, 141–143, 148, 149, 156–159, 163. These passages allow us some insight into the judicial thinking as well as into the penal system in force in the 3rd century before our era, and perhaps even earlier.[30]

The following pages[31] indicate what I believe to be important points. I must stress that I am a philologist and an historian, and not a jurist, nor a sociologist, and I will therefore have overlooked or misinterpreted points, which the latter type of scholar would have interpreted in a different manner.[32]

Starting with the judicial material, one is struck by the care bestowed on the investigation of criminal suits. It started with detective work, on which detailed reports[33] were required. A report on the corpse of a man found murdered on the highway describes the exact location of the body, the fatal wounds, the man's clothes, and even his shoes found at some distance from the body.

---

[27] See p. 1.

[28] Listed in *RHL*, pp. 32–47.

[29] See *RHL*, pp. 31–32.

[30] In the appendix to this introduction I have tried to provide a brief survey of the penal system.

[31] With the editor's kind permission adopted practically verbatim from my "Legalists", p. 11 f.

[32] See e.g. the critical remarks by Professor Jacques Gernet in his review of *RHL* in *Journal asiatique* 249 (1961), p. 95.

[33] *Yüan shu* 爰書; see note 8 to E 2.

Another contains the detailed description of a corpse found hanging on a roof-beam, attempting to discover whether the man had committed suicide or whether he had been murdered and then hung up so as to make his death appear as suicide. A final example of such an investigation is the report on a robbery, where the thieves had entered the house by digging through the pisé wall. The report presents numerous measurements for the size of the hole and the location of various objects; it even provides details on the old shoes worn by the thieves, based on a reading of the footprints.[34]

Once caught, a suspect was interrogated. The investigating officials are urged, not to lose their patience when the suspect continued to prevaricate and when it was evident that he was lying; they should not be too quick in applying torture in the form of beating, in order to obtain a confession, only doing so in cases where the statutes permitted this.[35] A confession wrung from a suspect by means of torture was considered inferior.[36] The same warning was voiced some two centuries later; when prisoners could no longer bear the pain, they would produce false confessions, or, as the author put it: "once the stick is applied, (the prosecutor) can obtain anything".[37] For the rest of the trial and the verdict, the texts under discussion do not provide more details,[38] except the rule that after the termination of the trial the accused could ask for another enquiry[39], a practice also known during the Han period[40]. In the present context it deserves notice that already at this early date there existed a difference between the written code and the precedents created by the courts[41], the latter either providing details lacking in the code[42], or modifying the rules laid down in the statutes by applying heavier punishments than those demanded there[43]. It seems quite likely that such precedents were collected by an agency of the central government (perhaps the Commandant of Justice) and issued together with the code; they can hardly have been local rules.[44]

Another aspect of the criminal law should be mentioned. In the 4th century B.C. Shang Yang had propagated what seems to have been a new idea, namely that in criminal suits no distinction was to be made between high and low.[45] However, whereas Shang Yang appears to have advocated that the law

---

[34] E 20, 21, 22.

[35] This probably means that children and aged person were not to be beaten; cf. *RHL*, p. 298 f.

[36] E 1, 2.

[37] This warning is found in a memorial, submitted in 74 B.C.; see *RHL*, p. 425 (*HSPC* 51.32a).

[38] For the Han period, when the conduct of trials must have been largely, if not wholly, identical with Ch'in practice—the Han having adopted the whole of the Ch'in legislation—see *RHL*, p. 80.

[39] D 95.

[40] See *RHL*, p. 79 f.

[41] *T'ing hsing shih* 廷行事. In principle, "the court" is not a circumlocution for the ruler or the government, but the Prefect's office, as shown by A 21.

[42] D 53, 126–128.

[43] D 30, 47, 53.

[44] For Han precedents and similar rules see *RHL*, pp. 48–51; the Han collections were certainly official compilations, but nothing is known of their binding force.

[45] See Duyvendak, *Lord Shang*, p. 273 f.

should be applied impartially to all offenders, the texts under discussion show that position in the hierarchy continued to count, with the result that superiors were often punished more lightly than their subordinates and in particular that the holders of aristocratic rank suffered less than ordinary commoners and slaves.[46] The principle remained that all offenders were to be punished, but nevertheless a certain gradation was introduced.

A completely different point concerns manslaughter. The Yün-meng texts show that in the 3rd century B.C. — and probably already earlier — a clear distinction was made between wounding or killing a person in a fight, resulting in involuntary, unpremeditated manslaughter, and killing somebody intentionally, committing murder with malice aforethought.[47] The two relevant terms occur frequently in Han texts, where a third term is also found: to hurt or kill a person when playing or frolicking[48], but this word does not occur in the texts under discussion. What we do find, however, are graduated rules for punishing people who in an unpremeditated fight attacked others with a needle or an awl, which was punished by a heavy fine[49], or who did so with a weapon which they first had to unsheathe, like a dagger or a sword or a halberd, for which they incurred a sentence to a long term of forced labour.[50] Other rules indicate the punishments for pulling out the adversary's hair, or tearing off an ear or biting.[51]

Special attention is paid to killing one's children. In case a father wished to kill his unfilial son, he was not allowed to do so, but he had to ask the authorities to execute him.[52] In the same way, he could request the officials to banish his son for life, going in chains like an ordinary criminal.[53] From other articles it becomes clear that a father or master could kill or mutilate his children or slaves, provided he had first obtained official permission to do so; unauthorized killing, however, was punished by being tattooed and serving a long term as a hard labour convict.[54] This prohibition was especially directed against infanticide, for we read that whereas killing a deformed newborn child was not considered a crime, killing a healthy infant because the family had already too many children was heavily punished;[55] this rule applied both to free persons and to slaves.[56]

Punishment for theft or robbery was determined in the first place by the

---

[46] See Huang Sheng-chang, "Pien cheng", p. 6 f., Hori, "Keimei", p. 120 f. and Kao Min, *Ch'u-t'an*, p. 244 f.

[47] D 60, 71; *tou shang sha* 鬭傷殺 and *tsei* 賊 *shang sha*. See the discussion in *RHL*, pp. 253–257.

[48] *Hsi* 戲; see *RHL*, p. 254.

[49] D 71.

[50] D 70.

[51] D 72, 66–68.

[52] E 18, cf. D 68.

[53] E 17.

[54] D 56, 58. The provision that a denunciation for such unauthorized killing was not to be accepted must have been restricted to the members of the family or the household (D 86), for otherwise the prohibition would have been meaningless.

[55] D 56.

[56] D 59, 62.

money value of the stolen goods, and secondly by the circumstance of the theft having been committed by a single person or by a band[57]. We therefore find the example of two men who had decided independently to rob the same place. If each of them had continued to act on his own, he was to be punished according to the value of what he had stolen personally, but if they had cooperated, they were both condemned for the total value of the stolen goods.[58]

The texts pay great attention to receiving stolen goods. Here, as well as elsewhere, no general principle is enunciated, but the texts show plainly that a person to whom stolen goods had been entrusted was only found guilty if it could be shown that he had been aware of the fact that the goods had been stolen. Furthermore, he was punished according to the value of the goods entrusted to him and not for the value of the thief's actual booty.[59] However, all persons who had known about the robbery and who had joined the thief in wining and dining on the proceeds were subject to the same punishment as the thief.[60]

The rather complicated matter of the punishments used in Ch'in is analyzed in Appendix I.

The bulk of the administrative statutes in this collection is directly or indirectly concerned with two subjects: labour and food, as already remarked above on p. 5.

The editors of these texts have rightly placed an article from the Statute on Agriculture[61] at the very beginning of this collection, stipulating that the local authorities had to report[62] on the state of the grain crop, including the exact area of cultivated and fallow land, and the acreage affected by seasonable rain as well as by rainstorms, inundations, drought or insect plagues. Agriculture was the mainstay of the economy and the size of the crop was of immediate local importance to an official responsible for feeding a host of labourers.

Of equal importance was the storage of the harvest. The grain had to be stored in heaps of 10.000 bushels, to which the seals of the officials in charge had to be attached[63]. The persons in charge of a granary were punished if there were leaks letting in the rain so that the grain was spoilt[64], or if the doors could not be tightly closed so that the grain escaped[65], or if there were more than three rat holes, three mouse holes being counted as one rat hole![66] There

57 D 1.
58 D 11.
59 D 13, 14.
60 D 15, 16.
61 A 1.
62 Such reports were still required under the Han, as shown by the rule that between February and August "the benefits of rain" had to be reported; see *HHSCC* Tr. 5.1a, and the remarks in the additional notes to this chapter: *chiao-pu* 5.1a.
63 A 19, 86.
64 A 83.
65 D 128.
66 D 130.

existed a separate Statute on Checks and Controls;[67] checks were made when grain was issued, but particularly when there was a change of personnel. If shortages were discovered, these had to be made good by the men responsible for the granary as well as by those directly in charge. All storage offices had a full set of weights and measures, which had to be checked every year; their loss resulted in punishment for the responsible officials.[68] A separate rule[69] indicates the deviations from the standard that were allowed: between one twentieth and one thirtieth for measures of capacity, but only one hundred and twentieth for weights. Appendix II provides a brief survey of Ch'in-Han weights and measures.

There existed rules for the quantities of seed to be used for sowing a standard surface of one *mu*, differing for the different kinds of grain; these were evidently to be followed by the managers of grain stores when distributing seed-grain to commoners, who eventually had to repay such loans.[70] Other rules[71] were set for the pounding or refining of grain, establishing the quantitites of more or less polished grain to be obtained from treating a certain amount of unhusked cereals; these rules applied perhaps to the work done by female hard-labour convicts with the telling appellations of "grain-pounders" and "sifters of white rice".[72] Of all these and similar activities reports had to be made, sometimes even to the central government.[73]

Not only the stocks of grain, but also the condition of the government horses and cattle were subject to a regular and strict control. If the cattle were fat, rewards were given; if they were thin, the men in charge were punished.[74] Calving cows as well as horses in the courier service were given extra rations.[75] When cows and sheep produced insufficient offspring, the personnel was fined.[76] The government horses were inspected and graded[77]; wounding these animals was punished[78]. When such horses or cattle died, detailed reports had to be made, and their hides, horns and bones had to be handed over.[79]

The origin of the grain in the goverment storehouses must surely be sought in the land-tax, which may have been as high as one fifth of the harvest[80]; local officials were punished for failing to report taxable fields and embezzling the tax.[81] Ultimately, the grain was destined to be distributed as rations: to

---

[67] *Chiao lü* 校律; A 82–89, and group B.
[68] A 104; A 54; D 124.
[69] B 3–4.
[70] A 27; see further my "Economy".
[71] A 29–30; see further my "Weights and measures".
[72] See Appendix I and my "Economy".
[73] A 21, 23, 25, 26.
[74] A 7.
[75] A 37; A 10.
[76] C 19.
[77] C 6.
[78] C 17.
[79] A 9; this rule shows similarities with the T'ang documents reproduced in Maspero, *Stein*, pp. 129–147.
[80] See my "Economy"
[81] D 135.

officials[82], to men serving in the army[83], and to hard-labour convicts[84]. Several rules were directed against abuses; for instance, no rations were to be issued to persons who had already been provided with food from another source,[85] whereas soldiers were prohibited to sell their rations.[86] All issues had to be carefully registered, in view of the demand that the number of the recipients had to be reported;[87] the hundreds of wooden strips found in the Edsin-gol defence lines, mostly dating from the 1st century B.C., furnish excellent examples of this type of meticulous bookkeeping.[88]

The Yün-meng texts also throw new light on the Ch'in system of conscription. It is well known that under the Ch'in and the Han all men, except the holders of the higher degrees of aristocratic rank[89], were obliged to perform two kinds of service: military service and labour service. During the Han period the former took two years: one year's training in the men's place of origin, and one year's garrison service, either in the capital or on the frontier. Labour service was, at least theoretically, one month each year.[90]

Here the Ch'in texts provide additional information. They show e.g. that young men were enrolled (*fu* 傅) already in their 15th year, whereas formerly it was assumed that their names were entered in the service registers at twenty, if not at twentythree years of age.[91] Failing to enter young men in the rolls was a punishable offence; in the same way, the responsible officials were punished if they did not remove the names of "old" men from the lists.[92] On the other hand officials were punished if they mobilized more than one person from the same household at the same time;[93] this is an additional indication that households were small and that they usually did not count more than five persons. As regards the men, once they had been called up, they were bastinadoed if they did not answer the summons or if they ran away from the work site.[94] Like the hard-labour convicts, their main task consisted in contruction work,[95] including the building of pisé walls; if these collapsed within one year, they had to rebuild them, but this extra work was not counted as labour service, and the Controller of Works and the men in charge were punished.[96]

These are some of the aspects of the Ch'in laws that I believe to be important, but there surely are many other points which trained jurists will discover and

82 A 31, 92, 93.
83 C 8.
84 A 12, 17, 65, 66, 68, 110.
85 A 32, 33.
86 C 8.
87 A 26.
88 See *RHA* I, p. 93 f. and II, pp. 64–93; cf. also the documents of the 2nd century B.C. discussed in *Wenwu* 1974/7, p. 51 f.
89 See Loewe, "Ranks", pp. 145 and 157.
90 For further details see Loewe, *RHA* I, p. 80 f.
91 See note 1 to A 13.
92 C 20, cf. C 4 and 5; "old" may have been 56 or 60.
93 C 25.
94 D 143, 144; E 6.
95 For further details known from Han sources, see my "Statute labour".
96 A 64.

discuss. But these texts also present other facets; one of these, the influenc of the Ch'in state on the economy in so far as this is reflected in these texts I have discussed in a separate study.[97] Another question which merits close study is the organization of Ch'in society, especially as regards the position of the farmers, as well as the related problem of slavery. These problems should be approached *sine ira et studio* — which is far from always the case at present — avoiding preconceived notions and dogmatic formulae, where the answers are already implied in the questions.[98] The documents should be allowed to speak for themselves, as they do in Wilbur's study, now forty years old, but still unsurpassed.[99]

By way of conclusion I should like to make a few remarks.

The first is that I am convinced that the beginnings of codified law in China lie much farther back than is usually assumed. These beginnings will have coincided with the growth of the large, increasingly centralized and bureaucratic states in the 8th and 7th centuries before the beginning of our era.[100] In principle I see no reason why the state of Ch'in should have lagged far behind — a view which is often encountered. And this brings me to my second point: the so-called backwardness of Ch'in.

The complexity and the sophistication of the Ch'in laws and regulations hardly bear witness to this backwardness, or to its semi-barbarian condition. These traits are always attributed to Ch'in, because of its position on the fringe of the Chinese culture area and of the fact that part of its population consisted of recently subdued "barbarian" tribes. To me, this view seems fallacious, or at least subject to strong doubt. As regards the "barbarian" tribes both Maspero and Průšek have stressed that the tribes were of the same stock as the Chinese of the nuclear area and that they differed only from these by being culturally less advanced; they were not completely alien nomads from the northern steppe.[101] And secondly, those who believe the Ch'in to have been backward, usually overlook that this state occupied the original homeland of the Chou, who were anything but backward.[102] It is therefore not logical to assume that this area lapsed into barbarity once the Chou king had fled East in the 8th century, when we observe that in a comparable situation a millennium later North China remained Chinese in spite of its occupation by nomadic tribes (real aliens, this time) during several centuries after A.D. 317, when part of the cultural elite had fled to the Yang-tzu region.

It is not logical to postulate that the Ch'in because of their "backwardness" were obliged to model their laws on those of the states farther East.[103] All these

97 See my "Economy".

98 See e.g. Thorpe, "Marxist perspective".

99 Wilbur, *Slavery*.

100 See my "Legalists", p. 3 f.

101 Maspero, p. 9 (pp. 10–11 of the 1927 edition); Průšek, *Statelets*, p. 13.

102 A striking exception is Yeh Hsiao-yen's article, where the influence of the Chou population is duly acknowledged, a point not discussed in the related study by Li Hsüeh-ch'in, "Ch'in-kuo wen-wu".

103 Huang Sheng-chang, "Pien-cheng", pp. 11–15.

laws were after all the written form of the ancient customary law, and this will not have been greatly different for the different groups of the same cultural community. New elements, however, may have come into being in the rules connected with the exercise of power in the new bureaucratic, and above all centralizing, states, and in this field Ch'in may well have produced original solutions.

The texts translated in this volume show that in the 3rd century B.C. the state of Ch'in aimed at extending its influence over all spheres of the life of its inhabitants. Although also the ancient customary law was all-embracing, here the ideas of the School of Law definitely played a determining role. Collective responsibility, for instance, is a general trait of primitive law, but its systematization is the work of the Legalists. It is not without reason that Shang Yang is credited with the idea of organizing all families in groups of five, whose members were to be held responsible for the misdeeds of other members of the same group[104]. Dr. Momiyama is probably right when he traces these measures to the military organization[105], for it is in a miliary context that the groups of five are mentioned in the Book of Lord Shang and in the military 70th chapter of the *Mo-tzu*. I believe that the relative newness of the idea of group-responsibility is shown by the need that was apparently felt to explain the relevant terms.[106]

I may leave it to the reader to find other points of interest: legal, social, historical or linguistic; as regards the latter, the way in which loan characters are used in these manuscripts of the 3rd century B.C. may be of some value to all those who are interested in ancient texts and their transmission.

It is only a few years ago that a chance discovery brought to light these remnants of Ch'in law, but already the Chinese archaeologists have presented us again with another valuable find[107]. We can therefore continue to hope that further additions to our knowledge of the laws of Ch'in will eventually be turned up by the searcher's spade.

---

[104] *SC* 68.7; Duyvendak, *Lord Shang*, pp. 14 and 58. The division of the population in groups of five appears to be older, but it was Shang Yang who introduced the element of mutual responsibility; see Vandermeersch, p. 93.

[105] Momiyama, "Hōka"; cf. Vandermeersch *loc. cit.*

[106] D 19 explains the term *t'ung chü* 同居, and D 82 *ssu lin* 四鄰.

[107] Translated in G.

APPENDIX I

A BRIEF SURVEY OF THE CH'IN PENAL SYSTEM

Because punishments are mentioned in many of the following articles, and because these punishments are indicated by traditional terms that are anything but self-explanatory, the following pages provide a brief survey of these matters, in order to facilitate the understanding of the Ch'in laws.

The Ch'in, like their successors, the Han, knew several types of punishments: the death penalty, hard labour, banishment and castration, as well as fines and redemption (it will be explained below, why redemption figures here as a punishment). Beside these, the bastinado was used during the questioning of suspects, and as an immediate punishment for labourers who had broken tools or who had absconded.

The usual death penalty was beheading, called "casting away in the market place", *ch'i shih* 棄市 (D 57, 151). There also existed a death penalty called *che* 磔, traditionally explained as "to be torn apart by carriages", but probably meaning "to be executed and exposed", but apparently not identical with "quartering" (D 69; see *RHL*, p. 110 f.). It is unknown how far this was the same as *sheng lu* 生戮. "dishonouring while alive", explained in the present texts as "first dishonouring and then cutting asunder" (D 41). The word *chan* 斬 is rendered here as "cutting asunder", because it may refer to a form of the death penalty frequently used in the Han period, but not mentioned in the Ch'in texts, namely *yao chan* 要斬, "cutting in two at the waist" (see *RHL*, p. 111f.). No less than thirty three cases of this form of execution are mentioned in the Han histories, whereas the term is rarely found in pre-Han sources[1]. Criminal lepers were to be drowned (D 101).

Persons condemned to hard labour were often also subjected to mutilating punishments; these mutilations never appear in isolation, but they are always combined with hard labour. The heaviest of the hard labour punishments was that of the "wall builders", *ch'eng-tan* 城旦, or, for women, "grain pounders", *ch'ung* 舂. Because many examples show that the main task of the men consisted in construction work, the word *ch'eng* doubtless means "wall (building)", but the meaning of *tan*, literally "morning", remains unclear; it cannot have meant "to stand guard since early dawn" as the commentators explain it. In this connection it should be noted that all walls—those of simple houses (see E 22) as well as those of palaces, and also defence works, including the Long Walls on the frontier—were made of pounded earth; in any traditional building in the Far East wooden pillars and cross beams form the essential structure, supporting the wooden frame of the roof, whereas walls are merely a filling between the pillars and have no supporting function.

[1] *SC* 68.8, Duyvendak, *Lord Shang*, p. 14; *SC* 87.43, Bodde, *Unifier*, p. 52; *Ch'in ts'e* iii, in *CKT* vol. i, p. 39.

These wall builders could be *wan* 完, "whole; intact", i.e. not subjected to mutilation, or they could be condemned to suffer a mutilating punishment in addition. The heaviest of these mutilations was the amputation of both feet, *chan yu chih* 斬右止, "cutting off (also) the right foot"; this is only known from a Han source (*HSPC* 23.14a; *RHL*, pp. 125 and 335) and it is not mentioned in the Ch'in laws. One degree less was cutting off the left foot, *chan tso chih* 斬左止 (D 1, 105). Again one degree less was cutting off the nose, *i* 劓; in the few cases it is mentioned in the Ch'in laws (it is to be remembered that the present collection only contains some fragments of the Ch'in code), it is combined with the lightest of the mutilations, namely tattooing, *ch'ing* 黥 (D 1, 100). Tattooing by itself occurs ten times, mostly combined with "wall building", *ch'eng tan* (D 27, 28, 56, 62, 71, 93, 99, 146, 154, 162, E 16), and once combined with amputation of the left foot (D 1).

All wall builders, including those who had not suffered a mutilating punishment, had their hair and their beard removed. This "shaving", *k'un* 髡, is evidently understood implicitly, for it is not mentioned in the official nomenclature, whereas Han practice was to record it always explicitly; it is, however, mentioned in articles dealing with fathers or masters who had on their own authority "killed, mutilated *or shaved*" their children or their slaves. A stone engraving from a Later Han tomb shows people (slaves or criminals) having their hair cut off.[2]

In a number of cases the Ch'in texts record that wall builders as well as convicts from the two following groups were "mutilated", *hsing* 刑, without further details; Professor Hori is probably right when he suggests that this indicates the lightest of the mutilating punishments, viz. tattooing.[3]

The next group of hard labour convicts were the "(gatherers of) firewood for the spirits", *kui hsin* 鬼薪, and their female counterparts, the "(sifters of) white rice", *pai ts'an* 白粲. One degree lower again were the "bond servants" and "bond women", *li ch'en* / *ch'ieh* 隸臣/妾. All these could also be mutilated.

The last two groups were the "robber guards", *ssu k'ou* 司寇, and the "watchmen", *hou* 候; for neither of these the Ch'in laws record cases of mutilation. The robber guards were either condemned to this punishment, or they were transferred to this status from one of the heavier hard-labour punishments. In the Ch'in texts this transfer is only known from that of wall builders, whom they were effectively made to guard in groups of twenty. Here, the Han reforms of 167 B.C. may have introduced a change: wall builders became gatherers of firewood after three years and served as such for one year, whereupon they became robber guards for another year, to be freed at the end of this term. Bond servants, however, became robber guards after two years, to be released after another year.[4]

Except the wall builders who, as was said above, had their heads completely shaved, all other hard labour convicts were *nai* 耐, i.e. they had their beard

[2] See "Chu-ch'eng", p. 18, and Huang Chan-yüeh, "K'un ch'ih t'u".
[3] Hori, "Keimei", p. 119.
[4] *HSPC* 23.14a–b; *RHL*, p. 336.

shaved off. This is always expressly mentioned, e.g. *nai wei li ch'en* 耐爲隸臣, "to have the beard shaved off and to be made a bond servant". In this way, in the Ch'in texts the single word *nai* comes to mean "hard labour without mutilation", but further specification is lacking; in some cases we find *nai tsui i shang* 耐罪以上, "crimes punishable by shaving off the beard and above (i.e. heavier)". So far, I have not been able to find any indication regarding the implications of the single word *nai*; that it had a specific meaning is clear from the many cases where culprits are condemned to *nai* for a great variety of crimes.

The hard labour convicts condemned to an additional mutilation, *hsing* (perhaps tattooing, as mentioned above) also had their beard shaved off. This is shown by the case of a man with privileged status, who had committed a crime "warranting mutilation and being made a bond servant", for in his case an order was given "do not mutilate him, but apply the shaving of the beard", *wu hsing hsing ch'i nai* 勿刑行其耐 (D 91 and 92).

In order to clarify the situation, I insert here the useful table made by Professor Hori[5]; + means that the combination of the two elements is found in the texts, whereas – indicates that it does not occur.

	mutilations specified	mutilated no details	"whole, intact"	beard shaved
ch'eng-tan, ch'ung wall builders and grain pounders	+	+	+	–
kui hsin, pai ts'an wood gatherers and rice sifters	–	+	–	+
li ch'en, li ch'ieh bond servants and bond women	–	+	–	+
ssu k'ou robber guards	–	–	–	+
hou, watchmen	–	–	–	+

To the uncertainties mentioned above – what were the implications of *hsing*, "mutilation"? which punishments were indicated by *nai*, "shaving off the beard"? – there are to be added other questions: what was the duration of the different hard labour punishments, and what were the tasks of the convicts? The last question is partly answered by the text of the laws: building walls for the wall builders, and sometimes also for the other groups; agricultural labour; work in government storehouses and workshops. But formal information is lacking, just as it is lacking for the Han period.[6]

As regards the duration of the punishments, the Ch'in laws do not offer any information,[7] with one exception of dubious value: in three cases we learn that privileged persons condemned to "gathering firewood for the spirits" or to bond service were "to be detained among the wall builders for six years"

[5] Hori, "Keimei", p. 119.

[6] See *RHL*, pp. 130–132.

[7] We are well informed for the Han period after the reforms of 167 B.C.; see *RHL*, pp. 130–132.

(D 89, 19, 92). The express mention of "six years" shows that this was an exceptional measure, but the only conclusion which it seems permissible to draw is that the normal duration of gathering firewood and bond service was less, but we cannot infer that the term for wall builders was six years. A negative indication is found in a father's request that his son should be banished for life (E 17), which shows that normally banishment was for a fixed period.

Personally, I am convinced that the duration of the hard labour punishments was the same during the Ch'in and the Han dynasty, not only because a change is nowhere mentioned, but also because I fail to see any reason for the Han to introduce such a momentous innovation. However, many Chinese authors believe that all condemnations to hard labour were for life, and that these convicts were in fact government slaves; they fail, however, to explain why distinctive names like "wall builder" or "bond servant" were nevertheless perpetuated.[8]

When the Ch'in laws — as well as the Han histories—note that a person was condemned to one of the hard labour punishments, they always carefully indicate whether he was also to be mutilated (either specifying the mutilation or merely writing *hsing*), or whether he was to be left intact, *wan* (for wall builders), c.q. to have his beard shaved off, *nai* (for the other groups of hard labour convicts). However, when such convicts are mentioned in other contexts, such as rules for the distribution of food rations or clothing, these details are not given, because such rules applied to the whole group, irrespective of their differences.

During the Han period, the general term for hard labour convicts of all types was *t'u* 徒, but in the Ch'in laws the meaning of *t'u* is uncertain; it seems rather unlikely that it meant "convicts".

Banishment, *ch'ien* 遷, was quite often used, but, with two exceptions, the place of banishment is not specified[9] (contrary to Han practice[10]), nor is the duration mentioned. The exceptions are the lepers, who are sent to the asylum[11] and one case where the man is sent to *Shu* 蜀,[12] i.e. modern Ssu-ch'uan, an area which had been conquered by Ch'in towards the end of the 4th century B.C.

Although the texts show that castration existed as a punishment,[13] the crimes

[8] See Kao Heng, "Li ch'en ch'ieh", p. 43; Kuan and Sung, "Li ch'en ch'ieh"; Wu Jung-tseng, "Shou kung-yeh", p. 49 f.; Wu Shu-p'ing, "Chieh-chi", p. 119 f.; Yü Hao-liang, "Nu-li", p. 131 f. Momiyama, "Reishinshō", argues in great detail that bond servants were in fact life-long government slaves with an hereditary status; by analogy, he assumes that also the other hard-labour punishments were for life. For the thesis—also adopted by several Chinese scholars—that the terms for the different hard-labour punishments established by emperor Wen in 167 B.C. (cf. *RHL*, p. 335 f.) were an absolute innovation, he finds support in a memorial submitted by Ch'ao Ts'o in 164 B.C., where among a series of this emperor's praiseworthy acts we find "for criminals there are (fixed) terms (for their punishment)", *tsui jen yu ch'i* 辠人有期 (*HSPC* 49.21a; not in *SC*). However, Liu Hai-nien, "Hsing-fa", p. 188 f., shares my view.

[9] A 72, 90; C 5, 7, 20; D 1, 48–50; E 24.

[10] See *RHL*, p. 112 f.

[11] D 102, 103.

[12] E 17.—In contrast to the practice in other civilizations, e.g. in ancient Greece, banishment in China left the exile still within the country and subject to Chinese authority.

[13] For the Han period see *RHL*, p. 127 f.

for which it was applied are unknown. It is recorded only once, in an article concerning the treatment of certain privileged persons, where we read: "those guilty of crimes punishable by 'rottenness' should redeem castration", *ch'i yu fu tsui shu kung* 其有府 (for 腐) 罪贖宮 (D 94). Eunuchs are also mentioned only once, namely as recipients of rations (A 93); the article does, of course, not enter into the origin of their condition. Also the *Shih-chi* mentions but a few cases: the highly doubtful story that the O-pang Palace of the First Emperor was built by 700,000 castrates,[14] the scurrilous tale about Lao Ai, the lover of the First Emperor's mother,[15] and the remark that the minister Chao Kao, who served the First Emperor as well as his son, was an eunuch, as were his brothers.[16]

Fines, *tzu* 貲, seem to have been a punishment mainly applied to officials. The amounts of these fines are not expressed in cash, but in arms, namely suits of armour, shields, and laces used to string the scales of a suit of armour together. Unfortunately, the value of these objects is nowhere indicated and consequently we do not know the amounts.[17] Sometimes the word "fine" is used for conscript service imposed by way of punishment; persons were "fined" with one or two years military service or thirty days statute labour.[18]

Both the Ch'in and the Han[19] allowed the redemption of punishments, called *shu* 贖, a term which is likewise used for obtaining the liberation of parents serving as bond-servants[20] and for slaves buying their freedom[21]. Redemption appears to have been frequently allowed, because we find cases of redemption mentioned for banishment (A 72), hard labour (A 68; C 20; D 52, 94, 136, 164), mutilation (A 68; D 164), tattooing (D 3, 25), castration (D 94), and even the death-penalty (A 68), Under the Ch'in, people could be *condemned* to redeem a punishment;[22] in other words, this peculiar type of redemption was equivalent to a fine. In case the persons condemned were unable to pay the redemption-fee at once, they were allowed to pay it by working for the government together with hard-labour convicts at the rate of eight cash per day, or six cash if they were fed by the authorities,[23] and the actual punishment was not executed. This system may have lapsed under the Han, because the famous historian Ssu-ma Ch'ien complains in 93 B.C. that he had to suffer the punishment to which he had been condemned, viz. castration, as he had been unable to pay the redemption-fee.[24]

---

14 *SC* 6.54, *Mh* II, pp. 175–176, further embellished in later works quoted in the commentary.
15 *SC* 85.11, Wilhelm, *Frühling*, p. xiv.
16 *SC* 88.4.
17 See my "Ch'in documents", p. 208 f.
18 C. 8, D 6; for a similar Han case see my "Weights", pp. 36–37.
19 See *RHL*, pp. 205–214.
20 A 35, 91.
21 *RHL*, p. 208.
22 See, e.g., below, C 20, 52; D 136.
23 A 68.
24 *HSPC* 62.21a. The statement occurs in his famous letter to Jen An, translated in *Mh* I, p. ccxxvi f.

APPENDIX II

CH'IN-HAN WEIGHTS AND MEASURES

More than forty years ago, Dubs presented a list of equivalents of Ch'in-Han weights and measures[1], based on experiments, earlier studies, and the measuring of actual Ch'in and Han objects; these equivalents were adopted by Dr. Loewe.[2] Since then, archaeological finds have continued to provide a large and constantly growing number of vessels etc. with inscriptions that indicate their measurements. In 1975 a scholar writing under the pseudonym "T'ien shih" published an illuminating study on Early Han weights and measures,[3] covering a large pumber of vessels, where his data show considerable variations in the measures actually used. The following table summarizes his findings, to which I have added Dubs' figures.

		T'ien shih	Dubs	remarks
ch'ih 尺,	foot	22,38 – 23,75 cm.	23,1 cm.	
sheng 升,	pint	185 – 207 cm^3	199,9 cm^3	majority of vessels c. 200 cm^3
liang 兩,	ounce	14,01 – 15,625 g.	15.25 g.	majority of weights 15 + g.
chin 斤,	catty	200 – 311 g.	244 g.	majority of weights 254 g.

The discovery of a small number of gold ingots with their weight inscribed in great detail shows the *shu* 銖 (1/24th of an ounce) to have been 0,66 g., the *liang* or ounce 15.84 g. and the *chin* or catty 253,44 g.[4]

In view of these findings we can therefore assume that the *liang* weighed nearly 16 grammes, the *chin* about 254 g., and the *shih* 石 or picul of 120 catties 3048 g.

The many hundreds of Ch'in and the thousands of Han bamboo and wooden strips show, that the Ch'in – Han foot was quite close to 23,1 cm. The *pu* 步 or pace of six feet was therefore 138,6 cm. and the li 里 of 300 paces 416 m., whereas the *mu* or *mou* 畝 of 240 × 1 pace or 1440 × 6 feet[5] must have been approximately 460 m^2. and the *ch'ing* 頃 of 100 *mu* about 4,6 hectare.

[1] *HFHD* I, pp. 279–280.
[2] Loewe, "Measurement", p. 65.
[3] See T'ien shih, and see also Wang Kuang-yung, as well as Ch'iu Kuang-ming, "Heng chih".
[4] See *Kaogu* 1980/4, p. 379. Cf. also *Wenwu* 1982/11, p. 11.
[5] In actual practice probably a plot of 8 × 30 paces or 48 × 180 feet; see note 8 to G below.

TRANSLATION

GROUP A

The texts belonging to the first group of strips, called by the editors *Ch'in lü shih-pa chung* 秦律十八種, "Eighteen kinds of Ch'in statutes," consist of 110 articles (A 1–A 110) in the division adopted in *Wenwu* 1976 / 7 and followed here. The 202 strips of this group have a length of c. 27 cm. or 1 ft. 2 in. Ch'in-Han measure. They were held together by three sets of strings: at the top, in the middle, and at the bottom, as is clearly apparent from the traces left by the decayed remains. Each article starts on a new strip, with the result that not a few strips are left partly blank. Strips fully covered with writing contain about 35 well-spaced characters. The strips of this group had been placed in the coffin at the right-hand side of the body, along the right thigh (SS, p. 23; CM, p. 74).

A 1 W 7.1a; S I.10a; S III.22a; SS 24–26; str. 1–3 (068–070).

[1] Whenever[1] the rain is beneficial[2] and affects[3] the grain in ear[4] a report in writing is to be made[5] concerning the favoured crop and the grain in ear, as well as the number of *ch'ing*[6] of cultivated fields and areas without crops.[7] Whenever it rains when the crop is already fully grown[8], also the quantity of rain and the number of *ch'ing* which were affected[9] [2] are to be reported in writing. Likewise, in cases of drought[10] and violent wind or rain, floods, hordes of grasshoppers or other creatures which damage the crops, the number of *ch'ing* concerned is always to be reported in writing. Nearby[11] prefectures have lightfooted runners deliver the letter, distant [3] prefectures have the courier service deliver it. By the end of the eighth month[12]. . . .it.

Statutes on Agriculture.[13]

1 This article has also been translated in Vandermeersch, "Procédure", p. 13. For *che* 輒 cf. *RHL*, p. 402, note 264.

2 The editors read the vague sign on the strip as *feng* 澍, "mud", which they believe to be a mistake for *shu* 澍, explained in SW as "timely rain, whereby the myriad things rise and grow".

3 In these texts *chi* 及 mostly serves as an emphatic conjunction, which I have consistently rendered by "as well as". In some cases it is used as a verb, "to reach; to implicate; to affect", and that is its meaning here.

4 The editors read *hsiu* 秀 for *yu* 誘. SS refers to the *Erh-ya* and explains *hsiu* as grain where the ears are forming (*Erh-ya* 8.12b (0344)).

5 Such reports were still required during the Han period, as is shown by *HHSCC* Tr. 5.1a (see also the explanatory remarks in the *chiao-pu* 5.1a): *tzu li ch'un. . . .chün kuo shang yü tse* 自立春.... 郡國上雨澤, "From the Establishment of Spring. . . .the commanderies and kingdoms report the benefits of the rain."

6 A *ch'ing* 頃 measured c. 4.6 hectare; see further Appendix II above. This size of the *ch'ing* is based on the new or large *mu* 畝 (100 *mu* being 1 *ch'ing*), which was probably adopted in the 4th century B.C; see e.g. *Hsin T'ang shu* (T'ung-wen edition), 215.3b, where Tu

Yu (735–812) is credited with this statement, as indicated in SS, p. 25, note 2. Satake, "Kazoku", p. 29, suggests that the introduction of the large *mu* may have been connected with the spread of using oxen for ploughing.

7 *Ch'ang* 暘. according to SW "without growth". SS mentions a remark by Yü Yüeh 俞樾 (1821–1907) to the effect that this *ch'ang* is the same as *ch'ang* 場, of which SW says that it can mean "uncultivated fields".

8 This is a tentative rendering of *chia i sheng* 稼已生.

9 Literally *shu* 澍, "benefitted".

10 The text reads *tsao* 早, which the editors have rightly corrected to read *han* 旱.

11 Presumably prefectures situated close to the Ch'in capital Hsien-yang.

12 I.e. before the beginning of the administrative year in the 10th month.—Strip 3 consists of two fragments which the editors have combined, but the central part, with a length of two or three characters, is missing.

13 *T'ien lü* 田律; cf. *RHL*, p. 37, no. 13.

A 2 W 7.1a; S I.10a; S III.22b–23a; SS 26–27; str. 4–7 (071–074).

[4] In the second month of spring one should not venture to cut timber in the forests or block water courses[1]. Except[2] in the months of summer one should not venture to burn[3] weeds to make ashes[4], to collect [indigo][5], young animals, eggs or fledglings. One should not......[6] [5] poison fish or tortoises or arrange pitfalls and nets. By the seventh month (these prohibitions) are lifted. Only when someone has unfortunately died and one fells (wood for) the inner and outer coffins,[7] this is not done according to the seasons. In settlements close to corrals[8] and other forbidden parks, in the season of young animals [6] one should not venture to take dogs to go hunting.[9] When dogs of the common people enter forbidden parks without pursuing and catching animals, one should not venture to kill them; those which pursue as well as catch animals are to be killed. [7] Dogs killed by the wardens[10] are to be completely handed over to the authorities[11]; of those that are killed in other forbidden parks the flesh may be eaten, but the skin is to be handed over.[12]

Statutes on Agriculture.

1 Flessel, *Huang-ho*, p. 26, refers to Wen I-to, *Shen-hua yü shih*, 聞一多, 神話與詩 (Peking, 1956), p. 51 (unaccessible), who believes that in the treaty of 651 B.C., mentioned only in the *Ku Liang chuan*, Duke Hsi 9 (*Ku Liang chuan chu-su* 8.3b (0184)), the phrase *wu yung ch'üan* 勿雍泉 means "(the signatories of the treaty) will not build dykes."

2 As stated by the editors, *pu* 不 is used for *fei* 非.

3 This rather indistinct character the editors interpret as *yeh* 夜, which is quite possible in view of the Later Han forms of this sign listed in *HLTY*, *ch'ü sheng* 47b. They believe that the phrase *yeh ts'ao wei hui* 夜草爲灰, means "to burn grass to ashes, so as to make fertilizer". *SS* suggests that *yeh*, *ziag (*GSR*, p. 211, no. 800j) should be a loan for *tse* 擇, *d'âk (*GSR*, p. 209, no. 790n). However, this loan is not attested, and one might as well suggest that *yeh* is a loan for *shao* 燒, *śńiog (*GSR*, p. 299, no. 1164t), which is the word used in similar passages in other texts. The simplest solution would be, of course, to assume that the scribe, who made several evident mistakes elsewhere, inadvertantly omitted the word "to burn". In the *SS* translation the editors completely neglect their own suggestion *tse*. But these same editors are right when they refer to the *Li-chi* chapter *Yüeh ling*, the Ordinances of the Months (*Li-chi chu-su* 16.3b (0756); Couvreur, *Li ki* I, p. 363; Legge, *Li ki* 27, p. 274), which reads *wu shao hui* 勿燒灰. So does the *Huai-nan-tzu*, ch. 5, p. 74, but *LSCC* 5/1, p. 45, reads *tan* 炭 (*Frühling*, p. 55), which has led both Couvreur and Legge to translate *hui* in the *Li-chi* passage as "charcoal". The present strip would seem to prove that *hui* is the correct reading. The strip shows in any case that the rule existed in the 3rd century B.C.,

so that the quarrel between Jung Chao-tsu and Tsou Shu-wen on the origin of the *Yüeh ling* included in the *Li-chi* loses some of its point.

4 To be used as fertilizer.

5 The editors read *li* 茘, "broom sedge; iris"; for the different ancient meanings of this word see Teng Ssu-yü, pp. 156–157. I fail to understand why *SS* suggsets that *li* should be a loan for *chia* 甲, for the ancient pronunciation of *li* is *—/ liei, whereas *chia* was *kap (*GSR*, p. 318, no. 1241, and p. 168, no. 629a). This impossible loan is nowhere attested. *SS* then explains *chia* as the husks around sprouting seeds (according to the—unaccessible—*Shih ming*, ch. *shih t'ien* 釋天) and translates the phrase *ch'ü sheng li* 取生茘, now equated with *ch'ü sheng chia*, as "to pick plants that are just sprouting"! In view of the *Li-chi* one would have expected *lan* 藍, "indigo", which is found there in the sentence preceding the prohibition to burn and make ashes (*Li-chi chu-su* 16.3b (0756); Couvreur, *Li-ki* I, p. 363; Legge, *Li-ki* 27, p. 274). For completeness' sake: *li*, "broom sedge" is found in the *Yüeh ling*, which states that this plant starts to grow in the second month of winter (*Li-chi chu-su* 17.11a (0825); Couvreur, *Li-ki* I, 0. 602; Legge, *Li-ki* 27, p. 305), without mentioning any prohibition to pick it.

6 About six characters effaced.

7 享 is not *hsiang*, but *kuo*, i.e. 椁 or 槨; see GSR, p. 204, no. 774.

8 *Tsao* 皀; see e.g. *Chuang-tzu*, the beginning of ch. 9, p. 149; Legge, *Chuang-tzu* 39, p. 276.

9 *Chih t'ien* 之田; the context makes it unlikely that this could mean "to go to the fields".

10 "Wardens" is a tentative rendering of *ho chin* 河 (explained by the editors as 呵) 禁. The editors, however, subordinate the following *so* 所 to *ho-chin* and explain *ho-chin so* as "an area where warnings have been established", i.e. a forbidden area.

11 *Kung* 公; in these texts *kung* refers to the authorities or the government.

12 Compare A 9 below, which stipulates that certain parts of dead government horses or cattle had to be handed over to the authorities.

A 3 W 7.1b; S I.10a; S III.23b; SS 27–28; str. 8–9 (075–076).

[8] The delivery of hay and straw per *ch'ing*[1] is to be done according to the number of fields bestowed.[2] Irrespective of whether the fields are cultivated or uncultivated the delivery per *ch'ing* is three bushels[3] of hay (or) two bushels of straw. From a raking of hay[4] or a bundle of whitlow grass[5] upward, everything will be received. When delivering hay and straw, substitution [9] of the one for the other[6] is allowed.[7]

Statutes on Agriculture.

1 See note 5 to A 1 above.

2 The text reads *shou* 受, taken by *S* to mean *shou* 授; I have followed this explanation. *SS* retains the normal meaning "to receive". The manner in which fields were bestowed, c.q. received, is unknown. Some authors believe that fields had been "bestowed" in rotation under the ancient "well-field" system, but that since Shang Yang's reforms in the 4th century B.C. they had become property with well-defined limits, and that, although in the present article the old name is retained, these fields actually were private property; see T'ang, "So-yu-chih", p. 60 f., Hsiung and Wang, "So-yu-chih", p. 76 f. and Lin Chien-ming, "T'e-tien", p. 9 f.

3 *Shih* 石, "bushel", of c. 20 litres. That bushels are meant and not piculs of c. 30kg. is clear from the Han tax-records of about a century later, as these note the receipt of the hay and straw tax in parts of bushels, namely in *tou* 斗, "pecks" of c. 2 l., and even of *sheng* 升 of c. 200 cubic centimeters; see Ch'iu Hsi-kuei, "Hu-pei", p. 58, where the author suggests that the hay and the straw may have been chopped.

4 The text reads *huang-x* 黄 X; the character X, being a combination of 黍 and 魚, is unknown. The editors of both *S* and *SS* think that it might be the same as *su* 穌, and they believe *huang su* to mean "dry hay". However, this explanation militates against the construction of the whole sentence and it disregards the fact that *SW* explains *su* as "grain raked together" (cf. *SWKL*, p. 3125b). *Huang* by itself might indicate "hay".

5 蘑 is unknown, but Morohashi, vol. 9, p. 1002, contains *li* 藶, identified as *inunazuna*, "whit-

low grass". *SS* remarks that 膺 should be read *li* 曆, which in the *Ta Tai Li-chi* (unaccessible), chapter *Tzu Chang wen ju kuan* 子張問入官, is explained as *luan* 亂 (Karlgren, *GSR*, p. 227, no. 858e, agrees), and so *SS* translates *li* as *luan ts'ao* 草, "weeds". Another suggestion by *SS* is that *li*—*liek, should be read *ti* 藡, which is identical with *ti* 荻, *d'iek (*GSR*, p. 227, no. 856d), indicating some kind of rushes.

6 Literally "mutually transferring and handing over", *hsiang shu tu* 相輸度. That the above translation is correct is clear from the tax records of the 2nd century B.C., discussed by Ch'iu Hsi-kuei, "Hu-pei", pp. 50–51 and 58, which show that hay was paid in lieu of, *tang* 當, straw at the rate of two to one. *SS* gives "to convert" as a second possibility, but translates *shu* and *tu* literally as "to transport" and "to weigh", neglecting *hsiang*, but this solution is grammatically unacceptable.

7 In the Yün-meng texts the Ch'in land tax is not mentioned. This tax is discussed in my "Economy"; some texts indicate that it was one tenth of the harvest, whereas others show that it may have been one fifth. Perhaps the amount depended on the type of tenure; it may also have differed during different periods.

A 4 W 7.1b; S I.10b; S III.24a-b; SS 28–29; str. 10 (077).

[10] Whenever[1] (from a storehouse for) grain, hay or straw the wood and the (bottom) matting[2] have been removed[3], the number of bushels is to be reported[4] to the Prefect's court.[5] Do not use it; cover it again with the matting.[6]

Statutes on Agriculture.

1 *Che* 輒 is used in the second part of the Chinese sentence, but it is to be translated by "whenever" at the beginning of the English sentence.

2 *Chien* 薦 is matting or a layer of grass spread under other objects. From D 129 it is clear that a straw mat formed the bottom of a grain store. According to "Liang ts'ang", p. 58, the bottom of the grain storage pits of the Warring States period, discovered in Lo-yang, was covered with planking, over which rush mats had been spread. The function of the wood—simply *mu* 木— is not clear; perhaps there was some kind of wooden structure.

3 *Ch'e* 徹 is used for *ch'e* 撤, "to remove".

4 Literally "to present", *shang* 上.

5 Both the Prefect's and the Commandery Administrator's office were called "court", cf. D 79 below.

6 Or, as *SS* translates this sentence, "The wood and the matting should not be used for other purposes; they should again be used as a bottom layer and a covering".

A 5 W 7.1b; S I.10b; S III.24b; SS 29; str. 11 (078).

[11] As regards rations for (official) carriage horses and draft oxen, if for more than two months rations have not been issued or forwarded, they are all to be stopped; they must not be issued or forwarded.[1] Those who are given rations by the Main (Office of) Agriculture[2] without having a permanent record[3] are to be given rations as from the day of the arrival of the certificate[4]; one must not exceed[5] (the stipulations of) the certificate.

Statutes on Agriculture.

1 The translation of this rule is highly tentative; for want of anything better it is mainly based on the indications provided by SS, although these are doubtful. The main difficulty is caused by the word *chih* 致 which seems to be used with two completely different meanings (see also note 4). *SW* explains *chih* as *sung-i* 送詣, "to forward", and this has been adopted here by both S and SS.

2 As indicated by SS, the title *ta t'ien* 大田 occurs in *LSCC*, p. 207 (Wilhelm, *Frühling*, p. 274, "Ackerbauminister"), and in *YTCC*, p. 101, but these passages do not furnish any indications concerning the position and the tasks of this official. Yü Hao-liang, p. 7, suggests that the title *ta t'ien* was eventually changed in *chih su nei-shih* 治粟內史.

[3] Following the explanation of the editors of S and SS.

[4] Here the editors of both editions give an explanation of *chih* 致 which differs completely from the one referred to in note 1. For they believe that here *chih* means "document" or "certificate", being led to this solution by a remark in *SWTHTS* in *SWKL*, p. 2318a. Here, in discussing the various meanings of *chih*, the author Chu Chün-sheng (1788–1858) notes that in one passage in the *Li-chi* chapter *Ch'ü li* (*Li-chi chu-su* 2.15b (0098)) *hsien t'ien chai che ts'ao shu chih* 獻田宅者操書致, the word *chih*, *t̂'i̯ĕd (*GSR*, p. 116, no. 413d) should be a loan for *chih* 質, *t̂'i̯ĕt (*GSR*, p. 135, no. 493a), meaning *ch'üan* 券, "document, contract". In view of the surrounding passages in the *Ch'ü li* paragraph, which enumerates a series of persons all presenting two objects, *chih* in the combination *shu chih* 書致 must be a noun, signifying some kind of writing. Karlgren, "Loan characters I", p. 42, no. 101 (based on Wang Nien-sun) considers this loan "plausible". He repeats this equation in his "Glosses on the Li ki", p. 6, no. 58, and in his "Gleanings", p. 11, no. 101. (Because the traditional commentators are silent on this point, both Couvreur, *Li ki* I, p. 42, and Legge, *Li ki* 27, p. 84, render *chih* by "to present"). However, whereas in the *Ch'ü li* passage *chih* has the specific meaning of "pledge" or "deed", it cannot have this technical meaning in the rule under discussion. That it is a noun is certain, for it is followed by the verb *tao* 到, "to arrive", but its exact meaning escapes me. For completeness' sake I add that Shen Chih-yü shows that about a millennium before the Ch'in strips were written, *chih* 至 (not 致) meant "to inform, to communicate" in the oracle bone inscriptions.

[5] The editors want *shen* 深 to be read as *shen* 甚, explaining the latter as "to exceed". Although I feel doubtful about using this typical "adverb" or "adjectival predicate"—excessively, to be excessive—as a "transitive verb"—to exceed something—I see no way out of this difficulty except the editors' suggestion. It should be noted, however, that in the first sentence of the present rule "to exceed, to pass beyond" is quite normally rendered by *kuo* 過 in the phrase "exceeding two months". S renders *shen chih* as "to exceed the date of the certificate", but SS translates "to exceed the stipulations . . ."; I have followed SS. Professor Li Hsüeh-ch'in, "Ku wen", p. 342, wants to render *shen* by "to increase, to add to", which amounts to practically the same.

A 6 W 7.1b; S I.10b; SIII.25a; SS 30; str. 12 (079).

[12] Commoners living in farms[1] should not venture to sell[2] wine. The Agricultural Overseer[3] and the Division Assistants[4] carefully restrain and stop them. Persons who do not obey the Ordinances[5] will have committed a crime.

Statutes on Agriculture.

[1] The term *t'ien she* 田舍 occurs repeatedly in literature, but it is nowhere explained; the impression gained from various passages is that *t'ien she* refers to an unwalled village or hamlet. The passages are *SC* 69.22; *SC* 91.17 (Watson, *Records* I, p. 206: "a field outhouse"; not in *HSPC* 34.21a); *HSPC* 37.1a (rendered by Wilbur as "a house among the fields"; *SC* 100.3 only has *t'ien*); *HHSCC* Mem. 41.2a; Mem. 68.8a; Lao Kan, *K'ao shih*, p. 53, no. 2628 (126) 127.7, and Ch'en Chih, *Liang Han*, p. 60. Ch'en Chih seems to assume that *t'ien she* is a farm.

[2] *Ku chiu* 醢 (酤) 酒 may mean both to buy and to sell wine The Annals of emperor Ching mention a prohibition to sell wine because of a drought (*HSPC* 5.6b; *HFHD* I, p. 331). Cf. the article of the Han code, mentioned in the commentary by Wen Ying (fl. 196–220) to *HSPC* 4.5a (*HFHD* I, p. 231, note 2): *Lü san jen i shang wu ku ch'ün yin fa chin ssu liang* 律三人以上無故羣飲罰金四兩, "(According to) the Statutes, when three or more people flock together to drink without (just) cause, they are fined four ounces of gold."

[3] See Hulsewé, "Ch'in documents", p. 201 ff.

[4] *Pu tso* 部佐. The term is unknown; it may refer to subordinate officials controlling a small area; cf. note 7 to C 8 below, and D 135, where SS identifies these officials with Commune Assistants.

[5] Not to obey the Ordinances was a punishable offence; see A 51, note 6, and especially D 120.

A 7 W 7.1b–2a; S I.10b; SIII.25b–26a; SS 30–32; str. 13–14 (080–081).

[13] In the 4th, 7th, 10th and 1st month the oxen used in agriculture are measured[1]; when the year is ended, in the 1st month they are subject to a great evaluation[2], For good results the Overseer of Agriculture is granted a bottle of wine and a bundle of dried meat; the corral keepers are relieved of one turn of duty[3] and the chief of the cattle men is granted in days three decades.[4] For bad results [14] the Overseer of Agriculture is berated[5], the corral menials[6] are fined two months[7]. In case the oxen have been used in agricultural work[8] and they have decreased in girth[9], the person in charge is bastinadoed[10] with ten strokes for each inch. They (viz. the oxen) are also evaluated per village. For good results the Village Chief[11] is granted in days one decade; for bad results he is bastinadoed with thirty strokes.

Statutes on Stables and Parks.[12]

1 For a brief illustrated account of the use of oxen in ploughing see Chang Chen-hsin.—According to Ho Hsiu's commentary to the *Kung Yang chuan*, Duke Hsi 31 (*Kung Yang chuan chu-su* 12.11b (0372)), one *fu* 膚 is the width of one hand; here *fu* is used as a verb, viz. "to measure". The editors believe that *fu* stands for *lu* 臚, which they translate as "to compare"—a meaning I have not found attested.

2 *Ta k'o* 大課; the scope of such a "great evaluation" is unknown, i.a. because the texts do not mention any "small evaluation". *K'o* meaning "to evaluate, to grade, to classify" is well known. Its use for the evaluation of domestic animals is also attested in literature, for in the economic chapter of the *Han shu* and its parallel in the *Shih-chi* we find it applied to the grading of the offspring of brood mares, *k'o hsi* 課息 (*HSPC* 24B.18b, *SC* 30.39; the word *hsi* has been misunderstood both by Chavannes, *Mh* III, p. 589, and by Swann, p. 309, although the former had correctly interpreted the word on its earlier occurrence in the same chapter, *SC* 30.37, as "progéniture" in *Mh* III, p. 591, note 1). A document found in the Edsin-gol defence lines, to be dated between 43 and 27 B.C., shows that draught oxen were inspected to determine their characteristics, *hsiang* 相 (note that *SW* defines *hsiang* as *hsing shih* 省視), the results being noted in ledgers that were presented to the Minister of Agriculture (see Lao Kan, *Shih-wen, k'ao-cheng*, p. 61). So far, we have no actual handbook for the inspection of cattle, but among the silk manuscripts found at Ma-wang tui there is a rather poetic (but also rather abstruse) text on the inspection of horses. This formed perhaps part of the *Hsiang liu ch'u* 相六畜, mentioned in *HSPC* 30.78a; see Loewe, "Manuscripts", p. 123, no. 11, and see also *Hsiang-ma ching* and Hsieh Ch'eng-chia. Chavannes, *Stein*, strip no. 395, Wang, *Liu sha* 1.11a, contains a fragment of a text which Wang Kuo-wei believed to be a *Hsiang-ma fa* 相馬法. See also Tsou Chieh-cheng and Mori, *Kan-kan*, p. 37 ff., as well as Ch'en Chih, *HSHC*, p. 356, who refers to *HSPC* 65.10a for training in this art.—*Tien* 殿 and *tsui* 最 denote poor and excellent results.

3 *Keng* 更. We do not how this system worked; in view of Han practice these men may have been freed of the obligatory month of statute labour per year (see *HSHD* II, p. 176 ff.).

4 The editors of SS correctly assume that this is a case of *ssu lao* 賜勞, "bestowal of extra service time" as mentioned in the Edsingol strips (see *RHA* II, p. 169) and in a Tun-huang strip (see Chavannes, *Stein*, str. 592; Wang, *Liu sha*, 2.10a).

5 The Ch'in documents contain several instances of an official being "berated", but we do not know what this implied; was it an oral reprimand, or was it entered in his service record and could influence his further career?

6 The word *jung* 冗 or 宂 poses problems. *SW* explains it as *san* 㪔, i.e. 散, and defines it as "people in the house who have no work in the fields", *jen tsai wu hsia wu t'ien shih* 人在屋下無田事, which is not very helpful. Apart from "to roam, to wander" (e.g. in *HHSCC*, Ann. 1A.17a; see further the passages in Fujita, vol. 1, pp. 614–615), the usual explanation of *jung* is "supernumerary", but that is not applicable to the use of *jung* in the Ch'in strips. The most helpful ancient explanation is found in Cheng Hsüan's commentary to the *Chou Chou li, t'ien kuan, kao-jen* 槀人 (*Chou li* 8/31, p. 99 f.; *Chou li chu-su* 16.13b–14a (0600–0601); cf. Biot I, p. 395), viz. that *jung* were subordinate clerks, fulfilling their duties in turn.

At the Han court, a body of eunuchs formed "the Extra Retinue of the Yellow Gate", standing guard in the inner apartments or forming a body-guard around the imperial equipage (*HHSCC*, Tr. 26.6a; Bielenstein, *Bureaucracy*, p. 65). The idea implied by *jung* seems to be "(undetermined) duties"; this comes out most clearly in an edict of Wang Mang of A.D. 10, concerning taxes (*HSPC* 24B.24a). This edict orders that persons unable to pay the tax should *jung tso* 冗作, "be assigned for service without fixed duties" (Swann, p. 339), or "work at incidental occupations" (*HFHD* III, p. 459). In the Ch'in texts I believe *jung* to mean "to be assigned to work at a particular place or for a particular person". This explanation fits the context in the twelve cases where *jung* occurs (see index, *s.v. jung*). I fail to understand why Professor Li Hsüeh-ch'in, "Ku wen", p. 342, wants to explain *jung* as "many".

7 This might perhaps mean "two months salary", as specified in other cases. The editors of *SS* suggest that this was the counterpart of *ssu lao*, for which see note 4 above. Unfortunately, we do not know the practical effect of this measure.

8 For the use of oxen drawing the plough, see the brief essay in *Ch'in hui-yao*, p. 461 f., Li Chien-nung, p. 154 f., and Chang Chen-hsin. See also Bodde, *Festivals*, pp. 230–241, and Amano, pp. 733–756.

9 *Hsieh* 絜 is "to measure", especially the circumference; it is explained as *wei tu* 圍度 in the commentary to *Kuan-tzu*, ch. 8, p. 37 (Rickett, p. 229). Similarly in Chia I's essay *Kuo Ch'in lun* (*HSPC* 31.28a; *SC* 6.99; *Mh* II, p. 231). SS refers to a Han strip from the Edsin-gol area, which mentions a black bull, measuring 7 ft. 3 in. (c. 169cm.); see *Chia pien*, p. 93, no. 2274 (misread in Lao Kan, *K'ao shih*, p. 35, no. 1685).

10 Here the bastinado is a separate punishment, and not a subsidiary aggravation, for which see *RHL*, p. 128.

11 The editors are right in correcting the *t'ien tien* 田典 of the text to *li* 里 *tien*. The original title of the village chief was *li cheng* 正 (mentioned in *Han Fei-tzu*, ch. 35, p. 253; Liao II, p. 124), but this was changed to *li tien* in order to avoid the tabooed personal name Cheng 政 of the First Emperor.

12 See note 4 above.

A 8 W 7.2a; S I.10b; S III.26b–27a; SS 32–33; str. 15 (082).

[15] When loaned[1] iron tools that have become worn, spoilt and unusable,[2] break, this[3] has to be noted in writing[4]; they are to be taken in without charging[5].

Statutes on Stables and Parks.

1 This article is also translated in Vandermeersch, "Procédure", p. 13.—The text has *chia* 叚, explained as *chia* 假, evidently based on *SW*. For the loan of government tools to commoners see A 56 and 57 below.

2 *Pu sheng* 不勝, evidently short for *pu sheng yung* 用.

3 The text has *wei* 爲, presumably meaning "for (this)".

4 *Yung shu* 用書; I presume that this means that the fact had to be entered in the appropriate ledger, and not that it had to be reported, which is the rendering adopted by SS. Strips from the Han period found in the Edsin-gol area show, that such ledgers were subject to periodical inspections; see Yoneda.

5 In view of the last line of A 41 below I think it is the borrower who is excused repayment, but cf. A 57.

A 9 W 7.2a; S I.10b–11a; S III.27a–28a; SS 33–35; str. 16–20 (083–087).

[16] When government horses and cattle are taken out to graze, and horses (or cattle[1]) die, the prefecture where they have died is to be speedily informed. The prefecture speedily inspects this and collects it (viz. the dead animal). In case this is not done speedily[2] and it becomes spoilt, the Prefect[3] refunds it with the value it had before it was spoilt.

If small[4] bond-servants die of sickness, this is to be reported to. . .[5] concerned. For those who die without having been ill, this is to be reported [17] to the office by means of an investigation report to judge[6] it.

When horses or oxen of the Great Stables, the Palace Stables[7] or palace stables[8] are concerned, their sinews, hides and horns as well as their value in cash are to be handed over[9]; [18] the persons concerned take[10] these to the office concerned. When those who use[11] government horses and oxen lose horses (or oxen[12]) . . .[13] the prefecture where they have died; the prefecture investigates and. . . .[14] sells the meat. It immediately collects the sinews, hides and horns, as well as fully[15] collecting its value in cash. In case the money (collected) is less than (the sum stipulated by) [19] the Statute[16], orders are given to the person(s) concerned to make good the deficiency[17], meanwhile informing the office. The office informs the prefecture (responsible for) the horses or oxen to remove (the animals from the register)[18].

Now, as regards the evaluation of oxen officially used by the prefectures and by the general offices[19], these will be evaluated once each[20]. If after a full year one third has died of (a number of) ten or more, or, if not fully [20] ten oxen, as well as for those who have received oxen for use, three or more have died after a full year, the officials in charge, the men[21] who fed the oxen, as well as the Prefect and the Assistant Prefect are all guilty. The Ministry of Finance[22] evaluates the prefectures, (whereas) the Great Granary[23] evaluates the general offices as well as those who had received oxen for use.

. . . .[24]

1 This article is also translated in Vandermeersch, "Procédure", p. 13.—In the text the reduplication mark = has been added to the character "horse", but it seems to have been inadvertently omitted before "ox". For the frequent use of this mark see also *RHA* II, p. 378 (1).

2 The editors rightly consider *ch'i ju chih* 其入之 as redundant.

3 *Ling* 令. Because it is the prefecture that is at fault, it seems likely that *ling* indicates the Prefect, but it is also possible to translate the sentence as "order (the persons in charge of the animals, or the responsible officials in the prefecture) to refund it. . . ."

4 *Li ch'en* (*ch'ieh*) 隸臣 (妾) are persons serving a three years' sentence as hard-labour convicts; see *RHL*, p. 130. They were not slaves, as demonstrated by Li Chien-ming; see also Introduction, p. 15 and 17. "Small" is defined in A 12 below as less than 6 ft. 5 in. in height (c. 1.50 m.). The rule in A 11 allows officials to "loan" young bondwomen to private persons, who had to clothe and feed them.

5 Two characters illegible.

6 *Lun* 論; see note 5 to E 4 below.

7 The *ta ch'iu* 大廄 and the *chung* 中 *ch'iu* in Han times were respectively one of the emperor's Six Stables, and the empress' stable; see *HSPC* 19A.12a and *HSPC* 63.2b (see also *HSPC* 16.53a) and cf. Bielenstein, *Bureaucracy*, p. 34 f.

8 The text reads *kung* 宮 *ch'iu*, correctly rendered in S and SS, whereas W 7 mistakenly has *kuan* 官 *ch'iu*. *Chung* 中, "the Centre", is a general designation of the imperial palace compound; *kung* is an individual palace building, like e.g. the Wei-yang kung. The term *kung ch'iu* is unknown.

9 *Chiao* 效 occurs frequently in these texts with the meaning "to check, to control", but in the present case, as well as in a few other instances, it is equivalent to *chiao* 交, as pointed out by the editors.

10 From the context it is clear that in many cases *i* 詣 does not simply mean "to go to, to proceed to (of an inferior to a superior)", but that it often is to be understood as "to bring, to take along".

[11] The word "use" here covers both *ch'eng* 乘 for carriage horses and *fu* 服 for oxen.
[12] I have added this word to conform to the foregoing.
[13] The editors of SS suggest that the scribe has omitted something in this passage.
[14] The text reads *tsa* 雜, which the editors of S explain as *hui-chi* 會集, "combined, united". *Tsa* with this meaning is frequently used in the Han histories, e.g. when several officials "combined try", *tsa chih* 治, a lawsuit; see also Ch'u Shih-pin, p. 182, last lines. However, I do not believe that *tsa* has this meaning in the passage under discussion. The editors of SS refer to the commentary of the *Kuo yü, Yüeh yü, hsia* (p. 236), where *tsa* is explained as *chü* 俱, i.e. "together", but they misunderstand this to mean "all", and as a result they translate "they completely sell the meat", which is unacceptable. Yen Shih-ku (581–645) knew better when in a similar case he explained *tsa* as *kung* 共 (*HSPC* 71.2b), an explanation which the editors of SS themselves adopt in SS, p. 37, note 4! Karlgren, "Loan characters IV", p. 23, no. 1745, adopts an ambiguous position. But all this leaves the word *tsa* in the present passage unexplained, for I cannot see any other authority, with whom the prefecture "together" could sell the meat.
[15] The text has 索 which the editors explain as *so* 索, here meaning "to exhaust, exhaustively; to empty", as indicated by the commentators to some passages in the classics, coveniently assembled by Karlgren in his "Glosses ... Documents", p. 228, no. 1513 A.
[16] I believe that this statute is the Statute on Equipment, *chi lü* 齎律, for which see note 6 to A 56 below.
[17] *Pei* 備. In these texts the expression *pu* 不 *pei* occurs many times, meaning "shortage". In this connection attention should be drawn to a Han strip from Tun-huang, which quotes an unnamed Han statute: "When stock animals wound or kill each other, one third (of the value) is paid (to the owner) to restore harmony"; the text continues with the order that one party should pay 3000 cash to the other party and give him the bones and the meat of the dead animal (Chavannes, *Stein*, p. 109, no. 494; Wang, *Liu-sha* 2.12a, no. 56; *RHL*, p. 257, no. b).
[18] *Ch'u* 出 mostly means "to issue", and as such the word occurs frequently in the Ch'in texts and in the Han strips found near Tun-huang and in the Edsin-gol defence lines. However, *ch'u* sometimes has the technical meaning "to consider as issued", viz. "to remove from the registers as being no longer held", or, more briefly, "to write off, to cancel". It is the latter meaning which has to be adopted here; SS has also done so.
[19] *Tu kuan* 都官, "General Offices", were regional branch-offices of government departments in the capital, mainly of those concerned with economic activities, like the Ministry of Finance and its organizations, like the Central Treasury and the Great Granary (all mentioned in the present texts), and, especially in Han times, the many agencies of the Privy Purse (see *HSPC* 19A. 14a f.). These General Offices were found in the provinces; certainly in the prefectures, as shown by these texts, and probably also in the commanderies (see Ch'iu Hsi-kui, "Se-fu", p. 221). Within the capital, such offices were called "General Offices of the Palace", *chung* 中 *tu-kuan*; in the prefectures these establishements are sometimes referred to as *li kuan* 離官, "detached offices" (see Kao Heng, "Chih-kuan", p. 222, and Ch'iu, *op. cit.*, p. 232). These offices are to be distinguished from the many offices which belonged to the prefectural organization and which where headed by *se-fu* 嗇夫, "Overseers" (see my "Ch'in documents", p. 201 f., and the extensive study by Ch'iu Hsi-kuei, mentioned above), whereas the General Offices were headed by a *chang* 長, "Chief" (see D 79 below). These Chiefs were certainly nominated by the central government, as is also assumed by Kao Min, *Ch'u t'an*, p. 217, and by Kao Heng, "Chih-kuan", p. 221; the Overseers, however, were appointed locally by the prefect and occupied a far more modest position (Ch'iu, *op. cit.*, p. 240). See also Emura, p. 191, and Yü Hao-liang, "Chih-kuan", p. 22. Professor Kudō, "Tokan", has a completely different explanation of the term *tu kuan*, which is hard to accept. He suggests that the *tu kuan* were in charge of the domains, *tu*, granted to members of the royal clan and to men of military merit; their organization was therefore similar to that of the prefectures.—A renewed study of the evidence and of the Chinese and Japanese studies mentioned above has led me to conclusions which differ considerably from those adopted on pp. 200–201 of my "Ch'in documents", which were written late in 1977.
[20] The text writes *ko i k'o* 各一課, which is ambiguous; it may mean that each animal was inspected.
[21] The meaning of *t'u* 徒 in the Ch'in texts is still unclear to me, see my "Ch'in documents", p. 214; perhaps the term designates statute labourers in some cases. It should be noted

that in Han times *t'u* were without exception hard labour convicts, whereas conscripts—both those who performed statute labour and those who served their term in the armed forces—were called *tsu* 卒. In view of these uncertainties I have used the neutral term "men".

22 For this rendering of *nei shih* 內史 see my "Ch'in documents", p. 194. Kudō, "Naishi", also arrives at the same conclusion; he sketches the historical development of the function of the *nei shih* and he believes that in Ch'in times the function of *chih-su nei-shih* 治粟內史, i.e. the Minister of Finance, was split off, leaving the traditional *nei-shih* the task of administering the capital area. Yü Hao-liang, p. 5 f., wrongly assumes that in the text under discussion the governor of the capital area is meant.

23 In the Han period the Great Granary was one of the departments of the Ministry of Finance; see *HSPC* 19A.14b; *HHSCC* Tr. 26.2a; Bielenstein, *Bureaucracy*, p. 43.

24 The title of this statute is practically illegible, but in view of its contents the editors have included it here.

A 10 W 7.2b; S I.12b; S IV.37a; SS 47–48; str. 47 (114).

[47] When horses of the courier service are used[1], they are given one feeding[2] of grain; when they return, they are again given one feeding of grain. Always[3] eight horses are (fed) together. When they are used repeatedly, they should be given one feeding without letting a day go by. When using horses of the prefecture[4] and these have done heavy work[5], they should again be given one[6] additional feeding of grain.

Statutes on Granaries.[7]

1 *Chia* 駕, lit. "to harness".

2 *I shih ho* 一食禾 might also be rendered as "to be fed wholly with grain", but that seems not to fit the context; SS translates as I have done.

3 Lit. *chieh* 皆 "all".

4 The editors of SS want *hsien* 縣 to mean "far", based on the commentary on a passage in the *Huai-nan-tzu*, ch. 9, p. 129, but it is evident that there the meaning of *hsien* is not "far" in a physical sense, being an abbreviation of *hsüan* (縣=懸) *ko* 隔 "apart, removed", as in *HSPC* 1B.8a, rendered by Dubs as "separated" in *HFHD* I, p. 110.

5 *Lao* 勞.

6 *Hu* 壺 is an evident mistake for *i* 壹 "one".

7 For a study of the Ch'in granary organization, see Ōda and the remarks by An Tso-chang, "Nung-yeh", p. 30 f.

A 11 W 7.2b; S I.12b; S IV.37a–b; SS 48–49; str. 48 (115).

[48] In case commoners wish to borrow[1] (bond)-women[2] who are not yet employed[3] and who are clothed and fed by the government, they are to be loaned; they are to be clothed and fed by them[4]. The officials will in every case stop[5] to make them serve.

Statutes on Granaries.

1 The text reads *chia* 叚, which according to *SW* means "to borrow or to lend". In the present case it seems that these girls are entrusted to the commoners without any payment being demanded, although in the Han history there are instances that for government land that was "loaned" to commoners a land-rent had to be paid; see the discussion in Hiranaka, pp. 83 f. and 133 f.

2 Although the text only has *ch'ieh* 妾 which in these texts means "slave woman" (see Lin Chien-ming), I assume that *li* 隸 *ch'ieh*, "bond-women", are meant, because they are said to be fed and clothed by the government, which would hardly be done for privately owned slaves.

3 It is to be noted that in Han times *wei shih nu* 未使女 were "pre-service girls", aged six years *and less* (see Yang Lien-sheng, p. 110), and this is the explanation adopted by S and SS, although this hardly seems to fit the context.

4 I.e. the commoners.

5 The editors explain *p'i* 柀 as *pa* 罷. Although this loan is not attested, it is phonetically acceptable, *p'i* being *p'ia and *pa* being *b'ia (*GSR*, p. 26, no. 25j and no. 26a). The editors of SS add another possibility, viz. that *p'i* should mean "partly" (cf. note 25 to A 19 below).

A 12 W 7.2b; S I.12b; S IV.37b–38a; SS 49–50; str. 49–52 (116–119).

[49] As regards bond-servants and bond-women engaged in work[1] for the government, a bond-servant (receives a ration of) two bushels[2] of grain per month, a bond-woman one and a half bushel; to those not engaged in work no rations are given. Small[3] *ch'eng-tan* and bond-servants who are working[4] (receive a ration of) one and a half bushel of grain per month; those not yet able to work one bushel of grain per month. Small [50] bond-women and grain-pounders[5] who are working (receive a ration of) one bushel and two and a half *tou*[6] per month; those not yet able to work one bushel of grain per month. Infants who have no mother (receive a ration of) half a bushel each; although they have a mother and they are with her while she is assigned[7] to (work for) the government, they are also given rations: per month [51] half a bushel of grain.

Bond-servants (assigned to) agricultural (work) as from the second month are given a monthly ration of two and a half bushels; at the end of the ninth month the half-bushel is to be stopped.

Grain-pounders (receive a ration of) one and a half bushel per month.

Bond-servants and *ch'eng-tan* whose height is not fully six feet and five inches (c. 1.50 m.), and bond-women and grain-pounders whose height is not fully [52] six feet and two inches (c. 1.43 m.) are all considered as "small". When their height is five feet and two inches (c. 1.20 m.) they are all put to work[8].

1 *Ts'ung shih* 從事, "to be engaged on". Hori, "Keimei", p. 123, mistakenly assumes that *ts'ung shih* was different from *tso* 作. The difference between the two terms is not material but grammatical, *ts'ung shih* meaning "to be engaged on a specified task", whereas *tso* means "to work", c.q. "to be made to work".

2 Issues of rations are expressed in measures of capacity; the occurrence of *tou*, one tenth of *a bushel*, makes it clear that *shih* 石 here means "bushel" (c. 20 litres), and not "picul" (c. 30 kg.).

3 The meaning of "small" is defined at the end of this rule.

4 Here *tso* is used; cf. note 2 above.

5 *Ch'ung* 舂, "to pound (viz. grain)" was the hard-labour punishment for women, equivalent to *ch'eng-tan* for men.

6 One *tou* 斗 was one tenth of a bushel.

7 This is a tentative rendering of *jung chü* 冗居; cf. note 6 to A 7. I believe the editors of SS are mistaken in attributing to *chü* 居, "to dwell, to stay", the technical meaning "to work off debts etc. in forced residence", for which see note 8 to A 39 below. As a matter of fact, the editors make this remark in a note, but they do not adopt it in their translation.

8 Cf. the Han Statute on the Great Music, *ta yüeh lü* 大樂律 (*RHL*, p. 37, no. 14), which stipulates that for dancers in the imperial ancestral temples boys from prominent families were to be chosen, over 5 ft. (c. 1.16 m.) tall, between 12 and 30 years of age (*HHSCC*, Tr. 26.3a, Bielenstein, *Bureaucracy*, p. 21, but cf. *Chou-li* 12/42, pp. 67–68, *Chou-li chu-su* 23.4a (0835)).

A 13 W 7.2a; S I.12b; S IV.38b; SS 50; str. 53 (120).

[53] Small bond-servants and bond-women are enrolled[1] in the eighth month as great[2] bond-servants and bond-women. As from the tenth month[3] their rations[4] are increased.

(Statutes on) Granaries.

[1] *Fu* 傅, see Meng K'ang's commentary to *HSPC* A1.34a, and cf. *HFHD* I, p. 80, note 2. Enrolment of free people entailed the performance of statute labour and military service. The height of 6 ft. 2 in., which marked the transition from "small" to adult bond-servants, also played a role in the life of free persons, because young men below this height were excused enrolment, according to Meng K'ang. Enrolment originally took place at fifteen years of age, as has been ably shown by Kao Min, *Ch'u t'an*, pp. 20–25; this age was raised to twenty in 155 B.C. (*HSPC* 5.3b; *HFHD* I, p. 312), and to twenty-three some time between 86 and 81 B.C. (*YTL*, ch. 15, p. 17; Gale, p. 97).

[2] *Ta* 大 were adults, aged fifteen and above; see Yang Lien-sheng, p. 110.

[3] The administrative year started in the 10th month.

[4] Lit. *shih* 食 "food".

A 14 W 7.2a; S I.12b; S IV.38b; SS 50–51; str. 54 (121).

[54] As regards bond-women who perform work in turns of duty[1], as soon as[2] there is an emergency, they will be assembled and assigned (their task)[3], receiving rations according to the Statutes[4]; if there is no emergency, they are not to be assembled.

(Statutes on) Granaries.

[1] *Keng* 更 is "a turn of duty". The term *keng li-ch'ieh* is unknown, but the situation is undoubtedly connected with that described in A 12, viz. that bond-women could "not work".

[2] *Chi* 即.

[3] See note 6 to A 7 above. According to S *tsung jung* 總宂 means "to fall in"; SS explains the term as "assembling those who are scattered", but translates it simply as "to assemble".

[4] I.e. according to A 12, one bushel of grain per month.

A 15 W 7.2b; S I.13a; S IV.39a; SS 51–52; str. 55–56 (122–123).

[55] *Ch'eng-tan* engaged in building walls as well as in other tasks where the hardship is equal to that of building walls (will receive a food ration) of half (a *tou*) in the morning and of one third (of a *tou*)[1] in the evening. Those who are present at their assigned place of duty[2] as well as those who perform other work are to be fed with one third (of a *tou* at both meals). Those who are ill will be fed in consideration of the circumstances[3], letting the officials decide[4]. [56] Grain-pounders[5], grain-pounder-robber-guards[6] and sifters of white (rice)[7] engaged in construction work will be fed one third (of a *tou* at both meals); when they are not engaged in construction work, they are to be fed according to the Statutes[8].

(Statutes on) Granaries.

[1] For this rendering of *ts'an* 參 see my "Weights", p. 38.

[2] *Shu* 署 is explained in *SW* as "post", *shu-pu* 部; also in *Wen hsüan* 2.3b the 3rd century commentator Hsüeh Tsung 薛綜 defines *shu* as *wei* 位, "position". Karlgren, *GSR* p. 30. no. 45r renders it as "to place; position". As a verb it means "to be posted; to assign, to be assigned (a certain task)", e.g. in a report from the Edsingol defence lines concerning the activities of the men in a certain station: "two men escorting prisoners, 38 men *shu*—posted in or assigned to the kitchen, the resthouse of the courier service, the gaol ..." (Lao Kan,

Kao shih, p. 80, no. 3992 (211) 34.9). In the present instance, the term *shou* 守 *shu* will have the same meaning as *chien* 見 *shu* and *chü* 居 *shu*, which occur frequently in the Edsin-gol documents (cf. my "Han time documents", pp. 29–30, where the translation "office" has to be corrected). The explanation by the editors of both S and SS, viz. that *shou shu* should mean "to stand at one's post and keep guard" is therefore incorrect, all the more so because hard labour convicts could hardly be entrusted with military duties. See also note 1 to C 21 below.

3 *Ch'eng i* 程議, lit. "weighing and considering".

4 *Ling li chu* 令吏主, lit. "ordering the officials to take charge".

5 The new strip starts with the words *ch'eng-tan*, but their presence here is inexplicable because these are men, whereas the grain-pounders and the following are all women. In view of the context, the editors have done right in placing this strip here, but the presence of these two words has not given rise to any remark on their part. It might be due to a mistake of the ancient scribe, because the expression *ch'eng-tan ch'ung* occurs so frequently.

6 When women condemned to pounding grain (the heaviest of the hard labour punishments) had served a few years, their status was changed to that of robber-guards; see *RHL*, p. 336, and cf. Hori, "Keimei", p. 124, and Huang Chan-yüeh, pp. 13–14.

7 *Pai ts'an* 白粲, in Han times a three year punishment for women; see *RHL*, p. 130.

8 See A 12 above, which stipulates that female convict labourers received a normal ration of 1 1/2 bushel per month or 1/2 *tou* per day. Combining the data of A 12 and A 15, one arrives at the following figures:

labour	normal ration		heavy work ration	
convicts	p/day	p/month	p/day	p/month
men	2/3 *tou*	2 bushels	5/6 *tou*	2 1/2 bushels
women	1/2 *tou*	1 1/2 bushel	2/3 *tou*	2 bushels

As a personal note I may add that during the Second World War the prisoners of war of the Japanese in Singapore received 500 grams of raw rice daily as their main rations, with 50 grams extra for heavy work (mostly moving earth, like the *ch'eng-tan*). This was supplemented by a modest quantity of vegetable fat (crude palm-oil) and some self-grown vegetables, including red peppers. Occasionally they received a small piece of dried fish, but meat hardly ever. This diet was sufficient to keep me at least in good physical shape. Whether the Ch'in hard labour convicts received the prescribed quantities is perhaps subject to doubt.

A 16 W 7.2b; S I.13a; S IV.39b–40a; SS 52–53; tr. 57–58 (124–125).

[57] When feeding *ch'eng-tan* by the day, at the end of the month one takes the surplus[1] to serve as rations for the later ninth month[2]. For increasing[3] their food when the *ch'eng-tan* perform easy[4] tasks, the official(s) in charge will be judged according to the Statute on infringing the Ordinances[5]. [58] The issues not fulfilled monthly for the grain-pounders and *ch'eng-tan*[6] will be deducted[7].

(Statutes on) Granaries.

1 The editors read *yü i* 餘益, where the second character might be *ying* 盈.

2 The chronological handbooks as well as Ch'en Chiu-chin show, that between the middle of the 3rd century B.C. and the reform of the calendar in 104 B.C. the intercalary month was inserted after the ninth month, thus forming a second or later ninth month.—The standard for rations being the month of thirty days, the authorities saved one day's rations during the "short" months of twentynine days. With an average of 60 short months during a ten-year period, the authorities saved 60 days' rations for the 4 intercalary months in the same 10 year period, or half the rations (60:4 = 15) for one intercalary month. The object of this rule will have been the prevention of embezzlement.

3 *I* 益. A 15 stipulates higher rations for heavy work.

4 *An* 安, lit. "quiet".

5 D 120 below only explains "infringing the Ordinances" as "when the Ordinances say 'do not do this', to do it", without indicating the measure of punishment.

[6] I fail to understand the purport of the inversion of the normal order "*ch'eng-tan* and grain-pounders".

[7] If this translation is correct, the text presumably refers to the reduction of the rations during months of 29 days. However, SS translates: "When grain-pounders and *ch'eng-tan* do not work a full month . . ."

A 17 W 7.2b; S I.13a; S IV.40a; SS 53; str. 59 (126).

[59] When dismissed[1] bond-servants and bond-women (as well as) bond-servants and bond-women build walls, as well as perform[2] other tasks equal[3] to wall building, the men are to be fed with half (a *tou*) in the morning and one third (of a *tou*) in the evening; the women (receive) one third (of a *tou* at both meals).

(Statutes on) Granaries.

[1] This rule is similar to A 15 above.—*Mien* 免, "dismissed", can only refer to ex-convicts, viz. bondservants and bond-women who had completed their term of hard labour, but it seems curious that such persons could be obliged to work again, or was this counted as normal statute labour?

[2] *Wei* 爲; this word does not occur in A 15 above.

[3] Here A 15 inserts *lao* 勞, "hardship".

A 18 W 7.2b; S I.13a; S IV.40 a; SS 53; str. 60 (127).

[60] For feeding starving[1] incarcerated (convicts)[2]: daily one third[3] of a *tou*.[4]

(Statutes on) Granaries.

[1] *O* 餓.

[2] Cf. *RHL*, p. 74.

[3] There existed two terms for indicating "one third", viz. *shao pan* 少半, very common in other texts, and *ts'an* 參, for which see my "Weights", p. 38.

[4] This means that these people received half the rations of an ordinary convict. The editors of SS may therefore well be right when they suggest that "starving" was a punishment for prisoners. That *o*, "to starve" can be used transitively is proved by *Mencius* VI B, xv, 2: "When Heaven is about to impose a great task on a man, it is sure first. . . . to starve his body and skin".

A 19 W 7.2b; S I.11a; S III.29a; SS 35–38; str. 21–27 (088–94).

[21] When grain in the ear[1] is entered in a granary[2], 10.000 bushels make one pile; they are ranged[3] so as to form a "house"[4]. The Prefectural Overseer[5] or[6] the Assistant (Prefect) as well as the Chief of (the Bureau of) Granaries[7] come together[8] to seal it, whereas one "house" each is given to the Granaries Overseer as well as to the Granary Assistants of the detached settlements[9] in charge of [22] ration issues to use for supplies[10]; (this "house") they seal personally and issue it directly[11]. When the remainder is exhausted[12], another "house" is assigned to them[13].

When an Overseer is dismissed[14], the controller[15] opens (the granary); when he observes that it has been sealed (by several persons) together[16], he checks it by means of the inscription[17], and it is again sealed [23] by (these several persons) together; he must not measure or weigh[18] it. Only the granaries that have been sealed personally (by the dismissed Overseer) are measured and weighed[19].

When issuing grain in the ear, in case the person who issues it is not the person who had entered it[20], it should be measured. If the measuring agrees with the inscription, it should be issued. In case there is a shortage, the person who issues it is to be charged with it[21]. [24] If there is a surplus, it is entered[22].

When (several authorities) together[23] issue grain, there must be no change[24].

When the entered grain is not fully ten-thousand bushels and it is desired to increase the stack thereto[25], it is permitted that the person who had entered (the grain) earlier, increases the stack. If somebody else increases the stack, the stackers [25] must first measure the old stack; if (the quantity) agrees with the inscription[26], the grain is entered thereto. If later there is a shortage, the person who entered (grain) last will solely be charged with it. And[27] write the name, status and place[28] of the person who entered the grain to increase the stack in the grain-store[29] register. When ten-thousand [26] bushel stacks as well as those of not fully tenthousand bushels are issued in portions[30], one should not venture to increase the stack.

In Yüeh-yang[31] 20.000 bushels form one stack. In Hsien-yang[32] 100.000 bushels form one stack.

Issuing and entering grain (and) increasing the stacks has to be done in accordance with the Statutes and Ordinances.

Leading officials[33] act [27] together[34] for entering grain in the granaries and opening[35] (them).

Stacks of grain[36] that have been attacked by weevils[37] should[38] be re-stacked[39] and should not be allowed to spoil.

(Statutes on) Granaries.

[1] It is to be noted that the word used here is *ho* 禾 and not *su* 粟, which is the normal word for untreated grain. Now *ho* is explained by the commentator Cheng Hsüan (A.D. 127–200) as *shih kao ping i che* 實稾并刈者, "(fruit=) grain and stalks harvested together", in his remarks to the *I li*, chapter *pin li* (*I li* 20.3a (0577)), aptly rendered by Steele, vol. I, p. 198, as "grain in the ear". This rendering of *ho* esplains why the grain was stacked in the form of "houses" (see note 4), which would be impossible to do with loose grains. However, in some cases *ho* refers to loose grains; see the index *s.v. ho*.

[2] The exact size of such granaries is unknown; Hayashi, *Bunbutsu*, plate 4.10–15, shows some representations of these buildings (text p. 162 f.), and so does e.g. Shen Chung-ch'ang. Early this century Sir Aurel Stein discovered near Tun-huang the ruins of an enormous granary, divided into three halls, each measuring c. 42 × 14,5 m.; see Stein, *Report*, plate 41, and Stein, *Tracks*, plate 78. *San fu*, p. 49, states that the Great Granary (see note 23 to A 9 above) in Ch'ang-an contained 120 space-units called *ying* 楹, but the size of these is unknown. Finally Wang Zhongshu, *Han civilization*, p. 5, notes that in the Ch'ang-an Arsenal the largest warehouse measured 230 × 46 m., incorporating four storage areas of c. 1500m² (the difference between the surface occupied by the storehouse, viz. 230 × 46m = 10580m², and the surface of the four storage areas, viz. 4 × 1500m² = 6000m², hence a difference of c. 4500 m², is easily explained by the enormous thickness of the walls, which on the average lies between 6 and 7 m.; see "Wu k'u", p. 262 f.). See Addenda et Corrigenda.

[3] *Pi-li* 比黎. This expression is unknown, but the editors of S are undoubtedly right in explaining it as "to range, to order in a row". Mao's commentary to verse 2 of Ode 257 (*Shih ching* 18/2.2a (1581), but Karlgren, "Glosses Siao-ya", p. 39, no. 430, rejects this) explains *li* as *ch'i* 齊, "to regulate, to arrange evenly". However, the editors of SS present

a completely different solution, which to me seems unacceptable. Having found that in the 11th century *Chi yün* dictionary (unaccessible) *pi-li* 茈莉 (note that 利 and 黎 are practically homophones; see *GSR*, p. 141, no. 519a and k: *liəd and *liər) denotes a kind of shrub, used to make hedges, they not only take *pi-li* as "hedge", but also turn this binome into a transitive verb, "to hedge in", translating *pi-li chih* 之 as "separate them by means of a thorn hedge" *ke i ching-pa* 隔以荊笆.

4 The text reads *hu* 戶. Even at present, in North China grain in the ear is stacked in piles that look like straw huts; clay models of the same shape are very common among the Han grave goods, although these are mostly provided with feet; see Hayashi, *Bunbutsu*, ills. 4/13–15. SS takes *wei hu* 爲戶 as "to instal a door", whereas Ōda, p. 144, suggests "close the door"!

5 *Hsien se-fu* 縣嗇夫. For lack of supporting evidence, it has so far not been possible to determine the position of this official with absolute certainty, nor that of the Great Overseer, *ta se-fu* 大嗇夫, a title which all authors consider as a synonym of *hsien se-fu*; see my "Ch'in documents", p. 203 f. Practically all authors believe that the *hsien se-fu* is identical with the *hsien ling* 令, the normal term for "prefect". S and SS (p. 16, note 2) do so, although in D 44 below SS renders *ta se-fu* as "the Prefect and his Assistant". Yü Hao-liang, pp. 20–21, also identifies these *se-fu* with the Prefect, and in support of this identification he quotes the *Ho-kuan-tzu*, ch. *Wang fu*, 鶡冠子, 王夫 (Ssu-pu pei-yao ed., ch. *chung* 中, p. 7b), which in its description of the local administration notes that the chief of a prefecture was the *se-fu*. Now Ch'ien Chien-fu, p. 140, provides a solution which, for the time being, seems to be the most acceptable. He suggests that the Ch'in *hsien se-fu* is the forerunner of the Han time *hsien chang* 長, i.e. the prefect of a small or unimportant prefecture (see Bielenstein, *Bureaucracy*, p. 100), whereas the head of a normal prefecture was called *hsien ling* 令.

Kao Min, *Ch'u t'an*, pp. 185–200 (practically identical with Kao Min, "Se-fu"), does not accept the identification of the *hsien*, c.q. *ta*, *se-fu* with the prefect. He believes that he was the chief of all the Overseers in a prefecture, in charge of offices concerned with economic matters. He considers this symptomatic for the (assumed!) state ownership of the land under the Ch'in; with the (assumed) increase of private ownership under the Han, the Prefectural Overseer disappeared. I cannot accept this highly hypothetical construction.—The article by Cheng Shih on the *se-fu* is confused and unclear.—Finally, having reconsidered all the evidence and the suggestions by ancient commentators and modern sholars, Ch'iu Hsi-kui, "Se-fu", pp. 226–229, concludes that both *hsien se-fu* and *ta se-fu* were alternative—and, I would suggest, older—designations for the *hsien-ling* or *chang*, i.e. the Prefect.

6 *Jo* 若.

7 The text here as well as in A 85 and B 11 reads *ts'ang ch'ing* 倉卿. The editors want to substitute *hsiang* 鄉 for *ch'ing*, but I believe that *ch'ing* is correct, and that *ts'ang ch'ing* is a honorific expression, indicating the director of the prefectual office in charge of granaries, the Han time *ts'ang ts'ao* 倉曹, for which see Yen Keng-wang, vol. I, p. 230. For the honorific use of *ch'ing* in Han texts see Ch'en P'an, *Ch'i chung*, pp. 26a–27a. For the honorific use of *ch'ing* after the name of an office or after a title, see Lao Kan, *K'ao shih*, p. 64, no. 3206 (155) 45.10A: *fu ch'ing* 府卿; p. 103, no. 4994 (297) 485.46, and no. 5006 (297) 485.53: *wei-shih ch'ing* 尉史卿; p. 114, no. 5482 (336) 287.17: *yin ch'ing* 尹卿 and *hou ch'ing* 侯卿.

8 Cf. note 14 to A 9 above.

9 I have translated *i* 邑 as "settlement"; perhaps it was a walled town, because the *tu i* 都邑 was the seat of the prefecture (see note 7 to A 21 below). It must have been larger than a *li* 里, "village", because Shang Yang is said to have combined *i* and other agglomerations to form prefectures (*SC* 68.11; Duyvendak, *Lord Shang*, p. 18). In Han times, *i* was the name for appanages granted to empresses, heirs-apparent and princesses (*HSPC* 19A.30a; *HHSCC* Mem. 30A.5a and Tr. 28.7a; cf. Swann, p. 150, note 139). Kao Min, pp. 203–204, throws no further light on the subject.

10 *I ch'i* 以氣; according to *SW* the original meaning of *ch'i* is "to send or give supplies".

11 *Che* 輒, "immediately", explained by the editors as "on their own authority".

12 Cf. note 15 to A 9 above.

13 *Wei* 爲; as *wei* here precedes a verb (*fa* 發) it must have the meaning "on behalf of, for the sake of", without mentioning the object, this being understood.

14 *Mien* 免.

15 *Chiao che* 效者, "the person who performs the check or control", and not necessarily an official with this title.

16 Cf. note 8 above.

17 The text reads *ti* 隄, "dyke", which the editors, doubtless correctly, consider as a loan for *t'i* 題, "inscription."

18 19 In two places on the same strip 23, and very close together, *to* 度, "to measure", is followed by *hsien* 縣. In view of their punctuation after *to*, the editors of W and S evidently consider *hsien* to mean "prefecture", but in the context this makes no sense. I prefer to consider *hsien* to have the well-attested meaning "to weigh", a rendering also adopted by SS. This remark also applies to the parallels of the present rule in A 86 and B 11 below.

20 Lit. "if it is not the person who had entered it who issues it".

21 *Fu* 負, "to carry on the back; to load; to impose a charge", i.e. "to impose responsibility for".

22 *Ju* 入, viz. in the store register; cf. the remarks on *ch'u* 出 in note 13 to A 9 above.

23 Cf. note 8 above.

24 Presumably this means that the responsibility for issuing the grain continued to rest with the same authorities who had entered it. I consider it unlikely that *keng* 更 would mean "to arrange anew", as in the Edsin-gol strips, where *keng chi* 積 occurs frequently for "stacking anew" the piles of bundles of rushes used for the signal fires; see Hsü P'ing-fang, "P'in yüeh", p. 453.

25 For a Han example of adding grain to an existing stock see Lao Kan, *K'ao shih*, p. 78, no. 3890 (202) 112.29: 入粟二十石增廩五千二百廿五石今五千卅石.

26 Cf. note 16 above.

27 I do not understand the function of *erh* 而 here, for the two sentences are not connected.

28 *Ming shih i li* 名事邑里; c.f. E 4 below, which reads *ming shih li* 名事里, and a strip from the Edsin-gol limes, reading *ming hsien chiao li* 名縣爵里 (Lao Kan, *K'ao shih*, p. 13, no. 594 (39) 239.46, which agrees literally with a passage in an edict of 66 B.C. in *HSPC* 8.11a, *HFHD* II, p. 228). Still another combination, *hsien chiao li nien* 年, is found on another Edsin-gol strip (Lao Kan, *K'ao shih*, p. 126, no. 6039 (383) 214.127). Referring to *SW* which explains *shih* 事 as *chih* 職, the explanation of *ming shih li* in the SS note to E 4 below as "name, status and place" is undoubtedly right, because in group E—and in many Edsin-gol strips—persons are identified by these very particulars.

29 *K'uai* 廥. According to *SW* this is a store for hay or straw, but here the word evidently refers to (part of) a grain store.

30 The text reads *pei* 被, which the editors take as a loan for *p'i* 柀, of which *SW* indicates as "another meaning" *hsi* 析, "to split".

31 *Yüeh-yang* 櫟陽 was the capital of the state of Ch'in between 383 and 350 B.C.

32 Hsien-yang was the later capital of the Ch'in kingdom and empire.

33 *Chang li* 長吏. This term presents a riddle, which I am unable to solve. It occurs many times in the Han histories, even more often than indicated by the indices. Sometimes it seems to indicate a single person, namely the Prefect, but there are cases where it seems to be used for the Prefect, his Assistant and his Police Officer. In the present passage it would appear to indicate several persons, in view of the verb *hsiang tsa*, "to come together". In his addition to *SC* 126, Ch'u Shao-sun (1st century B.C.) calls the Prefect of Yeh early in the 4th century B.C. *chang li* (*SC* 126.31; not in Watson, *Records*), but that need not be historically true. When in 202 B.C. emperor Kao warned the *shou wei* 守尉 *chang-li*, "the Commandery Administrators and Military Commandants (as well as) the *chang li*" (*HSPC* I B.5b; *HFHD* I, p. 106), *chang li* can only mean the Prefect together with his two subordinates. But in an edict of emperor Wen issued in 179 B.C., we find the *chang li* mentioned separately, apart from the Assistant Prefect and the Police Officer: special gifts and issues are to be supervised by the *chang li*, whereas the two other officials are to distribute them (*HSPC* 4.7a; *HFHD* I, p. 237). Here the *chang-li* can only be the Prefect. However, an edict of emperor Ching of 144 B.C. says that officials ranking at 600 bushels or more were all *chang li*! (*HSPC* 5.8a; *HFHD* I, p. 342). An edict of emperor Hsüan of 51 B.C. grants gifts to a Grand Administrator and to the *chang li* of a certain prefecture, but also to the Thrice Venerable and others there, so that the *chang li* might very well include the Assistant Prefect and the Police Officer (*HSPC* 8.23a; *HFHD* II, p. 260). This also seems to be stated by the chapter on the organization of the bureaucracy in the Han history (*HSPC* 19B. 29b). It enumerates the *hsien ling* and *hsien chang* 縣令, 長, and their salaries, adding that these different classes of Prefects all had an Assistant Prefect and a Police officer, and concluding the paragraph with the statement *shih wei chang li* 是爲長吏, "These are the *chang li*". This apparently clear statement, however, is ambiguous; hence the word "seems"

in the preceding sentence. For this statement may refer to the whole paragraph, but it may also refer to the Prefects alone, because this chapter often starts with the description of the functions of a superior official and then branches off into details about his subordinates, to add finally further remarks about the superior, without again mentioning his title.

The same uncertainty is felt in the dozens of passages, expecially in the history of the Later Han, where officials ranking at 2000 bushels and *chang li* are mentioned together. As the former term indicates the Grand Administrators of the commanderies, it would only be logical that *chang li* refers to the Prefect, and not also to his Assistant and his Police Officer. The question is not solved by emperor Kuang-wu's edict of 11 August A.D. 30, ordering the abolition or amalgamation of numerous prefectures (on this policy see Bielenstein, "Restoration III", p. 141), because the phrase *hsien kuo pu tsu chih chang li k'o ping ho che* 縣國不足置長吏可幷合者, "prefectures and kingdoms not worth (the trouble) to establish *chang li*, and which can be amalgamated", leaves the interpretation of *chang li* undecided. The specialist in the organization of local government, Yen Keng-wang, vol. I, pp. 7 and 220, does not enter into this curious problem but accepts the definition in *HS* 19 that *chang li* includes the Prefect and his two immediate subordinates, and so does Kamada, p. 142. Lao Kan, *K'ao-shih, k'ao-cheng*, p. 13, however, is aware of the difficulty, but he finally adopts the same solution as Yen Keng-wang. He even goes further, for he states that, contrary to the *shao li* 少吏, "lesser officials", who received a salary of 100 bushels or less, all members of the regional administration who had a salary between 200 and 1000 bushels were *chang li*! To me, the issue remains doubtful, also because Later Han inscriptions show *chang li* offering sacrifices to the mythical emperor Yao, to Confucius and to a sacred mountain (*Li shih* 1.1b, 1.15b, 1.26b, 3.19b), a task surely performed by the Prefect personally and not by one of his aides.

34 See note 8 above.

35 *Fa* 發, and not *ch'u* 出, "to issue".

36 Whereas up to here the text has constantly used the word *ho* 禾, "grain in the ear", it here suddenly writes *su* 粟, "threshed, but further untreated grain"; could this be a scribal error?

37 The text has the unknown character 𧒒, which the editors explain as *yüan* 蝝, "maggot, locust larva".

38 The text reads *i* 義, which in many passages in the classics is explained as *i* 宜, "right and proper, fitting", here rendered by "should."

39 The grain was probably to be re-stacked; cf. note 23 above.

A 20 W 7.2b; S I.11b; S III.29a; SS 38–39; str. 28 (095).

[28] When grain[1], hay or straw is entered, a store-register[2] is made; this is presented to the Minister of Finance. ○ Of both hay and straw 10.000 bushels form a stack; in Hsien-yang 20.000 bushels form a stack. The issuing, entering (and) increasing (their) stacks, as well as checking conform (to the procedures prescribed for) grain in the ear.[3]

(Statutes op) Granaries.

1 This article is also translated in Vandermeersch, "Procédure", p. 14.—In stead of *ho* 禾 the text writes *ho chia* 禾稼, a comparatively rare term, best rendered by "grain crop" (cf. my "Han documents", pp. 26–27).

2 Cf. note 28 to A 19 above.

3 I.e. A 19 above.

A 21 W 7.2b; S I.11b; S III.31b–32a; SS 39; str. 29–30 (096–097).

[29] On the day when grain in the ear, hay or straw have been completely issued, the surplus or shortage is reported to the Prefect's court. When they have not been completely issued and it is already sufficient[1], the Prefect's court is informed. The court orders the leading officials[2], who together had sealed the storehouse, to take part in issuing[3] it, immediately reporting the

figures [30] to the court. If, when (the) quantity is small[4], it is desired to weigh[5] everything[6], this is permitted. When the storehouse is located in the chief settlement[7], it is warranted . . . [8] take part in clearing it.

(Statutes on) Granaries.

[1] This evidently means that the amount noted on the "inscription" had already been reached before the store had been completely emptied.

[2] See note 33 to A 19 above.

[3] *Yü ch'u chih* 與出之. *Yü* meaning "to take part in" is common. *Ch'u* is to be taken literally as "to take out, to empty, to clear".

[4] *Shao* 少 is to be taken literally as "few, little, small", and not as "too little; short", for that is indicated by *pu pei* 不備.

[5] It is to be noted that this small quantity is to be weighed and not to be measured.

[6] *I* — evidently means "the whole", and not "once"; this is also the view of the editors.

[7] *Tu i* 都邑, the seat of the prefecture; see Lao Kan, *K'ao shih, k'ao cheng*, p. 18.

[8] About nine characters are missing, but the photograph is so poor, that it is impossible to distinguish whether the central part of the strip is missing; the editors make no remark.

A 22 W 7.2b–3a; S I.11b; S III.32a–b; SS 40; str. 31–32 (098–099).

[31] . . . . .[1] shortage, orders are given to the former official to take part together with the new official in issuing[2] it completely as a first step. If the former official does not wish it, he is not to be compelled. In case there is no former official, orders are given to the Rank Holder[3] and the Prefectural [32] Clerk[4] . . .[5], together with the Granary . . .[6] to take it out. When it is wholly empty, the shortage will be judged[7]. No change should be made in the persons who acted together[8]; if they are changed and there is a shortage, the Prefect and the Assistant (Prefect) will be ordered to take part in making good the shortage.

(Statutes on) Granaries.

[1] It is impossible to judge from the poor photograph, whether the top of this strip is missing, or whether the characters have become illegible. To judge by other strips, five or six characters are missing.

[2] I.e. emptying the store.

[3] *Yu-ch'ih* 有秩. Kao Heng, "Chih-kuan", p. 220 f., shows that Rank Holders were locally appointed officials ranked at the rather modest level of 100 bushels, and sometimes even less. Rank holder is a general term and does not denote a specific office, as is clear from the passages where it is used in these texts and also from *HSPC* 5.3a, *HFHD* I, p. 311 (Dubs' rendering "anyone who has official rank" goes too far). On this rather complicated problem see also Kao Min, "Yu-ch'ih", and Ch'iu Hsi-kui, "Se-fu", pp. 233–237, as well as the much older remarks in Yen Keng-wang I, pp. 237–240. In Han times, the Rank Holder *yu ch'ih* 有秩 with a salary of 100 bushels, was in charge of a District, *hsiang* 鄉.

[4] As has been demonstrated by Ikeda, pp. 48–54, under the Ch'in the Prefectural Clerk, *ling shih* 令史, appears to have occupied a rather elevated position among the subordinate prefectural personnel, being i.a. in charge of the investigation of law-suits. They were probably of the same rank as the Overseers and they seem to have been immediately subordinate to the Assistant Prefect. In Han times, their position seems to have been lower. Yen Keng-wang I, pp. 221–222, and Yü Hao-liang, "Chih-kuan", p. 21, believe that *ling shih* was a general designation for the scribes working in the different offices of the prefectural administration; see also Bielenstein, *Bureaucracy*, p. 7 and *passim*.

[5] The next two words are barely legible; the editors' reading *chu* 主 seems doubtful, and so is the translation in SS: "in charge".

[6] One character effaced.

[7] See note 5 to E 4 below.

[8] *Tsa che* 雜者.

A 23 W 7.3a; S I.11b; S III.32b; SS 40–41; str. 33 (100).

[33] When measuring grain, millet ....[1] in writing, report the year[2], keeping the figures apart. Use it for issuing rations to people.[3]

(Statutes on) Granaries.

[1] This article is also translated in Vandermeersch, "Procédure", p. 14.—About ten characters are missing. The photograph is indistinct; CM, p. 76, shows that the editors have combined a small and a large fragment without indicating this.

[2] S believes this to be the year in which the cereals were entered in the granary, whereas SS thinks it is the year of production.

[3] *Jen* 人 is a very general term, which might cover both officials and convicts; in C 12 below *jen* indicates convicts.

A 24 W 7.3a; S I.11b; S III.33a; SS 41; str. 34 (101).

[34] When accounting[1] grain in the ear, the yellow, white and blue-green[2] and the glutinous millet are to be kept separate; do not use them for issuing rations to the people[3].

(Statutes on) Granaries.

[1] This article is also translated in Vandermeersch, "Procédure", p. 14.—*Chi* 計, "to calculate; to book accounts".

[2] I do not know which varieties of grain are indicated by these colours; the traditional agricultural and pharmaceutic works quoted by the editors of SS do not contain any indications on the subject.—*Ch'ing* 青 may mean green, blue-green, blue-grey and even black.

[3] See note 3 to A 23 above.

A 25 W 7.3a; S I.11b; S III.33a–b; SS 41–42; str. 35–36 (102–103).

[35] As rice[1] ripens after[2] grain, rice is to be accounted for the next year.[3] When the harvest is finished, the figures are to be reported, distinguishing between non-glutinous grain,[4] glutinous grain[5] and rice, (also) distinguishing between the stalks of non-glutinous rice.[6] They are to be stacked according to the difference in year; stacks are not to be increased. Use it to provide strangers.[8] In the tenth month[9] note the figures on writing strips[10] and [36] report these to the Minister of Finance.[11]

(Statutes on) Granaries.

[1] *T'ao* 稻. For the cultivation of rice in southern and central North China during the Warring States period see Nishijima, p. 206, and Hsü Cho-yün, p. 84 f.—This article is also translated in Vandermeersch, "Procédure", p. 14.

[2] S and SS read *hou* 後, where *Wenwu* 7 has a blank.

[3] *Hou nien* 後年, lit. "the later year".

[4] *Ts'an* 粲 normally means "refined grain", obtained by polishing *su* 粟; see below, A 29, strip 43. However, this makes no sense here. I therefore follow the suggestion made by the editors of SS that *ts'ân might be a loan for *śân 秈, which is another name for non-glutinous grain.

[5] *No-k'u* 穤秙; the editors rightly suggest that the second character (which means grain that does not bear seed) should be a loan for *hu* 黏.

[6] Cf. note 1 above.

[7] I follow the suggestion by the editors of SS that *hsiang* 襄 stands for *hsiang* 穰, which, ac-

cording to *SW* means "threshed-out stalks"; the suggestion in S that *hsiang* should be a loan for *jang* 釀, "to brew" is impossible, also grammatically.

8 *K'o* 客, "passing strangers" rather than "guests"; cf. D 75 and D 180 below.

9 *Tao shih yüeh* 到十月, lit. "when having come to the 10th month", in other words "once the new administrative year has started".

10 *Tieh* 牒, small, c.q. short, writing-strips.

11 For the effaced character the editors rightly suggest *shih* 史.

A 26 W 7.3a; S I.12a; S III.33b–34a; SS 42–43; str. 37 (104).

[37] The prefecture sends the register of persons who have received rations[1] as well as (the records of) other expenses to the Great Granary[2]; they go together with the accounts.[3] The general officials at the time of accounting[4] check the registers of persons who have received rations.

(Statutes on) Granaries.

1 This article is also translated in Vandermeersch, "Procédure", p. 14.—*Shih-che chi* 食者籍, lit. "register of eaters". For a detailed study of the Han time lists found in the Edsin-gol defence lines, called *shih p'u* 食簿 and *lin ming chi* 廩名籍, see Mori, *Kankan*, pp. 95 f. and 121 f.; see also *RHA* II, p. 64 f., esp. pp. 76–77, no. 1; pp. 78–79, no. 13; pp. 80–81, no. 18.

2 As remarked in note 23 to A 9 above, the Great Granary was subordinate to the Minister of Finance. *HHSCC* Tr. 26.1b states that "in the four seasons the commanderies and kingdoms submit (viz. to the ministry of Finance) the registers of cash and grain actually available." According to the present rule, under the Ch'in it was the Prefects who sent the registers.

3 The accounts were sent annually to the capital, see *HFHD* II, p. 42, note 7.4, and especially Kamada, pp. 369–412, and Yen Keng-wang, vol. II, pp. 252–256.

4 This is one way of rendering *shih* 時; it has also been adopted in SS. Another way would be to take *shih* as "all the time, constantly", leading to the translation "the officials ... use the accounts to check constantly the registers of the eaters."

A 27 W 7.3a; S I.12a; S III.34a; SS 43; str. 38–39 (105–106).

[38] Sowing: for rice and hemp per *mu*[1] use 2 2/3 *tou*[2]; for wheat and barley per *mu* 1 *tou*; for millet and red beans per *mu* 2/3 *tou*; for peas per *mu* 1/2 *tou*. If profitable use is made of the fields,[3] it is permissible that some do not fully have this quantity.[4] When there are roots,[5] [39] (these fields) are to be sown according to the circumstances.[6]

(Statutes on) Granaries.

1 I am unable to judge whether the "old" *mu* of c. 190 m^2 is meant, or the "new" *mu* of c. 460 m^2.

2 *Ta pan* 大半 is "two thirds".

3 This is a tentative rendering of *li t'ien ch'ou* 利田疇. To me, the translation in SS simply as *liang t'ien* 良田 "good, or fine fields" is unacceptable. The editors refer to a note by Yen Shih-ku (581–645) to *HSPC* 1B.14a *yü li t'ien-chai* 與利田宅, where he explains *li* 利 as *pien-hao* 便好; Dubs and his Chinese collaborators rendered the *HS* phrase correctly as "gave them the advantage of its fields and dwellings" (*HFHD* I, p. 122) and did not take *li* as an adjective—nor did Yen Shih-ku.

4 Namely, of the seed grain.

5 The text clearly reads *pen* 本, explained in S as "roots of crops", which I fail to understand, because such roots, if not torn out and used as fuel, are normally ploughed under. The involved reasoning in SS, leading to the translation "if there already are crops" seems unacceptable. The "roots" may well refer to tree stumps, left in place in "slash and burn" agriculture.

6 Lit, "weighing and discussing (what to do)".

A 28 W 7.3a; S I.12a; S III.34b; SS 44; str. 40 (107).

[40] The Prefecture gives[1] barley, to be used as seed[2]; it is to be stored like[3] grain in the ear.

(Statutes on) Granaries.

[1] SS translates *i* 遺 as "to retain", rendering the text as "The barley retained by the prefecture to be used as seed is to be stored like grain."

[2] The editors of S and SS have rightly corrected the transcription in *Wenwu* in two respects. In the first place they have removed the signs for an hiatus after "barley", and secondly, they punctuate after *yung che* 用者 in stead of before.

[3] *Yao* 殽 is explained as "to imitate, to act conformably to", with a reference to the commentary to the chapter *Li yün* in the *Li-chi*, which explains *yao* as *fa* 法, "(to take as) model" (*Li-chi chu-su* 21.4a; Couvreur I, p. 501; Legge 27, p. 367). This is in fact more reasonable than to render *yao* by "to mix".

A 29–30 W 7.3a; S I.12a; S III.35a–b; SS 44–46; str. 41–43 (108–110).

A 29 [41] Grain[1] (untreated)[2] weighing one picul[3] constitutes sixteen and two thirds pecks[4]; when pounded, this becomes one bushel[5] of husked grain[6]. One bushel of husked grain becomes nine pecks of polished grain.[7] Nine pecks of polished grain become eight pecks of refined grain.[8] Rice[9] weighing one picul[10] [43] constitutes twenty pecks of untreated grain; when pounded this becomes ten pecks of (refined)[11] grain. Ten pecks of refined grain (when further pounded produce) six and two thirds pecks of refined rice.[12] Ten pecks of barley are equal to three pecks of coarse flour.[13] Fifteen pecks of beans, peas, or hemp[14] are equal to one bushel. When issuing refined grain or rice,[15] ten pecks are equal to one bushel.[16]

(Statutes on) Granaries.

A 30 [41 continued] When treated grain[17] has been bestowed as a gift,[18] it is issued from the government grain.[19] If by the end of the ninth month[20] [42] the person concerned has not[21] fetched it, it is not to be given[22] (to him).[23]

(Statutes on) Granaries.

[1] This rule has been discussed in my "Weights", written in the summer of 1977; this is a new version.—Strip 41, in spite of the rather clear writing, is in a poor condition. In the first place, the top is missing, and secondly, the copyist made mistakes, i.a. by inserting part of the text of a wholly different rule (see below, note 10). Fortunately, it is possible to restore the text of the missing top from *SW*, which quotes parts of the present rule under different entries. To judge from the photograph, the missing part of the strip may have contained three or four characters, and with "one", *i* 一, written very close to the following word, even five signs. Under *lai* 糲 *SW* writes *su chung i shih wei shih liu tou ta pan tou* 粟重一䄷爲十六斗大半斗. This rendering is corroborated by a similar statement on the present strip and twice by *SW*, under the entries *shih* 䄷 and *ts'an* 粲, reading *t'ao chung i shih wei su erh shih tou* 稻重 (*chung* is omitted *s.v. shih*, whereas the Ch'in copyist misreads it as *ho* 禾) 一䄷爲粟二十斗. SS, p. 44, is therefore wrong in supplementing only two characters, viz. 粟一. —I am unable to judge the correctness of the difference in weight for the same cubic measure of unhusked grain and rice, riz. c. 0.75 kg for c. 1 litre of rice, and c. 0.9 kg for the same quantity of grain. The local grain chandlers, the Société d'agriculture de Romont et Environs, kindly told me that the average weight of 100 litres of wheat is c. 78 kg, whereas that for rye is c. 73 1/2 kg; they had, understandably, no figures for rice The calculations,

which *HSPC* 21A.19b (cf. *HFHD* I, pp. 276–280) allows us to perform, lead to figures similar to those on the strip. *HSPC* states that a *yüeh* 龠 of c. 10 cubic cm of millet weighed 12 *shu* 銖 of c. 0.64 gr. With the picul of the *HSPC* source at c. 29.5 kg, this means that 16 2/3 pecks weighed c. 25.6 kg, and 20 pecks c. 30.7 kg.

2 *Su* 粟 indicates the loose grains or seeds of any kind of cereal that have not been treated in any way; this is also the conclusion of Yoshida, p. 25.

3 The *shih* 石 (written 柘 in *SW*) weighed nearly 30 kg.

4 The *tou* 斗 or peck measured c. 2 litres. That the Ch'in *sheng* 升 or pint contained c. 200 cubic cm, and the *tou* c. 2 litres is conclusively shown by Ch'iu Kuang-ming, esp. pp. 65–66 and 70.

5 The *shih* 石 or bushel of ten pecks contained c. 20 litres.

6 *Lai* 糲 is husked grain, unpolished.

7 *Tso* 鑿, i.e. 糳; according to *SWKL*, p. 3177b f., this loan is frequent in classical literature.

8 *Hui* 毇, i.e. 毇.

9 *T'ao* 稻. Wang Jen-chün (1866–1913) 2, p. 7, rightly suspected that the *SW* text was a quotation of a Han statute (overlooked by Ma Tsung-huo). For Wang Jen-chün see also my "Shuo-wen", p. 240, note 3.

10 Here the text on the strip suddenly introduces a wholly different rule, translated below as A 30.

11 *Mi* 米, loose grains of cereal; in view of *CCSS*, p. 23, *mi* seems to be used for treated grain.

12 *Ts'an* 粲.

13 *Shih* 麱, according to *SW* this is wheat mixed with fragments of chaff, or, as Tuan Yü-ts'ai (1735–1815) formulates it in his commentary, "wheat flour from which the bran has not yet been separated" (*SWKL* 2311b). *SW* writes *shih chin wei san tou* 十斤爲三斗, but here *chin* 斤 is obviously a mistake for one of the forms of *sheng* 升 (see Loewe, "Measurement", p. 87 f.). *CCSS*, p. 23 (cf. Vogel, p. 17), distinguishes between large and small *shih*, giving a ratio of 50: 13 1/2 for untreated grain versus small *shih*, i.e. nearly 4 to one, whereas in the present rule it is 3 1/3 to 1.

14 Hemp seed was used for making oil.

15 *Pai* 粺, which *SW* explains as *hui* 毇, so that the two terms appear to be interchangeable. Tuan Yü-ts'ai believes that *pai* is refined rice and *hui* refined wheat.

16 The frequently recurring ratio 5: 3 is the standard ratio between grain in the rough—and therefore unedible in this form—and the cleaned product, fit for consumption. Five to three is also the ratio between the large bushel, *ta shih* 大石, and the small bushel, *hsiao shih* 小石, mentioned many times in the Edsin-gol documents and repeatedly discussed (see Loewe, "Measurement", p. 78 f.). The present text shows that Professor Yang Lien-sheng was undoubtedly right when he stated (in Dr. Loewe's paraphrase) that "when husked, or grain of better quality was being measured, it was counted in units termed *ta shih*; when rough, unhusked grain was measured it was counted in *hsiao shih*. But the actual unit of measurement was . . . one and the same" (Loewe, "Measurement", p. 81).

17 Cf. note 11 above.

18 *Wei ssu* 委賜.

19 *Lin ho-chia kung* 稟禾稼公. In spite of the curious construction the meaning must be as in the translation. For *ho-chia* see note 1 to A 20 above.

20 The ninth month was the last month of the Ch'in administrative year.

21 For the use of *fu* 弗 as an emphatic negative see Pulleyblank, pp. 117–125.

22 *Shu* 鼠, lit. "rat", is used for *yü* 與 "to give". This unattested loan is quite acceptable, in view of the ancient pronunciation, *shu* being *śi̯o and *yü* being *zi̯o (see *GSR*, p. 42, no. 92a, and p. 41, no. 89b).

23 Except for the title *ts'ang* 倉, "granaries", the rest of this strip has been left blank.

A 31 W 7.3a; S I.12a; S III.36a; SS 46; str. 44(111).

[44] When court dignitaries,[1] (officials of) the general offices[2] and personnel[3] of the general offices in the service of the court[4] are in charge[5] (of a group), the prefecture is ordered to lend[6] them (provisions), immediately informing[7] the prefecture where they (normally) receive rations. The prefecture where they (normally) receive rations decreases their rations by (the amount received

elsewhere).[8] If rations have already been issued, the prefecture where they are staying is informed to charge them.

(Statutes on) Granaries.

[1] Contrary to the editors of SS, I do not think that *huan-che* 宦者 here means "eunuchs", but that it has the same meaning here as in D 170 below where the same editors accept the meaning "those who serve" the emperor as officials. Also the fact that in the present case they are mentioned before the *tu-kuan li* 都官吏 "officials of the general offices", is an argument in favour of my view.

[2] Cf. note 4 to A 26 above.

[3] As *jen* 人 is used in contrast to *li* 吏, "officials", I suppose that *jen* refers to subordinate personnel.

[4] I have followed the editors' explanation of *yu shih shang* 有事上 as *wei ch'ao-t'ing pan shih* 爲朝廷辦事.

[5] *Chiang* 將 is used *passim* in these texts for "to be in charge of" a group of workmen or convict labourers. The editors gloss this word by *tu sung* 督送 "to be in charge of a convoy".

[6] The text clearly writes *t'e* 貣, lit. "to beg", which the editors no doubt correctly take as a loan (or a mistake?) for *t'ai* 貸, "to lend or to borrow"; not only the graphs are confusingly similar, but also the ancient pronunciation of the two words was nearly the same: *t'e* being *t'ək, and *t'ai* being*t'əg (*GSR*, p. 242, nos. 918h and 918p).

[7] *I* 移, "to transfer", but also "to transfer a document", hence "to inform"

[8] As is often the case, the object of *i* 以 is omitted, because *i* refers back to the preceding phrase.

A 32 W 7.3a; S I.12a; S IV.36a; SS 46; str. 45(112).

[45] Those[1] who have a task[2] in the army or[3] in a subordinate prefecture[4] are provisioned with food; they must not use their passport[5] to borrow[6] (rations) from the prefecture.[7]

(Statutes on) Granaries.

[1] This refers, I believe, to the officials of the general offices mentioned in A 31.

[2] I assume that they have a special task to perform, for which they are sent out, and not that they have been appointed there.

[3] *Chi* 及, lit, "as well as", but that is less elegant in English.

[4] The prefecture was subordinate to the commandery. It is, of course, also possible to render *hsia* 下 as "to go down", namely from the capital or from the commandery; the latter explanation is followed in Oda I, p. 151.

[5] *Chuan* 傳; see Oba, "Pasupōto." For the connection between *chuan* and the courier service see Hamaguchi, *Shin Kan* II, pp. 965–974.

[6] Again *t'e* is used for *t'ai*; see note 6 to A 31 above.

[7] Cf. the Han statute found in the Tun-huang defence lines: "In all cases concerning messengers not mentioned by name on the passport, conscripts are taken. Defensive and offensive arms and grain entered in the official registers are not to be issued to them without authorization"; see my "Han documents", p. 26.

A 33 W 7.3a; S I.13b; S IV.36b; SS 47; str. 46(113).

[46] Persons receiving food rations by the month and who have already been given their rations, when on an official mission where they receive food on (the strength of) their passport,[1] as well as those on leave[2] who have not come (to fetch their rations) by the end of the month, will have their food rations stopped at the next new moon[3] and will be given food rations as from the day of their return.[4] Rank-holding officials[5] will not have (their rations) stopped.

(Statures on) Granaries.

[1] Some rules for the issue of rations to holders of passports are found in A 92–94 below; see also note 7 to A 32 above.
[2] For this explanation of *hao* (not *kao*) *kuei* 告歸 see my "Ch'in documents", p. 204 f.
[3] I.e. the beginning of the month.
[4] *Lai* 來, lit." (their) coming".
[5] As the present rule applies to subordinate personnel, who as a class are called *yüeh shih* 月食, "those who receive rations by the month", the term "rank-holding officials", *yu ch'ih li* 有秩吏, will not refer to the district officials of that name (see note 1 to A 22 above), but to all officials of a higher rank.

A 34 W 7.3a; S I.13a; S IV.41a; SS 54–55; str. 63(130).

[63] Chickens are to be reared away from the granaries.[1] Where dogs are used, they are to be reared so that there are enough.[2] The offspring of pigs and chickens[3] which are not used, are to be sold; a separate account is to be kept for the money (obtained from their sale).

(Statutes on) Granaries.

[1] *Li ts'ang* 離倉. I have taken *li* as a verb, "to separate, to keep apart", but the word might also be considered as a qualifier of "granaries", leading to the translation "at a separate granary".
[2] This seems to imply that surplus pups were to be killed, in contrast to the chicks and piglets of the next line.
[3] Pigs and chickens being reared close to the cattle corrals are shown in a tomb wall-picture of the late 2nd century of our era; see Wu Jung-tsung, "Ho-lin-ko-erh", p. 27.

A 35 W 7.3b; S I.13a; S IV.40b; SS 53–54; str. 61–62 (128–129).

[61] When a bond-servant wishes to be redeemed by two adult persons[1], this is to be allowed. When old ones, warranted to be dismissed for old age[2] (or) small ones of five feet and less in height[3] as well as bond-women wish to be redeemed by one adult person, this is to be allowed. For redemption [62] always men are used; those who redeem are made bond-servants. Women[4] engaged in embroidery-work[5] as well as clothing must not be redeemed. For those in border prefectures, the population register[6] is to be returned to their prefecture.[7]

(Statutes on) Granaries.

[1] *Lin* 粦 must be a loan character; the editors suggest that this is *ling* 齡, "age". They refer to the commentary of the so-called "reply to the letter from Su Wu" in *Wen-hsüan* 41, which explains *ting ling* 丁齡 as *ting nien* 年, "the age of an adult worker". The term *ting ling* seems to be applicable both to men and to women, because in the following sentence it is expressly stipulated that only men could be used for redemption.
[2] See note 1 to A 17 above. However, it remains strange that hard-labour convicts—for bond-servants and bond-women were convicts—could have their punishment remitted for reasons of age.
[3] See A 12 above.
[4] *Nü-tzu* 女子 is currently used for "women"; see e.g. *HSPC* 76.28a: *fei nü-tzu so chih yeh* 非女子所知也, "this is not a thing women know about".
[5] The editors suggest that *min* 敃, "to exert oneself", is a loan for *min* 緍, which, according to the *Fang yen* 方言, ch. 6, quoted in Morohashi, vol. 8, p. 1122, no. 27652, sub 6, is a Ch'in expression, meaning "to decorate". The editors then equate *min* with *min-hsiu* 繡, which occurs in A 60 below, and which they rightly think to have the same meaning as *wen-hsiu* 文繡 in the *Yüeh-ling* chapter of the *Li chi* (*Li chi chu su* 16.2a (0773); Couvreur, *Li ki* I, p. 379; Legge, *Li ki* 27, p. 288). For *nü hung* 女紅 = *nü kung* 女工 see *HSPC* 5.9a (*HFHD* I, p. 328).

[6] The editors explain *fu shu* 復數 as "to send back the population register," because they consider *shu* to mean *ming* 名 *shu*, which the commentary to *HSPC* 1B.4b (*HFHD* I, p. 104) renders by "population register". As indicated by Hsiung, "Chün-shih", p. 43, *SC* 6.109 (*Mh* II, p. 240) writes that population registers, *hu chi* 戶籍, were introduced in Ch'in in 375 B.C.; it is to be noted that the texts under discussion use *chi* to designate all kinds of registers, i.a. for grain.

[7] This rule shows, that female convict labourers could be sent out for work elsewhere, and that eventually they were sent back to their home prefecture.

A 36 W 7.3b; S I.13b; S IV.43a; SS 58; str. 70–71(137–138).

[70] When offices transfer[1] (goods) to one another, they are to report in writing the year for which these (goods) were cancelled[2] in the accounts; the recipient accounts it as entered. When there are transfers during the eighth and the ninth month, the distance of the place where they are transferred is to be calculated. If it is not possible to arrive there before[3] (the closing date of) the accounts[4] of the place where (the goods) are transferred [71] ....[5] shift the account to the next[6] year. The accounts must not be confused with each other.[7] When tribute of artisans[8] is transferred to an office, this is always to be accounted accurately[9] for the (actual) year.[10]

Statutes on Currency.[11]

[1] This article is also translated in Vandermeersch, "Procédure", p. 14. —*Hsiang shu* 相輸; cf. note 6. to A 3 above.

[2] *Ch'u* 出; see note 18 to A 9 above.

[3] *Tai* 逮, lit. "to reach, to attain, to catch up with". To put it more simply, the sentence means "if it is impossible to have the goods arrive there before the closing date. . ." For a similar use of *ta* 遝, which also means "to reach, to attain", see A 57, note 7, below. To judge by the ancient pronunciation indicated in *GSR*, the two words do not seem to be related, *tai* being *d'âi, and *ta* being *d'əp (*GSR*, p. 139, no. 509c, and p. 180, no. 678e).

[4] Cf. note 1 to A 24 above.

[5] The top of strip 71 of a length of six or seven characters is missing.

[6] *Ch'i hou nien* 其後年, lit. "the later year."

[7] *Wu hsiang niu* 勿相繆; SS translates "must not contradict each other".

[8] *Kung hsien* 工獻. The expression is anything but self-explanatory. It occurs once more in C 12 below, which contains the phrase *hsien kung hsin hsien tien* 縣工新獻殿, "when the new 'tribute' of the prefectural artisans is of inferior quality. . ." This might be connected with the *sui kung* 歲功, the "annual work", the year's production, mentioned earlier in C 12. From these uncertain indications one might deduce that prefectural workshops had to fulfil an annual quotum. This impression is reinforced by references to *sui hsien* 歲獻, "annual tribute", and *sui kung* 功, "annual work", in the ritual handbooks. The *Chou-li* contains at least three references to the custom that women presented the textiles they had woven to different authorities: the *nei tsai* 內宰 assisted the ruler's wife in receiving "the tribute work (of the palace women) at the end of the year", *sui chung. . . . shou hsien kung* 歲終....受獻功; other palace women, *nü yü* 女御, "according to the seasons of the year presented their work", *i sui shih hsien kung* 以歲時獻功: the *tien fu kung* 典婦功 received the women's work, and "when autumn came and the work was presented", *chi ch'iu hsien kung* 及秋獻功, he judged its quality (*Chou-li* 4/13, p. 53, 4/14, pp. 71 and 75; *Chou-li chu-su* 7.10a (0261), 8.1b (0286), 8.2b (0288); Biot I, pp. 146, 156, and 159–160), In the *Chou-li* we also find that the feudal lords in autumn "presented work", *hsien kung*, explained by the commentators, as Biot puts it, as "le résultat de leur gestion", but it may well have consisted in actual objects (*Chou-li* 21/72, p. 1; *Chou-li chu-su* 37.13b (1744); Biot II, p. 410). The same annual presentation of tribute, *sui hsien*, is mentioned in the chapter on ceremonial archery, *she i* 射義, in the *Li-chi* (*Li-chi chu-su* 62.2b (2418); Couvreur II, p. 671; Legge 28, p. 448, where *hsien* is wrongly translated as a verb governing what follows). SS in commenting on C 12 believes that the prefectural workshops mentioned there were the "work offices", *kung kuan* 工官, casually mentioned in *HSPC* 24B.8a and 19b (Swann,

pp. 308, 315), but that is rather doubtful, in view of the ten localities which had *kung kuan* in the geographical chapter of the Han history, one of which was at Huai 懷 hsien (*HSPC* 28AI.61a; for the others see the *HS* Harvard-Yenching index under *kung kuan*). The extensive studies on Ch'in—Han handicraft industries by Ch'en Chih (see his *Liang Han*, p. 79 f. and p. 201 f.) and by Satō throw no light on this problem.

9 In note 5 to A 5 above, *wu shen chih* 勿深致 was explained as "one must not *exceed* (the date or the stipulations of) the certificate", but here the editors of SS have a completely different suggestion: they believe that *shen* 深 is a loan for *shen* 審, "to examine; to determine" (which is phonetically not impossible, both being *śiəm), inspired by the commentary to *LSCC*, p. 88 (Wilhelm, *Frühling*, p. 109), which explains *shen* 審 as *ting* 定. I have accepted the loan, but I have translated differently.

10 *Ch'i nien* 其年. I suppose that this means the year when the goods had been manufactured.

11 *Chin-pu lü* 金布律. In view of A 43 below, *pu* does not refer to the shovel-shaped coin, but to an actual piece of cloth used as a medium of exchange. "Metal (rather than 'gold') and cloth" therefore means "currency", but cf. A 44 below. For the Han *chin-pu lü* see *RHL*, pp. 38–39.

A 37 W 7.3b; S I.13b–14a; S IV.43b–44a; SS 58–60; str. 72–75 (139–142).

[72] Officials of the general offices, rank-holding officials[1] as well as Overseers of detached offices[2] each have one cook;[3] their Assistant Clerks[4] will be cared for together with them.[5] For ten men one carriage and an ox,[6] with one ox herd. Assistant Clerks who have been assigned to[7] the general offices have one cook for ten men; [73] for fifteen men one carriage and an ox, with one ox herd. Groups of less than[8] ten men will share the cook, the carriage and the ox with the chief of their office. Not fully fifteen Assistant Clerks of general offices but seven or more will be given[9] a carriage, an ox and [74] a servant;[10] less than seven, but three or more will be given a cook. Minor offices which have no Overseer will be given a servant, a carriage and an ox, based on this (rule). In case of. . . . birth,[11] its mother is fed with one *tou* of unhusked grain daily during one decade and five days, whereupon this is stopped. Separately [75]. . . .[12] in order to loan them.

Statutes on Currency.

1 For the rank-holding officials see note 5 to A 33 above. — SS translates "the rank-holding officials of the general offices", which is also possible; to me this seems less logical, for the officials of the general offices were *ipso facto* holders of higher ranks.

2 For *li kuan* 離官 see note 19 to A 9 above.

3 *Yang* 養, "cooks", occur *passim* in the Tun-huang and Edsin-gol documents; cf. Wang, *Liu-sha* 2.25a–b.

4 The editors punctuate after *tso*, hence "Assistants *and* Clerks".

5 *Yü kung* 與共, "together and in common with".

6 *Niu* 牛; it might be more correct but less elegant to translate *niu* by "bovine", because it seems that also cows were used as draught animals, as further on we read about *niu* giving birth.

7 For *jung* 宂 see note 6 to A 7 above.

8 *Pu ying* 不盈, lit. "not fully."

9 For the use of *shu* 鼠 for *yü* 與, "to give", see note 22 to A 30 above.

10 *P'u* 僕; "servants and cooks" occur in A 62 below; they are evidently to be distinguished. SS wants *p'u* to mean "coachmen", but this is illogical in view of the preceding where only ox carts are mentioned, whereas coachmen were used in horse-drawn carriages.

11 The text clearly reads *k'en* 豤, "to root, to grub" according to *SW*, but this makes no sense here. S wants this to be *shan* 犍 (*SW*: "cattle"), which they explain as "calf", although the *Chi yün* (unaccessible; quoted in Morohashi, vol. 7, p. 661, no. 20139) says that it may mean "cow". On the other hand, SS suggests that it should be read as *chien* 艱, "difficult", translating "when a cow has had difficulties in giving birth". The ancient pronunciations

are *k'en* = *k'ən, *shan* = *śan, *chien* = *kɛn (GSR, p. 117, no. 416c; p. 70, no. 194a (?); p. 132, no. 480c). Impossible to say what is the correct solution. Only one thing seems certain: a cow, after having giving birth, received extra rations.

12 The editors have placed strip 75 after strip 74, but SS considers this uncertain. This uncertainty renders the translation of this sentence highly doubtful. The first character is read *peng* 絜, identical with 紺, "hempen shoes or sandals". If str. 75 is actually the sequel of str. 74, one would expect a word meaning "to pen up" or "to corral", or, more vaguely, "to tie", in view of the preceding *pieh* 別, "separately". If "to tie" is meant, *peng* could be a loan for the cognate *pang* 綁. SS suggests that *peng* is a loan for *feng* 奉 (which is phonetically possible; se *GSR*, p. 301, no. 1197a and i), meaning "to feed or to rear", because in *HSPC* 23.10b Yen Shih-ku explains *feng* as *yang* 養 (in *RHL*, p. 331, I rendered *feng* by "maintain"), but this seems unacceptable. In short, this short sentence is unclear, and what is to be "loaned" remains a riddle.

A 38 W 7.3b; S I.14a; S IV.44b; SS 60; str. 76(143).

[76] Whenever persons, having debts towards the government, as well as those (owing) fines[1] and redemption fees,[2] live[3] in another prefecture, the prefecture where they are living is informed[4] to charge them. When the government owes debts to commoners, the prefecture concerned is likewise informed; the prefecture repays them.

Statutes on Currency.

1 For *tzu* 貲, "fines", see my "Ch'in documents", p. 208 f.

2 For the redemption of punishments see the introduction, p. 18, and *RHL*, p. 205 f. The editors correctly distinguish between fines and redemption fees.

3 Here *chü* 居 must have the normal meaning "to dwell", and not the technical meaning "to work off debts etc. in forced residence"; see A 39, note 8 below.

4 *I* 移; see note 7 to A 31.

A 39 W 7.3b; S I.14a; S IV.44b–45a; SS 60–61; str. 77–79 (144–146).

[77] When commoners borrow government tools, as well as when they have debts[1] that have not been repaid, and the days for collecting or charging[2] these have been fulfilled,[3] (then) not to collect or charge them, whilst the persons concerned die or abscond[4]—[5] Likewise, when bond-servants or bond-women loose government tools or cattle,[6] as from that date [78] their issues of clothing and food are to be decreased, but not more than one third is to be taken. The quantity of what they have lost is to be accounted; if by the end of the year the food and clothing (deducted) are insufficient to repay (the losses) completely,[7] they are to be ordered to work these off.[8] If they are not ordered to work these off, and the persons concerned [79] die or abscond—[9] orders are to be given to the Overseer of the office concerned as well as to the officials in charge to make repayment in their stead.

(Statutes on) Currency.

1 *Tse* 責 is used as a loan for *chai* 債.

2 The text reads *shou tse* 收責, which in SS is simply translated as "to collect", with a reference to *HSPC* 7.3b (*HFHD* II, pp. 156–157). This is not correct, for *shou* refers to the objects (the tools in the present case, seed grain in *HS* 7), and *tse* refers to the debts.

3 The character 踐 is unknown, but, as indicated by the editors, its meaning must be the same as *tsu* 足, "enough, fully, to fulfil". For commoners borrowing iron tools see A 8 above.

4 *Ssu wang* 死亡 can mean "to die", but here the two words do not form a binome; they are to be taken independently. In D 48 below we find a condemned prisoner mentioned who

ssu jo wang 死若亡 "dies or runs away". Except in C 3 below, where *wang* is equivalent to *wu* 無 (very frequent in the historical texts), the fundamental meaning of *wang* is "to loose"; when the context mentions objects (as here in A 39, and in A 68, C 14 and D 158), the natural translation is, of course, "to loose"; sometimes living beings are lost, like convicts which one is guarding (D 96, 105). In all other cases the subject "looses himself", i.e. he "absconds", even an ox (E 11).

5 The rule does not end here, for the final injunction that the officials concerned will have to pay these debts covers both this paragraph and the next.

6 *Ch'u sheng* 畜生, a general term for domestic animals.

7 *Shao* 稍 usually means "a little, little by little, gradually", but SS refers to the *Kuang ya, shih ku* 釋詁 1 (unaccessible), which glosses *shao* by *chin* 盡, "exhaustively"; *SWTHTS*, quoted in *SWKL* 3126b, states that it is a loan for *hsiao* 消.

8 *Chü* 居 has the technical meaning of "to work off debts etc. in forced residence"; details concerning this procedure are found in A 66 and A 68 below. It is sometimes called *chü tso* 作; see Ch'en P'an, *Ch'i chung*, pp. 91b–92b. Ch'en refers i.a. to an edict of A.D. 143 which permits the redemption of punishments by means of the payment of different quantities of silk, but those unable to pay the redemption fees were to be sent to Lin-ch'iang Prefecture (near present—day Hsi-ning in Ch'ing-hai Province) "to work these off during two years", *chü tso erh sui* 居作二歲 (*HHSCC*, Ann. 6.13a). The combination *chü tzu* 居貲, "to work off a fine" is found on a number of grave-markers that indicate the shallow burials of mainly convict labourers, working probably as stone cutters or brick makers near the tomb of the First Emperor; see "Hsing-t'u mu", pp. 6–7. It is likewise found in an Edsingol strip, but the context is too fragmentary to allow further conclusions (Lao Kan, *K'ao shih*, p. 93, no. 4520 (257) 154.4 and 210.14). Chang Ming-hsin has rightly stressed that *chü* was not a punishment; he also remarks that this system provided the authorities with another supply of cheap labour.

9 Here begins the injunction which covers both the first and the second paragraph.

A 40 W 7.3b; S I.14a; S IV.45a–b; SS 61–62; str. 80–81 (147–148).

[80] When (members of) prefectural or general offices[1] are adjudicated (for irregularities found when) checking[2] and accounting, and they have been charged with repayment,[3] after sentence has been pronounced the Overseer[4] immediately proportionately charges the Chief of the office concerned as well as the officials who work there[5] with the value[6] in cash, giving each person the third part of a triplicate tally[7] to be presented[8] to the Treasury.[9] The Treasury [81] uses this to collect and to charge (viz. the allotted amounts). In case a surplus is entered, tallies are likewise given to the office (concerned)[9] to enter it. As regards these charges, one should not venture to exceed[10] one year. If the year is exceeded and (the amounts charged) have not been entered, as well as if the Ordinance have not been followed[11], in both cases[12] this will be sentenced according to the Statutes.

Statutes on Currency.

1 The text merely reads *hsien tu-kuan* 縣都官, but in view of what follows, this lapidary phrase will have the meaning given in the translation. The modern Chinese translation in SS repeats *hsien tu-kuan* without any further explanation.

2 This is the first mention in these texts of the very important practice of checking or controlling, *chiao* 效, grain stores, equipment etc.; numerous rules in the present collection are devoted to this administrative routine. Also the strips discovered near Tun-huang and in the Edsin-gol defence lines provide many examples of the application of these rules during the Han period. An instructive example of checking a grain store is found in Lao Kan, *K'ao shih*, p. 88, no. 4279 (238) 142.32a:

tsui-fan su 最凡粟	2590	*shih*	7	*tou*	2 1/3	*sheng*
fan ch'u 凡出	1857	–	3	–	1	–

chin yü su 今餘粟	733	–	4	1 1/3	–
chiao chien su te 校見粟得	754	–		2	–

The difference between the calculated and the actual amount of nearly twenty bushels may well be the result of the imperfection of the measures used; cf. B 3–6 below.

3 *Shang* 賞 is used for *shang* 償.

4 Probably the Overseer of the office concerned.

5 See note 6 to A 7 above.

6 *Chin* 直 is used for *chih* 値.

7 The editors offer a tentative solution for the cryptic phrase *erh jen yü ts'an pien ch'üan* 而人與參辨券. Taking *pien* to mean *fen* 分 (it is to be noted that *SW* defines *pien* as *p'an* 判, "to split") they suggest that a *ts'an pien ch'üan* was a tally divided into three parts, adding, however, that archaeologists so far have not discovered these, although seals divided into three pieces have been found. One part was for the Overseer, one for the Treasury and one for the person condemned to repay, to serve as a certificate. However, in the translation of *SS* the word *ts'an* is conveniently overlooked. Being unable to provide a better solution, I have followed the editors' suggestion, but with some misgivings, i.a. because of the attributive use of *ts'an*. The expression *ts'an pien ch'üan* is also found in an Edsin-gol report on the death of a conscript (Lao Kan, *K'ao shih*, p. 21, no. 1058 (50) 7.31) but the text is of no help for understanding the expression.

8 For *chiao* 效 "to present" see note 9 to A 9 above.

9 As I tried to show in my "Ch'in documents", p. 199, the *shao nei* 少內 "are treasuries—i.e. offices receiving and disbursing money—attached to all organs, both metropolitan and regional, whose tasks included financial transactions"; see also Kudō, "Shōnai", pp. 22 and 30. To the few examples given there I can now add another: the residences of the kings in the capital Ch'ang-an each had a *shao nei*, "treasury", as is shown by two bronze tripods discovered in Hsi-an in 1940, one of which had the inscription *Ch'ing-ho ti shao-nei ti wu ting* . . . 清河邸少內第五鼎 . . . "Tripod no. 5 of the Treasury of the residence of (the king of) Ch'ing-ho" (see Ch'en Chih, *HSHC*, p. 314). Both the editors of SS and Yü Hao-liang, "Chih-kuan", p. 9, are wrong in connecting the *shao-nei* with the imperial court; Ch'en Chih, *HSHC*, p. 387, is unclear.

10 *Yü* 隃 is used for *yü* 逾; this is also done in Han texts, e.g. by the poet Ssu-ma Hsiang-ju (*SC* 117.44; Watson, *Records* II, p. 314; Hervouet, *Chapitre 117*, pp. 105b and 108; *HSPC* 57A.39a–b).

11 D 120 below stipulates that transgressing the Ordinances was a punishable offence, but without providing further details.

12 *Chieh* 皆, lit. "all".

A 41 W 7.3b–4a; S I.14b; S IV.45b–46a; SS 62–64; str. 82–85 (149–152).

[82] When the Overseer of an office, having been dismissed and again made Overseer, is adjudicated[1] for (misdemeanours in) his former office, for which he is fined and has to make repayments,[2] as well as having other debts, is (so) poor that he has no means of repayment, his salary and monthly food ration[3] are slightly[4] reduced in order to repay these (debts). It is not allowed to make him [83] work off[5] (these debts). In case he has been dismissed, orders should be given to have him work these off, in accordance with the Statutes.[6]

When the Overseer of an office is dismissed and on checking his office there are shortages, orders should be given that he is to share these with his subordinates according to their duties.[7]

When an official[8] is adjudicated for (misdemeanours in his) office for which he is charged with repayment, but before (his share has been established)[9] [84] he dies, as well when he has committed a crime and therefore is under arrest,[10] his share is to be cancelled.[11] When his share has already been allotted and he dies, as well as when those who normally work[12] in a government storehouse[13] have in this way been charged with repayments, (or) when herdsmen in charge of government cattle kill or lose them and have not yet repaid them, as well as when working (these obligations) off they have not yet [85] completely done so, and they die—in all these cases these (debts) are to be cancelled;[14] they must not be charged to their wife or to family members living in their household.[15]

(Statutes on) Currency.

1 For *tso* 坐, "to be adjudicated", see note 5 to E 4 below and *RHL*, p. 397, note 239.

2 This must be the meaning of *tzu shang* 貲賞; it cannot be "payment of fines", because *shang* is not used in this way. The fines would have been for official misdemeanours and the payments for shortages.

3 I fail to understand this combination, because normally the higher echelons in the bureaucracy received a salary, whereas subordinate local officials were given "monthly food (rations)".

4 *Shao* 稍 normally means "little, a little" and the editors of both S and SS explain it in their notes as "gradually", but in the translation SS renders it by "periodically". None of these explanations seem satisfactory; Morohashi, vol. 8, p. 590, *s.v. shao*, 5, quotes the *Kuang yün* saying that it means *chun* 均, "equitably", but without textual support.

5 See note 8 to A 39 above.

6 See the beginning of A 68 below.

7 *Shih* 事.

8 On strip 83 the word *shih* is followed by the reduplication marker; in their transcription, the editors have replaced *shih* by *li* 吏, correctly so, in view of Karlgren's remark in *GSR*, p. 256, no. 971a and 975a, that in the archaic graphs for these two characters there is no fundamental difference. However, in the Han "clerks' writing" the two characters are clearly different, if *HLTY, ch'ü-sheng*, p. 11a–b, may be taken as a guide.

9 As remarked by the editors, the verb *fen* 分 is understood.

10 *Shou* 收. The fundamental meaning of this word appears to be "to collect", but in the strips it is used with at least three different meanings. In D 13 and 14 below it signifies "to accept or receive stolen goods"; in A 41, 110; D 61, 91, 92, it means "to arrest" (which is the *SW* explanation of *shou*, viz. *pu* 捕), or, perhaps more accurately, "to keep in custody", whereas in D 55, 96 and 174 *shou* means "to confiscate", namely persons who are made government slaves. In D 149 and 150 a female criminal is *shou*, "arrested", whereas her slaves and property are likewise *shou*, "confiscated"; that this latter rendering is correct is proved by the addition of the alternative that both might also be returned to the criminal's husband, for her property, lit. "clothes and vessels", could hardly he "arrested." It is to be noted that the expression *ju kung* 入公, meaning "to be handed over to the government", occurs only; in D 147; in view of the context it certainly means "to be confiscated" (*ju kung* is not to be found in Morohashi, nor in the *P'ei-wen yün-fu*), like the later *ju kuan* 入官.

11 *Yüeh ch'u* 抉出, "lifted out (or: picked up) and removed".

12 This is a tentative translation of *heng tso kuan fu* 恒作官府. The editors believe that *heng tso* refers to artisans working in a government workshop, *tso wu* 作務, mentioned in A 51 below.

13 The meaning of *kuan fu* 官府 is not clear; the editors leave the term unexplained and untranslated. It can hardly be a government workshop, because that is indicated by *kung shih* 工室 in A 54. *Kuan fu* occurs seventeen times in the Ch'in strips, and this allows us to observe: see further p. 244, "Addenda et corrigenda".

14 See note 18 to A 9 above.

15 *T'ung chü* 同居 is a technical expression. In D 19 below it is simply identified with the household, *hu* 戶, whereas D 181 provides the curious explanation "only the mother of the household", which SS believes to mean "members of the household who have the same mother". After an extensive discussion, Hiranaka, pp. 320–336 and 341, arrives at the conclusion that *t'ung chü* 同居 refers to relatives living in the same household, including, of course, parents and children. The term therefore seems to exclude persons not related to the head of the house, such as servants or slaves; the latter are evidently included in the term *shih jen* 室人, likewise explained in D 181. *HFHD* I, p. 178, note 1, is incomplete. In

certain cases *t'ung chü* is a verb, as in the standing phrase "the brothers A and B *t'ung chü*: lived together", implying that they had not established separate households after the death of their parents; see e.g. *HSPC* 50.1a; *HHSCC* Mem. 25.11a; 42.12b, or 50B.1b. *T'ung chü* is not to be confused with *t'ung ch'an* 同產, which means "sons of the same father", but not necessarily of the same mother; see *RHL*, p. 394, note 240. A72 mentions *t'ung sheng* 同牲 (i.e. *sheng* 生), "children of the same father".

A 42 W 7.4a; S I.13b; S IV.41b; SS 55–56; str. 64–65 (131–132).

[64] In government storehouses which receive cash, one thousand cash (form) one basket;[1] it is sealed with the seals of the Assistant (Prefect) and the Director.[2] Those of not fully one thousand (cash) are likewise sealed. Cash good and bad are put in together. When cash is to be disbursed, the seal impression is presented to the Assistant (Prefect) and the Director [65] and thereupon (the basket) is opened and (the cash) are used. When commoners in their deals use cash, fine and bad[3] (pieces) are to be used together; one should not venture to differentiate between them.[4]

(Statutes on) Currency.

1 According to *SW pen* 畚 is a receptacle made of rushes, used for storing grain.
2 In two places on this strip the text has *ch'eng ling* 丞令, which excludes the possibility that *ling* would indicate the Prefect. *Ling* is therefore either a "director" (further unknown in these texts, but frequent in the departments of the ministries in the capital), or, less probable, an abbreviation for *ling shih* 史 (see note 4 to A 22 above).
3 The text employs two expressions with the same meaning: *shan pu shan* 善不善, and *mei o* 美惡.
4 A 45 below, when treating the same subject, uses another expression, viz. *tse hsing* 擇行, "to circulate selectively". A reference to this practice is found in the *Han Fei-tzu*, ch. 32, p. 204 (Liao II, p. 44), where an employer is said to give his labourers not only good stew, but also "to select cash and cloth", *t'iao ch'ien pu* 調錢布 (corrected according to the commentators) in order to keep them; see also Vandermeersch, p. 213.

A 43 W 7.4a; S I.13b; S IV.41b; SS 56; str. 66 (133).

[66] The "cloth" has a length of eight feet;[1] its width[2] is two feet five inches.[3] If the cloth is bad,[4] (or) if its width and length are not in accordance with the model, it is not put into circulation.

1 With the foot at c. 23.1 cm, this is c. 1,85 m. SS refers to *HSPC* 24B.1b (Swann, p. 221; not in *SC* 30), which indicates the standard measures for bolts of textiles: width 2 ft. 2 in. (c. 51 cm.) and length 40 ft. (c. 9.30 m.).
2 *Fu* 福, "happiness" is used for *fu* 幅, "width".
3 C. 57 cm.
4 *O* 惡 is often used for "of bad quality".

(Statutes on) Currency.

A 44 W 7.4a; S I.13b; S IV.41b; SS 56; str. 67 (134).

[67] Eleven cash[1] are equivalent to one "cloth". When cash are disbursed or entered to serve as an equivalent of gold or cloth,[2] this is done in accordance with the Statutes.

(Statutes on) Currency.

1 In B 5 below the value of shortages, and in D 1, 7, 14, 15 below the value of illegally acquired goods is expressed in multiples of eleven. I have noticed at least one case where in Han

times the same multiple is used: *tsang man erh pai nien* 贓滿二百廿, "the illegal profit was fully 220"; see Chavannes, *Stein*, p. 49, no. 173; Wang, *Liu-sha*, 2.12a, no. 53.

2 Here *chin* 金 and *pu* 布 are to be taken separately, and not as a binominal expression for "currency". Whereas this text informs us about the equivalent of one "cloth" in cash, the Ch'in texts do not indicate the cash value of gold; in Han times this was nominally 10.000 cash for a gold "cake" weighing one catty of c. 244 gr. (cf. *CICA*, p. 134, note 333, where "224" is a mistake for "244"), but *CCSS* pp. 99–100 and 113 (Vogel, pp. 63 and 72) mentions as the value of one catty gold 6250 and 9800 cash. The Ch'in are said to have had a gold piece which, according to Meng K'ang's commentary, weighed 20 ounces, i.e. c. 300 gr., and which was called *i* 溢 or *i* 鎰 (*SC* 30.4; *Mh* III, p. 540, note 2, and p. 603; *HSPC* 24B.3b; Swann, p. 238). *HSPC* 40.4b reports that in 206 B.C. Chang Liang received a gift of 100 *i*. I do not know whether such Ch'in gold pieces have ever been found. See also Ch'iu Kuang-ming, "Heng chih", pp. 523 and 526–527.

A 45 W 7.4a; S I.13b; S IV.42a; SS 57; str. 68 (135).

[68] Traders who occupy stalls, as well as officials of government storehouses should not venture to circulate cash or "cloth" selectively.[1] When in case of (selective circulation of cash or cloth)[2] the chiefs of the groups of five[3] of the stall keepers do not denounce[4] this, and the officials are not diligent when making their rounds, all are guilty of a crime.

(Statutes on) Currency.

1 Cf. A 42 and note 4 above.

2 The words between brackets are indicated in the text by reduplication markers being added to the preceding characters.

3 As rightly pointed out by the editors of SS, this text shows that also tradesmen were organized in groups of five, implying mutual responsibility.

4 *Kao* 告 appears to be the term for accusations brought forward by private persons, whereas accusations by officials were called *he* 劾; see *RHL*, p. 74.

A 46 W 7.4a; S I.13b; S IV.42b; SS 57; str. 69 (136).

[69] When there is buying as well as selling,[1] to each (object) the price[2] is to be attached.[3] To small objects, each not worth[4] one cash, it must not be attached.

(Statutes on) Currency.

1 The characters for "to buy" and "to sell" are identical on the strip, both being 買.

2 *Chia* 賈 is used for *chia* 價.

3 *Ying* 嬰, "to hang around the neck as an ornament". The editors refer to the *Chou li, t'ien kuan, tien fu kung* 典婦功 (*Chou li* 4/14.76; *Chou li chu-su* 8.2b (0288); Biot I, p. 160 f.), which mentions price tags, *chieh* 楬.

4 *Neng* 能, to be taken in the sense of *nai* 耐 or chi 及.

A 47 W 7.4a; S I.14b; S IV.46b–47a; SS 64–65; str. 86–88 (153–155).

[86] In the seventh month the prefectural and general offices[1] discard[2] government tools that cannot be mended; those that have marks[3] are scraped.[4] The bronze[5] and iron tools among these are taken in to make bronze.[6] The general offices transfer these to the Main Treasury;[7] the Treasury[8] receives and buys [87] them. By the end of the seventh month (these transactions) are concluded.[9] Those metropolitan offices which are far away from the Main Treasury transfer (the discarded tools) to the prefecture; the prefec-

ture receives and buys them. As regards discarding, when there are objects which cannot wait for the right moment (to be sold), it is requested[10] to sell these earlier; at that moment the circumstances are reported to the Minister [88] of Finance.[11] In all cases of discarding, things that cannot be sold but which can be used as fuel or as coverings,[12] they are to be so used. If they are useless, burn them.

(Statutes on) Currency.

[1] Cf. note 1 to A 40 above.

[2] *Fen* 糞 usually means "manure", but *SW* explains it as "to remove dirt".

[3] *Chiu shih* 久識. This might be a binome for marks in general, but to me the two words appear to mean two different things, viz. "brand marks" and "(other) marks", in view of A 56 below, which mentions brand marks, carved marks and painted marks. *Shih* 識 may also mean "inscription", as noted in Morohashi, *s.v. shih.* In view of a phrase in the word list included in the collection entitled "How to be a good official" (see my "Ch'in documents", p. 184) reproduced in SS, p. 286, *shih* is also used as a verb, "to mark": *chiu k'o shih wu* 久刻識物, "to mark objects by branding and carving". Contrary to the editors, who suggest that *chiu* is a loan for *chi* 記 (unattested, but phonetically possible, *chiu* being *kiŭg (*GSR* 993a) and *chi* being *kiəg (953j)), I am inclined to believe that *chiu* 久 will have meant "to mark with a branding iron". The character may even have been a picture of this tool, although the dictionaries do not say so (see the endless expatiations in *SWKL*, pp. 2360a–2362a). This would explain the derivative *chiu* 灸, "to cauterize". In *RHA* II, 302, Dr. Loewe tentatively renders *chiu* 久 as "to cauterize", but to me it seems obvious that a brand on cattle is meant. Definite proof that *chiu* means "to brand" I find in an edict of emperor Kuang-wu of A.D. 35, prohibiting the branding, *chiu cho* 灸灼 of slaves (*HHSCC* Ann. 1B.7b; Wilbur, p. 468, no. 138). In addition it is to be noted that in E 20 below, moxa-burns are called *chiu* 久.

[4] The editors' suggestion that *mi* 靡 stands for *mo* 磨 is fully acceptable (see *GSR* 17f and h), although it is not attested. The character following *mi*—small, and apparently simple, but which I am unable to identify—the editors, rather surprizingly, read *ch'ih* 蚩 and consider it as a loan for *ch'e* 徹. This is phonetically impossible, for *ch'ih* was *t̂'iəg, whereas *ch'e* was *d̂'i̯at or *t̂'i̯at. Still, whatever the form and meaning of this second character, the meaning of the binome is clear.

[5] *Chin* 金; that pure red copper would be meant seems most unlikely.

[6] The editors read *t'ung* 銅, but I am not sure whether this decipherment is correct; also the idea of mixing bronze with iron is strange. SS translates the word by "metallic raw materials".

[7] For this rendering of *ta nei* 大內 see my "Ch'in documents", p. 199; the Main Treasury was a subdivision of the Ministry of Finance. See also Yü Hao-liang, "Chih-kuan", p. 8 f. Lists of metal objects were kept and checked; *Chia pien*, no. 2284 (as corrected in *Kaogu* 1960/10, p. 49) mentions *t'ieh ch'i p'u* 鐵器簿,

[8] In the text the words *ta nei* should have been repeated, but the scribe added a repetition marker only to the word *nei.*

[9] The editors read this word as *pi* [illegible] and take it to be a loan for *pi* 畢, which is quite acceptable in view of *GSR* p. 321, no. 1257g, and p. 115, no. 407a, giving the identical pronunciation *pi̯ĕt. *Pi* is constantly used in adminstrative documents and in contracts to signalize that full payment had effectively been made; see my "Contracts", p. 20.

[10] *Ch'iu* 求.

[11] Cf. note 22 to A 9 above.

[12] The editors read 蓋蘙, explained as "to screen, to cover". For the last character they substitute *i* 鷖, taken to mean *i* 翳, also "to screen, to cover".

A 48 W 7.4a; S I.14b; S IV.47b; SS 65–66; str. 89 (156).

[89] As regards wheels of carriages of the courier service or of big carts,[1] it is permissible to repair[2] those which are irregular.[3] Leather and textiles[4]

(are used) for repairing.[5] Take out[6] those which cannot be repaired and discard[7] them.

(Statutes on) Currency.

[1] Big carts, *ta chü* 大車, are two-wheeled heavy carts, drawn by oxen and used for transport; see Hayashi, *Bunbutsu*, p. 347 and ills. 7/15 and 16, and Biot II, p. 485 f.

[2] *Pao* 葆 is used for *pao* 保, "to preserve". The binome *pao shan* 繕 is unknown, but, as also remarked by the editors, it means "to repair".

[3] The binome *ts'an hsieh* 參邪 is unknown; it is probably synonymous with *ts'an-ch'a* 參差.

[4] *Hung ch'i* 紅器, lit. "red vessels or utensils", but the editors are undoubtedly right when they explain the term as "objects made of textiles".

[5] The text reads *hsiang pu shan* 相補繕, meaning presumably that worn textiles or leather goods are to be repaired by using pieces of other worn objects of the same material.

[6] The use of *ch'ü* 取 seems curious; perhaps it means "to sort, to select".

[7] Cf. note 2 to A 47 above.

A 49 W 7.4a–b; S I.14b–15a; S IV.47b–48a; SS 66–67; str. 90–93 (157–160).

[90] As regards the bestowal[1] of clothes, summer clothing will be issued from the fourth till the end of the sixth month; winter clothing will be issued from the ninth till the end of the tenth month. No issues are to be made beyond these times. Account[2] for the winter clothes in next year's (account). For incarcerated (convicts) who suffer from the cold, clothes of coarse hemp[3] are to be made.[4] [91] To make one head-cloth[5] use three catties[6] of hemp.[7] To make jackets for issuing as clothes: for one large jacket eighteen catties of hemp are used; value 60 cash. For one medium jacket fourteen catties of hemp are used; value 46 cash. For a small jacket use [92] eleven catties of hemp; value 36 cash.[8] When clothing has been issued and there remain ten jackets or more, these are to be transferred to the Main Treasury, together with the presentation of the (annual) accounts.[9] When metropolitan officials have a need for. . . .[10] their office; for bond-servants, bond-women, grain pounders and *ch'eng*-[93] *tan* this does not apply. (Offices) in Hsien-yang send[11] these clothes to the Main Treasury; in other prefectures they are sent to the prefectures were they[12] are engaged in work. The prefectures and the Main Treasury all allow that the offices concerned send them. The clothes are to be issued according to the Statutes.

(Statutes on) Currency.

[1] The editors rightly take *shou* 受, "to receive", as *shou* 授, in view of the first line of Ode 154: *chiu yüeh shou i* 九月授衣; see also note 1 to A 3 above.

[2] I do not understand the function of the word *hou* 後, "after, later", at the beginning of this sentence. It is conveniently overlooked in the SS annotation and translation.

[3] *Ho* 褐, explained by *SW* as "coarse clothes". That these were made of hemp is clear both from the following and from the commentaries to the classics.

[4] This seems to be the only way to render *wei* 爲.

[5] *Meng* 幪, "a cover", but also "a head-cloth."

[6] To me the character 𠀌 on the strip presents a riddle. Although at first sight it resembles the modern form of *chin* 斤, the catty of c. 245 gr., it is unlike the form of *chin* on another strip, viz. on strip 6 in S I.23a; the latter is practically identical with the signs reproduced in *GSR*, p. 123, nos. 443a and b. Moreover, a headcloth weighing three catties or about 0.75 kg., and even worse, a jacket of 18 catties or c. 4.5 kg., seem rather extraordinary. I am unable to suggest an alternative; the character is not an aberrant form of *ping* 秉, "a

handful", used in *CCSS*, p. 137 (Vogel, p. 88, no. 15; his rendering "Garbe", i.e. "sheaf", seems exaggerated).

7 *Hsi* 枲; the edible variety of hemp is *ma* 麻.

8 As remarked in SS, these figures imply a price of 3 cash for ten units of hemp.

9 Cf. note 3 to A 26 above.

10 Five, if not six, characters have disappeared from the strip; not only four, as indicated by *SS*.

11 As in A 5 above, the editors of SS take *chih* 致 to mean "certificate", which they now are forced to use as a verb. I have maintained the usual sense of *chih*, "to arrive, to cause to arrive—to send, to present".

12 Probably the convict labourers.

A 50 W 7.4b; S I.15a; S IV.48b–49a; SS 67–68; str. 94–96 (161–163).

[94] As regards the issue of clothing: bond-servants and storehouse bondsmen[1] who have no wife, as well as *ch'eng-tan*, in winter per person[2] 110 cash,[3] in summer 55 cash; those of small stature[4] in winter 77 cash, in summer 44 cash; grain-pounders in winter per person fifty [95] five cash, in summer 44 cash; those of small stature[5] in winter 44 cash, in summer 33 cash. Bond-servants and bond-women who are old, as well as those who are small[6] and unable to provide their own clothes are to be clothed like grain-pounders. Those[7] who have absconded[8] or who are unpleasant[9] to their master or their office [96] are to be clothed like bond-servants and bond-women.

(Statutes on) Currency.

1 These *fu li* 府隸 are unknown; as they are mentioned together with bond-servants, it seems likely that they were unfree persons.

2 On these strips the characters *jen* 人 and *ju* 入 are easily confused; here *Wenwu* writes *ju*, which has been corrected in the later editions.

3 The relation between these sums and those mentioned in A 49 above is not clear. SS refers to A 68 below, which stipulates that such issues had to be *chü* 居, "worked off"; the same rule mentions the values obtained per work-day: 8 cash without food, or 6 cash with food provided by the authorities.

4 According to A 12 above: men shorter than 6 ft 5 in, or c. 1.5 m.

5 According to A 12 above: women shorter than 6 ft 2 in, or c. 1.44 m.

6 Hence c. 1.5 for men and c. 1.44 for women.

7 It is not clear who these runaways etc. are; they cannot be bond-servants, for they are to be clothed "like", *ju* 如, bond-servants.

8 Because it is not possible to clothe people who have run away, these must be persons who had run away but who had been caught again.

9 The text reads *pu jen* 不仁, explained by the editors as *pu chung-shih* 不忠實, "disloyal, unfaithful"; in view of its occurrence in D 51 below, I have rendered the term as "unpleasant". The binome is found in *HHSCC*, Mem. 37.10a, where Pan Chao says of her brother Pan Ch'ao that he is old and that his hands and feet are *pu jen*, which the T'ang commentator Li Hsien explains as *pu sui* 不遂, perhaps to be rendered by "do not function".

A 51 W 7.4b; S I.15a; S IV.49a; SS 68–69; str. 97 (164).

[97] For transactions by work shops[1] as well as government store houses[2], whenever cash are received, these must be entered in the money-box.[3] Order the dealers to observe that it is entered. Those who do not obey the Ordinances[4] will be fined one suit of armour.[5]

(Statutes on) Passes and Markets.[6]

1 *Tso wu* 作務, according to the editors' explanation; the term recurs in A 68 below, coupled

with "traders", from which it can be deduced that such workshops were private establishments and not government institutions.

[2] See note 13 to A 41 above.

[3] *Hsiang* 缿 is defined by *SW* as "a vessel for receiving money".

[4] *Pu ts'ung ling* 不從令. D 120 mentions *fan* 犯 *ling* and *fei* 廢 *ling*; *pu ts'ung ling* is evidently identical with *fei ling*, which is defined as "not to do what the Ordinances say".

[5] On the problem of fines see my "Ch'in documents", p. 208 f.

[6] *Kuan shih* 關市 is a term currently used in classical literature; see the examples collected by Morohashi, vol. 11, p. 772, where the best known is probably the passage in the *Mencius* I B, v, 3. But no commentator explains what the term really means. In the present instance I prefer the rendering "passes and markets" to "markets at the passes". The latter existed in Han times, when markets were held at the passes or control points leading into non-Chinese territory; there the Chinese traded with the Nan-Yüeh in the South (*HSPC* 95.8a) and with the Hsiung-nu in the North (e.g. *HSPC* 94A.15b, misunderstood in de Groot, *Urkunden* I, p. 91). For passes see further note 6 to D 46 below.

A 52 W 7.4b; S I.15a; S IV.49b; SS 69; str. 98(165).

[98] When making[1] vessels of the same type,[2] their size, length and width should also be identical.[3]

Statutes on Artisans.[4]

[1] In view of the context, *wei* 爲 can only mean "to make".

[2] The editors rightly explain *wu* 物 as "type".

[3] *Teng* 等, lit. "equal".

[4] *Kung* 工; that the meaning of *kung* is "artisan, craftsman" and not "work, labour" is shown by A 61 and 62 below.

A 53 W 7.4b; S I.15a; S IV.50a; SS 70; str. 99 (166).

[99] When making accounts, items that are not of the same norm[1] must not be listed[2] in the same way.

Statutes on Artisans.

[1] *Ch'eng* 程, "norm" or "quota". One would have expected to find this rule in the following group, *kung jen ch'eng* 工人程, i.e. A 58–60.

[2] The evidently technical meaning of *ch'u* 出 escapes me; it cannot mean" to issue", nor "to cancel", like e.g. in A 41 above. SS renders it by *ch'u chang* 出帳, which seems to mean "to charge an account". I have therefore rendered it by the neutral term "to list".

A 54 W 7.4b; S I.15b; S IV.50a; SS 70; str. 100 (167).

[100] Prefectures as well as (government) workshops[1] let the office[2] correct their balances and weights[3] (and their cubic measures) *tou*,[4] *yung*[5] and *sheng*;[6] one must not let a year pass (without doing so) once.[7] When there are artisans, these must not undertake the correction; when (these weights and measures) are loaned for use,[8] they are corrected.

Statutes on Artisans.

[1] *Kung-shih* 工室. The editors of SS note the occurrence of clay seal imprints of "Assistant of the Workshop of the Right" and "Seal of the Workshop of the Left" in collections of such seal imprints; a department of the Han Privy Purse was the *k'ao kung-shih* 考工室 (*HSPC* 19A.15a).

[2] The text merely has *kuan* 官, "office"; this must have been a special office, which inspected and corrected weights and measures.

[3] The editors believe *lei* 贏 (*GSR* p. 24, no. 14c *lwia) to be a loan for *lei* 絫 (not in *GSR*,

but cf. *lei* 絫, *GSR* p. 155, no. 577f *li̯wər), and the latter means "weight". On the one hand it is a definite weight of ten grains of millet, or the tenth part of one *shu* 銖 of 0.64 gr., according to *SW* and the commentary of Ying Shao (A.D. 140–206) to *HSPC* 21.3a. On the other hand it is a general term for weight as is shown by Huang Sheng-chang, p. 44, who refers to Ch'in and Han inscriptions on weights, containing the word *lei*.

4 A *tou* or peck was equal to nearly 2 litres.

5 The *yung* 甬 (*diung), used for *t'ung* 桶 (*t'ung), was a measure of capacity, mentioned here in A 54 and in B 3 below. The word is found in two identical passages in the *Yüeh ling* chapter of the *Li chi* (*Li-chi chu-su* 15.3b (0712) and 16.14b (0778); Couvreur, *Li ki* I, pp. 343 and 382; Legge, *Li ki* 27, pp. 260 and 289), and in the *Lü-shih ch'un-ch'iu* (*LSCC*, pp. 13 and 76; Wilhelm, *Frühling*, pp. 15 and 93). It also occurs in a similar passage in the biography of Shang Yang (*SC* 68.11; Duyvendak, *Lord Shang*, p. 19). The only explanation of the term is found in the commentary of Cheng Hsüan (A.D. 117–200) to the first *Li chi* passage, where he says that the *yung* was equal to "the present-day bushel". However, *SW* explains *t'ung* as *mu fang shou liu sheng* 木方受六升, "(made of) wood and square; receives six *sheng*". Some commentators, quoted in *SWKL* 2588a, want to insert *ch'i* 器, "vessel", after *fang*, but Tuan Yü-ts'ai wants *mu fang* corrected to *fang hu* 方斛, "a square bushel" because that is the reading in the (unaccessible) *Kuang ya*, chapter *shih ch'i* 廣雅, 釋器. Tuan also suggests that *sheng* 升 is a mistake for *tou* 斗 (for the frequent confusion between these two words see Loewe, "Measurement", p. 86 f); the correctness of this suggestion is proved by the text of B 3 below. However, there remains the difference in interpretation given by *SW*, namely 6 *tou*, and by Cheng Hsüan: 1 *hu*, i.e. 10 *tou*. Ch'en Chih, *Liang Han*, p. 163, mentions two dated Han dynasty *t'ung*—83 and 53 B.C.—both with an inscription, stating that each contained 10 *sheng*! However, these inscriptions are only found in the Sung epigraphic work *Li-tai chung-ting i-ch'i k'uan-shih* 歷代鐘鼎彝器款識 by Hsüeh Shang-kung 薛尚功, so that mistakes are not to be excluded. One of these is *sheng* for *tou*; another—far from imaginary—could be that the 12th century author took the top of a partly effaced character *liu* 六, "six", for *shih* 十, "ten". Still, the modern author Ch'iu Kuang-ming, p. 66, continues to accept that the *t'ung* contained ten *tou* and was therefore equal to the bushel. Nevertheless, I believe that the *t'ung* contained six *tou*. My reason for doing so lies in the figures quoted in B 4. These figures indicate the minimum punishable difference for measures of capacity. There we find:

1	*tou* of	10	*sheng*:	punishable	difference	1/3	*sheng*	or 1/30.
1/2	– –	5	–	–	–	1/3	–	– 1/15.
1/3	– –	3 1/3	–	–	–	1/3	–	– 1/20.
1	*sheng*			–	–	1/20	–	– 1/20.

Now for the *t'ung* the punishable difference is placed at 2 *sheng* (or between 1 and 2 *sheng*). Applying the fractions indicated in the above table for the largest unit mentioned, the *tou*, we obtain, with 2 *sheng* as the punishable difference for the *t'ung*, that 2 *sheng* would be equal to 1/30 *t'ung*, so that the *t'ung* would have a volume of 30 × 2 *sheng* = 60 *sheng* = 6 *tou*. Because the point at issue is the dispute between ten and six *tou*, the other theoretical possibilities—2 *sheng* = 1/15, or 2 *sheng* = 1/20, leading to a *t'ung* of 3 or 4 *tou*—are not relevant. Finally, the normal unit for ten *tou* was the *shih* or bushel, and it is this word which occurs at least a dozen times in the Ch'in strips, whereas *t'ung* only occurs twice. If the *t'ung* had really been the usual term for a ten *tou* measure, it would have been more frequent.

6 The *sheng* 升 or "pint" contained c. 0.2 litres.

7 The editors read *hu* 壺, "pot, flask", to be read as *i* 壹, "one".

8 According to *SW*, the meaning of *shih* 試 (normally: "to try", etc.) is *yung* 用, "to use".

A 55 W 7.4b; S I.15b; S IV.50b; SS 70–71; str. 101 (168).

[101] When for statute labour in the capital area[1] as well as for official work[2] on government buildings[3] there is borrowing of government (tools),[4] and the borrowers die or abscond,[5] orders are likewise[6] to be given to the statute labourers[7] and the retainers[8] to stand surety for[9] those borrowers, as in the case of participating in levies for frontier service.[10]

Statutes on Artisans.

1 The many examples of *pang chung* 邦中 and *kuo chung* 國中, collected in Morohashi, vol. 11, p. 222, and vol. 3, p. 83, show that this expression refers to the capital and the capital area.

2 *Kung shih* 公事.

3 *Kuan she* 官舍, where the editors explain *kuan* 官 as *kuan* 館. The examples in Morohashi, vol. 3, p. 967, and vol. 12, p. 416, show that *kuan she* is an ancient binome, meaning "office buildings" or "official residences"; *kuan* 館 *she* may also mean "hostel" (cf. A 64: *kung she* 公舍, "government residences"). The editors, however, apparently feel the lack of a verb and therefore take *kuan* 官 to be a substitute for *kuan* 館, which they render by "to lodge in", viz. to lodge in an official building, giving a double function to the single word *kuan* 官 on the strip.

4 What is borrowed is not indicated, but tools seem to be the most likely objects.

5 Cf. note 4 to A 38 above.

6 The occurrence of *i* 亦, "likewise", seems to indicate that the present rule formed part of a larger set.

7 Because the rule deals with statute labour, *yao* 繇, the *t'u* 徒 mentioned here can only refer to statute labourers and not to convicts.

8 S explains *she jen* 舍人 as *chia ch'en* 家臣, "family slaves or retainers", but SS considers them to be "members of the suite of the persons on official business". In many instances *she jen* are in fact members of the suite of prominent persons; Chavannes calls then "clients" in *Mh* II, p. 102 (*SC* 6.3).

9 *Jen* 任.

10 The Ch'in strips contain one article from the Statute on Frontier Service, *shu lü* 戍律 in C 25 below, whereas the Han had a Statute on Levies, *hsing lü* 興律 (see *RHL*, pp. 34–35), mainly concerned with statute labour.

A 56 W 7.4b; S I.15b; S IV.50b–51a; SS 71–72; str. 102–103 (169–170).

[102] Government armour and arms are each to be incised or branded[1] with the name of the office concerned; on those that cannot be incised or branded, it should be written with vermillion or lacquer. When armour and arms are loaned to commoners, it is essential to record the brandmark; they are to be bestowed[2] according to the brand-marks. When loaned (armour and arms) are handed in and[3] [103] they have no brand-mark, as well as when it is not the brand-mark of the office concerned, (such armour and arms) are all to be confiscated by the government;[4] they are to be charged[5] according to the Statutes on Equipment.[6]

(Statutes on) Artisans.

1 For *chiu* 久 meaning "to brand" or "brand-mark" see note 3 to A 47 above. The expression *k'o chiu* 刻久 is also found in the early abecedarium *Ts'ang Chieh p'ien*; see "Ts'ang Chieh p'ien", p. 26, fragment C 037, and p. 30, note 31.

2 The text reads *shou* 受, which I take to mean *shou* 授; cf. note 2 to A 3 above, but SS takes it as a loan for *shou* 收, "to collect".

3 The last word on strip 102 is *erh* 而, but the scribe has started the next strip with the same word. The mistake is the scribe's and not that of the editors, who, in view of the context, have been fully justified in placing strip 103 after 102.

4 Does this mean that these arms etc. were turned over to another government authority? The editors avoid the question.

5 To whom? To the office concerned or to the borrower?

6 *Chi* 齎, "to provision, to equip" (*SW* explains it simply as "to bring"), is found several times in the Ch'in strips; in A 32 above and in A 57 and D 75 I have translated it literally. The Statutes on Equipment are mentioned here, in A 56, as well as in A 88 (and in B 15, which is a doublet of A 88); *chi* occurs furthermore in D 182, where I believe it to stand for *chi lü*. These passages give the impression that this statute not only listed equipment, but also indicated its value.

A 57 W 7.4b; S I.15b; S IV.51a–b; SS 72–73; str. 104–107 (171–174).

[104] Government tools and office. ...[1] branded,[2] brand them; those that cannot be branded, brand them with lacquer. When somebody has borrowed government tools and returns these, these are only to be accepted when the brand-mark is correct.[3] From those that are spoiled and discarded[4] the brand-mark is scraped off.[5] The office every time[6] informs the person who borrows [105] a tool, saying: "When a tool is spoiled and it is to be feared that the brand-mark will be rubbed of, then, before it is rubbed off,[7] you should request to renew the mark." When the mark has been rubbed off and is unrecognizable,[8] (the borrower) must be ordered to provide (another tool) in repayment.[9] Whenever the work of the person who borrowed the tool is terminated, as well as when he is dismissed,[10] the office should [106] collect the tool; not collecting it quickly constitutes a crime. In case[11] the borrower dies or absconds[12] or commits a crime, it[13] is not to be charged; the official(s) repay(s) it in his stead. One must not unauthorizedly loan[14] government tools; all those who unauthorizedly loan government tools are guilty of a crime. Those who destroy or break government [107] tools as well as those who ...[15] are to be ordered to repay them.

(Statute on Artisans).[16]

1 One, perhaps two, characters effaced.

2 For *chiu* 久, "brand-mark, to brand", see note 3 to A 47 above.

3 *Pi* 必, lit. "certain".

4 See note 2 to A 47 above.

5 See note 4 to A 47 above.

6 *Che* 輒.

7 The text reads *ta ch'i wei mo* 逮其未(靡=) 磨, lit. "reaching its not yet being rubbed off", meaning, as in the translation, "before it is rubbed off".

8 The text has *chih* 智 for *chih* 知.

9 Because in these lapidary texts every word is significant, the fact that the strip does not simply read *shang* 賞(=償), "to repay", but has *chi* 齎 *shang*, has led me to the present rendering. SS translates "repays with money", taking *chi* (*GSR*, p. 159, no. 593u, *tsiər and *tsi̯ər) in the sense of *tzu* 資 (*GSR*, p. 149, no. 555h, *tsi̯ər), used i.a. in the *Chou li, t'ien-kuan, tien fu kung* 典婦功 (*Chou-li* 4/14.74; *Chou-li chu-su* 8.2b (0288); Biot I, p. 160).

10 I believe that "dismissed" refers to persons who had reached the age limit, when they were no longer obliged to perform statute labour.

11 The text has a slightly damaged character *chih* 之, which resembles *yeh* 也, and it is the latter reading which the editors have adopted, forgetting that in these texts the place of modern 也 is taken by 殹.

12 Cf. note 4 to A 39 above.

13 This will mean that the wife or relatives were not to be ordered to repay the tool, as in A 41 above.

14 Although *chia* 叚 can both mean "to lend" and "to borrow", it is only reasonable to suppose that officials who "loaned" are idicated, for it seems hardly imaginable that commoners would have been able to "borrow" without authorization.

15 *Wenwu* reads 及令 ... 賞, but this has been corrected in S and 22, reading 及 ... 者令賞; from the photograph it is difficult to judge how many characters are missing.

16 Strip 107 is the top of a strip, of which the lower half—which would have included the title of the statute—is missing. The suggestion by the editors that strip 114, which is the lower half of a broken strip, might form the sequel of strip 107, is quite unlikely, because A 57 is quite similar to A 56 and will therefore have belonged to the Statutes on Artisans, whereas the title mentioned on strip 114 is *chün kung* (*lü*) 均工(律), which forms a separate group, including A 61 and 62 below.

A 58 W 7.5a; S I.15b; S IV.52a; SS 73–74; str. 108 (175).

[108] For bond servants, persons under detention[1] (and) *ch'eng-tan* who are working together with artisans, the winter norm is the applied norm;[2] three days imposed[3] on them are equivalent to two days in summer.[4]

Personnel norms for Artisans.[5]

[1] For want of a better solution I follow the editors' suggestion; I fully agree with the editors of SS that *hsia li* 下吏 cannot mean low-ranking, c.q. subordinate officials. The term *hsia li* occurs many times in the histories, meaning that a person was *hsia* "sent down" to the *li*, "(judicial) officials". Now the editors turn this verb-object construction into a composite noun, meaning "a person sent down to the officials" for trial, but not yet sentenced. Kao Heng, "Chih-kuan", p. 210, has the dubious idea that *hsia li* were officials in detention.

[2] I follow the punctuation of *Wenwu* and S, as well as the latter's suggestion as regards *shih* 矢 (replaced by an open space in *Wenwu*) meaning *shih* 施. The equation is ancient, as shown by Karlgren, "Loan characters III", pp. 105–106, nos. 1511, 1512. There we find *shih* to mean "to spread out and set forth", but also "to apply", and in certain contexts even "to impose", viz. a certain task. Examples of the latter usage are found in the *Chou-li* (*Chou-li chu-su* 7.10b (0262); *Chou li* 4/13.54; Biot I, p. 147, seems mistaken), where the *nei tsai* "imposes working tasks upon them", *shih ch'i kung shih* 施其功事, and in the pseudo-K'ung An-kuo commentary to *Lun yü* 5, 25, 3: *pu shih lao* 不施勞, explained as "not to impose hardship (on others)" (*Lun yü* 5.7a (0117)). This explanation was later given up in favour of Chu Hsi's exegesis that the phrase meant "not to display one's meritorious actions"; this was accepted by Liu Pao-nan (1791–1855), p. 111, and the occidental translators of the *Analects*. However, the editors of SS take *shih* 矢 to mean *ch'ih* 弛, "to relax, to release", as stated in *Erh-ya* 2.6b (0058), overlooking that Hao I-hsing 郝懿行 in his *Erh-ya i-su* 爾雅義疏 indicates that 弛 was a mistake for 施 (according to Morohashi, vol. 8, p. 276, no. 23929, *sub* 11). Moreover, SS places a comma after *tung tso* 冬作 and translates "... perform hard labour during winter, the standard must be relaxed", smuggling the word "must", *tei* 得, into their text.

[3] As *fu* 賦 is followed by *chih* 之, *fu* must be a verb; beside "tax" it sometimes means "to impose a tax". Cf. also the use of *fu* in A 61 below.

[4] This indicates a ratio of two to three. This ratio is not found in *CCSS*, pp. 67–69 (Vogel, pp. 45–46), where the norms for men engaged in digging are mentioned: in winter 444 cubic feet, in spring 766, in summer 800, and in autumn 300. However, this ratio of 2:3 happens to be the ratio used for computing extra service time for personnel on the borders; see *RHA* II, p. 169.

[5] The editors explain *jen ch'eng* 人程 as "the number of men and the time needed for production". That *ch'eng* by itself means "norm" is shown by the passage in the *CCSS* referred to in note 4 above, for this reads *tung ch'eng* 冬程, *ch'un* 春 *ch'eng*, etc. That *kung* 工 means "artisans" is clear from its use in A 59, 61 and 62 below. SS explains the title as "legal rules concerning the fixed quantities to be produced by government handicraft industries". Perhaps the aim of this rule was that a smaller quotum was expected from the untrained convict labourers working together with trained artisans.

A 59 W 7.5a; S I.16a; S IV.52b; SS 74; str. 109 (176).

[109] For bond-women assigned to work[1] (the labour of) two bond-women is equivalent to that of one artisan. (The labour of) four bond-women taking their turn of duty[2] is equivalent to that of [one][3] artisan. For small bond servants and bond-women who can be employed,[4] (the labour of) five persons is equivalent to that of one artisan.

Norms for Artisans.

[1] For *jung* 宂 see note 6 to A 7 above.

[2] For *keng* 更 see note 1 to A 14 above.

[3] The editors are quite justified in adding this figure, which has been omitted on the strip.

[4] As indicated in A 12 above, bondservants of 6 ft. 5 in. (c. 1.5 m.) or less, and bond-women

of 6 ft. 2 in. (c. 1.43 m.) or less in height were considered as "small", but both were made to work when their height was 5 ft. 2 in. (c. 1.2 m.). Note that in Han practice *shih nan* and *shih nü* 使男/女, "serviceable males and females" were between 7 and 14 years of age; see Yang Lien-sheng, p. 110.

A 60 W 7.5a; S I.16a; S IV.52b; SS 74–75; str. 110 (177).

[110] For bond-women as well as women[1] who use the needle to make embroidery[2] and other things, one woman is equivalent to one man.

Norms for Artisans.

[1] For *nü-tzu* 女子 see note 4 to A 35 above; these women must have been free.
[2] Cf. note 5 to A 35 above.

A 61 W 7.5a; S I.16a; S IV.52b–53a; SS 75–76; str. 111–112 (178–179).

[111] When a new artisan begins his work as an artisan, in one year (he obtains) half the work;[1] in the year thereafter the work imposed[2] on him is equal to that of an old hand.[3] If the Master of the Artisans[4] teaches him well, what the old artisan accomplishes in one year, the new artisan accomplishes in two years. When somebody is capable of accomplishing his training before the term, [112] this is reported to the superior; the superior will have means to reward him. When somebody does not accomplish his training within the term, this is noted in his register and reported to the Minister of Finance.[5]

Statutes on Equalizing Artisans.

[1] *Hung* 紅 is used for *kung* 功.
[2] *Fu* 賦; see note 3 to A 58 above.
[3] Note the use of the word *ku* 故.
[4] *Kung shih* 工師. This title is found in several ancient texts as well as on bronzes and other objects, as indicated by Yü Hao-liang, "Chih-kuan", p. 10, and by Wu Jung-tseng, "Shou kung-yeh", p. 39. It is clear that he was in charge of artisans, and Wu, *loc. cit.*, is surely right when he states that he also directed official workshops. The translators of the classical texts have often rendered the term in a way which shows that they considered the *kung shih* as a kind of minister of works, but the inscriptions discussed by both Yü, *op. cit.*, and Ch'en Chih, *Liang Han*, pp. 218–222, show that this is incorrect. Legge, translating *Mencius* I B, ix, 1, writes "the Master of the workmen", and in the *Yüeh-ling* chapter of the *Li-chi* once correctly "the chiefs of works" (*Li-ki* 27, p. 265), but then wrongly "the chief Director of works" (*op. cit.*, p. 299), where "works" should be "workmen". But Dubs correctly renders *kung shih* as "the Superintendent of the Artisans" in his *Hsüntze*, p. 141, in his translation of the *Wang chih* chapter of the *Hsün-tzu*, p. 107, and so does Wilhelm (*Frühling*, p. 28), "der Meister der Handwerker", in his rendering of *LSCC*, p. 24.
[5] For T'ang rules for the training and testing of apprentices see des Rotours, *Fonctionnaires* I, p. 459, and *TLT* 22.11b–12a.

A 62 W 7.5a; S I.16a; S IV.53a; SS 76; str. 113(180).

[113] When bond servants are clever and could be made artisans, they must not be made servants or cooks[1] of other people.

(Statutes on) Equalizing (Artisans).[2]

[1] Cf. A 37 above.
[2] The title is defective, only *chün* 均 being legible.

A 63 W 7.5a; S I.16a; S IV.53b; SS 76; str. 114(181).

[114]. . . .Equalizing Artisans.[1]

1 This is the lower half of a broken strip, which only contains the title of the statute. I do not think that this fragment forms the sequel to strip 107, as suggested by the editors; see note 16 to A 57 above.

A 64 W 7.5a–b; S I.16a–b; S IV.53b–55a; SS 76–80; str. 115–124(182–191).

[115] When a levy is raised for the Court,[1] to be remiss[2] and not to carry it out is fined two suits of armour; to miss the term[3] by three to five days (results in) a reprimand; from six days to a decade the fine is one shield; beyond a decade the fine is one suit of armour. When (the men) have been obtained,[4] (the levy) quickly[5] proceeds; if it rains, the levy is cancelled. [116] When levying conscripts[6] for work[7] inside a settlement, order is given to guarantee[8] the earth walls[9] for a full year. In case the walls collapse before (the year) is over, the Controller of Works[10] who had directed the work, as well as the Master[11] in charge of the wall (building) will have committed a crime. The conscripts concerned will be ordered to build it again: [117] (this work) must not be accounted as statute labour.[12] ○

Whenever prefectures, which maintain[13] Forbidden Parks[14] (or) parks for government horses and cattle, levy statute labourers because the ditches and walls have fallen apart and they quickly repair these,[15] the park officials are informed about this. The park officials[16] inspect these (repairs). In case within a year some[17] collapse [118] or show cracks,[18] the prefecture is ordered to levy conscripts again to do (the repairs), whereas this must not be accounted as statute labour. In case they would show cracks or collapse when the year is over, for more than three sections[19] the prefecture which maintains (the parks) repairs them. For less than three sections and also, although [119] the year is not yet over, when some have been surreptitiously breached for passages in and out, the park (officials) are ordered to repair these themselves immediately. In Forbidden Parks, regardless of their being close to or far from the hills,[20] where the soil is bad[21] and does not resist[22] rain, so that in summer there are [120] (walls) which collapse, these must not be repaired piecemeal;[23] this is to be done by means of statute labour when autumn has come, the season without rain.

When for fields near (to these parks) it is feared that animals as well as horses or cattle would break out and eat the crops, the Prefectural Overseer[24] will make an estimate[25] for a levy among those who have fields close by [121] regardless of their status, to provide men according to the number[26] of their fields in order to build walls or repair these; it is not allowed to consider this as statute labour.

The prefecture must not venture unauthorizedly to demolish or change[27] government buildings, storehouses[28] as well as (the prefect's) court.[29] When it is desired to demolish or change (such buildings), this must be requested.[30] [122] When it is desired to use *ch'eng-tan* and grain-pounders to enlarge[31] government buildings and storehouses, as well as to repair these, let it be done; it should not be requested.

When the prefecture undertakes routine work[32] as well when it has requested (permission) to undertake work, the officials apply the norms to the work.[33] In case (the estimate proves to be wrong by) an excess [123] of the (labour) force,[34] or a shortage, of two days or more, this is considered as "lack of perspicacity".[35] When for levies raised by superiors[36] the application of the norms to the work is incorrect,[37] (punitive measures[38]) are like those for the prefecture. When estimating[39] the work, it is imperative to have the Controller of Works estimate it together with the Builder;[40] one must not only order [124] the Builder (to estimate it). In case of carelessness[41] the persons who made the estimate are to be adjudicated according to the Statutes, whereas the actual amount[42] is to be accounted as statute labour for the conscripts.[43]

Statutes on Statute Labour.

1 *Yü chung* 御中; the binome seems to be unknown in Chinese traditional literature, because it is not to be found in the *P'ei-wen yün-fu*. *Yü* is commonly used for objects for the personal use of the ruler; see e.g. the *Wang chih* 王制 chapter of the *Li-chi* (*Li-chi chu-su* 11.98 (0518); Couvreur, *Li ki* I, p. 269; Legge, *Li ki* 27, p. 212). The editors' suggestion that *yü chung* refers to the court seems therefore quite justified.

2 Cf. D 154 below.

3 According to the biography of Ch'en She, "to miss the term", *shih ch'i* 失期, was punished by beheading (*SC* 48.3, *Mh* VI, p. 8; *HSPC* 31.1b). *Ch'i* is related to *ch'i hui* 會, "to assemble at the appointed time"; see *RHL*, p. 444, and cf. D 143 below for *pu hui* 不會.

4 The text only has *te* 得, which the editors explain as *tsu* 足, translating *ch'i te yeh* 其得也 by "when the number of the men levied is already sufficient". However, this explanation of *te* is only based on a gloss in the *Li-chi*, where Cheng Hsüan says "*te* is like *tsu* 足", whereas the *Li-chi* text shows that something like "proportionate" is meant (*Li-chi chu su* 12.16b (0586); Couvreur, *Li ki* I, p. 297; Legge, *Li ki* 27, p. 230). I have preferred to take *te* literally.

5 The editors are undoubtedly right in taking *chi* 及, "to reach, to extend to", to mean *chi* 急, "hastily". They refer to the manuscript of the *Sun-tzu ping-fa*, which has the first character, whereas the traditional text has the second; see *Sun-tzu, Yin-ch'iao shan*, p. 35, note 12, and *Sun-tzu shih chia chu*, p. 28. The same substitution is also found in the *P'an keng* chapter of the Book of Documents, the *Shu ching*; see Karlgren, "Glosses, Documents", p. 210, gloss 1480. 及 is the phonetic element of 急, and the pronunciation of the two words was quite similar: *g'i̯əp and *ki̯əp (*GSR*, p. 180, no. 681 a and g).

6 See note 7 to A 55 above.

7 Again, *hung* 紅 is used for *kung* 功.

8 *Ku* 結 is taken as a loan for *ku* 嫴, explained by *SW* as *pao jen* 保任, "to guarantee"; cf. *RHL*, p. 271.

9 *Tu* 堵 is a section of a wall of tamped earth, 2 ft thick and 10 ft high, its length being either 8 or 10 ft; different opinions of the commentators to the classics are cited in Morohashi, vol. 3, p. 222, no. 5280, *sub* 1.

10 *Ssu k'ung* 司空. This prefectural official was in charge of conscripts and convicts, especially those engaged in building activities; see *HSPC* 19A.14a with Ju Shun's remarks, as well as 48.28b–29a, 66.14b, 88.19a (*SC* 121.18). Ch'en Chih, *HSHC*, p. 96, indicates the existence of many Han bricks and tiles stamped with the words *ssu-k'ung*, whereas Yen Keng-wang, vol. I, pp. 109 and 232, shows that both the commandery and the prefecture had *yü* 獄 *ssu-k'ung*, "Controllers of Works for Prisons", attached to the *wei ts'ao*, "Bureau of the Commandant" and in charge of conscripts and convicts. For completeness' sake it should be added that there were also *ssu-k'ung* in the army (*HSPC* 60.3a and 79.1b). When in 8 B.C. the title of one of the highest functionaries in the central government, the Grandee Secretary, was changed to *ssu-k'ung* "in conformity with the institutions of the Chou dy-

nasty", the word *ta* 大 was expressly added, so as to distinguish this title from that of the local *ssu-k'ung* (in 5 B.C. the old title was restored, but changed again in 1 B.C., see *HSPC* 10.15b, 11.4b, 8a; *HFHD* II, p. 416; III, pp. 28, 38; *HSPC* 19A.5b; in A.D. 51 the word *ta* was removed, see *HHSCC* Ann. 1B.19b, Tr. 24.6a, commentary. See also Bielenstein, *Bureaucracy*, pp. 15–16).

11 *Chün-tzu* 君子. This is not the Confucian "gentleman", but the title of a local official. *Chün* (without *tzu*) occurs twice in the *Han shu* account of the Western Regions (*HSPC* 96A.10b and 16a); Dr. Loewe and I have rendered this title of a local official in the Central Asian states of Lou-lan and Wu-mi in charge of small bodies of native troops as "master" (*CICA*, pp. 84 and 96) and I have retained this translation here. The title *chün-tzu* is found four times in the strips: in the present case and in the practically parallel C 26, where the *chün-tzu* are in charge of labour conscripts building pisé walls; in C 21, where they are in charge of military conscripts, and in A 81, where a *chün-tzu* temporarily assumes the duties of an Overseer. In their note 1 to A 81 the editors of SS remark, that the *chün-tzu* might have been holders of aristocratic rank, because the commentator Tu Yü 杜預 (222–284) explains *chün-tzu* as *tsai wei che* 在位者, "a person in a position of authority" (Duke Hsiang 13th year; *Tso chuan* 32.2b (1302); Couvreur, *Tch'ouen-ts'iou* II, p. 285); they combine this with the information in C 1 below, which stipulates that a temporary Overseer had to possess at least the second aristocratic rank, viz. that of *shang tsao*. Considering his duties and his position below the Overseer and the prefectural Controller of Works, the Master was evidently a low-ranking local official, as stated above. Like any other man he could acquire aristocratic rank and then become eligible for the post of Probationary Overseer, but I do not think that rank was a prerequisite for becoming a Master. Rather we shall have to acknowledge our ignorance as regards the origin of this high-sounding title. See also note 2 to C 21 below.

12 This is an indication that *t'u* 徒 were not convicts but free men, performing statutory labour.

13 I have chosen this rather vague term to render *pao* 葆 (i.e. 保), which can mean both "to protect" and "to guarantee"; SS, however, renders it by "to repair".

14 Probably hunting parks of the ruling house.

15 For the rendering of *chi* 及 as "quickly" see note 5 above.—The editors of *Wenwu* and of S suggest that *chan* 斬, "to hack", is a loan for *ch'ien* 塹, "moat, trench"; SS also opts for the other meaning of *ch'ien*, viz. "to dig". For *san* 散 SS suggests reading *fan* 藩 and then takes *li san* 離散 to mean *li fan* 籬藩, "a hedge"! This obliges SS to smuggle the word "to construct" into their translation: "... construct trenches and walls and hedges", or rather, they make *ch'ien* serve first for "to construct" and then again for "trenches". This is unacceptable. The normal meaning of *li san* is "torn apart and scattered", said of families separated because of war or social unrest; I have taken it literally. Needless to say, the pronunciation, ancient and modern, of *san* and *fan* is completely different.

16 These two words are indicated by repetition markers in the text.

17 Here, as well as later in the text, the word *huo* 或 is used.

18 *Chüeh* 昳.

19 See note 9 above.

20 *Fu* 傅, *pi̯wo (*GSR*, p. 47, no. 102*u'*) can be used as a loan word for *fu* 附, *b'i̯u (*GSR*, p. 56, no. 136k), meaning "to adhere to; close to".

21 Cf. note 4 to A 43 above.

22 *Neng* 能 used as a loan for *nai* 耐, "to endure, to withstand" (both *nəg; see *GSR* p. 236, no. 885a and p. 259, no. 982h).

23 *Shao* 稍, "somewhat; little by little"; cf. note 7 to A 39 above.

24 See note 5 to A 19 above.

25 *Ts'ai* 材 used as a loan for *ts'ai* 裁.

26 *Shao-to* 少多.

27 According to *CS* 30.11a (cf. Uchida, p. 104 and note 11), the Han had a similar rule: "Among the (Han) Rulings (for this term see *RHL*, p. 51) there is mention of 'unauthorized construction or repair of buildings'", *k'o yu shan tso hsiu she shih* 科有擅作脩舍事. See also *HSPC* 8.13a, *HFHD* II, p. 232, for unauthorized levies to decorate relay stations of the courier service.

28 For *kuan fu* 官府 see note 13 to A 41 above.

29 *T'ing* 廷; from the context, i.a. in A 21 above, this must be the meaning of *t'ing*, but in D 79 below it indicates the court of the Commandery Administrator.

30 *Yeh* 讞 is an accepted variant of *yeh* 讞, "to refer to a superior"; see *SWKL*, p. 5103b sq. and *RHL*, p. 339 and note 211, as well as *HFHD* I, p. 326. The present text does not indicate which superior is to be addressed.

31 *I wei* 益爲, lit. "to increase and make"; the text does not contain a technical term for "to build".

32 *Heng shih* 亘(=恒) 事, lit. "constant or permanent tasks".

33 *Ch'eng* 程; one might also render the word by "to measure".

34 *Yüan* 員 is explained in *SW* as *wu shu* 物數 "the number of things"; for persons it often means "fixed number, personnel, complement, staff". In the chapter on the organization of the bureaucracy in the Han histories the phrase "*yüan* so and so many persons" occurs frequently. In the present case *yüan* not only includes the number of persons, but also the number of days.

35 *Pu ch'a* 不察; in view of the context, this must have entailed punishment for the officials who had made the wrong estimate.

36 *Shang* 上. This word is to be taken as a general term, referring to authorities superior to the Prefect; in view of the context it cannot refer to the ruler.

37 *Pu tang* 不當, lit. "not corresponding, not matching"; cf. *RHL*, p. 80 f.

38 Cf. note 35 above.

39 Here the word *to* 度 is used in stead of *ch'eng* 程.

40 *Chiang* 匠, defined in *SW* as *mu kung* 木工 "artisan in wood", i.e. "carpenter". I have used the word "builder" because here the work involves more than carpentry; in this connection it should be noted that part of the title of the Court Architect was *ta chiang* 大匠.

41 *Pu shen* 不審, lit. "not to look into, not to investigate" implies a reprehensible lack of care or attention, resulting in an untrue or false report, without, however, any criminal intent (cf. also *RHL*, p. 263). *Pu shen* is therefore radically different from *pu chih* 不直, "not straight or upright", which implies conscious dishonesty; see D 77 below. Furthermore, *pu shen* can be said of any person, whereas *pu chih* was only applied to officials.

42 *Ch'i shih* 其實.

43 *Erh i ch'i shih wei yao t'u chi* 而以其實爲繇徒計, lit. "take the actual (amount) and make it the account of (or for) the statute labour conscripts".

A 65 W 7.5b; S I.17a; S IV.58b; SS 87–88; str. 134–135(208–209).

[134] Bond-servants and bond-women, and robber-guards of the *ch'eng-tan* and grainpounders,[1] who work off[2] fines, redemption fees or debts, and who are detained[3] among the *ch'eng-tan* and grainpounders, must not be charged for clothing and food. Those who work together with the *ch'eng-tan* and grainpounders are to be clothed and fed like the *ch'eng-tan* and grainpounders. When a bond-servant has a wife [135] and this wife performs turns of duty,[4] as well as when he has a wife outside,[5] he is to be charged for his clothing. When a person's male or female slaves are detained among the *ch'eng-tan* and grainpounders,[6] they are to be loaned[7] clothing and fed by the government. If they die before their time has been completed,[8] their clothing and food[9] are to be cancelled.[10]

(Statutes concerning) the Controller of Works.

1 It is clear from A 69 below, that *ch'eng-tan* after three years could be made *ch'eng-tan* robber-guards; this was apparently optional. According to the Treatise of the norms of punishment in the *Han shu* (*HSPC* 23.14a, *RHL*, p. 336) the Han bond-servants and bond-women, whose full term was three years, became robber-guards after two years, but this is not said in connection with *ch'eng-tan*.

2 See note 8 to A 39 above.

3 The text has *ch'i* 毄 for *chi* 繫 see *RHL*, p. 74.

4 Cf. note 1 to A 14 above. This seems to imply that the wife was a bond-woman. in contrast to the separately mentioned "wife outside", who was free.

5 "Outside" must imply that she had no servile status; the editors also think so.

6 *Nu ch'ieh* 奴妾; the term recurs in A 68; D 18, 62, 86, 88, 119; in other passages, slaves are called *ch'en ch'ieh* 臣妾 (D 4, 43, 60, 89, 149, 150, 153; E 3). Lin Chien-ming has proved that these persons were slaves, and not convicts (abstracted in my "Additional remarks"). A source not utilized by Lin (nor by Wilbur) is the chapter on divination in the *Shih-chi*, still untranslated. *SC* 128.36, 40 etc. shows that *ch'en* and *ch'ieh* were bought and sold like horses and cattle. This part of *SC* 128 was written by Ch'u Shao-sun around the middle of the 1st century B.C. (see Wilbur, p. 318, note 7), but it is clear that Ch'u was copying a manual of divination, which may have been many years, if not centuries, older.—There exists only one reason I can think of, why these slaves were detained among the convict labourers, and that is that they were punished at the request of their owners (cf. D 89 and E 15 below), for otherwise the expression "before their time has been completed" in the following lines would have no sense. In case they would have been arrested and condemned by the authorities, they would have been automatically fed and clothed by them, whereas in case they were working off their owners' obligations (see the last lines of A 68 below), there could hardly have been a time limit.

7 *T'e* 貣; see note 6 to A 31 above.

8 *Jih wei pei* 日未備, lit. "the days are still incomplete"; *pu pei* 不備 is the usual expression for "shortage" in these texts.

9 Note that clothing and food were "loaned", so that cancellation profitted the slaves' owner.

10 See note 18 to A 9 above.

A 66 W 7.5b; S I.17b; S IV.59a; SS 88; str. 136 (210).

[136] For persons detained[1] among the *ch'eng-tan* and grainpounders and receiving government food whilst making good[2] their debts, the bushel is reckoned at thirty cash.[3]

(Statutes concerning) the Controller of Works.

1 See note 3 to A 65 above.

2 The text is highly abbreviated; in stead of the long construction with *chü* 居, "to work off", like in A 65, 67 and 68, the text simply writes *tang* 當, "to counterbalance, to outweigh".

3 In A 68 below we find that one day's work repaid 8 cash of the debt, but only six cash when the person received government rations. This means that the value of the food was 2 cash per day. For one month of thirty days (cf. note 2 to A 16 above) this amounts to sixty cash, i.e. the value of two bushels according to the present rule. This agrees with A 12 above, which stipulates that the ration for convict labourers was two bushels per month.

A 67 W 7.5b; S I.17b; S IV.59a; SS 88–89; str. 137(211).

[137] Persons who work off fines, redemption fees or debts return (home) for agricultural work at the time of sowing and at the time of weeding,[1] on both (occasions) two decades.

(Statutes concerning) the Controller of Works.

1 I do not know the meaning of the expression *chih miao* 治苗, "to treat the sprouts"; the SS translation "to control or regulate the sprouts" is of no help. According to the subcommentary of a phrase in the *Li-chi*, quoted in the *P'ei-wen yün-fu*, it would seem to mean some kind of weeding: "removing (the plants) which bear no fruit". The term might mean "to thin out". It seems to follow from this rule that these persons must have performed their convict tasks in their home prefecture.

A 68 W 7.5b–6a; S I.17b–18a; S IV.59a–60b; SS 84–87; str. 138–145(200–207).

[138] Persons who have committed crimes and who therefore (have to pay) fines or redemption-fees, as well as those who have debts[1] towards[2] the govern-

ment are to be asked[3] on the day the order is given.[4] Those who are unable to pay[5] or to refund are to work off (their obligations) as from the day the order is given. Per day they work off eight cash; those fed by the government work off six cash per day. For those who work off (their obligations) in government storehouses, and who are fed by the government, (the rations are) for men one third[6] (of a *tou* for the morning meal and again for the evening meal[7]); [139] for women one quarter.[8] As regards persons with the aristocratic rank of *kung shih*[9] or less,[10] who are working off the redemption of a mutilating punishment[11] or the death penalty and who work this off among the *ch'eng-tan* and grainpounders, their clothes are not to be made red[12] and they are not to be manacled or fettered.[13]

Gatherers of firewood for the spirits and sifters of white rice,[14] and persons under detention[15] who have not had their beards shaved off[16], or people's slaves who work off redemption fees, fines or [140] debts, who work these off among the *ch'eng-tan*, will all have their clothes made red and are to be manacled and fettered.[17] The person who leads or supervises[18] them and who lets them escape will have committed a crime.

(Persons with the status of) *pao-tzu*[19] or higher who work off the redemption of a mutilating punishment or more, up to the redemption of the death (penalty), work these off in government storehouses;[20] none of these must lead or supervise (other convict labourers).

In case persons have not been asked,[21] but [141] have been detained for a long time, the Great Overseer[22] and the Overseer of the office concerned[23] will have committed a crime.

When it is desired to replace those who work off fines, redemption fees or debts, and the ages are equivalent, this is to be allowed. (Owners of) workshops[24] as well as traders who owe debts are not allowed replacement.

When in one household[25] two persons or more are made to work off [142] fines, redemption fees or debts and there is nobody to look after their household, one person is to be released;[26] they should be made to work off (their obligations) in turn.[27]

In case persons who work off fines, redemption fees or debts wish to borrow[28] another person to work these off together, this is to be allowed, but (the other person) is not to be excused from statute labour or military service.[29]

In all cases [143] when persons are unable to provide their own clothing, they are to be clothed by the government; they are to be ordered to work off (the value of) these clothes according to the Statutes.[30] If, before their term is complete, they want to pay cash in instalments,[31] this is to be permited. Those who by means of days (of labour) equate a mutilating punishment, but who are unable to provide their own clothing and food, are also to be clothed and fed [144], but they are to be ordered to work these off.

When by working for a government office[32] persons work off fines, redemption fees or debts and they are distant from the office which keeps their accounts, (then) at the end of the eighth month the office which keeps their accounts is to be informed[33] for each one about the days they have worked and the number of clothes (issued to them); one must not let the ninth month pass before the finalized accounts[34] have reached [145] the office concerned. When offices are close[35] to each other, the office which keeps their accounts is to be informed at the end of the ninth month; these (figures) should be accounted for the year in which they worked.[36]

When commoners[37] have fines, redemption fees or debts, and they have a[38] male or female slave, or they have a horse or an ox, with which they wish to work off (their obligations), this is to be permitted.

(Statutes concerning) the Controller (of Works).[39]

1 *Tse* 責 for *chai* 債.

2 The strip reads *yü* 於 which the editors have "modernised" as *yü* 于. In the other cases on this strip the transcription 于 is correct.

3 *Wen* 問 is rendered in SS as "to interrogate", but the technical term for "to interrogate" is *hsün* 訊; see E 2 below and cf. *RHL*, p. 79. I think that in the present case these persons were simply asked, whether they were able to pay the required amount.

4 *Ling jih* 令日 is explained in S as "the day when the order is given", without explaining this further. I assume that these words indicate the day when the sentence was to be executed; cf. note 1 to D 48 below. SS wants *ling jih* to mean "the term fixed by the judgement", but that does not explain anything. *Ling jih* certainly cannot mean "auspicious day" as in *HSPC* 73.15b.

5 *Ju* 入, in the sense of *na* 納, "to pay in".

6 For this meaning of *ts'an* 參 see my "Weights", p. 38.

7 That this is implied is clear from A 15 above.

8 *Ssu* 駟, lit. "a team of four horses", is used here for "four", or rather "one fourth", just as *ts'an* 參, "a set of three" is used for "one third". Morohashi, vol. 12, p. 515, gives only one example of *ssu* 駟 being used for "four"; this is found in the chapter *Yüeh chi* 樂記 of the *Li chi* (*Li-chi chu-su* 39.6a (1665); Couvreur, *Li ki* II, p. 98; Legge, *Li ki* 28, p. 123).

9 *Kung shih* 公士 was the first or lowest of the aristocratic ranks; cf. Loewe, "Rank", pp. 99 and 103.

10 The addition "or less" is surprising, because it implies that the following privileged treatment would also be given to commoners without aristocratic rank.—Professor Hori, working only with the Ch'in texts as published in *Wenwu*, where the division into strips is not indicated, assumes the occurrence of "misplaced strips" in the following passage, but the photographs show, that this is not the case; see Hori, "Keimei", p. 122, and Hori, "Yakuchū", p. 96, no. 4, note 7.

11 Hori, "Keimei", p. 119, believes that in these texts the single word *hsing* 刑 indicates the lightest of the mutilating punishments, viz. tattooing.

12 *Ch'ih ch'i i* 赤其衣. I do not know whether this means "dye their clothes red" or "clothe them in red".

13 The dictionaries do not indicate these meanings for the four words *chü* or *kou* 枸 (explained as "crooked"), *tu* 櫝 (box), *lei* 欙 (clogs), *ti* 杕 (tree), nor does Shen Chia-pen discuss these or similar terms in his *Hsing-chü k'ao*. However, the *lei-ti* must be fetters or leg-irons, i.e. the *ti* 鈦, already mentioned in the *Kuan-tzu* (see *GSR*, p. 95, no. 317 l; the chapter is not indicated), and in the treatise on the economy in both *Shih-chi* and *Han shu* (*SC* 30.23, *Mh* III, p. 571; *HSPC* 24B.13a, Swann, p. 277). Incidentally, the occurrence of *lei* in this context might solve a question hotly debated during many centuries, for it seems that the *lei* worn by the Great Yü as one of his "four conveyances" when draining the waters of the great flood (Karlgren, "Documents", p. 9) were some kind of clogs. For the quarrel among the learned see especially *SWKL*, p. 2604 ff., the commentary of the pseudo-K'ung An-kuo to the chapter *I chi* in the *Shu-ching* (*Shu-ching* 5.1a), and the commentaries to *SC* 29.1 (*Mh* III, p. 520) and *HSPC* 29.1b. The explanation by the editors that *lei* would be a loan for *lei* 縲, the "black ropes" in *Lun-yü* V. i (*Lun-yü chu-su* 5.1a (0105)), said to be tied around the neck of a convict, seems highly improbable. For *ti*, "leg-irons", see also Hamaguchi; archaeological finds of leg-irons are described in "Hou Ma", Chin Chung-

hsing, and "Lin-t'ung", pp. 40–41. Because *lei-ti* are "leg-irons", *chü-tu* are evidently "manacles".

14 Respectively male and female convicts, in Han times condemned to three years hard labour; cf. *RHL*, p. 129 f.

15 See note 1 to A 58 above.

16 *Nai* 耐; cf. *RHL*, p. 130.

17 The punctuation in all editions is wrong; the sentence ends here.

18 That this is the meaning of *chiang ssu chih* 將司之 is clear from the next sentence, which forbids this.

19 The term *pao-tzu* 葆子 is unknown; in the Ch'in strips it is found also in D 89–92 below. Different explanations have been offered. S believes that it means "persons under arrest, but not yet sentenced", evidently inspired by Ch'en Chih, *Liang Han*, p. 44, who suggests that *pao* might mean *pao shih* 保釋, "released on caution". This explanation of *pao-tzu* is unacceptable, not only because *pao-shih* is a late term, but especially because in D 89–92 the words "whose cases have not yet been judged" is added to the words *pao-tzu*. Now Ch'en Chih, *loc. cit.*, also suggests that *pao* might stand for *pao chü* 保舉, a Sung term: high officials were allowed to recommend *chü* a person, but they had to guarantee *pao* his capacities and his probity. SS seems to have preferred this second explanation, for they equate *pao-tzu* with *jen tzu* 任子, a well known Han term: Han officials ranking at 2000 bushels (and therefore including commandery administrators) were entitled to have one of their brothers or sons appointed as *lang* 郎, Gentleman, for whom they stood surety, *jen* (see *HSPC* 11.13a, *HFHD* III, p. 23). This explanation looks acceptable, but a better solution has been found. This solution is offered by Chang Cheng-lang. Basing himself on passages in the military chapters of the *Mo-tzu*, he concludes that *pao-tzu* were hostages, taken from the families of leading officials in order to ensure their loyalty, a practice frequently resorted to, both in antiquity and later, as demonstrated by Professor Yang (Yang Lien-sheng, p. 43 ff.) with references to the same passages in the *Mo-tzu*. This explanation of *pao-tzu* as "hostage" is also valid for the Edsin-gol strips discussed by Dr. Loewe in *RHA* II, p. 202 ff.; there *pao* serves to indicate the position of the person, whose further personalia are listed immediately afterwards (*pao* therefore does not define the following place name, as suggested by Dr. Loewe). For *tzu* 子, the second element in the term *pao-tzu*, two explanations are possible. The first is that *tzu* serves to indicate a person, like in the ubiquitous *nan-tzu* 男子, or in *nü-tzu* 女子 (see note 4 to A 35), or *ch'ien-tzu* 鉗子, "collar-man", i.e. a hard labour convict wearing an iron ring or collar around his neck (see *RHL*, p. 129), or *ch'e-tzu* 車子, "carter" (see Ch'en P'an, *Ch'i chung*, p. 71a ff.), or *k'o-tzu* 客子, "stranger" (see *Chia-pien*, p. 23, no. 524). The second possible explanation of *tzu* is to take the word literally as "children" or "sons", because then the following words *i shang* 以上, "and higher", become understandable; they would indicate senior family members of the person who had to provide hostages. Because such persons were leading officials, their family members taken as hostages evidently enjoyed the privileged treatment in criminal cases indicated in the rule under discussion.—The conclusion which Ch'iu Hsi-kui, "Chü-yen", pp. 109–110, draws from the same Edsin-gol documents that were used by Ch'en Chih and Dr. Loewe, namely, that *pao* would indicate hired labourers, does not fit the context, although *pao* does have this meaning in other cases.

20 See note 13 to A 41 above.

21 Cf. note 3 above; here the meaning is perhaps that these persons had never been asked whether they could pay the required amounts, but had been immediately put to work.

22 See note 5 to A 19 above.

23 Perhaps the Overseer of the office in which the debtor had been put to work.

24 See note 1 to A 51 above.

25 See note 15 to A 41 above.

26 *Ch'u* 出, lit. "made to leave".

27 This seems to be the meaning of *ling hsiang wei chien chü chih* 令相爲兼居之 ; the editors of SS are of the same opinion.

28 *Chi* 籍 for *chieh* 藉, i.e. *chieh* 借.

29 The end of this paragraph is marked by a black dot.

30 See A 49 and 50 above.

31 For *p'i* 柀, "to split; in parts", see note 29 to A 19 above.

32 *Kuan tso* 官作; perhaps "for a government agency".

33 Here *kao* 告 is used in its usual sense of "to report, to inform", and not as "to denounce".

34 Cf. note 9 to A 47 above.

35 In stead of the normal character for "near", viz. *chin* 近, which occurs several times in these strips, strip 145 reads 䜣, evidently to be pronounced *chin*. The character is not to be found in *SW*; Morohashi, vol. 8, p. 991, no. 37321, only quotes a late dictionary, which indicates the pronunciation *chiu* and the meaning "mirror"!

36 As the administrative year started with the tenth month, the figures were to be entered for the year just past, and not for the year in which the figures had been received.

37 *Pai hsing* 百姓. This is a very general term, whereas *shu jen* 庶人 seems to be used for persons who did not possess aristocratic rank. SS, p. 91, note 4, refers to Ch'ien Ta-hsin 10.5a, who remarks that *shu jen* is used in contrast to slaves and convicts, whereas *shu min* 民 is a general term. Wu Shu-p'ing, "Chieh-chi", p. 84 f., believes that *pai-hsing* denotes persons of certain means, because the present article shows that these commoners could own slaves, cattle and horses, whereas other articles show that they gave loans to the authorities (A 38), that they engaged in deals in the market (A 42), and that they bought army rations (C 8), but I believe that this explanation is exaggerated and that *pai-hsing* embraced all free people, rich and poor. The contention by T'ang Tsan-kung, "Nu-li", p. 143, that the most general term for "people", *jen-min* 人民 would signify "slaves" is unfounded. It is based on CM strip 752, where this mantic text indicates that certain days were favourable for *ju jen-min* 入人民 as well as cattle, horses and grain, but he overlooks that similar passages (CM str. 837, 839) have the normal term for "slaves", *ch'en ch'ieh* 臣妾, which shows that in the text he quotes *jen-min* must have its usual meaning.

38 The use of the numeral *i* 一, "one", is curious.

39 Because there was no more room on the strip, the scribe has imply written *ssu* 司 in stead of the full title *ssu-k'ung lü* 司空律.

A 69 W 7.6a; S I.18a; S IV.61b; SS 89; str. 146–147(212–213).

[146] Do not place (persons who) work off fines, redemption fees or debts in charge[1] of *ch'eng-tan* and grainpounders. If there are not sufficient *ch'eng-tan* robber-guards[2] to lead them, then order bond-servants or bond-women to lead them. As regards persons who work off fines, redemption fees or debts who are warranted to work together with *ch'eng-tan* and grainpounders, as well as *ch'eng-tan* enrolled as strong[3] [147] *ch'eng-tan* and grainpounders warranted to be led and supervised, twenty persons are led by one *ch'eng-tan* robberguard. If (the number of) robber-guards is insufficient,[5] dismiss[6] *ch'eng-tan* who have laboured[7] for three years or more and make them *ch'eng-tan* robber-guards.

(Statutes concerning the Controller of Works).[8]

1 *Chiang* 將, lit. "to lead".

2 See note 1 to A 65 above.

3 The strip reads *fu chien* 傅堅. As shown by A 13 above, young men were enrolled, *fu*, on having reached a certain height; *chien* means "hard soil" according to *SW*, but it can also mean "strong", so that here it may indicate that these young men had the necessary strength. The suggestion by the editors of S that *fu chien* could be a name for convicts, *hsing t'u ming* 刑徒名, seems unacceptable. SS suggests that *fu* should be read as *po* 搏, "to beat" (the phonetic element in both characters is the same, but according to *GSR*, p. 47, no. 102u', and p. 204, no. 771d, the ancient pronunciation was different: *pi̯wo and*pak, but apparently also *pi̯wo), and that *chien* should actually mean "hard soil", so that the binome might indicate *ch'eng-tan* who specially worked as builders of pisé walls. However, *po* primarily means "to knock, to fight" and not "to pound".

4 The contents of strips 146 and 147 are undoubtedly connected, but the transition here is embarrassing. The easiest solution would be to assume that either a full strip is missing, or that the scribe made a mistake by omitting some words concerning the control of the different groups, mentioned in the second half of strip 146. The first sentence on strip 147 looks very much like an independent general statement.

5 Here the same character is used as in A 39 above.

6 I have taken *mien* 免, "to dismiss", as an imperative, and not as qualifying the following noun. This stipulation is evidently connected with the Han rule that *ch'eng-tan* after three years were to be made "(cutters of) firewood for the spirits" (a three year punishment), who eventually became robber-guards (see *RHL*, p. 336).

7 *Lao* 勞. For *lao* meaning "length of service" see *RHA* II, p. 19.

8 The lower part of this strip is missing; it must have contained the title. The editors are fully justified for including this strip among the rules concerning the Controller of Works, although, as noted in note 4 above, there is some doubt whether strip 147 directly follows after strip 146.

A 70 W 7.6a; S I.18a; S IV.62a; SS 89–90; str. 148–150 (214–216).

[148] *Ch'eng-tan* and grainpounders are to be dressed in red clothes and to wear red head-cloths[1]; they are to be manacled and fettered.[2] Capable[3] *ch'eng-tan* are not to lead or supervise (others); those who have been nominated[4] to lead and supervise, lead and supervise them. Grainpounders[5] and *ch'eng-tan* who are going out for statute labour[6] must not venture to go to the market as well as to remain outside the outer gate of the building.[7] In case they would be obliged to pass through[8] the market [149], they are to make a detour;[9] they must not pass through. When *ch'eng-tan* or grainpounders break pottery vessels or iron tools, or wooden tools,[10] or when making carts[11] they break wheel rims, they are to be bastinadoed[12] immediately ten strokes for the value[13] of one cash; if the value is twenty cash or more, they are to be thoroughly[14] beaten. The tool (or vessel) is to be written off.[15] If they are not immediately [150] beaten, the official in charge is to be charged with half (the value).

(Statutes concerning) the Controller of Works.

1 This rather indistict character is transcribed in all three editions as *t'an* 幨, which according to the dictionaries means a loose garment, but the editors take it to mean *chan* 氈, "felt". Because the object is to be *mao* 冒, "worn on the head", it must indicate some kind of head covering; could it perhaps be *tse* 幘, which is found in the commentary to *HSPC* 9.2a, rendered by Dubs as "a conical cap" in *HFHD* II, p. 302, note 2.1.

2 See note 13 to A 68 above.

3 *Wenwu* transcribes *chi* 伎, whereas S and SS have *chang* 仗. S suggests that this might mean "a *ch'eng-tan* bearing arms, *chang ping* 仗兵 and standing guard", but I cannot imagine a manacled and fettered convict being given arms and made to perform guard duties. SS wants to explain *chang* 仗 as *chang* 杖, "staff", which they then believe to indicate "elderly", because in *Lun-yü* X, x, 1 *chang che* 杖者 are explained by the commentators as "elderly men over sixty, needing a staff". To me, *chi* 伎 seems quite clear, and as *chi* means "handy, practical, clever", I have taken it literally, with A 62 in mind, which forbids the use of "clever" bond-servants as cooks or servants, although there the word for "clever" is not *chi* but *ch'iao* 巧.

4 *Ming* 名 "(indicated by) name".

5 Here again, like in A 49, we find the inexplicable inversion of grainpounders and *ch'eng-tan*.

6 Also here convict labour is called *yao* 繇, the normal term for statute labour.

7 The editors reproduce the *SW* explanation of *hui* 闠, "the outer gate of the market", but because this rule forbids convicts to pass through the market this explanation is unacceptable. Moreover, *hui* here is determined by *she* 舍, so that the whole expression can only mean "the outer gate of the building". In their translation, the editors of SS take *liu she* 留舍 together and render this by "to stay and rest".

8 *Hsing* 行.

9 *Hui* 回, "to turn around, to make a detour".

10 *Ch'i* 器 can mean both "vessel" and "tool".

[11] For *ta chü* 大車, "carts", see note 1 to A 48 above.
[12] *Chih* 治 is used for *ch'ih* 笞, "to bastinado".
[13] *Chih* 直 is used for *chih* 値, "value".
[14] *Shu* 孰 is used for *shu* 熟, "ripe, well cooked".
[15] Cf. note 18 to A 9 above.

A 71 W 7.6a; S I.18a; S IV.62b; SS 91; str. 151(217).

[151] Robber-guards should not be used as servants or cooks;[1] they guard government storehouses as well as being appointed for tasks.[2] In case superiors order that they be appointed (as servants or cooks),[3] one should be sure to request this again.[4]

(Statutes concerning) the Controller of Works.

[1] For a similar rule see A 62 above.
[2] The editors read *yu wei* 有爲, but on the strip the second character is practically effaced.
[3] The addition between brackets seems to be necessary in view of the preceding. However, SS takes the first sentence as one whole, including the guarding of storehouses and the other tasks within the prohibition.
[4] Namely to reconsider or to rescind the order in view of the present rule.

A 72 W 7.6a; S I.18a; S IV.62b–63a; SS 91–92; str. 152–153 (218–219).

[152] Commoners who have a mother or a sister[1] who are bond-women, and (these commoners) are not being punished[2] for a crime, whereas they wish to be assigned[3] to the frontier for five years without remuneration for the days they have been levied, in order to free one person to become a commoner,[4] this is to be permitted. If someone [153] for the redemption of banishment[5] wishes to pay money, this is eight cash per day.[6]

(Statutes concerning) the Controller of Works.

[1] The text reads *t'ung sheng* 同牲 for *t'ung sheng* 生, children of the same father; because the text refers to women, these are sisters.
[2] The text reads *shih* 適 for *che* 讁, "to blame, to punish"; as indicated by SS, the same substitution is found in Chia I's *Kuo Ch'in lun* as quoted in *SC* 6.98 (*Mh* II, p. 230) and 48.24 (*HSPC* 31.19b). SS is wrong, however, when it renders the word by "banished".
[3] For *jung* 冗 see note 6 to A 7 above.
[4] Cf. note 37 to A 68 above.
[5] For the punishment of banishment see the introduction, p. 17, Ōba, "Shisen-kei", and *RHL*, p. 132 f.
[6] The editors may have been right in inserting strip 153 here, after the vague word *huo*, which being preceded by a black dot, starts a new sentence. The rule seems rather surprising, because redemption already implies a payment. Could it be that, similar to the situation given in strip 152, somebody wishes to redeem a person already banished? Another possible explanation could be that redemption fees were normally "worked off", and that actual payments were so rare that an extra rule was deemed necessary. The stipulation about eight cash per day is also found in A 68 above. An important point brought out in the present rule is, that banishment was not permanent, for otherwise it would not have been possible to redeem it.

A 73 W 7.6a; S I.16b; S IV.56a; SS 80–81; str. 125(192).

[125] When prefectural or general offices use posts[1] and boards[2] for making frames[3] and planks,[4] as well as . . . .[5] posts[6] for suspending[7] bells, they use the transverse beam,[8] and none of these withstand the charge and

break, as well as when the shafts of carts are unable to withstand the charge and break above the curve,[9] these (objects) are to be considered as "used"[10] and to be written off.[11]

(Statutes concerning) the Controller of Works.

[1] *Chen* 貞 used as a loan for *chen* 楨, "posts at both ends of a wall".
[2] *Ts'ai* 栽, defined by *SW* as "long boards for building (pisé) walls".
[3] *P'eng* 傰 used as a loan for *p'eng* 棚, "frames".
[4] *Yü* 牏, defined by *SW* as "short planks for building walls".
[5] The meaning of *tsai* 載, normally "to load" is unclear; SS neglects it.
[6] I am unable to decipher the character on the strip, but the editors read *yü* 虞 (*GSR* p. 36, no. 59h: *ngi̯wo) and consider it as a loan for *chü* 虡 (*GSR* p. 40, no. 78e: *g'i̯o); although not attested the loan is justified in view of the context. *Chü* are the vertical posts of the frame on which bells or sounding stones are suspended.
[7] *Hsien* 縣 is a loan for *hsüan* 懸, "to hang, to suspend", very common.
[8] The strip has *li* 輻 (not in *GSR*, but cf. *GSR* p. 226, 855a 鬲= *gliek), identified by the dictionaries with *li* 轢 "to crush" (*GSR*, p. 289, no. 1125g: *glåk or*gliok). The editors take this as a loan for *ko* 槅 (*GSR*, p. 226, 855e: *klĕk), the horizontal beam of a bell-frame; cf. *SC* 23.21, *Mh* III, p. 225.
[9] The technical meaning of *ku* 軲 is unknown; the 11th century dictionary *Chi yün* merely says "carriage". S says "part of a carriage", but I would suggest, that it indicates a section of the shaft. In Tai Chen the curved end of the single shaft of a horse-drawn carriage is called *ch'ien hu* 前胡; Tai's sketch is reproduced in Morohashi, vol. 10, p. 1015. In A 74 below, *ku* recurs, again in connection with a cart; there the *ku* is spoilt by having become bent or crooked, which reinforces the impression that *ku* is a part of the shaft. I arrived at my conclusion by means of Tai Chen's picture, whereas the editors of SS did so by means of passages in the *Mo-tzu*, namely *Mo-tzu* 43, p. 222, and 71, p. 374, where Sun I-jang quotes Cheng Chung's commentary to the *Chou li* (*Chou-li* 20/71, p. 75; *Chou-li chu-su* 37.8a (1333), Biot II, p. 402). See also ill. 16 on p. 90 of "Chiang-ling". This illustration shows that, at least in certain types of carriage, the curved part of the shaft was constructed of several separate elements, forming a curious bulge which could be said to resemble a *hu* 胡, "dewlap". This composite, and therefore potentially weak, structure might explain, why the shaft would break above the curve. But also a shaft made of a single piece of wood might break at this point, for it had been artificially bent by heating, and the *Chou-li* already warns against forcing the curvature, as this might cause a break (see *Chou-li* 22/77.55 and 58; *Chou-li chu-su* 40.2b (1455) and 3b (1458); Biot II, pp. 485, 486). These concrete indications militate against accepting Professor Li Hsüeh-ch'in's suggestion ("Mo-tzu", p. 333) that 軲 might be a variant of *chou* 軸, which, however, does not mean "shaft" but "axle-tree".
[10] The editors of SS believe that *wei yung* 爲用 is the same as *wei yung shu* 書 in A 8 above, which they interpret as "this has to be reported in writing", but see note 4 to A 8 above.
[11] See note 18 to A 9 above.

A 74 W 7.6a; S I.16b–17a; S IV.56b; SS 81–82; str. 126–127(193–194).

[126] When government storehouses loan[1] government carts and oxen....[2] In case the borrower[3] perhaps[4] privately uses the government carts and oxen, as well as when the borrower does not feed the oxen well, and the oxen grow thin;[5] if he does not repair[6] the cart, if the cart is neglected,[7] if the cart's shafts[8] are crooked,[9] as well as when the cart has not been covered,[10] or if the carriage's [127] hood[11] or canopy have been violently broken or torn,[12] the person in charge of the carriage as well as the official (and) the head of the office[13] will have committed a crime.

(Statutes concerning) the Controller of Works.

1 For providing official carriages to specified persons see *HSPC* 12.9b, *HFHD* III, p. 84, note 9.6; for the lending of objects see A 39 above.

2 The first few words are on one fragment, the rest on another, which in view of the contents belong together, but a third piece, containing perhaps three or four characters, is missing.

3 Note the use of *so* 所 in *chia jen so* 叚（=假）人所.

4 This is a tentative translation of *huo* 或.

5 Here oxen are said to be *tzu* 訾 (*tsi̯ăr or *dziăr), lit. "to slander", whereas in C 18 horses are said to be *tz'u* 柴 (*dz'i̯ăr?), lit. "a lamb" (? see *SWKL*, p. 1570b). In both cases the editors brilliantly suggest that both words are loans for *tz'u* 胔 (*dz'iar), lit. "carcass; animal bones with flesh still adhering", here used for "thin", as in *HSPC* 43.12a, where Yen Shih-ku (581–645) explains *tz'u* as *chi* 瘠 (*dz'i̯ĕk), "thin, emaciated" (this *lectio facilior* has been adopted in *SC* 99.39; Watson, *Records* I, p. 288).

6 *Kung-chien* 攻閒; this unknown binome, which recurs in A 76 below, the editors explain as "to repair"

7 This is a tentative translation of *k'ung-shih* 空失, where I have tried to keep close to the original meaning of the words; the binome is found in *HHSCC* Mem. 11.5b for territory, which, as a result of army movements, would be "needlessly lost". SS believes that *k'ung shih* should be read *k'ung tieh* 控跌, an unknown binome, taken to mean "to fall over, to overturn".

8 See note 9 to A 73 above. However, it should be noted that the two shafts of a cart are called *yüan* 轅.

9 The text clearly reads *chih* 紩 (not in *GSR*), "rope"?, which the editors believe to be *li* 盭, "crooked".

10 This character the editors read *chieh* 芥, which is undoubtedly correct, considering the forms listed in *HLTY*, *ch'ü sheng* 27a, and they take this to be a loan for *chieh* 介 (*kad), which they explain as "to cover". It is to be noted that the normal word for "to cover", *kai* 蓋, also had the ancient pronunciation*kâd (cf. *GSR*, p. 171, no. 642q).

11 *Fan* 蕃 is rightly taken as *fan* 藩 (both *pi̯wăn; see *GSR*, p. 71, no. 195 m and s): the editors refer to Cheng Hsüan's commentary to the *Chou-li* (*Chou-li* 15/52, p. 31; *Chou-li chu-su* 27.6b; not noted in Biot II, p. 126) who says that in his day, i.e. in the 2nd century A.D., carts had a hood of varnished matting.

12 *Lieh* 列 is rightly taken as a loan for *lieh* 裂.

13 The exact meaning of *li kuan chang* 吏官長 is not clear to me.

A 75 W 7.6a; S I. 17a; S IV. 57a; SS 82; str. 128–129 (195–196).

[128] It is permitted that office chiefs as well as officials use government carriages and oxen to draw their monthly food (allowance) as well as the rations for government oxen and carriage horses. Offices which have ready cash[1] take care themselves of buying grease and glue.[2] Those who have no ready cash will monthly ask for[3] grease and glue, so that it suffices [129] for the period.[4] They undertake iron work[5] in order to repair[6] government carts.

(Statutes concerning) the Controller of Works.

1 *Chin ch'ien* 金錢 must be a binome here, meaning money or coins.

2 *Chih ch'iao* 脂膠 appear to be two distinct goods; the binome is found in the *Yüeh-ling* chapter of the *Li-chi* (*Li-chi chu-su* 15.8b (0722); Couvreur, *Li-ki* I, p. 351; Legge, *Li-ki* 27, p. 266). The editors of SS remark that some parts of carriages were glued.

3 *Yen* 言 in Ch'in-Han usage means "to report to a superior".

5 *Wei t'ieh kung* 爲鐵攻, which SS translates: "they should establish workshops for iron work"

6 *Kung* 攻; cf. note 6 to A 74 above.

A 76 W 7.6a; S I.17a; S IV.57a–b; SS 82–83; str. 130(197).

[130] For one lubrication when repairing[1] one cart[2] use one ounce of glue and two *ch'ui*[3] of grease. When repairing[4] (pieces which have) fallen apart,[5]

the glue is divided according to their number In this way, the cart will not (move with) difficulty;[6] it is to be greased according to the circumstances.[7]

(Statutes concerning) the Controller of Works.

[1] Cf. note 6 to A 74 above.

[2] Note the use of *liang* 兩, later amplified to *liang* 輛, as the numerative for vehicles.

[3] According to *SW*, one *ch'ui* 錘 contained 8 *shu* 銖 of c. 0.64 gr. and was therefore equivalent to c. 5 gr.

[4] Cf. note 6 to A 74 above.

[5] *Pien chieh* 扁解, where the editors of SS say that *pien* is to be read as *pien* 辨 (a loan indicated in *SWKL*, p. 921a), meaning *fen* 分, "to divide"; they refer to the very last sentence of *YTL* 59, which does not bring us much further. For want of a better solution I have followed the editors' suggestion.

[6] I have taken *pu lao* 不勞 as literally as possible, but the editors of SS have a wholly different suggestion. They suggest that *lao* (*log) should be read *t'iao* 佻 (*t'iog or *d'iog) and the latter may mean "lightly, hurriedly"; to me this equation—which is nowhere attested—seems impossible. They also punctuate differently, because they include *i chih* 以之 in the foregoing sentence, taking *i* to mean *yung* 用, "to use". *Wei* 爲 they render by "if", with a reference to a modern study of Chinese "particles". Their translation therefore runs: "When repairing carriages which have become unstuck, according to the number of detached elements divide the glue and use it. If the carriage does not move fast, it can be lubricated according to the circumstances."

[7] Cf. note 3 to A 15 above.

A 77 W 7.6a–b; S I.17a; S IV.57b–58a; SS 83–84; str. 131–132(198–199).

[131] Let the prefectural and the general offices select willows as well as (other) wood that is soft[1] and can be used for writing, and make it square[2] in order to write on it; when there are no square (pieces), use "boards".[3] In prefectures where there are many sedges[4] in the hills, write on sedge tied together; where there is no sedge, use rushes,[5] stitched[6] together with hemp. [132] All these should be piled up when there are many to be harvested.[7]

(Statutes concerning) the Controller of Works.

[1] This article is also translated in Vandermeersch, "Procédure", p. 9.—The text writes *mu* 楘, according to *SW* "strips of leather wound around the shafts of a carriage", which the editors explain as *jou* 柔, "soft".

[2] *Fang chih* 方之, "make it (viz. the wood') square". *Fang* are writing strips of greater width; see Ōba, *Mokkan*, p. 21.

[3] *Pan* 版 are writing strips; it seems to be a general term; see Ōba, *Mokkan*, p. 22.

[4] *Ch'ien* 萆 is a kind of medicinal herb; the editors want to read it as *chien* 菅, "sedge".

[5] *P'u-lin* 蒲藺. That rushes were used to write on is also apparent from *HSPC* 51.30b (*RHL*, p. 423; around 100 B.C.).

[6] *Hsiao* 蕭 the editors explain as *hsiao* 絜, "to sew, to stitch".

[7] 槫 is unknown; the editors suggest that this should be *huo* 穫, "to harvest".

A 78 W 7.6b; S I.17a; S IV.58a; SS —; str. 133(?).

Strip 133 is a fragment of c. 5.5 cm., forming the lower end of a strip and only containing the words "Controller of Works."

A 79 W 7.6b; S I.18b; S IV.64a–b; SS 94; str. 158–159(224–225).

[158] When prefectures, general offices or the twelve commanderies[1] dismiss or appoint officials[2] as well as assistants[3] and subordinates[4] of the multitude

of offices, they dismiss and appoint them as from the first day of the twelfth month, ceasing to do so at the end of the third month. In case of death or abscondence as well as when there are old vacancies,[5] in order to fill [159] these, one should not wait for the time (mentioned above).

Statutes for the establishment[6] of officials.

1 This enumeration proceeds from the lower to the higher: first the organizations within the prefecture, then the general offices, and finally the offices within the commanderies. The editors think that the mention of twelve commanderies indicates a time before the 5th year of the First Emperor, or 242 B.C.; Huang, "Pien cheng", p. 2, believes that this refers to the last years of Chao, who reigned between 306 and 256 B.C. For an exhaustive study of the Ch'in commanderies and their gradual increase in number see Kamada, pp. 3–101, and Yen Keng-wang, I, p. 32 ff.

2 *Li* 吏, implying holders of rank. The rule shows that in the Ch'in system, as later under the Han, local and regional authorities, including the prefects and commandery administrators, nominated their subordinate staff locally; see Yen Keng-wang, pp. 108, 223, 351 f.

3 *Tso* 佐, to be clearly distinguished from the Assistant Prefect, *ch'eng* 丞, who was an imperial appointee.

4 *Shu* 屬.

5 *Ku yu chüeh che* 故有夬者; *chüeh* (or *kuai*) has been used for *ch'üeh* 缺 (cf. GSR, p. 93, no. 312a and h).—I have taken *ku* to mean "of old", and so have the editors of S, who explain the phrase by "originally there was (already) a vacancy", whereas SS renders it by "when for some reason a vacancy occurs".

6 Whereas "to appoint" is *ch'u* 除, "to establish" is *chih* 置; this is shown by the use of *chih* in A 99 below and by the frequent use of this term in the chapter of the bureaucratic organization in the Han history, *HSPC* 19A.

A 80 W 7.6b; S I.18b; S IV.65a; SS 94–95; str. 160–161(226–227).

[160] When appointing (subordinate) officials and....,[1] (only) when they have been already appointed they should be ordered to handle business[2] as well as to be sent out. Those who should not have been appointed but who venture to handle business previously, as well as to make an agreement[3] to have them sent out will be sentenced according to the Statutes. When Overseers are transferred[4] to [161] handle business[5] in another office, it is not allowed to appoint assistant officials of their former office to go to the new office.[6]

Statutes concerning the establishment of officials.

1 The editors read this character *wei* 尉 and it does look like it. However it would be most surprising to find *wei* mentioned here, for they were imperial appointees, both in the commanderies (where they were in charge of military affairs) and in the prefectures (as Chief of Police); do we have to assume a scribal error? SS explains in a note the duties of a *wei*, forgetting that *wei* could never be appointed locally.

2 *Shih shih* 視事, "to observe affairs"; SS refers to the use of this expression in *HSPC* 76.21a.

3 *Hsiang t'ing* 相聽, "to listen to, c.q. to obey, each other's (suggestions)". SS refers to the *Kuang ya* (unaccessible), which explains *t'ing* as *mou* 謀, "to plot". SS translates: "they secretly plot together to despatch him to the post".

4 The editors all read this character *sung* 送, which they believe to be a mistake for *hsi* 徙; I think it is *ch'ien* 䙴 (i.e. 遷), which has the same meaning as *hsi*.

5 The text simply has *chien* 見.

6 In other words, the Overseer is not allowed to take his former subordinates with him.

A 81 W 7.6b; S I.18b; S IV.65a; SS 95–96; str. 162(228)

[162] If an Overseer is absent,[1] a Master[2] who is "without evil",[3] or a Prefec-

tural Clerk is ordered to fill the office on probation.[4] Do not order office assistants or clerks (to fill the office) on probation.

Statutes for the installation of officials.

[1] *Pu ts'un* 不存; this might be a euphemism for "to die", but the dictionaries do not say so, and the translation in SS as *pu tsai* 不在 is ambiguous. In D 81 below *pu ts'un* definitely means "absent".
[2] For this rendering of *chün-tzu* see note 11 to A 64 above.
[3] *Wu hai* 無害. The consensus of the commentators—conveniently collected by Sun I-jang in *Mo-tzu*, p. 358—is that *wu hai* means "just and fair". Iijima, pp. 69–70, believes that the term implies ability in practical tasks; he stresses that the use of the term in historical literature shows, that possession of this qualification was a prerequisite for promotion in the administration.
[4] *Shou* 守, lit. "guarding; keeping", is used for appointments made on probation, pending definitive appointment, usually after one year.

A 82 W 7.6b; S I.19a; S IV.65b; SS 96–97; str. 163–164 (239–230).

[163][1] When assistants or clerks of offices concerned with grain storage[2] are dismissed,[3] retired or transferred, the Overseer of the office concerned,[4] together with the departing (official) must check and transfer[5] (the stores) to the person who is replacing him. If[6] the Overseer of the office retires and makes a check (but later) a shortage (is discovered)[7] the person who has replaced him will be adjudicated for this, together with the officials still there.[8] If the former official has not made a check and the new official [164] has been in office for less than a year, the departed (official) will be adjudicated for this, together with the officials still there; the new official will not be adjudicated. After a full year, although no check has been made,[9] the new official will be adjudicated, together with the officials still there; the departed official will not be adjudicated. Other (matters are to be handled) according to the Statutes.

(Statutes concerning) Checking.

[1] This article is wholly identical with B 8 below.
[2] *Shih* 實 is sometimes used for "grain"; SS refers to *Kuo yü, Chin yü* 3, p. 118.
[3] *P'i* 柀 used for *pa* 罷; cf. note 5 to A 11 above. I do not understand why SS translates *p'i* here by *fen pieh* 分別.
[4] Cf. my "Ch'in documents", p. 203.
[5] Although there is no repetition marker after *chiao* 效, this twofold translation is necessary, on the one hand because the sequel mentions checks, and on the other because it is not the new appointee who is checked but the stores, and these, as well as the result of the check, are handed over to him; the editors of SS also arrived at this conclusion.
[6] *Chieh* 節 is used for *chi* 即.
[7] The sentence reads (*chieh* =) *chi kuan se-fu mien erh chiao pu pei* (節=) 即官嗇夫免而效不備. *Wenwu* and S IV punctuate after *mien*, but SS puts a stop after *chiao*, so that *pu pei* becomes a separate phrase. In the first case the translation would be "If the Overseer of the office *has* retired, and a check is made (showing) a shortage ...", but in the second case "If the Overseer upon retirement makes a check (*and later*) there is a shortage ...". The second version, although extremely lapidary, must be correct, because it explains why it is the new appointee who is condemned. I have adopted the second version, following SS.
[8] *Chü li* 居吏, "the officials in residence", i.e. those still in their original position.
[9] The foregoing shows that a check should have been made.

A 83 W 7.6b; S I.19a; S IV.66a; SS 97; str. 165–167 (231–233).

[165][1] When a granary leaks, causing rot among the grain,[2] as well as when piling up grain one lets it become spoilt, (then) in case the uneatable[3] part is less than one hundred bushels, the Overseer of the office is reprimanded; in case it is one hundred bushels or more[4] up to one thousand bushels, the Overseer of the office is fined [166] one suit of armour; in case it exceeds one thousand bushels, the Overseer of the office is fined two suits of armour. (Furthermore) orders are to be given to the Overseer of the office and to the officials assigned to work there[5] to repay[6] together the spoilt grain. If the grain though spoilt can still be eaten, it is to be measured;[7] according to the number of bushels wasted[8] (the persons concerned) are condemned[9] [167] to be charged for these.

(Statutes concerning) Checking.

1 This article is wholly identical with B 9 below.
2 The text writes *ho su* 禾粟, lit. "grain in the ear and untreated grain". This seems to be a binome; it occurs e.g. in the *Tso chuan*, Duke Hsiang 30 (*Tso chuan* 40.4a; Couvreur, *Tch'ouen-ts'iou* II, p. 549).
3 In B 9 below, *shih* 食 is written *ssu* 飤, which can mean both "food" and "to feed".
4 In B 9 below *shang* 上 has been omitted.
5 *Jung li* 宂吏; cf. note 6 to A 7 above.
6 The text has *shang* 賞 for *shang* 償.
7 *Ch'eng* 程; SS translates *ch'eng* by "to estimate".
8 The text distinguishes between *pai* 敗, "to become spoilt", and *hao* 秏, which also means "to spoil", but evidently in a worse manner; hence the translation.
9 This last character on strip 166 is practically illegible; the editors' reading *lun* 論 is based on the parallel version in B 9; its use here implies that the persons concerned were tried.

A 84 W 7.6b; S I.19a; S IV.66b; SS 97–98; str. 168 (234).

[168] When measuring[1] grain in the ear, hay or straw there is (found) a shortage of one tenth or less, orders should be given to restore the former number (of bushels). If it exceeds one[2] tenth, it is first to be emptied[3] and used to give rations to people, but (the officials concerned) are to be condemned for this shortage.

(Statutes concerning) Checking.

1 This article is identical with B 10 below, except for two mistakes in the present rule, which have been corrected, based on B 10. The first mistake occurs in the very first word, where A 84 reads *ju* 入, "to enter", where B 10 has the obviously correct *tu* 度, "to measure".
2 Here A 84 omits the word "one".
3 For this rendering of *so* 索 see note 15 to A 19 above.

A 85 W 7.6b; S I.19a; S IV.66b–67a; SS 98–99; str. 169–171 (235–237).

[169][1] When grain is entered (in a granary),[2] ten-thousand bushels make one pile; these are ranged[3] to form a "house".[4] This[5] is to be registered as "So and so many bushels of grain in the ear in grainstore[6] X; the Granaries Overseer X, the Assistant X, the clerk X, the Storekeeper[7] X". In case the grain is entered by the prefecture, the Prefectural [170] Overseer[8] or the Assistant (Prefect) as well as the Chief of the Granary Bureau[9] come together

to seal it with their seals,[10] whereas one "house" each is given to the Granaries Overseer as well as to the Granary Assistants of the detached settlements in charge of ration issues, in order to give people[11] supplies.[12] When grain is taken out, again[13] [171] note the person who takes it out, as is done in the case of entering grain.

(Statutes concerning) Checking.

[1] This article is practically identical with B 11 below and with the beginning of A 19 above. This article is also translated in Vandermeersch, "Procédure", p. 15.
[2] Added according to A 19.
[3] For this rendering of *pi-li* see note 3 to A 19 above.
[4] Cf. note 4 to A 19 above.
[5] The following sentence, down to "...by the prefecture" is not included in A 19. In B 11 this sentence is preceded by *chi* 及, "as well as".
[6] Cf. note 28 to A 19 above.
[7] *Lin jen* 禀 (presumably identical with 廪) 人. *SW* says that this type of store had a door and (a) window(s); see also Hayashi, *Bunbutsu*, pp. 162–165 and ill. 4/12. For *lin-jen* SS refers to the notes on this official in the *Chou-li* (*Chou-li* 8/31, p. 88 f.; *Chou-li chu-su* 16.11a–b (0595–6); Biot I, p. 384 f.), and in the *I li* (*I-li* 16/47. 4b (1372); Steele II, p. 161).
[8] See note 5 to A 19 above.
[9] See note 7 to A 19 above.
[10] A 19 does not contain the word *feng* 封.
[11] A 19 does not contain the word *jen* 人.
[12] The following sentence does not occur in A 19.
[13] *Yu* 有 is used for *yu* 又.

A 86 W 7.6b–7a; S I.19b; S IV.67a; SS 99–100; str. 172–174 (238–240).

[172][1] When an Overseer is dismissed and a check is made,[2] the controller[3] looks at the seals as well as at the inscription in order to check it;[4] he must not measure or weigh it.[5] Only the granary that had been sealed by (the Overseer) personally is measured or weighed.[6] When the year ends, a general survey of issues is made:[7] "Grainstore X has issued grain in the ear so and [173] so many bushels; the remaining grain is so and so many bushels." When Granary Overseers as well as assistants or clerks are dismissed or they leave, the new Granaries Overseer, the new assistant or clerk in charge of grain stores must measure it (viz. the stock) without fail by means of the grain store register. In case of doubt [174] they report to the Prefectural Overseer. The Prefectural Overseer orders others[8] to measure it again, as well as to issue it together with....[9] If there is a surplus of grain, it is to be entered,[10] whereas those (reponsible for) a shortage are to be condemned according to the Statutes.

(Statutes concerning) Checking.

[1] The contents of this article are identical with the second half of B 11 and the first part of B 12 below, as well as with the second paragraph of A 19 above.
[2] The wording here differs slightly from that in A 19; hence the difference in translation.
[3] See note 14 to A 19 above.
[4] Again a slight difference with A 19 above.
[5] See note 17 to A 19 above.
[6] Here ends the parallel passage in A 19.
[7] *Ch'u fan* 出凡, lit. "the generalities, i.e. the totals of the issues"; Lao Kan, *K'ao shih, k'ao cheng*, pp. 11–12 shows that in the Edsin-gol strips *fan tsui* 凡最 or *tsui* alone means "total". For an example see note 2 to A 40 above.

8 *Jen* 人.
9 I do not understand which persons are to cooperate: the newly appointed weighers and the former officials? And does *ch'u* 出 mean "issue" here?
10 The manner of "entering" is not clear. SS translates *ju chih* 入之 by "it must be handed over to the officials", without explaining what they mean by this cryptic phrase.

A 87 W 7.7a; S I.19b; S IV.67b; SS 100–101; str. 175–177 (241–243).

[175][1] When grain, hay or straw is stacked in a grainstore, and there is a surplus or a shortage, to hide this and not to report it, as well as all cases of transferring a surplus to repay[2] a shortage, or for the multitude of other objects for which repayment[2] has to be assumed, fraudulently to write these off[3] in order to use[4] them for repayment[2]—all these cases will be dealt with in the same manner as theft.[5] [176] When the Great Overseer[6] and the Assistant[7] are aware[8] of this and do not punish it, they will be sentenced according to the Statutes for ordinary criminals;[9] moreover,[10] they will share in the repayment of the shortage with the person(s) in charge of the grain store.

When[11] the accounts are sent in, the grain store registers are to be presented to the Minister of Finance.[12]

When on entering grain[13] [177] one opens a leaking granary, the leading officials[14] must be made to come together to observe this. Hay and straw are (dealt with) like grain in the ear.

(Statutes on) Checking.

1 This rule occurs in the second half of B 12 below.
2 The text writes shang 賞 for *shang* 償.
3 Cf. note 18 to A 9 above.
4 The text reads *i pi shang* 以彼賞, where I take *pi* in the normal sense of the demonstrative "this, these". SS, however, believes that *pi* is a loan for *pi* 貱, explained in *SW* as *i-yü* 迻予, "to transfer".
5 For *t'ung fa* 同法 see D 18 below.
6 See note 5 to A 19 above.
7 Normally, *ch'eng* 丞 indicates the Assistant Prefect; this strengthens the identification of the Great Overseer with the Prefect.
8 The text writes *chih* 智 for *chih* 知.
9 This is a tentative rendering of *i p'ing tsui jen lü lun chih* 以平罪人律論之. *P'ing jen* 平人 being sometimes used for "commoners", *p'ing tsui jen* could perhaps be an attributive construction. The aim of this rule would be that in this case the hierarchically superior officials should not receive a more lenient treatment. However, SS renders *p'ing* as *hsiang-teng* 相等 "equal" in a note, and translates *i yü tsui-fan t'ung-teng-ti fa-lü lun-ch'u* 以與罪犯同等的法律論處, "are to be condemned by laws of the same kind as the criminals", which I fail to understand.
10 The text writes *yu* 有 for *yu* 又.
11 This paragraph is not found in B12 nor in the other rules in group B.
12 Cf. note 22 to A 9 above.
13 The parallel in B 13 below reads *ju ho chi*.. 入禾及. .., where I cannot understand the insertion of *chi*.
14 Cf. note 32 to A 19 above.

A 88 W 7.7a; S I.19b; S IV.68a; SS 101; str. 178(244).

[178][1] When checking government tools (there is found) a surplus or a shortage, (the responsible persons) are to be sentenced according to the

Statutes on Equipment[2] as well as having to repay.[3] In case (a tool) is not listed as equipment, then (its value) is to be estimated.[4]

(Statutes concerning) Checking.

[1] This rule is practically identical with B 15 below.

[2] The editors rightly read this character *chi* 齎, as this is quite clear in strip 30 of rule B 15. — As remarked in note 6 to A 56 above, the context in which *chi* and *chi lü* occur gives the impression that this statute not only listed equipment, but also indicated its value. S is therefore justified in paraphrasing the final sentence of this article by "In all cases when the text of the Statute does not determine an amount of money, an estimate is made". SS assumes that *wu chi* 毋齎 means that the statute did not indicate the amount of money, but translates "if the statutes do not contain a provision".

[3] The text has *shang* 賞 for *shang* 償.

[4] The text has *chih* 直 for *chih* 値, meaning literally "price it!"

A 89 W 7.7a; S I.19b; S IV.68a; SS 101; str. 179(245).

[179][1] For government tools that are not branded or carved,[2] the Overseer of the office is fined one shield.

(Statutes concerning) Checking.

[1] This article is identical with B 16 below.

[2] Cf. note 3 to A 47 above.

A 90 W 7.7a; S I.18b; S IV.63b; SS 92; str. 154–155 (220–221).

[154] When a person who had joined the army is warranted for a decision (to award him an aristocratic rank)[1] because of his meritorious service,[2] as well as to be rewarded,[3] but he dies before having been invested[4] (with an aristocratic rank), ...,[5] none are allowed to receive rank or reward. If he has already been invested [155], but he dies before having been rewarded, as well as. . . .,[6] the reward is to be given.[7]

Statutes concerning aristocratic rank for military action.

[1] See note 5 to E 4 below; for the aristocratic ranks see Loewe, "Ranks", as well as further details in Chu Kuo-chao, pp. 28–29.

[2] *Lao* 勞, lit. "hardship", or "length of service"; see *RHA* II, p. 172.

[3] *Tz'u* 賜, "to bestow; bestowal, gift".

[4] *Pai* 拜, "to make obeisance", is consistently used for "to be appointed to high office."

[5] The text reads *yu tsui fa nai ch'ien ch'i hou chi fa nai ch'ien che* 有辠（=罪）灋（=法）耐䙴（=遷）其後及法耐遷者 on strip 154 and again on strip 155 *chi fa nai ch'ien che*. Although the individual terms are more or less clear, I cannot understand the full statement. *Yu tsui* is "to (have) commit(ted) a crime." As mentioned in my "Ch'in documents", p. 180, *fa* (*pi̯wăp) is used in these texts as a loan-word for *fei* 廢 (*pi̯wăd); this loan had been suggested by the commentators to the classics, but had been rejected by Karlgren in his "Loan characters I", p. 72, whereas the present texts fully demonstrate the correctness of this suggestion. But, whereas *fa* is definitely used for *fei* in C 1, 2, 8 and 13 below, its use here is unclear. In a note the editors of SS suggest two posibilities. The first is to retain *fa* as it stands, but explaining it as in *HSPC* 90.8a: *sui yu pai tsui fu fa* 雖有百罪弗法, "although they had committed a hundred crimes, he did not *apply the law* to them", but this seems unlikely, because *fa* meaning "law, norm" does not occur in other strips. The second possibility is to take *fa* as a loan for *fei*, meaning "to dismiss"; *fei* is evidently a much stronger term than *pa* 罷 or *mien* 免, and the editors suggest that it means "to be removed from office, never to be reappointed"; it might be similar to the Han practice of *fei ku* 錮 or *chin* 禁 *ku*, for which see *RHL*, p. 135 f. and Liu Hai-nien, "Hsing-fa", p. 199 f. *Nai ch'ien* is "to have the beard shaved off and be banished". *Ch'i hou* 其後 is "his successor", viz. as head of the family; the tables

in the Han histories contain many examples of fiefs being abolished because the last incumbent *wu hou* 無後 "had no heir". However, the meaning of the full sentences escapes me. SS offers a highly hypothetical translation. In the first case they write "...and his heir has committed a crime for which, according to the law, he should have his beard shaved off and be banished, as well as when the man himself according to the law should have his beard shaved off and be banished..". In the second case they likewise translate "...if the man himself has already died and according to the law he should have had his beard shaved off and be banished, the reward should still be given"; similarly Yü and Li, p. 165. I can only call this an inspired guess, which leaves the curious construction of the text unexplained. Summarizing the rule under discussion, I arrive at the following conclusion: if a man dies before having received an aristocratic rank and a reward, his successor as head of the family will receive neither of these in two cases, which both imply punishment in the form of shaving off the beard and banishment; if the man dies after having been given an aristocratic rank, but before having received the reward, the reward is given (presumably to his heir), again related to the above mentioned punishment. But the how and why of this rule escape me; could the copyist have made a mistake?

6 See note 5.

7 For the use of *shu* 鼠 for *yü* 與 see note 20 to A 30 above.

A 91 W 7.7a; S I.18b; S IV.63b–64a; SS 93–94; str. 156–157 (222–223).

[156] Persons who desire to return two degrees of aristocratic rank in order to liberate[1] one person—their own[2] father or mother—who is a bond-servant or bond-woman, as well as bond-servants who have been made *kung shih*[3] for having cut off the head (of an enemy),[4] and who request to return the rank of *kung shih* in order to liberate their wife[5] who is a bond-woman (viz.) one [157] person, this is to be permitted; they are liberated and made commoners.[6] Artisan bond-servants who cut off the head (of an enemy) as well as persons for whom others have cut off a head in order to have them liberated, are all ordered to become artisans; those who are "incomplete"[7] are to be made artisans in the hidden offices.[8]

(Statute concerning) aristocratic rank for military action.

1 *Mien* 免.

2 *Ch'in* 親, implying their physical parents, and not step-parents or adoptive ones; cf. the use of *ch'in tzu* 親子 in E 17 below.

3 The first or lowest of the aristocratic ranks.

4 Rank was bestowed as a reward in proportion to the number of enemy heads cut off; cf. Loewe, "Ranks", pp. 99 and 103. Hsiung T'ieh-chi, "Chün-shih", p. 54, stresses that not only Ch'in, but also other states gave rewards for the capture of enemy heads.

5 The text has *ku ch'i* 故妻, where *ku* means "as of old", hence the wife the man had always had.

6 Cf. note 37 to A 68 above.

7 *Pu wan* 不完. In his commentary to *HSPC* 2.3b (*HFHD* I, p. 177, note 2) Meng K'ang notes that *wan* meant that neither a mutilating punishment not shaving off the beard and the hair had been applied to the condemned person.

8 The text reads *yin kuan* 隱官; this might refer to the ruler's harem as in the stipulations in the *Chou-li* concerning the tasks of mutilated convicts (Biot II, p. 370). SS suggests that these mutilated people were put to work in places where they could not be observed. D 105 below provides a case of men whose left foot had been cut off and who were "placed in the hidden office". The editors of SS believe that such mutilated men had not been castrated, which seems implied in the term *yin kung* 宮 found in *SC* 6.54 (Mh II, p. 176) and in *SC* 88.4 (not in Watson, *Records*).

A 92 W 7.7a; S I.19b–20a; S IV.68a–b; SS 101–102; str. 180–181 (246–247).

[180] Royal Secretaries[1] and *tsu-jen*[2] who are messengers[3] are fed with half a

tou of refined grain,[4] one quarter of a *sheng* of sauce,[5] and for vegetable soup they are given leeks and onions. Those who possess aristocratic rank, from the fifth rank[6] and above are fed according to their aristocratic rank. Messengers' [181] followers are fed with half a *tou* of husked grain,[7] and servants[8] with one third of a *tou*.

Statutes concerning Food rations for holders of Passports.

1 *Yü shih* 御史, "Royal (later: Imperial) Secretaries". I do not know, when these functionaries were created. They are briefly mentioned in the *Chou-li* (*Chou-li* 15/52.8; *Chou-li chu-su* 27.1a (0981); Biot II, p. 120f.) and i.a. in *SC* 81.8–9 (Kierman, p. 29: "recorders") in a story situated early in the 3rd century B.C.; see also *Ch'in hui-yao*, p. 202. These passages show that such Royal Secretaries existed in several of the Warring States. Because in the present case these men acted as messengers, it seems more likely that they were Royal Secretaries in Attendance, *shih* 侍 *yü-shih*, than that they were *chien* 監 *yü-shih*, inspectors of a commandery (see *Mh* II, p. 531); they can hardly have been the prefectural functionaries who, as indicated in S III, 18b, note 45, are mentioned in the *Chan-kuo ts'e* (*CKT* 28.54).

2 *Tsu-jen* 卒人. Whereas *tsu* is the normal word for commoners fulfiling their statutory service, usually translated as "conscripts", the binome *tsu-jen* is so rare, that it is not even found in the *P'ei-wen yün-fu*. Still, as pointed out by the editors of SS, it occurs in the *Lun-heng*, vol. II, p. 572 (Forke, *Lun-heng* II, p. 83, is of no help). There Wang Ch'ung says that when two commanderies exchange letters, they write *kan kao tsu-jen* 敢告卒人, "I beg to inform the *tsu-jen*", and he asks, why prefectures do not use this terminology—without providing an answer. The modern commentator Huang Hui suggests, that this is a form of politeness: not addressing the governor directly, but merely his subordinates, and he refers to a similar usage in the *chen* 箴, "admonitions", by Yang Hsiung (53 B.C. – A.D. 18), for which see Yen K'o-chün I, p. 417 ff. However, Wang, *Liu-sha* 2.21a (Chavannes, no. 460 verso, as corrected by Wang), shows that during the Former Han also lesser officials addressed each other in this way. This is confirmed by a recently discovered Edsin-gol document of 51 B.C.; see Ch'u Shih-pin, p. 179, strip no. 10. Still, all this does not help to clarify the status of the *tsu-jen* in the present instance. It is perhaps more useful to point out that, according to the chapter *Wang chih* in the *Li-chi*, thirty states formed a *tsu* and were governed by a *tsu cheng* 正 (*Li-chi chu-su* 11.9b (0518); Couvreur, *Li-ki* I, p. 270; Legge, *Li-ki* 27, p. 213); in A.D. 14 Wang Mang replaced the normal title of the Commandery Administrator, *t'ai shou* 太守, by *tsu cheng* (*HSPC* 99B.24a; *HFHD* III, p. 338). Because the editors of SS neglect the phrase-marker between *yü-shih* and *tsu-jen*, and therefore translate "the tsu-jen *of* the yü-shih", they conclude that these *tsu-jen* were "members of the staff of an official". However, this is unacceptable, because the phrase-marker shows that the two terms are to be taken independently; moreover, the editors overlook that the "followers", i.e. the staff, of these functionaries are mentioned separately at the end of the article. — The only conclusion which I can draw from all this is, that *tsu-jen* indicates officials with an elevated position, but unfortunately further unknown.

3 *Shih-che* 使者. I have used the neutral term "messengers", because on the one hand they could be legates, sent to the other states, and in Han times to the states in Centeral Asia and beyond, whereas on the other hand they could be lowly conscripts, as shown in Maspero, p. 14, no. 3 (as amended in my "Han documents", p. 26).

4 Cf. note 15 to A 29 above. — One *tou* equalled c. 2 litres.

5 Cf. note 8 to A 68 above. — One *sheng* equalled c. 0.2 litres.

6 The text reads *kuan shih fu* = 官士夫 =, transcribed as *kuan shih ta* 大 fu, which is correct in view of C 5 (strip 7) below. The editors explain this as indicating the fifth and the sixth of the Ch'in ranks, viz. *ta-fu* 大夫 and *kuan ta-fu* 官大夫 (cf. Loewe, "Ranks", p. 99), but then they neglect the word *shih*; it is to be noted that the only title which contains *shih* is the first and lowest, namely *kung shih* 公士.

7 Cf. note 6 to A 29 above.

8 Cf. note 9 to A 37 above; SS renders *p'u* 僕 again by "coachmen", as in A 37 and 62 above.

A 93 W 7.7a; S I.20a; S IV.68b; SS 102–103; str. 182 (248).

[182] (Holders of the rank of) *pu keng*[1] down to that of *mou-jen*[2] (will receive)

one *tou* of refined grain, half a *sheng* of sauce, vegetable soup, and half a bushel each of hay and straw. ○ Eunuchs[3] (will be treated) like *pu keng*.

Statutes concerning Food rations for Holders of Passports.

[1] *Pu keng* 不更 is the fourth of the aristocratic ranks; see Loewe, "Ranks", p. 99.

[2] The title *mou jen* 謀人 is unknown; the editors suggest that it might be equivalent to the third of the Ch'in ranks, i.e. *tsan niao* 簪裊, for which see Loewe, "Ranks", p. 99.

[3] *Huan-yen* 宦奄. *Huan* may mean "to serve" (cf. note 1 to A 31 above), but *huan kuan* 宦官 are eunuchs, and "eunuch" has been one of the meanings of *yen* since antiquity. Since these persons were to receive privileged treatment, these eunuchs will have been palace functionaries. — The comma, which the editors of S have placed between *huan* and *yen*, has been rightly omitted in *Wenwu* and SS.

A 94 W 7.7a–b; S I.20a; S IV.69a; SS 103; str. 183 (249).

[183] (Holders of the rank of) *shang-tsao*,[1] down to office assistants and clerks who do not possess aristocratic rank, as well as diviners, astrologers,[2] chief-coachmen,[3] attendants[4] and storehouse keepers[5] (will receive a daily ration of) one *tou* of husked grain, vegetable soup, and two twenty-seconds[6] of a *sheng* of salt.

Statutes concerning Food rations of Holders of Passports.

[1] *Shang-tsao* is the second of the aristocratic ranks. In view of the context one may expect that the following persons belonged to the royal (or imperial) establishment, where the diviners formed part of the staff of the Grand Diviner, *t'ai pu*.

[2] Because they are mentioned together with diviners, these *shih* 史 will not have been clerks—already mentioned in the first part of this article—but members of the staff of the Grand Astrologer, *t'ai shih*.

[3] *Ssu yü* 司御; the editors of SS refer to *HSPC* 41.9a (*SC* 95.19), which says that Hsia-hou Ying was *ssu-yü* of the stables of P'ei commandery. Watson, *Records* I, p. 255, translates the term as "carriage driver", but *ssu* in titles indicates a position of control.

[4] The text has *ssu* 寺, for which the editors suggest reading *shih* 侍.

[5] The editors are right in suggesting that *fu* 府 here does not indicate a storehouse, but a storehouse-keeper; they refer to the *Chou-li* (*Chou-li* 2/6.51 f., *Chou-li chu-su* 3.7a (0107); Biot I, pp. 4 and 60). See also Biot's remarks in III, p. 117 f.

[6] Whereas in weights the figures 4, 8 and 12 play a role, measures of capacity progress by tens. Here, however, the figure eleven appears, as it does in the rule that the "cloth" medium of exchange was worth eleven cash (see A 44 above). I do not know whether these small measures have ever been found.

A 95 W 7.7b; S I.20a; S IV.69b; SS 103–104; str. 184 (250).

[184] When forwarding (royal) commands[1] as well as documents marked[2] "urgent", these are to be forwarded immediately. Those that are not urgent are to be fully dealt with within a day;[3] one must not venture to detain them. Cases of detaining are to be condemned according to the Statutes.

(Statutes concerning) the forwarding of documents.

[1] This article is also translated in Vandermeersch, "Procédure", p. 10. — The text reads *ming shu* 命書, lit. "order documents". The editors of S explain this term as "proclamations of the court", whereas SS refers to *SC* 6.22 (*Mh* II, p. 126), which states that in 221 B.C. the First Emperor decided that henceforth *ming*, "commands", emanating from him, should be called *chih* 制, "decrees".

[2] *Shu* 署 here has the meaning "to note, to mark", as e.g. in *HSPC* 54.23a (Watson, *Courtier*, p. 44), which relates that the office, aristocratic rank, family name and personal name were

shu "marked, inscribed", on the portrait of the brave Su Wu. *Shu* also has this meaning in the statute from the state of Wei, translated in F 1 below.

[3] *Jih pi* 日𩞄 (畢), "within the day terminate"; cf. note 9 to A 47 above.

A 96 W 7.7b; S I.20a; S IV.69b–70a; SS 104; str. 185–186 (251–252).

[185] When forwarding documents by the courier service and receiving documents, be sure to write day and month, morning or evening[1] of their despatch and their arrival, in order to acknowledge[2] immediately. When documents are lost, the office is to be quickly informed. Bond-servants and bond-women, who are old and weak, as well as those who are not trustworthy[3] must not be... [186] When written orders[4] and summonses by the office[5] say: "Report',"[6] persons who should have arrived but who have not come, should be traced.[7]

(Statutes concerning) the forwarding of documents.

[1] This article is also translated in Vandermeersch, "Procédure", p. 10. — *Su mu* 夙莫 (for 暮).

[2] *I che hsiang pao yeh* 以輒相報殹 (=也); SS translates: "so that a reply can immediately be given".

[3] *Pu k'o ch'eng jen che* 不可誠仁者; because *ch'eng* means "upright, reliable", I have followed the editors' suggestion.

[4] *Ling* 令, "order, to order, to cause to do", is the first word on strip 196. The editors believe that *wu* 勿, the prohibitive "do not ..., must not...", governs *ling*, but then the action which is prohibited is lacking; nevertheless SS translates "Bondservants .... must not (be despatched to transport documents)". Although the original text may well have contained this provision, I believe that this must have been spelled out on a strip which is missing, and that strip 186 is not the continuation of strip 185, although both deal with the mail service. If this is admitted, *ling* can be combined with the following *shu* 書, the binome *ling shu* being comparable to the expression *ming shu* in A 95 above. *Ling shu* would then be "written orders", issued by some superior authority, perhaps, but not necessarily, the court. Moreover, *ling shu* would then have a parallel in the following *t'ing pi*.

[5] *T'ing pi* 廷辟. *T'ing*, lit. "the court" is used both for the office of the prefect (e.g. in A 21 and 64 above), and for that of the commandery administrator (as in D 79 below).

[6] Beginning the sentence with *shu* 書, S translates the first phrase by "On documents containing a summons there should be written 'you must reply' ", but SS offers another solution. SS proposes that *pao* 報 *pôg, should be interpreted as *fu* 赴 *p'iug, a loan already suggested in the 2nd century of our era and mentioned, but rejected, by Karlgren, "Loan characters" III, p. 29, no. 1156. SS therefore takes *pao* to mean "to hurry", translating "When on documents containing a summons there is written that they should come quickly, the persons who should already have come, but who have not arrived, should be investigated (rendering *chui* 追 as *chui ch'a* 查)". The explanation of SS seems unacceptable, for in this way two widely different meanings are given to *pao* in one and the same document.

[7] *Chui* 追, "to pursue, to trace".

A 97 W 7.7b; S I.20a; S IV.70a; SS 104–105; str. 187 (253).

[187] The prefectures each inform the general offices in their prefecture to copy[1] the statutes used in their office.

(Statutes concerning) the Ministry of Finance;[2] miscellaneous.

[1] This article has been wrongly translated in Vandermeersch, "Procédure", p. 20. — Is the prefecture informing the offices that it will copy their rules or is it warning them that they should copy their own rules? The translation in SS manages to be as ambiguous as the text.

[2] For this rendering of *nei shih* 內史 see my "Ch'in documents", p. 194 f. However, SS thinks that *nei shih* here and in the following articles refers to the Governor of the Capital area.

A 98 W 7.7b; S I.20a; S IV.70b; SS 105; str. 188 (255).

[188] When in the case of business requests have to be made, these must be made in writing. They must not be made orally, nor through another person.[1]

(Statutes concerning) the Ministry of Finance; miscellaneous.

1 This article is also translated in Vandermeersch, "Procédure", p. 20. — *Chi* 羈 is taken as a loan for *chi* 寄 ; this is quite acceptable, because also the ancient pronunciation seems to have been identical, both being *kia (see *GSR*, p. 19, no lx, and p. 317, no. 1238a); the loan is also attested in literature, see *SWKL*, pp. 3395b and 3251a.

A 99 W 7.7b; S I.20a; S IV.70b; SS 106; str. 189 (256).

[189] When the Overseer of an office is dismissed......[1] in this office an Overseer is to be installed[2] speedily. If after two months an Overseer has not been installed, the Prefect and the Assistant (Prefect) are considered as not having obeyed the Ordinances.[3]

(Statutes concerning) the Ministry of Finance; miscellaneous.

1 The editors have doubtless been right in combining two fragments, where the central piece, of a length of about seven characters, is missing.

2 For this use of *chih* 置 see note 6 to A 79 above.

3 In view of D 120 below, *pu ts'ung ling* 不從令 would seem to be identical with *fei ling* 廢令, as in A 51 above.

A 100 W 7.7b; S I.20b; S IV.71a; SS 106; str. 190 (257).

[190] When appointing (clerical) assistants, these must be of adult age[1] and above; one must not appoint persons newly enrolled as members of the rank and file.[2] When a Park[3] Overseer is absent,[4] the Prefecture for this purpose instals a probationer,[5] according to the Statutes on Stables.[6]

(Statutes concerning) the Ministry of Finance; miscellaneous.

1 The editors of SS state that *chuang* 壯 denotes persons of thirty years of age, i.e. they have adopted the explanation of the *Ch'ü-li* chapter of the *Li-chi* (*Li-chi chu-su* 1.8b (0036); Couvreur, *Li-ki* I, p. 8; Legge, *Li-ki* 27, p. 65). However, actual practice shows that adulthood was reached at 23, if not earlier; see Kao Min, *Ch'u-t'an*, p. 22; Hulsewé, "Statute labour", and cf. *CICA*, p. 216, note 806.

2 For *fu* 傅, "to register, to enrol", see note 1 to A 13 above. *Shih-wu* 仕五, "members of the rank and file" were adult commoners, liable for statutory labour and military service. That *shih-wu* means commoners has been shown again recently by Liu Hai-nien. The translation in SS wrongly stresses the negative fact that *shih-wu* had no aristocratic rank, which must inevitably lead the uninformed reader to the mistaken conclusion that clerical assistants had to possess rank.

3 Cf. note 14 to A 64 above.

4 See note 1 to A 81 above.

5 See note 4 to A 81 above.

6 Some of the Statutes on Parks and Stables are reproduced in A 7–9 above.

A 101 W 7.7b; S I.20b; S IV.71a; SS 106–107; str. 191 (258).

[191] According to the Ordinances[1] ...[2] clerks must not be made to work[3] in government storehouses. If (persons) are not sons of clerks,[4] they must not venture to study in the study-room.[5] Those who transgress this Ordinance will have committed a crime.

(Statutes concerning) the Ministry of Finance; miscellaneous.

[1] *Ling* 令 cannot mean "to order", for that would lead to the strange translation: "Order ... clerks not to work in offices". *Ling* must therefore be taken in isolation, meaning "ordinance", indicating that an ordinance stipulated the following. SS neglects *ling* in the translation.

[2] The character 敖 is unknown. SS suggests that it could be *she* 赦, "to amnesty" and translates "clerks who have committed a crime and who have been amnestied". This seems hardly possible, for it would imply that they could be made to work elsewhere, which would be violating the Statute concerning the appointment of officials (C 1 below) which expressly forbids the appointment of dismissed officials. Iijima, p. 72, note 11 suggests that this unknown character might be a variant of *ao* 敖, "proud, overbearing", and he thinks that this might be a reference to the bad officials who boast of their power, mentioned in the appendix to Governor T'eng's letter (SS, p. 20; see my "Ch'in documents", p. 183). In view of the present context, this seems most unlikely.

[3] *Ts'ung shih* 從事; see note 1 to A 12 above.

[4] Without offering any proof, the editors of SS state that "in antiquity the function of clerk was transmitted from generation to generation".

[5] *Hsüeh shih* 學室; so far, these schools are unknown. In Han times there were *hsüeh kuan* 官 or *hsüeh kung* 宮, for which see Yen Keng-wang, vol. I, pp. 252–256; for the training of these pospective clerks see my "The *Shuo-wen*".

(Statutes concerning) the Ministry of Finance; miscellaneous.

A 102 W 7.7b; S I.20b; S IV.71b; SS 107; str. 192 (259).

[192] Persons in detention[1] who are able to write must not be made to engage in the work of clerks.

(Statutes concerning) the Ministry of Finance; miscellaneous.

[1] For these *hsia li* 下吏 see note 1 to A 58 above. This article is also translated in Vandermeersch, "Procédure", p. 20.

A 103 W 7.7b; S I.20b; S IV.71b; SS 107–108; str. 193 (260).

[193] *Hou*,[1] robber guards as well as the multitude of persons under detention[2] one should not venture to make assistants or clerks of government storehouses, as well as guards[3] of the Forbidden Parks.

(Statutes concerning) the Ministry of Finance; miscellaneous.

[1] The text writes *hou* 矦 for *hou* 候. This was a hard labour punishment, as is clearly apparent from C 2 and 4, and D 97 below. Hori, "Keimei", p. 118, is undoubtedly right when he suggests that this was the lightest of these punishments. The idea of the editors of SS that, because *hou* means "to watch", these *hou* were "convicts watching enemy movements" can hardly be taken seriously.

[2] See note 1 to A 58 above.

[3] All editions read *hsien tao* 憲盜, which they explain as "thief-catcher", and which they believe to be synonymous with the *hai tao* 害盜 mentioned in D 1 and 2 below. The binome *hsien tao* is unknown; in view of the context it should indicate a guard or a game-keeper.

A 104 W 7.7b; S I.20b; S IV.71b; SS 108; str. 194 (261).

[194] Grain storage offices[1] which engage in measuring each have scales and weights[2] and *tou* and *yung*[3] (measures) so that these are sufficient for calculations.[4] The office concerned must not loan[5] these to commoners. Those that are not used are to be corrected[6] like those in use.

(Statutes concerning) the Ministry of Finace; miscellaneous.

[1] See note 2 to A 82 above.

[2] See note 3 to A 54 above.

3 See note 5 to A 54 above.
4 All three editions put a stop after *kuan* 官, undoubtedly induced to do so because of the open space on the strip after this word. However, I am convinced that this space was left open for the binding strings, for the same space can be observed on other strips, with sometimes a clearly visible trace left by the decomposed string. This mistaken interpunction forces the editors of SS to a rather strained translation.
5 *Chia* 叚 is used for *chia* 假.
6 *Cheng* 正; SS also adopts this translation of *cheng*. A 54 shows that weights etc. were checked annually. Lu Ch'i refers to a remark by Wang Yün 王筠 (1784–1854), included in *SWKL*, p. 1871a, who believed that standard weights in the Han period were called *tse* 則.

A 105 W 7.7b; S I.20b; S IV.72b; SS 109; str. 197–198 (26–265).

[197] One must not venture to enter into storehouses or archives[1] with fire. When the officials have finished collecting the stores, the Overseer of the office as well as the officials nightly in turns inspect the office; when there is no fire, they close the doors. The Prefectural Clerks must be ordered to patrol the (Prefect's) office[2] and the storehouses. In case of new construction [198] of official hostels, these must not adjoin[3] storehouses or archives.

(Statutes concerning) the Ministry of Finance; miscellaneous.

1 *Shu-fu* 書府; this seems to be the earliest occurrence of this term. Much later it is found in the pseudo-K'ung An-kuo preface to the Book of Documents (*Shu-ching* 1.8a (0027)).
2 *T'ing* 廷; see note 5 to A 96 above.
3 *I* 依, lit. "to lean on".

A 106 W 7.7b; S I.20b; S IV.72a; SS 108–109; str. 195–196 (262–263).

[195] For offices concerned with grain storage[1] the walls must be made high; as regards other walls connected with these, only the walls of stores where grain is placed[2] and of granaries covered with thatch should be made high. Order should be given that outsiders[3] should not come close[4] to the buildings;[5] those who are not personnel of the office concerned must not venture to lodge there. [196] A good watch should be kept, and whenever the gates have been closed, nearby fires should be extinguished.[6] Keep guard carefully and be diligent. If these orders are not obeyed[7] and there are losses[8] or decay,[9] or a fire breaks out, the officials of the office will have committed a serious crime and the Great Overseer[10] and the Assistant will be held responsible.[11]

(Statutes concerning the Ministry of Finance).[12]

1 Cf. note 2 to A 82 above.
2 *Chih* 置; this usage is surprising, at least to me.
3 *Jen* 人, "others".
4 *Chiu* (?) 斪 used for *chin* 近; see note 35 to A 68 above.
5 *She* 舍; cf. note 3 to A 55 above. SS translates "dwell close by".
6 The editors explain *mi* 靡 as *mieh* 滅; although the pronunciation was different (*GSR*, p. 25, no. 17h: *mi* = *mia; p. 89, no. 294 b: *mieh* = *mi̯at or *miät) the early 1st century *Fang yen* 方言 equates the two words (see Morohashi, vol. 12, p. 138, no. 42612, *sub* ii.5). Karlgren, "Loan characters III", p. 10, no. 1063, suspects that *mi* might be "a mere variant" of *mi* 糜, "to destroy, to crush", in the final paragraph of the *Shao i* 少儀 chapter of the *Li-chi* (*Li-chi chu-su* 35.15a (1523); Couvreur, *Li-ki* II, p. 27; Legge, *Li-ki* 28, p. 81).
7 Cf. note 3 to A 99 above.
8 *Wang* 亡; *wang* is often used for persons who "abscond".
9 *Pai* 敗; see note 5 to A 82 above.

[10] See note 5 to A 19 above.

[11] *Jen chih* 任之, where *chih* probably refers to the lower personnel, whom the superiors have to guarantee (cf. note 19 to A 68 above). The text does not say *fu chih* 負之, which would have meant that the Great Overseer and the Assistant were to be "charged" with the repayment of the damage.

[12] The end of the strip, c. 2cm. long, is missing; the fragment of a character on the broken edge the editors read *nei* 內.

A 107 W 7.7b–8a; S I.21a; S IV.73a; SS 105; str. 199 (154).

[199] General offices annually present the figures[1] for the tools that have been cancelled[2] and for which they request replacement. Accounts[3] are presented to the Ministry of Finance in the 9th month ...... miscellaneous.[4]

[1] According to the editors, the text reads *shu* 數; I am unable to decipher it.

[2] For *ch'u* 出, "to cancel", see note 18 to A 9 above.

[3] *Hui* 會, "annual accounts", see the remarks by Cheng Chung (A.D. 5–83) to the articles *hsiao-tsai* and *tsai-fu* in the *Chou li* (*Chou-li* 2/5, p. 33 f. and 2/6, p. 61 f.; *Chou-li chu-su* 3.3b (0100) and 10a (0113); Biot I, pp. 53 and 63).

[4] Strip 199 is a fragment, 13.5 cm. long; the word *tsa* 雜, "miscellaneous". is found on another fragment, less than 2.5 cm. in length, which formed the bottom of a strip. The editors have placed this fragment here, but this is not correct, because on these strips the title is usually written only some five or six centimetres below the end of the text, and in effect an undecipherable fragment of a character appears on the ragged edge of the first strip. However, in view of the context this strip will have belonged to the Statutes concerning the Ministry of Finance; miscellaneous.

A 108 W 7.8a; S I.21a; S IV.73a; SS 109–110; str. 200 (266).

[200] Annually, the penal statutes are checked with the Royal Secretary.
(Statutes concerning) the Commandant; miscellaneous.

The writing on the strip is clear, but the purport of this article escapes me, for there are too many uncertain factors, which render the above translation most unreliable. The occurrence of an apparently similar rule in the *Chou-li, ti kuan, hsiang shih* (*Chou-li* 6/21, p. 31; *Chou-li chu-su* 11.8b (0410); Biot I, p. 233) *i k'ao ssu-k'ung chih pi* 以考司空之辟 is of no help, because here the *hsiang shih*, the District Leader, checks the norms (of public works) established by the Controller of Works. The binome *pi lü* 辟律 is not to be found in the dictionaries. One of the meanings of *pi* is "law, rule" and so *pi-lü* could be a general term for "laws"; another is "ruler", providing "the ruler's statutes". But *pi* can also mean "punishment", leading to the translation "penal laws" and this is the solution adopted by the editors of SS, and here.—It seems likely that *yü shih* 御史 refers to the royal secretaries (see note 1 to A 92 above), or to their chief, the Grand Secretary, and this explanation has been adopted by the editors of SS. Still, the possibility remains that the *chien* 監 *yü shih*, the inspector of a commandery, is meant (see note 1 to A 92 above, and *Ch'in hui-yao*, pp. 201, 216, 468–470, 520, and *Mh* II, p. 531, no. 1), for we must not lose sight of the fact that this collection of regulations belonged to a subordinate local official.—Uncertainty also surrounds the word *wei* 尉 in the title of this statute. The editors of SS believe that is refers to the *t'ing* 廷 *wei*, the Commandant of Justice (for whom see

RHL, p. 86, and my "Commandant of Justice"). This is a possibility, but on the other hand I expressed the belief that the *Wei lü* 尉律, mentioned in *HSPC* 30.24b and in Hsü Shen's preface to the *Shuo-wen chieh-tzu* (*SWKL*, p. 6710b) were statutes concerning the Military Commandant of the commanderies (see my "The *Shuo-wen*", p. 244, and Ju Shun's quotation of this statute in *HSPC* 7.9a, *HFHD* II, p. 176). Furthermore, there were also other functionaries in the Ch'in bureaucracy, whose title included the word *wei*, like the Supreme Commander, *kuo wei* 國尉 (*Ch'in hui-yao*, pp. 201, 468, 515–516), and the Military Commandant for Deciding Lawsuits, *tuan yü tu-wei* 斷獄都尉 (*op. cit.*, pp. 217, 521). See also the historical survey in Yü Hao-liang, pp. 12–16. Finally, there remains the problem of "checking", *ch'ou* 讎. Here one may refer to the curious passage in the *Shang-chün shu*, p. 93 (Duyvendak, *Lord Shang*, p. 329), reading 一歲受法令以禁令. The modern commentator paraphrases this as "Each year the officials and the people receive the laws, using the laws of the forbidden chamber (the palace archives mentioned earlier in the text) *as the standard*", where the addition in italics is only an intelligent guess.

A 109 W 7.8a; S I.21a; S IV.73a–b; SS 110; str. 201 (267).

[201] ...[1] the officials of the office concerned......[2] statutes, register of standards, one should not venture to proceed;[3] proceeding is a punishable offence.

(Statutes concerning) the Commandant; miscellaneous.

[1] The top of this strip, of a length of c. 2.5 cm., is missing.

[2] Here twelve characters are completely illegible, being nearly effaced. The thirteenth the editors read as *fa* 灋, i.e. 法, possibly as a loan for *fei* 廢 (see note 5 to A 90 above), but I am unable to decipher it.

[3] *Hsing* 行; cf. the similar phrase on a Ch'in bronze tiger tally: *nai kan hsing chih* 乃敢行之: "only then one may presume to carry out (the levy of troops)" (*RHL*, p. 35 f., as corrected by Professor Ch'ü T'ung-tsu in *HJAS* 19 (1956), p. 422); the same inscription is found on a recently discovered tally, for which see *Wenwu* 1979/9, p. 93.

[4] Because of its lacunose condition, it is impossible to say what were the contents of this article; it may have dealt with statute labour.

A 110 W 7.8a; S I.21a; S IV.73b; SS 110–111; str. 202 (268).

[202] When offices in the (border) marches[1] transfer[2] bond-servants and bondwomen to each other, and the people have been collected,[3] one must note the years, days and months (during which) they were already given rations, whether they did or did not receive clothing,[4] whether they do or do not possess a wife.[5] Those who have received (food and clothes) will continue to be fed and clothed according to the Statutes.[6]

(Statutes concerning) Dependent States.[7]

[1] The editors read the first, rather defaced, character as *tao* 道, which they define as "a prefecture where minorities are living". This is a modernized version of the information for the Han period, found in *HSPC* 19a.30b; *HSPC* 28Bii. 48b–49a says that in A.D. 2 there were 32 such "marches", which Ch'i Shao-nan enumerates in his commentary *ad loc.* (*HHS CC* Tr. 5.6b and Tr. 28.7a contain no further information). It is quite possible that "marches"

existed already under the Ch'in; see the detailed studies by Hisamura and P'ien, and cf. *RHA* I, p. 59

2 See A 36 above.

3 For *shou* 收 see note 10 to A 41 above. The editors explain *shou jen* 人 as "persons who have been arrested", but this seems unacceptable, because this would imply that they had not yet been tried, which would preclude their being transferred to another jurisdiction. *Shou* can also mean "to confiscate", but I doubt that *shou jen* could mean "confiscated persons".

4 Cf. A 49 above.

5 Cf. A 50 above.

6 See A 12 and 17 above.

7 *Shu pang* 屬邦. The editors equate this term with the Han term *shu kuo* 國 and explain it in modern parlance as "an organ for controlling minorities". *Shu pang* is not to be found in the *P'ei-wen yün-fu*; Morohashi, vol. 4, pp. 174-175, includes it and states that the term is equivalent to *shu kuo*, without, however, providing any references. The identification is undoubtedly correct, because in Han times the word *pang* was tabooed, being the personal name of emperor Kao, and replaced by *kuo*. Under the Han the dependent states were alien tribes under Chinese control in the frontier areas; see Kamada, pp. 329–336. For the Ch'in we only have the Han time indication in *HSPC* 19A. 19b, that the *tien* 典 *shu-kuo*, the Director of Dependent States, was a Ch'in institution "in charge of barbarians who had submitted"; this functionary is mentioned for 157 B.C. in *HSPC* 4.20a (*HFHD* I, p. 271; *SC* 10.43, *Mh* II, p. 490; see also *Mh* III, p. 523, no. xxii). If the reading of the first character on the strip as *tao* 道 is correct, it is quite likely that *shu pang* is identical with the later *shu kuo*, but the possibility remains that *shu pang* refers to Chinese states, allied with or conquered by Ch'in. The difference between dependent states and vassal states (D 99, note 4) is not clear.

GROUP B

The text belonging to the second group of strips called by the editors *chiao lü* 校律, consist of 29 articles, B1–29, in the division adopted in *Wenwu* 1976/7 and followed here. The sixty strips have a length of nearly 27 cm or 1 ft. 2 in. Ch'in-Han measure; they were held together by three sets of strings: at the top, in the middle, and at the bottom. Each article is started on a new strip with the result that several strips are left partly blank. Strips fully covered with writing contain between twenty-eight and thirty characters, clearly written and widely spaced. Although the writing seems to be slightly more archaic than that on the strips of the other groups, the editors of SS suggest (p. 112) that groups A and B might have been written by the same hand. According to SS, p. 112 (cf. SS, p. 127 and CM, p. 74) this group was found together with group A and "Governor T'eng's letter" and the collection of essays, called "How to be a good official" underneath the belly of the corpse.

B 1 W 7.8a; S I.23a; S V.75a; SS 113; str. 1 (269).

[1][1] (These) are the Statutes on Checking by the general offices as well as the prefectures.[2] When there is a surplus or a shortage, the goods are to be evaluated, and (the persons responsible) are to be held guilty for the highest value among them; they are not to be totalized.[3]

[1 reverse] (Statutes on) Checking.

1 This is a complete strip, and as the title of the collection is written on the reverse, it is evidently the first strip.—The initial *wei* 爲, however, is curious, and my translation remains tentative; the editors of SS have reached a similar conclusion.

2 The insertion of dots in the *Wenwu* transcription, indicating illegible characters, is a mistake, for the photograph shows that the text continues without a break; the editors of S and SS have corrected this.

3 The text reads *lei* 贏, "to entangle", which the editors explain as *lei chi* 累計, "total; to totalize"; I have adopted this explanation.

B 2 W 7.8a; S I.23a; S V.75a; SS 113; str. 2 (270).

[2] The Overseer of the office concerned and the officials assigned to work there[1] all together repay goods that are short, whereas a surplus is "entered".[2]

1 See note 6 to A 7 above.

2 Presumably booked as newly entered into the store.

B 3 W 7.8a; S I.23a; S V.75b; SS 113–114; str. 3–4 (271–272).

[3][1] If the weight-picul[2] is not correct (to the extent of) sixteen ounces or more, the Overseer of the office concerned is fined one suit of armour; (if the difference) is not fully sixteen ounces down to eight ounces[2] he is fined one shield. If the *t'ung*[3] is not correct (to the extent of two) [4] *sheng*,[4] he is

fined one suit of armour; (if the difference) is not fully two *sheng* down to one *sheng*[5] he is fined one shield.

[1] This, as well as the following article are discussed in my "Weights".
[2] The picul of about 30 kg was divided into 120 *chin*, catties, of about 250 gr; the catty was divided into 16 *liang*, ounces, of about 15 1/2 gr.
[3] I.e. between c. 250 and c. 125 gr.
[4] See note 5 to A 54 above.
[5] One *tou* of nearly two litres was divided into ten *sheng* of c. 200 cubic cm.

B 4 W 7.8a; S I.23a; S V.75b; SS 114–115; str. 5–7 (273–275).

[5] If the *tou* is not correct (to the extent of) half a *sheng* or more, he is fined one suit of armour; (if the difference is) not fully one *sheng* down to one third of a *sheng*, he is fined one shield. If the half-picul is not correct (to the extent of) eight ounces [6] or more, if the *chün*[1] is not correct (to the extent of) four ounces or more, if the catty is not correct (to the extent of) three *shu*[2] or more, if the half-*tou* is not correct (to the extent of) one third of a *sheng* or more, if the *ts'an*[3] is not correct (to the extent of) one sixth [7] of a *sheng* or more, if the *sheng* is not correct (to the extent of) one twentieth of a *sheng* or more, if the weights[4] of a balance for weighing gold are not correct (to the extent of) half a *shu* or more[5]—in all these cases he is fined one shield.

[1] The *chün* 鈞 was one quarter of a picul; hence c. 7 1/2 kg.
[2] The *shu* 銖 was one twentyfourth of an ounce, hence c. 0.64 gr.
[3] The *ts'an* 參 was most probably one third of a *tou*; see my "Weights", note 45 and the supplementary note on *ts'an*.
[4] The editors explain *lei* 羸 as *lei* 累, i.e. *lei* 絫; for further details see my "Weights", note 46.
[5] The editors rightly add *i* 以 in conformity with the preceding phrase.

B 5 W 7.8a; S I.23a–b; S V.76a; SS 115–116; str. 8–10 (276–278).

[8] When counting[1] (objects) (there is found) a surplus or a shortage (and) the value[2] is from 110 cash up to 220 cash,[3] the Overseer of the office concerned is reprimanded.[4] If it exceeds 220 cash up to 1100 [9] cash, the Overseer is fined one shield. If it exceeds 1100 cash up to 2200 cash, the Overseer of the office concerned is fined one suit of armour. If it exceeds 2200 cash [10] the Overseer of the office concerned is fined two suits of armour.

[1] *Shu* 數; S renders this by "making accounts", SS by "checking the number of objects".
[2] The text has *chih* 直 for *chih* 值.
[3] Cf. note 1 to A 44 above.
[4] See note 5 to A 7 above.

B 6[1] W 7.8a–b; S I.23b; S V.76b;77a; SS 116–117; str. 11–16 (279–284).

[11][1] When in weighing (there is found) a shortage, always[2] note the figures of the weighing.[3]

[1] In *Wenwu* the text of this strip is followed by that of the next without interruption, but the photograph shows that strip 11 is an independent strip, not fully covered with writing, and it is treated as such in S and SS. I have adopted the numbering B 6[1] and B 6[2] in order to conform to the arrangement in *Wenwu*.
[2] The text reads *ch'in* 欽 (GSR, p. 173, no. 652f *k'i̯əm), which the editors take as a loan for

hsien 咸 (GSR, p. 178, no. 671a *g'ɛm). So far, this loan had not been attested in literature, but the editors point out that in the text of the *I ching*, the Canon of Changes, found at Ma-wang tui the 31st hexagram *hsien* is consistently written *ch'in*. I have adopted this, translating *hsien*, lit. "all", as "always." If this is not adopted, *ch'in*, lit. "respectfully", might be rendered as "carefully".

[3] I do not understand the value or function of the word *i* 殹, consistently used for *yeh* 也 in these texts, in the phrase *shu ch'i hsien* (= *hsüan*) *liao i chih shu* 書其縣（=懸）料殹之數.

B 6² [12] When in weighing (there is found) a shortage of one fifth or more of the available[1] figures, the value is to be estimated; reprimands and fines are like those for (shortages in) counting.[2] If (the shortage) is one tenth up to not fully [13] one fifth, and the value exceeds 220 cash up to 1100 cash, the Overseer of the office concerned is reprimanded; if it exceeds 1100 cash up to 2200 cash [14] the Overseer of the office concerned is fined one shield; if it exceeds 2200 cash, the Overseer of the office concerned is fined one suit of armour. If (the shortage) is one hundredth up to not fully one tenth [15] and the value exceeds 1100 cash up to 2200 cash, the Overseer of the office concerned is reprimanded; if it exceeds 2200 cash, the Overseer of the office concerned is fined [16] one shield.

[1] The text reads *chien shu* 見數; the editors suggest reading *hsien* 現 for *chien*.

[2] I.e. B 5 above.

B 7 W 7.8b; S I.23b–24a; S V.77a–b; SS 117–118; str. 17–18 (285–286).

[17] (Although serving in) the same office, each (official) has a (particular) assignment,[1] (and so) each one is adjudicated for (misdemeanours in) his assignment. When the Overseer of an office is dismissed, the Prefect orders another person to check his office; the Overseer of the office is adjudicated for (the results of) the check and fined (but) the Great Overseer[2] and his Assistant are exempt of punishment.[3] When the Prefect is dismissed and the new Overseer personally makes a check, the former Overseer and his Assistant are not allowed to go free of punishment.

[1] *Chu* 主, "to be in charge of".

[2] See note 5 to A 19 above.

[3] *Ch'u* 除, "to be excused punishment or duty".

The articles B 8–16 are identical with the articles A 19 and A 82–89 above, except for minor differences, indicated in the notes to these articles. For completeness' sake I provide the references.

B 8 W 7.8b; S I.24a; S V.77b; SS 118; str. 19–21 (287–289).
B 9 W 7.8b; S I.24a; S V.78a; SS 118; str. 22–24 (290–292).
B 10 W 7.8b; S I.24a; S V.78a; SS 119; str. 25–26 (293–294).
B 11 W 7.8b; S I.24b; S V.78b–79a; SS 119; str. 27–31 (295–299).
B 12 W 7.8b–9a; S I.24b–25a; S V.79a; SS 119; str. 32–36 (300–304).
B 13 W 7.9a; S I.25a; S V.79b; SS 120; str. 37 (305).
B 14 W 7.9a; S I.25a; S V.79b; SS 120; str. 38 (306).
B 15 W 7.9a; S I.25a; S V.79b; SS 120; str. 39 (307).
B 16 W 7.9a; S I.25a; S V.79b; SS 120; str. 40 (308).

B 17 W 7.9a; S I.25a; S V.79b–80a; SS 120; str. 41 (309).

[41] When parts[1] of a suit of armour or scales[2] are in excess of their register as well as when they are short, the excess parts and scales are entered,[3] whereas parts[4] and scales that are short are charged.[5]

1 *Chia* 甲 is a suit of scale armour; according to the commentators to the article *han jen* 函人 in the *K'ao-kung chi* section of the *Chou-li*, *lü* 旅 are the top and the bottom of one suit (*Chou-li chu-su* 40.11b (1468); *Chou-li* 23/79, pp. 2–3; Biot II, p. 507). This explanation has been followed both by the editors and by Hayashi, *Buki*, p. 398. The latter work, pp. 404–415, contains an illustrated account of early Chinese armour, whereas Han armour is discussed in the same author's *Bunbutsu*, pp. 469–471. Ancient Chinese armour is also described in Yang Hung, "Chia chou".

2 *Cha* 札 are the individual scales.

3 Presumably entered in the register as having been newly introduced into the arsenal.

4 As noted by the editors, on this strip *lü* 旅 is not written with 氏 but with 衣; this manner of writing continued even on Later Han stelae, as is shown by *HLTY*, *shang sheng* 16a. On this strip, *lü* is twice followed by the repetition marker = and the editors explain the construction *lü* = as a *ho-wen* 合文—usually a single sign, made of the *ad hoc* combination of two characters—for *lü-i* 旅衣; this is also adopted by Professor Li Hsüeh-ch'in, "Ku wen", p. 341. But the technical meaning of this expression is not given by either, and in the translation in SS it is completely neglected. It should be noted that, at least in later literature, *lü i* means "travelling clothes", the sonorous *tabigoromo* of Nō-drama. I would suggest that a) the repetition-marker was omitted after the first *lü*, and b) that in all three cases the meaning is "parts of a suit of armour (*lü*) and scales on these parts (*lü cha*)", contrary to the translation in SS, which makes it appear as if only scales are meant.

5 The persons to be charged are not mentioned, but they will have been the officials directly concerned with the arsenal.

B 18 W 7.9a; S I.25a; S V.80a; SS 120; str. 42 (310).

[42][1] When government storehouses store hides and leather, these should be repeatedly dried[2] and aired; if there are any that have been bored by insects,[3] the Overseer of the office is fined one suit of armour.[4]

1 This article is practically identical with C 10 below.

2 The unknown character 暘 is explained as *yang* 煬, "to dry".

3 *Tu* 蠹, "wood-worm".

4 In C 10 below, in addition the Prefect and his Assistant are each fined one shield.

B 19 W 7.9a; S I.25a; S V.80b; SS 121; str. 43 (311).

[43] In case the sequence of marks[1] on tools does not correspond to the register[2]—for big ones the Overseer of the office is fined one shield; for small ones he is excused.

1 The strip clearly reads *chih* (for *shih*) *erh* 職 (for 識)耳. There is no doubt that marks are meant, but I do not understand the function of *erh*. The editors assume that *erh* is a loan for *erh* 佴, correctly explained as *tz'u* 次, "order, sequence", but the meaning of "the order or sequence of the marks" is unclear to me, especially because of the following "big" and "small" ones.

2 Cf. A 56 and 57 above.

B 20 W 7.9a; S I.25a; S V.80b; SS 123; str. 44 (312).

[44] For horses and cattle that have been wrongly marked,[1] as well as for objects that cannot be replaced,[2] the Overseer of the office is fined one shield.

1 For "mark" the same term *chih erh* 職耳 is used as in B 19 above.
2 *Pu neng hsiang i* 不能相易, lit. "cannot be exchanged". I have followed the translation in SS, although the meaning of the sentence escapes me, because a verb is lacking, like e.g. "to lose".

B 21 W 7.9a; S I.25b; S V.80b; SS 121–122; str. 45 (313).

[45] When quarterstaffs,[1] halberds[2] and crossbows (marked) in black or red[3] have become exchanged,[4] this is not to be considered as a surplus or a shortage but it is to be condemned according to the Statute concerning marks[5] not corresponding (to the register).

1 According to the texts and the representations in Hayashi, *Buki*, pp. 237–241, a *shu* 殳 was a kind of quarterstaff or riot-stick, made of bamboo strips tied together, and c. 1.70 m. long. This must have been the length of the Han time *shu*, because according to the pre-Han *Chou-li* this length was 12 feet or c. 2.80 m (*Chou-li* 21/74.89–90, cf. 18/61.4; *Chou-li chu-su* 39.5b (1414), cf. 32.4a (1151); Biot II, pp. 464, cf. p. 239.—Biot calls the *shu* "bâton de combat"). However, in a princely tomb, datable in c. 433 B.C., seven *shu* of quite a different type were found with inscriptions identifying these objects as *shu*. These *shu* have a length varying between 3.29 m. and 3.40 m. The shaft consists of bamboo strips with a wooden core. At the top they have a three-cornered spear-point, but the most striking characteristic is provided by two perforated bronze ball-shaped objects, one right under the spear-point, the other between 33 and 51 cm. lower. On one *shu* the balls had spikes, so that it looks like a gigantic morning-star; on the other six these bronze balls had flower designs, making them look like an out-size mace or a knob-kerrie; see "Sui-hsien", p. 9 and plate VI-2. A suggestion by the authors of this article, namely that fourteen poles, 3.13–3.23 m. long, with a bronze tube at the foot and a ring-shaped knob at the top might be "the ancient *shu*" is worth considering, because of the discovery of similar long poles, some of solid wood, some of bamboo strips, tied together with silk and lacquered black, in a tomb of the middle of the 4th century B.C.; see "Chiang-ling", p. 87 (for the dating see p. 111). The inordinate length of these *shu* indicates that they were used in fighting between war chariots, as described in Yang Hung, "Chan chü"; on p. 84 f. of this article special stress is laid on the length of the weapons needed for this type of warfare. However, the only passage in ancient literature which mentions the use of the *shu* in this connection seems to be the *Shih ming* 釋名 (inaccessible), section *shih ping* 兵 (quoted in Morohashi, vol. 6, p. 763).
2 For halberds, *chi* 戟, see Hayashi, *Bunbutsu*, p. 452 f. and ills. 10–1 f.
3 Literally "lacquer and cinnabar".
4 Cf. B 20 above; here *hsiang i* 相易 must mean "to become exchanged or confused".
5 For "mark" the same term *chih erh* 職耳 is used as in B 19 and 20.

B 22 W 7.9a; S I.25b; S V.81a; SS 122; str. 46–48 (314–316).

[46] When artisans are issued lacquer from another prefecture, they test it on arrival at the office. When absorbing[1] water, the water is decreased by more than 200 *tou*,[2] the artisans as well as the official in charge (of them)[3] are each fined two suits of armour; if it is not fully [47] 200 *tou* down to 100 *tou*, they are each fined one suit of armour; if it is not fully 100 *tou* down to 10 *tou*, they are each fined one shield. If it is not fully 10 *tou* [48] as well as when they have been issued lacquer in (their own) prefecture and there is a shortage, they have to restore it to the original amount.[4]

1 It is the lacquer which "drinks" the water, this being a test for the lacquer's quality. The editors of SS refer to *LSCC* 25/2, p. 319 (Wilhelm, *Frühling*, p. 435), which says that lacquer and water are both liquids, but that on combining them, they become hard, and that when lacquer is moistened, it becomes dry. Nevertheless the rule remains unclear, i.a. because the technique is unknown to me and because the quantity of lacquer is not indicated.

Ch'en Chih, *Liang Han*, p. 99 f., discusses the manufacture of lacquer objects, but without mentioning the preparation of the raw material.

2 With a *tou* of c. 2 litres, this figure indicates a quantity of c. 200 l.

3 Persons in charge of subordinates *chiang* 將 "lead" the latter; when in charge of an undertaking they *chu* 主 "master" it.

4 The text on the strip reads very clearly *chi lin chi hsien chung erh fu che fu chih ju ku* 及稟縣中而負者負之如故. This sentence presents one minor and one major problem. The minor one concerns the question: in which prefecture was the lacquer issued? Because the article starts with issues from another prefecture, one is lead to think that *hsien chung* refers to the artisans' own prefecture, but SS translates *kai* 該 *hsien*, "the prefecture referred to", hence: the other prefecture.—The major problem is the meaning of *fu* 負. Literally *fu* means "to bear", c.q. "to charge; to be made to bear", and in these texts *fu* usually means "to shoulder" debts etc. A literal translation would then be "Those who have received issues of lacquer . . . and they have to bear ???, let them bear it, to the original amount", but then it remains unknown, what these people have to bear. The editors suggest a different solution, namely that *fu* should mean "to be deficient"; this meaning the 7th century commentator attributes to *fu* in two passages in the History of the Later Han (*HHSCC* Mem. 22.4b and 51.3b). This meaning fits the first *fu* in the sentence and I have adopted it. But this meaning is impossible for the second *fu*. Without any further explanation SS renders *fu chih ju ku* as "to make good/to indemnify up to the original amount", but I believe that they are right. For I believe that the ancient scribe has made a mistake, confusing two words with a nearly identical pronunciation: for *fu* 復 *b'i̯ok or b'i̯ôg, "to restore" he simply repeated the first *fu* 負 *b'i̯ŭg (GSR, p. 219, no. 1034d and p. 263, no. 1000a).

B 23 W 7.9a; S I.25b; S V.81b; SS 123; str. 49 (317).

[49] When superiors[1] mobilize (people) for transport, commoners who might go to the prefecture (to ask for their) hire,[2] as well as those who transfer the transport to others will be sentenced according to the Statutes.

1 The text reads *shang* 上, which usually refers to the ruler. SS translates *shang* by "the court".

2 The editors rightly refer to *Shang-chün shu*, ch. 2, p. 9 (Duyvendak, *Lord Shang*, p. 184 and note 2), which says: *Ling sung liang wu ch'ü chiu wu te fan yung* 令送糧無取僦無得反庸, "According to the Ordinances, when transporting grain, no wage is to be asked, and on the return journey (the carter) must not be hired."

B 24 W 7.9a; S I.25b; S V.81b; SS 123; str. 50 (318).

[50] When in accounting due to lack of attention[1] to the Statutes there is a surplus or a shortage, this is to be fined according to the Statutes concerning checking (and finding) a surplus or a shortage,[2] but (those responsible) must not be made to repay.[3]

1 See note 41 to A 64 above.

2 Cf. B 5, 6, 9 and 10 above.

3 *Shang* 賞 for *shang* 償.

B 25 W 7.9a; S I.25b; S V.82a; SS 123–124; str. 51–53 (319–321).

[51] When[1] the Overseer of an office is fined two suits of armour, the Prefect and his Assistant are fined one suit of armour. When the Overseer of an office is fined one suit of armour, the Prefect and his Assistant are fined one shield. The officials in charge are adjudicated and fined or reprimanded [52] like the Overseer of the office. The other officials assigned to work there[2] and the prefectural clerks who compile accounts,[3] as well as Overseers of the Chief Granary,[4] of Arsenals, of Fields and of Guard posts[5] who are adjudicated (for

misdemeanours occurring) in the detached offices (under their control)[6] which are [53] subordinate to a commune,[7] (will be dealt with) in the same manner as the Prefect and his Assistant.

[1] In view of the similar construction of the following sentences this seems to be the correct translation.
[2] See note 6 to A 7 above.
[3] The text reads *yuan* 掾. In the Han period a *yüan* was the head of a department or office, *ts'ao* 曹, in the regional administration, and this is the only meaning of this word indicated by most dictionaries; it has been adopted by SS which renders *ling-shih yüan* as one single term: "the chief of the prefectural clerks". However, here *yüan* must be a verb, governing *chi* 計, and this view finds support in the *Shuo-wen* and its commentators (*SWKL*, p. 5402b f.). That *yüan* does not indicate some kind of official is also quite clear from B 27 below, where the other titles mentioned before *yüan* occur, whereas *yüan* does not. My rendering of *yüan* as "to compile" is tentative. Note that SS has been compelled to smuggle in a verb before *chi*, namely "to participate in".
[4] *Tu ts'ang* 都倉.
[5] *T'ing* 亭. The literature on the *t'ing* is endless; here I wish to refer only to Kao Min, "T'ing", who shows: a) that such guard-posts were established in towns, both at the gates and on the main thoroughfares; b) that they were also placed along the highroads, at intervals of ten *li* 里, or slightly over 4 km.; c) that their main function was the maintenance of law and order; d) that they also functioned as relay stations for the courier service and were often equipped with a hostel; e) that they were subordinate to the prefectural Chief of Police, *hsien wei* 縣尉, and f) that they were not territorial units (like the *hsiang* 鄉, districts, or *li* 里, villages or city-wards), as has been often assumed.
[6] The Overseers are punished for misdemeanours occurring in "their", *ch'i* 其, detached offices; these may have been local agencies under the Overseer's control, as suggested in Koga, p. 140.
[7] Like in A 19 (see A 19, note 7), the text writes *ch'ing* 卿; in this case I agree with the editors who believe that this character should be read *hsiang* 鄉.

B 26 W 7.9b; S I.26a; S V.82b; SS 124; str. 54 (322).

[54] In case the Commandant's[1] Accountant[2] as well as officials in the Commandant's office are accused,[3] the Prefect and the Assistant Prefect concerned[4] are adjudicated for their (misdemeanours), as in the case of other offices.[5]

[1] Probably the prefectural Chief of Police is meant; this is also assumed in SS.
[2] *Chi* 計 is quite clear on the strip. In view of the context, the word must refer to a person; hence the translation. The handbooks are silent on the subject. But cf. B 27 below.
[3] Note the use of *ho* 劾, implying an official accusation.
[4] *Ch'i* 其, lit. "their" Prefect.
[5] See B 25 above.

B 27 W 7.9a; S I.26a; S V.82b; SS 124–125; str. 55 (323).

[55] When the prefectural clerk[1] of the Controller of Horses[2] compiles[3] the accounts of a stud-farm, and there is an accusation[4] because of the accounts, the prefectural clerk of the Controller of Horses is adjudicated for this, like prefectural clerks being adjudicated for accusations concerning accounts of (their) office.

[1] See note 4 to A 22 above.
[2] Under the Han a *ssu-ma* 司馬 was a military officer subordinate to the *hsiao-wei* 校尉; in *HFHD*, *passim*, Dubs renders *hsiao-wei* by "colonel" and *ssu-ma* by "major". Recently, Sung Chih-min. p. 459, has shown that under the Han there were also *ssu-ma* attached to the

Grand Administrators of the border commanderies; this type of "major" had the name of the commandery attached to his title. Ch'en Chih, *HSHC*, p. 343, shows that such *ssu-ma* were also stationed in commanderies in the interior, at least during the 2nd century B.C.; cf. also Yü Hao-liang, pp. 16–18. However, in the present context "major" seems to be unsuitable, all the more so because C 6 below mentions a *hsien* or prefectural *ssu-ma*, and military officers had no place in the prefectural administration. I therefore suggest that the term will have to be taken literally as "the controller of horses", probably in charge of a stud-farm, *yüan* 苑, subordinate to a prefecture as mentioned in A 64 above. We find a similar literal use of *ssu* in the terms *ssu k'ung* "Controller of Works" (see note 7 to A 64 above) and *ssu k'ou* "Controller of Robbers" (see note 6 to A 69 above), the first being a subordinate functionary and the second even a convict, in charge of other convicts. A parallel to the rise in status of the *ssu ma* may be found in that of the French "maréchal" and the English "marshall", which originally meant "horse servant".—Next to nothing is known about the government rearing of horses in Ch'in times, if the *Ch'in hui-yao* is to be trusted. This compilation refers to *HSPC* 41.9a which mentions a *chiu ssu yü* 廄司御 (*SC* 95.19; Watson, *Records* I, p. 255, "carriage driver"); the *Han chi*, 1.3 writes *chiu tsou* 騶, which, in view of the explanation in *SW*, is identical with *chiu ssu-yü*. But this is of no help; nor, for that matter, are the seven *tsou* mentioned in the *Yüeh-ling* chapter of the *Li-chi* (*Li-chi chu-su* 17.3a (0809); Couvreur, *Li ki* I, p. 388; Legge, *Li ki* 27, p. 294), or the six *tsou* found in the *Tso chuan*, duke Ch'eng 18 (*Tso chuan* 28.16b (1144); Couvreur, *Tch'ouen-ts'iou* II, p. 171). These persons were all coachmen or grooms; perhaps they had a supervisory function. We are only slightly better informed about the Han; see *HLCI*, ch. 13, and Yen Keng-wang I, pp. 193 and 205–215.

3 For *yüan* ... *chi* 掾 ... 計 see note 2 to B 25 above; SS again takes *yüan* as part of the title, again smuggling in the indispensable verb, this time "controls" (cf. note 3 to B 26 above).

4 Cf. B 26.

B 28 W 7.9a–b; S I.26a; S V.83a; SS 125; str. 56–57 (324–325).

[56] When in checking the accounts there are mistakes, for 220 and less the Overseer of the office is reprimanded; if (the mistake) exceeds 220 cash, up to 2200 cash, he is fined one shield; [57] if it exceeds 2200 cash, he is fined one suit of armour. For one household,[1] horse or ox he is fined one shield; for two or more he is fined one suit of armour.

1 I have followed the translation in SS, which takes *jen-hu* 人戶 together.

B 29 W 7.9b; S I.26a; S V.83a–b; SS 125–126; str. 58–60 (326–328).

[58] When in accounting stores[1] are omitted, or when issuing stores one issues more than the norm (established by) the Statutes, as well as when one issues what should not be issued, the value[2] is estimated.[3] If it is not fully twenty two cash, it is excused; from twenty [59] two cash up to 660 cash, the Overseer of the office is fined one shield. If it exceeds 660 cash,[4] the Overseer of the office is fined one suit of armour and he is furthermore [60] charged with (the value of) what he had issued. One household,[5] horse or ox, or more is a serious mistake;[6] if he traces[7] (the mistake) himself, the punishment is decreased by one degree.[8]

1 For this rendering of *shih* 實 see note 2 to A 82 above.

2 *Chia* 賈 is used for *chia* 價.

3 *Chih* 直 is used for *chih* 値.

4 See note 6.

5 Cf. B 28 above.

6 The same stipulation occurs in D 189 below, which adds "goods whose value is more than 660 cash".

7 The editors suggest that *chung* 重 stands for *chung* 踵, which is explained in *SW* as *chui* 追, "to pursue, to trace"; in view of the context, *chung* cannot mean "heavy".

8 The exact steps in the Ch'in system of decreasing punishments are not known.

GROUP C

The texts belonging to the third group of strips, called by the editors *Ch'in lü tsa ch'ao* 秦律雜抄, "Miscellaneous excerpts of Ch'in statutes", consist of 26 articles (C1–C26) in the division adopted in *Wenwu* 1976/7 and followed here. The 42 strips have a length of c. 27.5 cm. or 1 ft. 2 in. Ch'in—Han measure; they were held together by three sets of strings: at the top, in the middle, and at the bottom. Each strip contains about thirty characters. In contrast to the writing on the strips of the other groups (A, B, D and E) the text on these strips is continuous; there are no blank spaces left at the end of an article. However, considerable use is made of heavy black dots to indicate the end of a sentence; in the translation these dots have been replaced by a small circle. For clarity's sake I have started a new paragraph with each new article, although the writing on the strips is continuous. According to SS, p. 127, (cf. CM, p. 74), these strips were found between the thighs of the corpse.

C 1 W 7.9b; S II.28a; S V.85a; SS 127–129; str. 1–4 (329–332).

[1] To (recommend and) guarantee[1] as an official a person who has been (permanently) removed from office[2] is fined by two suits of armour. ○

When there is a levy, there are appointed as probationary[3] Overseers and temporary Assistants[4] on probation (persons with the rank of) *shang tsao*[5] or higher; not to follow the Ordinances[6] is fined two [2] suits of armour. ○

When appointments to Sergeant Major[7] and Overseer of the crossbow archers[8] are not made in accordance with the Statutes,[9] as well as when crossbow archers when shooting do not hit (the target),[10] the Commandant[11] is fined two suits of armour. ○

When the Overseer of the crossbow archers when shooting does not hit (the target), [3] he is fined two suits of armour and dismissed; the Overseer guarantees him.[12] ○

When a coachman has been appointed since four years and he is unable to drive, the person who taught him is fined one shield. He is dismissed and he has to make good four years' statute labour and military service.[13]

[4] Statutes (concerning) the appointment of officials.[14]

[1] *Jen* 任 is not "to appoint", for that is *ch'u* 除. In *HSPC* 36.6a the commentator Fu Ch'ien (c. A.D. 125–195) explains *jen* as *pao* 保 *jen*, "to guarantee; to stand surety for". The editors of SS refer to *HSPC* 50.14b, where the commentator Su Lin (fl. 196–227) explains *jen* as *pao chü* 保舉, "to guarantee and recommend"; I have adopted the latter explanation.

[2] For the use of *fa* 法 for *fei* 廢 see note 5 to A 90 above.

[3] Cf. note 4 to A 81 above.

[4] Cf. note 3 to A 79 above.

[5] *Shang tsao* 上造 was the second lowest of the aristocratic ranks. Contrary to the editors of *Wenwu*, S and SS, I punctuate after *shang tsao i shang* and I consider the translation in SS unacceptable.

[6] For *pu ts'ung ling* 不從令, i.e. "not to do when the Ordinances say 'do this' ", see D 120 below.

7 The *shih li* 士吏, lit. "warriors' official", was a subordinate military officer; considering his status I render the term by "sergeant major". Yü Hao-liang, pp. 19–20, shows that he was senior to the *t'un-chang* 屯長, the leader of a squad of five men, "corporal", and to the *p'u yeh* 僕射, leader of a group of ten to fifty men, "sergeant", and that he could temporarily replace the *hou* 候, "captain", in view of an Edsin-gol strip (Lao Kan, *K'ao shih*, p. 22, no. 559 (28) 10.31). Another Edsin-gol strip summarises the duties of a *shih li*: he was in charge of a beacon-tower, to keep a look-out, to transmit sail- and fire-signals, and to be prepared against attack (Lao Kan, *K'ao shih*, p. 53, no. 2658 (128) 465.4). The *shih li* is mentioned in a Han statute quoted in the commentary to *HSPC* 94a.16a (cf. *SC* 110.43, not included in de Groot I, p. 96): "In commanderies close to the (frontier) defence works there is installed a Commandant for every forty *li* (cf. 10 miles or 17 km.) and two *shih li* and Commandant's Clerks each, to patrol the border area". The *shih li* also appears in other Edsin-gol strips; see *RHA* I, p. 96 and II, p. 387 (Dr. Loewe leaves the term untranslated); see also Fujieda, p. 637 f.

8 Both Yen Keng-wang I, p. 204, and Ch'en Chih, *HSHC*, p. 145, indicate that *HSPC* 28-AII.17a mentions a *fa nu kuan* 發弩官, "office for crossbow shooting", in Nan commandery. According to the early 7th century commentator Yen Shih-ku this office was in charge of instruction in archery. Both Yen and Ch'en transcribe seals with this title from other commanderies. Yü Hao-liang, pp. 18–19, also discusses this office. See also *HSPC* 45.8b and 58.10a, and Ch'en, *op. cit.*, p. 280.

9 This statute is unknown.

10 In Han times archery tests were held before the 9th month. Of the twelve arrows to be shot, six had to hit the target; for each further hit, fifteen days extra service-time were awarded. See *RHA* II, pp. 46–60; to the literature mentioned there in note 1 on p. 49, there can be added Lao Kan, "Ping chih", pp. 216–217 (30), and Ch'en P'an I, pp. 311–312.

11 *Wei* 尉. This must have been a military officer, whose status is still unknown; *SC* 48.6 (*Mh* VI, p. 11; Watson, *Records* I, p. 21; *HSPC* 31.3a) shows several *wei* in command of a convoy. It seems most unlikely that the Prefectural Commandant is meant, because this official was in charge of the local police.

12 For *jen* 任 see note 1 above. — It is unclear which Overseer is meant; SS believes that it was the *hsien se-fu*, the Prefectural Overseer, identified with the Prefect, but see note 5 to A 19 above.

13 In spite of the construction of this sentence, it seems likely that it was the coachman who was to repay or indemnify, *shang* (賞=) 償 these obligations, from which he must have been relieved during his training. *Yao shu* 徭戍 together might mean "military service", but in the strips *yao* occurs repeatedly by itself, meaning "statute labour". Moreover, it would be illogical that only the military service and not the statute labour should have had to be made good.

14 The third strip has room for at least two more characters, but this space has been left blank. In view of the contents, the editors were justified in placing strip no. 4 here.

C 2 W 7.9b; S II.28a; S V.86a; SS 129; str. 4 (332) continued.

[4 continued] Pretending[1] to obey a (royal) command,[2] setting it aside and not carrying it out (is punished by) shaving off the beard and being made a *hou*.[3] Not to retire from one's mat[4] is fined by two suits of armour and being (permanently) removed (from office).

1 The strip reads *wei* 爲 which the editors take to be a loan for *wei* 僞 "to falsify"; the translation follows the rendering in SS.

2 See note 1 to A 95 above.

3 For the hard labour punishment called *hou* 候 see note 1 to A 103 above.

4 Not to slide off the mat on which one had been kneeling when another person, and certainly one's superior, entered, was considered impolite; the custom is still observed in Japan. The suggestion by the editors of S that *li* 立 should be read *wei* 位 is correct, because one did not stand up, but, continuing to kneel, brought one's forehead to the ground. However, SS maintains *li* and translates it as "to stand up", which I believe to be contrary to ancient usage. But there is much to recommend their idea that this sign of politeness was to be observed when listening to a royal command. It should not be forgotten that the chair was intro-

duced into China several centuries after these texts had been written; see Fitzgerald and the excellent supplementary article by Holzman.

C 3 W 7.9b; S II.28a; S V.86a–b; SS 129–130; str. 4–5 (332–333).

[4 continued] When *yu shih*[1] are staying (somewhere)[2] without credentials,[3] the prefecture where they dwell will be fined [5] one suit of armour; at the end of the year it[4] will be charged.[5] ○ . . . .[6] (members of) the old Ch'in population[7] leave (the country)[8] . . . .[9] remove from the (population) register, (persons with the aristocratic rank of) *shang tsao*[10] and above will be made *kui-hsin*,[11] and (those with the rank of) *kung shih*[12] and lower[13] will suffer a mutilating punishment and be made *ch'eng tan*.[14] ○ Statutes (concerning) *yu shih*.

1 *Yu shih* 游士. S thinks that the "wandering warriors" were some kind of irregular troops, whereas SS takes the term in is usual meaning of "wandering scholars", the men who went from court to court to propagate their political ideas, decried i.a. in *Shang-chün shu*, ch. 3, p. 13, and 6, p. 27 (Duyvendak, *Lord Shang*, p. 193 f. and 220). Both these solutions seem equally unacceptable, for it seems hard to imagine either irregular troops or political propagandists wandering through the countryside; unfortunately, I have nothing better to offer, although Professor Li Hsüeh-ch'in, "Mo-tzu", p. 324, is convinced that "wandering scholars" are meant, in view of the very remarks in the *Shang-chün shu* referred to above.

2 The text has simply *tsai* 在.

3 *Fu* 符 are tallies or credentials, on which the name and function of the bearer could be inscribed; see Lao Kan, *K'ao shih, k'ao cheng*, pp. 318–323, esp. p. 322 (cf. my "Han documents", p. 24) and cf. Ōba, "Dōko-fu". The editors of S take *fu* to mean *wu fu* 伍符, which they explain as a certificate of membership of a squad of five soldiers, apparently based on the commentary in *HSPC* 50.8a, where *wu fu* is explained as a mutual guarantee of the members of a squad of five to prevent treachery. Lao Kan's explanation is preferable; it is followed in principle by SS.

4 The text reads *chih* 之, which may refer to the prefecture as well as to the *yu shih*.

5 *Tse* 責, the prefecture or the *yu shih* will have to pay the fine.

6 The meaning of *yu wei* 有爲 in this context is unclear to me; it can hardly be a complicated way of saying "if". The editors of SS translate the term by "persons who help people of Ch'in to leave."

7 I.e. the original inhabitants of the state of Ch'in, in contrast to immigrants from the states in the East; cf. *Shang-chün shu*, ch. 15, p. 55, Duyvendak, *Lord Shang*, p. 270. Shang Yang proposed that the original Ch'in population should furnish soldiers, whereas the immigrants should engage in agriculture.

8 I follow the editors' suggestion.

9 I have left a blank here, because I do not understand the relation between the different actions mentioned here. The persons to be punished with hard labour can only be the persons who tried to leave Ch'in, but they can hardly have removed their names from the registers. The editors of SS believe that the persons who helped them also removed their names from the registers.

10 *Shang tsao* is the one but lowest of the aristocratic ranks.

11 *Kui hsin* was the three years' hard labour punishment under the Han, but the length of the Ch'in punishment in unknown.

12 *Kung shih* was the first and lowest of the aristocratic ranks.

13 Hence commoners without rank; were unfree persons also included?

14 *Ch'eng tan* was the four or five years' hard labour punishment under the Han, but the length under the Ch'in is unknown.

C 4 W 7.9b; S II.28a; S V.86b–87a; SS 130–131; str. 6–7 (334–335).

[6] When (a person) is warranted[1] to appoint retainers[2] (but) the population

register does not allow this,[3] (or) when appointments[4] are made carelessly,[5] (such cases) are all[6] punished by shaving off the beard and being made a *hou*.[7] Employment of one's retainers in excess (of the norms established by) the Statutes,[8] as well as beating them, is fined one suit of armour; if the skin is broken[9] (the fine is) two suits of armour. [7] Statutes concerning the appointment of retainers.

1 The editors of SS explain *tang* 當 as *t'ang* 儻, "if", which is an accepted loan. However, its use here would be most surprising, in view of the hundreds of cases where these very texts use the bare statement to serve as a supposition, contrary to modern Chinese and western languages, which need an introductory "if". I prefer to take *tang* literally as "to be warranted" (see *RHL*, pp. 80–81). The following *ch'u* 除 the editors explain as "to remove", namely from the register *chi* 籍, referring to *SC* 88.4, where the phrase *ch'u ch'i kuan* (or *huan*) *chi* 除其官 (or 宦) 籍 effectively can only mean "remove him from the register of the officials". However, in the present context it would be very strange that *ch'u ti-tzu* would first mean "to remove retainers" and then have the identical words in the title of the statute mean "to appoint retainers", which is the interpretation adopted by the same editors!

2 I agree with the editors that the *ti-tzu* of the text are to be identified with the *shu-tzu* 庶子 mentioned in the *Shang-chün shu*. ch. 19, p. 71, where Duyvendak, *Lord Shang*, p. 295, renders the term as "bodyguards". According to Shang Yang, the holders of degrees of aristocratic rank were entitled to a number of retainers, who had to work for them six days a month and who had to follow them in war. The *Huai-nan-tzu*, ch. 12, p. 200, notes that there existed special registers for the retainers.

3 The editors of SS want *pu te* 不得 to mean "unsuitable, unfitting", referring to Cheng Hsüan's commentary to the last word of paragraph 2 of The Great Learning (*Li-chi chu-su* 60.1a (2343); there *te* is explained as *te shih chih i* 得事之宜. I do not think that this explanation is applicable here.

4 The text reads *chih jen* 置任, "to instal and give tasks", which I prefer to render as "to appoint", but which SS translates as *jen-yung pao-chü* 任用保舉, "to appoint and to recommend and guarantee", no doubt inspired by the presence of the word *jen*. I do not think that this is acceptable.

5 See note 41 to A 64 above and cf. *RHL*, p. 263.

6 The word *chieh* 皆, "all", I believe to refer to the preceding misdemeanours; consequently, the persons to be punished were the men who wrongly put persons to work. I think so because of a case which shows some similarities with the rule under discussion. This case is reported in *HSPC* 15A.11a: in 112 B.C. a noble was condemned i.a. because "knowing that persons had evaded registration, he had employed them as hired labourers", *chih jen t'o wang ming shu wei pao* 知人脫亡名數以爲保 (for *pao* meaning "hired labour" see Lao Kan *K'ao-shih, k'ao-cheng*, p. 56); the case is briefly cited in *RHL*, p. 219.

7 For *hou* see note 1 to A 103 above.

8 *Ying* 贏, besides meaning "surplus" as in several articles in groups A and B above, can also mean "excess, to exceed". *HSPC* 16.28b and 49a report cases of nobles who had "employed inhabitants of their fief in excess of the fixed number, *yüan* 員", c.q. "of the Statutes", *lü* 律, *shih kuo jen kuo yüan/lü* 事國人過員/律; here, however, the word for "exceed" is not *ying* but *kuo*.

9 *Kuai* 夬, "to make a breach", and therefore identical with *chüeh* 決. In these texts it is repeatedly used for skin wounds (C 17, D 64, 65, 72).

C 5 W 7.9b; S II.28a; S V.87a–b; SS 131–132; str. 7–9 (335–337).

[7 continued] ○ When a former[1] Grandee[2] cuts off heads,[3] he is banished. ○ Those who divide (a group of soldiers in) armour[4] into two during the hunt[5] (are punished by) shaving off the beard.[6] ○ The prefectures must not venture to keep[7] conscripts[8] and make them retainers; (in that case) the Commandant [8] is fined two suits of armour and he is dismissed; the Prefect (is fined) two suits of armour. ○ The prefectures must not venture to take away the dried meat[9] conveyed[10] to the army by (soldiers of) the light chariots,[11] crossbow-men,[12] archers,[13] and conscripts of the Central (Army).[14] If they take away the dried meat of the conscripts of the Central (Army), the Prefect and the Commandant [9] will each be fined two suits of armour.

1 SS renders *ku ta-fu* 故大夫 as "a person whose original rank had been *ta-fu*", referring to HSPC 1B.5a (*HFHD* I, p. 104). There we do find *ku ta-fu* with this meaning, but the editors overlook that in the imperial decree in which these words occur, these *ku ta-fu* are contrasted to other *ta-fu*: whereas the latter had just been given this rank, the former already possessed it and were now further promoted. This contrast is absent in the present article and the true meaning of *ku* remains unclear to me.

2 The strip reads 夫=; as in A 92 above, this will have to be read *ta fu* 大夫. There existed three aristocratic ranks with the title *ta fu*, namely the 5th, *ta-fu*; the 6th, *kuan* 官 ta-fu, and the 7th, *kung* 公 *ta-fu*.

3 The editors rightly refer to ch. 19 of the *Shang-chün shu*, p. 72 (Duyvendak, *Lord Shang*, p. 296, is mistaken), which states that during a battle, officers were not allowed to cut off heads, *ch'i chan pai chiang t'un-chang pu te chan shou* 其戰百將屯長不得斬首.

4 *Chia* 甲 is "a suit of armour", but in ancient literature (see the examples quoted in *SWKL* p. 6558b f.) it occasionally means a group of soldiers in armour; SS therefore suggests that it is a fixed group.

5 The great hunts were in fact military manoeuvres; cf. Biot II, p. 171 f.

6 The hard labour punishment which included shaving off the beard has been omitted.

7 The editors believe that *pao* 包, "to envelop", should be explained as "to hide"; in view of *SWKL*, p. 4051b, this is not unusual.

8 *Tsu* 卒 is the current Han expression for men fulfilling their labour and military service.

9 The text reads *tsu so tsai fu tao chün. . . . .tsu fu. .* 卒所載傅到軍 . . . . 卒傅, where the editors belive that *fu* 傅 is a mistake for *chuan/ch'uan* 傳. SS translates: ". .conscripts using (1) carriages (2) of the courier service (*chuan*) to transport goods (3) to the army. . . .goods (4) which the conscripts transmit (*ch'uan*)", . . *tsu yung* (1) *chuan-chü* (2) *yün sung tao chün ti wu-tzu* (3) . . . *tsu ch'uan-sung ti wu-tzu* (4) . . . 卒用 (1) 傳車 (2) 運送到軍的物資 (3) . . . 卒傳送的物資 (4); here the words followed by the figures 1, 2, 3 and 4 are "fillers", needed to produce an intelligible sentence out of a text that has been misunderstood. In the first place there is no need to assume that *fu* is a mistake for *chuan*; the scribe knew the character for *chuan*, because he used it correctly in A 32, 33, 92, 93 and 94 above. In the second place, the grammatical object of *tsai* 載, "to load, to charge, to convey" is *fu*; *tsu so tsai fu tao chün* is therefore "the *fu* which the conscripts convey to the army". It is clear, that *fu* here cannot have one of its accepted meanings ("to assist; assistant; teacher; to enroll"), but that it must be a loan for another character. I suggest that this is *fu* 脯 (both words have the same pronunciation *pi̯wo; see GSR, pp. 46–47, nos. 102r and 102u'), or perhaps *p'o* 膊 (*p'ak; GSR, p. 204, no. 771), "dried meat" (cf. *SWKL*, p. 1793a–b). In case the character is read *chuan/ch'uan*, I cannot think of *chuan* that could be "loaded" or "conveyed" — certainly not "passports", which is one of the meanings of *chuan*; in the second phrase *tsu ch'uan*, "the conscripts transmit", makes no sense.

10 *Tsai* 載.

11 For the use of chariots in warfare see Yang Hung, "Chan-chü".

12 *Ch'e chang* 趆張, "bending (the crossbow) by kicking". The archer grasped the string and pushed the bow away with both feet, eventually hooking the string behind the projecting part of the trigger mechanism. According to *SW*, *s.v. ch'e*, there existed a Han ordinance, *ling*, concerning these crossbow archers; these men are called *chüeh chang shih* 蹶張士, and the commentator Ju Shun (fl. 221–265) adds that this expression was found in the Statutes, a piece of information repeated in the *Han-kuan i* 漢官儀 (see *HKCC*, ch. A, 31b) quoted in *HHSCC* Ann. 1B.4a. A reproduction of a Han stone carving, representing an archer stretching a crossbow with his feet, is found in Mayer, p. 6, Hayashi, *Bunbutsu*, ill. 10/58, and *Kaogue xuebao* 1976/1, p. 41.

13 *Yin ch'iang* 引强, lit. "(those who) pull strong (bows)"; see the early commentaries to *HSPC* 40.20a.

14 I follow the editors' explanation of *chung tsu* 中卒; they have adopted the commentary to *Shang-chün shu*, ch. 19, p. 75 (Duyvendak, *Lord Shang*, p. 302, leaves the term untranslated).

C 6 W 7.9b; S II.28a–b; S V.88a; SS 132–133; str. 9–10 (337–338).

[9] When riding[1] horses of five feet eight inches[2] and higher are not fit for their task and when their running and ....[3] is not according to the Ordinances[4] the prefectural Controller of Horses[5] is fined two suits of armour, and the Prefect and the Assistant (Prefect) are each (fined) one suit of armour. First [10] (a quotum of) riding horses is imposed[6]; when (the number of) horses is complete, then those that are to join the army are selected.[7] Upon arrival in the army they are graded.[8] When the horses are of poor quality,[9] the Prefect and the Assistant (Prefect) (are fined) two suits of armour; the Controller of Horses is fined two suits of armour and he is (permanently) dismissed.[10]

1 The text has *mo*, with the repetition marker, 驀=, which the editors rightly read as *mo ma* 馬. *SW* explains *mo* as *shang ma* 上馬 and the few rare instances of the use of this word show that this means "to mount a horse", but the editors of S (not those of SS) suggest that it is "a fine horse".
2 With the Ch'in—Han foot at c. 23cm., this height is equal to c. 1.35 m.
3 The text reads *chih* 摯, "to catch, to seize"; according to GSR, p. 181, no. 685k, this could be a loan for *chih* 致 or *chih* 輊, and Karlgren, "Loan characters I", p. 50, nos. 137–139, mentions other suggested loans, but the editors take it as a loan for *chih* 縶, "a rope; to tether". As it is the performance of the horse which is being judged—note that it is the Controller of Horses who is punished and not the rider—this cannot explain the meaning of *chih*, for a horse cannot tether itself. The correct solution is surely provided by Yü and Li, p. 161. They suggest that *chih* 摯 is used for *chih* 驇 (explained in SW as "to go slowly and heavily"), and according to the *Kuang ya* (unaccessible), quoted in Tuan Yü-ts'ai's commentary in *SWKL*, p. 4332 a, the latter is the same as *chih* 駤, "to stop"! Phonetically, this seems not impossible: *chih* 驇 was *ti̯əb, whereas characters with the phonetic element 至 were *ti̯ĕd (see *GSR*, p. 181, no. 685j and p. 116, no. 413).
4 In view of the frequent occurrence of *pu ju lü* or *ling* 不如律 or 令, this must be the meaning, and not, as SS translates "it does not obey the commands".
5 See note 2 to B 27 above.
6 For this rendering of *fu* 賦 see note 3 to A 58 above.
7 *Lin* 厀 is a loan for *lin* 遴, "to select", as suggested by the editors, but I do not think that their explanation is correct that it was the cavalrymen who were selected.
8 For *k'o* 課, "to evaluate, to grade", see note 2 to A 7 above.
9 For *tien* 殿 see note 2 to A 7 above.
10 For this rendering of *fei* 廢 see note 5 to A 90 above.

C 7 W 7.9b; S II.28b; S V.88b; SS 133; str. 10 continued–11 (338–339).

[10 continued] When officials (with a position of) Assistants and Clerks or [11] higher load pack-horses or. ....[1] and order (them) to sell[2] these and take money, they will all be banished.[3]

1 The translation of this article is tentative, although the writing on the strip is clear. There are two elements whose meaning is obscure: *fu ts'ung-ma* 負從馬 and *shou shu ssu tsu* 守書私卒. In connection with the first, the 18th century scholar Wang Nien-sun remarked that these were "accompanying horses, loaded with wearing apparel" (see *HSPC* 94A.19b, de Groot, *Urkunden* I, p. 134; cf. *CICA*, p. 220). This explanation is tacitly followed by the editors, but S adds, that *fu* might also be rendered as a verb, so that *fu ts'ung-ma* would come to mean "to load pack-horses". As regards the second phrase, this is a complete enigma, although the individual terms are clear. *Ssu tsu*, "private conscripts" (assuming that *tsu* had this meaning in the Ch'in kingdom) are unknown, as are the *ssu li* 私吏, "private officials", in E 13 below. *Shou shu* can only mean "to guard documents" whatever this may imply, and that is how SS translates it. But when they translate the whole first sentence,

they write "officials.... *who possess* horses transporting baggage and document-guarding private retainers, and they barter these for gain...", they smuggle the word *yu* "to possess" into the text, and they neglect the word *ling* 令, "to order; to cause to do". The officials being the grammatical subject of *ling*, they must also necessarily be the subject of *fu*, "to load" (the variant suggested by S) and therefore unavoidably also of *shou* 守, although the meaning of this word here escapes me, as does the purport of the whole phrase *shou shu ssu tsu.*

2 *Shih* 市, "to deal", rendered in SS as "to barter for profit".

3 This article is not separated from the preceding and the following by a black dot.

C 8 W 7.9b–10a; S II.28b; S V.89a–b; SS 133–135; str. 11–15 (339–343).

[11 continued] Whereas the issue of rations (to certain persons) in the army is not warranted[1] still to issue these entails a fine of two suits of armour for both[2]; they are (permanently) dismissed. [12] If they are not officers,[3] (the fine is)[4] two years' military service. If (such persons') messmates,[5] corporals or sergeants do not denounce this, the fine is one year's military service. If the Prefect, the Commandant[6] or the sergeant-major do not arrest them, they are fined one suit of armour. ○ Men in the army who sell[7] their rations at the place where these rations were issued [13] as well as in the prefectures they pass through, will be fined two years' military service; if their mess-mates of the same chariot (troop),[8] corporals or sergeants do not denounce them, (they are fined) one year's military service. If the prefectural Controller of Works, the Assistants and clerks of the Controller of Works and the sergeant major in charge[9] do not arrest them, [14] the fine is one suit of armour; the State Controller of Works[10] (is fined) one shield. ○ If in the place where the rations were issued or in the prefectures passed through (by the recipients) commoners buy these rations, they are fined two suits of armour; the rations are confiscated.[11] If officials have been posted[12] and they do not arrest them, (they) as well as [15] the Prefect and the Assistant (Prefect) are each fined one suit of armour. ○ When arms issued to conscripts are not complete or in (good) repair,[13] the Arsenal Overseer and officials (there) are fined two suits of armour and they are (permanently) dismissed. ○

1 Cf. A 31–33 above for the prevention of the issue of double rations.

2 Viz. the persons who issued the rations and those who received them.

3 *Li* 吏.

4 The words between brackets occur in the next sentence.

5 *T'u shih* 徒食; here *t'u* probably means "infantry; foot soldier". As SS puts it: "soldiers who receive rations together". *T'u shih* cannot mean "vagrant; idler".

6 In Han times, the prefectural Commandant was the chief of the police.

7 Both "to buy" and "to sell" are expressed by the single character 買; cf. note 1 to A 46 above.

8 *T'ung chü shih* 同車食; according to Yang Hung, "Chan-chü", p. 87, one chariot was accompanied by ten foot soldiers, but judging by the An-yang finds, in the Shang period their number was thirty.

9 *Chiang* 將, lit. "who leads them".

10 *Pang ssu-k'ung* 邦司空. SS translates this title as "the Court Controller of Works". Yü Hao-liang, p. 11, suggests that this official will be identical with the *kuo* 國 *ssu-k'ung*, mentioned in the 19th chapter of the *Shang-chün shu*, p. 74 (Duyvendak, *Lord Shang*, p. 301), where in Han times *kuo* was substituted for *pang*, in order to avoid the tabooed name of emperor Kao. In the *Shang-chün shu* the *kuo ssu-k'ung* is shown to be present when towns were besieged;

he estimated the size of the walls. In the *Chou-li* the *ssu-k'ung* is the Minister of Works, whose main task consisted in building.

11 *Ju lin kung* 入稟公.

12 The text reads *li pu* 吏部, but the editors suggest that this is a copyist's mistake for *pu li*, and they refer to a few passages in the Han histories, where the term *pu li* occurs, viz. *HSPC* 99C.15b (*HFHD* III, p. 419) and *HHSCC*, Mem. 39.8b; they might have added others, e.g. *HSPC* 78.17b. Whereas S explains *pu li* as "prefectural officials in charge of this affair", SS understands the term as "officials in the areas of the districts and the communes". I only know of one case where *hsiang pu* 鄉部 is explained as "the officials of a district" (*HSPC* 72.13b); in *HHSCC*, Mem. 67.5b *pu li* indicates prefectural officials. However, in the passages quoted by the editors *pu* is a verb, meaning "to post"; in *HSPC* 78.17b "he immediately posted officials to arrest.." Similar instances are found in *HSPC* 90.19b and in an inscription of c. A.D. 150, included in *Li shih* 3.10a; in *HSPC* 69.10b we find *pu shih* 部士, "to post soldiers". With *pu* meaning "to post", there is no need to assume a copyist's mistake in the present instance. In addition, it should be noted that in Ch'in—Han usage *pu* as a noun did not mean "department", i.e. a government office, as it did in later ages. *Pu* indicates "an area", with a size that differed according to the circumstances; already in ch. 70 of the *Mo-tzu*, p. 348 (Forke, *Mê Ti*, p. 691), it designates a section of a city ward. The largest *pu* were the thirteen Regions, inspected by Regional Inspectors, *pu tz'u-shih* 部刺史, created by emperor Wu in 106 B.C. (*HSPC* 6.30a; *HFHD* II, pp. 96–97). At a lower level, the commanderies were divided into several *pu*, "divisions", varying in number between two and five and named after the four directions and the centre. These divisions, each consisting of several prefectures, were likewise inspected, in this case by the Inspector of Faults, *tu yu* 督郵 (for *yu* 尤), appointed locally by the Commandery Administrators (see the excellent survey in Lao Kan, *K'ao shih, k'ao cheng*, p. 15, under *tu-li* 都吏, and cf. *Li shih* 3.10a and 5.14a). This must have led the commentator Li Hsien (651–684) to explain *pu li* as being the *tu yu* and the *yu chiao* 游徼, the prefectural policemen, in his remarks to *HHSCC*, Mem. 36.12a. Similarly, many border commanderies which contained "barbarians who had surrendered" were divided into *pu*," sections", again named after the four directions. However, these were not inspectorates, but administrative divisions, under the control of Military Commandants, *tu wei* 都尉; see Kamada, p. 315 f. and p. 335. At a still lower level, *pu* are found on the silk maps discovered at Ma-wang tui; Chou Shih-jung, p. 20, believes that such *pu* were either earth-works (or forts), or minor administrative units, perhaps equal to a *hsiang* or district (cf. also *Kuan-tzu*, p. 15). Finally, a *pu* was an army unit of 400 men, commanded by a *ssu-ma* 司馬, "major"; Dr. Loewe was therefore quite right when he translated *pu li* as "officers of (a) unit" (*RHA* II, pp. 105 and 113, no. 14).

13 The editors rightly read *shan* 繕 for *shan* 善. *Wan* 完, "complete", occurs *passim* in the Edsin-gol documents.

C 9 W 7.10a; S II.28b; S V.90a; SS 135–136; str. 15–16 (343–344).

[15 continued] Persons who venture greatly[1] to increase the number of their years of hardship[2] [16] are fined one suit of armour and the hardship is cancelled.[3] ○ Statutes on hardship. . . . .[4]

1 *Shen* 深, in the sense of "greatly, extremely".

2 In the Han period, service in the distant border defences was counted as "hardship", *lao* 勞. According to an Ordinance, discovered in the Edsin-gol defence lines and translated in *RHA* I, p. 119 (where Dr. Loewe renders *lao* by "extra servic etime"; cf. also *RHL*, p. 47), two days' service in the outposts was counted as three days, and the Edsin-gol records show that servicemen were *tz'u* 賜, "granted", far over a hundred days in this manner; see Lao Kan, *K'ao shih*, p. 93, no. 4543 (259) 159.14, and *Chia pien*, no. 941.

3 *Ch'i* 棄, "to throw away".

4 SS points out that *chung lao* 中勞 occurs repeatedly in the Edsin-gol material. In discussing the latter, Dr. Loewe has reached the conclusion that *chung* 中 is an assessment of the degree of merit, *kung* 功, namely "medium", because *shang* 上 and *hsia* 下 are also found. However, this solution is of no help in the present instance.

C 10 W 7.10a; S II.28b; S V.90a; SS 136; str. 16 (344).

[16 continued] When in storing hides and leather these are attacked by insects,[1] the Overseer is fined one suit of armour, and the Prefect and the Assistant (Prefect) are (fined) one shield. ○ Statutes on Storage.[2]

[1] *T'o* (*t'âk) 橐, "bag", is an accepted loan for *tu* (*tâg) 蠹, "wood-worm"; see GSR, p. 209, no. 795p and r.

[2] This rule is practically identical with B 18 above.

C 11 W 7.10a; S II.28b; S V.90a–b; SS 136–137; str. 17–18 (345–346).

[17] When (the quality of manufactured objects) upon inspection is poor,[1] the Master[2] of the Artisans is fined one suit of armour; the Assistant[3] as well as the Head of the work-squad[4] (are fined) one shield, and the men[5] (are fined) twenty sets of laces.[6] When (the quality) upon inspection is poor during three consecutive years, the Master of the Artisans (is fined) two suits of armour, the Assistant and the Head of the work-squad [18] one suit of armour, and the men fifty sets of laces.

[1] In contrast to C 12 ff. below, no object is indicated, but the sense is clear; for *tien* 殿, "of inferior quality", see note 2 to A 7 above.

[2] See note 2 to A 61 above.

[3] *Ch'eng* 丞, "Assistant, Vice-", is combined with many titles; here it will indicate the Assistant-Instructor.

[4] *Ts'ao* 曹 indicates a group of workmen; cf. D 12 below.

[5] See note 21 to A 9 above.

[6] The editors are surely correct when they suggest that *lo tsu* 絡組 are the cords or laces with which the scales of a suit of armour were strung together; such "strung armour", *tsu chia* 組甲, is mentioned in the *Tso chuan*, duke Hsiang, 3 (*Tso chuan* 29.6a (1177); Couvreur, *Tch'ouen ts'iou* II, p. 189). Yang Hung, "Chia chou", pp. 31 and 36, and ill. 13 on p. 33, gives a detailed account of the method for stringing the scales, but without indicating the technical name for the laces; see also "P'i chia chou" p. 542 for the silk cords used for assembling armour of lacquered leather scales, found in a tomb of c. 433 B.C. (cf. *Wenwu* 1979/7, p. 13), again without technical names, not provided either in Yang Hung, "Chia ho k'ai", nor in Hayashi, *Buki*, p. 412, ill. 581. The meaning of *chi* 給, normally "to furnish; to supply", is less clear from the context; it must be either "a set" of laces, or a numerative, "a length" of such strings, and it is the latter meaning which SS adopts. The dictionaries are silent on this point. SS believes that *chi* should be "read as" *ch'i* 緝, "a connected row" (perhaps inspired by a remark by Hao I-hsing, quoted in *SWKL*, p. 5823a, that *chi* was "more or less the same" as *ch'i*), but phonetically this is impossible, because *chi* was *ki̯əp, whereas *ch'i* was *ts'i̯əp. The additional information in SS that according to the *Shih ming* 釋名 (unaccessible) *ch'i* (not *chi*!) in Later Han times was called *keng* 綆, "well-rope", is particularly useless. I would venture to suggest that in the character 給 both elements appear to be significant: the "silk radical" because the text deals with textile laces, and the "phonetic element", meaning "to combine", because the text deals with sets of objects. The character may therefore have been adopted for this technical purpose, disregarding its usual meaning in the early texts (cf. the remarks in this direction by Hao I-hsing, *loc. cit.*).

C 12 W 7.10a; S II.28b–29a; S V.90b–91a; SS 137; str. 18–20 (346–348).

[18 continued] Venturing to make other objects when these do not belong to the annual production,[1] as well when there has been no royal command,[2] the Master of the Artisans[3] as well as his Assistant are each fined two suits of armour. When a prefectural workshop[4] for the first time[5] [19] presents (work)[6] and it is poor, the Prefectural Overseer,[7] his Assistant, his (subordinate) officials and the Heads of the worksquads[8] are each fined one shield. When *ch'eng-tan*[9] working as artisans[10] are rated as inferior, (each) man is given a hundred strokes.[11] When carts[12] [20] are inferior, the Controller of Works and[13] the Overseer (are fined) one shield; the men[14] are given fifty strokes. ○

1 See note 8 to A 36 above.
2 See note 1 to A 95 above.
3 See note 2 to A 61 above.
4 In these texts *kung* 工 means "artisan", but here the strip reads *hsien* 縣 *kung*. I therefore believe that the editors of SS are right when they suggest that *hsien kung* is a prefectural workshop; Koga, *Chō-an*, p. 536, also adopts this rendering. SS bases this suggestion on passages in the Treatise on the Administrative Geography in the Han History (*HS* 28A) which note the presence of Offices of Artisans, *kung-kuan* 工官, in several prefectures. However, these offices were not perfectural establishments. As remarked in Yen Keng-wang I, p. 194 (see also Bielenstein, *Bureaucracy*, pp. 95 and 97), these Offices of the Artisans were the concern of the commandery administration and they were ultimately subordinate to authorities in the central government. Nevertheless, I am convinced that in the present case it is workshops and not single artisans that are indicated, in consideration of the heavy fines inflicted on the managers.
5 This would seem to be the meaning of *hsin* 新, lit. "new(ly)".
6 *Hsien* 獻, "to offer to a superior", has no object here; one may also translate *hsien* as a noun and render *hsin hsien* as "the new, i.e. first, tribute". Professor Koga has the strange idea that the Ch'in government organised competitions ("concours" in the text) between official workshops, ordering the presentation of products manufactured on trial (Koga, p. 536).
7 See note 3 to A 19 above.
8 See note 4 to C 11 above.
9 Hard labour convicts; see the introduction, p. 14.
10 Cf. A 62 above.
11 The text has *chih* 治 for *ch'ih* 笞.
12 *Ta chü* 大車; see note 1 to A 48 above.
13 It seems unlikely that a single official is meant, but SS translates "the Overseer of the Controller of Works".
14 *T'u* 徒; for the uncertainty concerning the meaning of this word see note 21 to A 9 above. As *ch'eng tan* hard labour convicts have been mentioned, the rendering of *t'u* as "convicts" could be justified.

lacquer

C 13 W 7.10a; S II.29a; S V.91a; SS 138; str. 20–21 (348–349).

[20 continued] When (the produce of) the lacquer (tree) plantations[1] is inferior, the Overseer is fined one suit of armour; the Director, the Assistant (Director)[2] and the assistants[3] (are fined) one shield each; the men[4] (are fined) each [21] twenty sets of armour laces.[5] When (the produce of) the lacquer (tree) plantations is inferior during three consecutive years, the Overseer is fined two suits of armour and he is (permanently) dismissed; the Director and the Assistant (Director) are each (fined) one suit of armour.

1 *Yüan* 園, "garden"; Ch'en Chih, *HSHC*, p. 147, mentions an early Former Han seal of a Major (*sic*) of the Ch'ang-shan lacquer gardens.
2 *Ling* 令 and *ch'eng* 丞 do not refer to a prefect and his assistant, but to a director and his aide; Bielenstein, *Bureaucracy*, pp. 254–257, lists dozens of government organizations, including parks and orchards, headed by a Director.
3 *Tso* 佐 are subordinate personnel.
4 *T'u* 徒; see note 21 to A 9 above.
5 See note 6 to C 11 above.

C 14 W 7.10a; S II.29a; S V.91a–b; SS 138–139; str. 21–23 (349–351).

[21 continued] When the weight[1] (obtained from) mining[2] is inferior, the Overseer is fined one suit of armour [22] and the assistants (are fined) one shield; when it is inferior during three consecutive years, the Overseer is fined two suits of armour and he is (permanently) dismissed. When (the weight) is inferior, but no expense is incurred,[3] no fines are to be imposed.

When the imposed[4] annual work is lost before it has been collected and inspected[5] [23], as well when there is a shortage,[6] the Head of the work-squad concerned is fined one shield.

[1] Translating *chung* 重 as "weight" seems preferable to the editors' suggestion that *chung*, read *ch'ung*, should mean "twice" or that *ts'ai shan chung* 采山重 together should stand for "mining".
[2] *Ts'ai shan* 采山.
[3] This is a tentative rendering of *pu fu fei* 不負費. SS translates: "there is no deficiency" (for *fu* = "deficiency" see note 4 to B 22 above), but the usual term for "deficiency, shortage" is *pu pei* 不備, which even occurs in the present article. I therefore believe that *pu fu fei* must have another meaning.
[4] See note 2 to A 64 above.
[5] This is a tentative rendering of *ch'ü hsing* 取省.
[6] *Fu pei* 弗備; on other strips *pu* 不 *pei*.

C 15 W 7.10a; S II.29a; S V.91b–92a; SS 139; str. 24–25 (352–353).

[24] When artisans in selecting posts[1] mark[2] a post that can be used as unfit for use, they are fined two suits of armour. ○ When an artisan marks posts as unfit for use, thwarting[3] the builders,[4] and the builders upon request (still) use it,[5] [25] the artisan who said that they were unfit for use is fined two suits of armour.

[1] *Kan* 榦 (also 幹) are posts used to reinforce a wall of rammed earth.
[2] For *chiu* 久, "to mark", see note 3 to A 47 above.
[3] *Fu* 負 is not only "to carry on the back", but also "to turn the back on", i.e. "to neglect; to repudiate"; I have rendered it here by "thwarting". This seems to me preferable to the forced use of other meanings of *fu* by the editors; S wants it to mean "to repay" and SS renders it by "shortage" (cf. note 4 to B 22 above).
[4] It is evident that *chiu* 久 here cannot have its usual meaning "a long time", nor the technical meaning "to mark". The editors of SS are undoubtedly right when they refer to the *K'ao-kung chi* section of the *Chou-li* under *lu jen* 廬人 (*Chou li* 23/82, p. 83; *Chou-li chu-su* 41.13a (1517); Biot II, p. 552), where *chiu* 灸 (written *chiu* 久 in *SW* when quoting the *Chou-li* pasage) means "to shore; to prop up", namely the boards between which the earth is pounded to make a pisé wall. The term *chiu che* 者 is unknown; I have followed SS in rendering it as "builders".
[5] *Erh* 而, the last word on strip 24, is awkward; SS wants it to mean *nai* 乃, "then, thereupon".

C 16 W 7.10a; S II.29a; S V.92a; SS 140–141; str. 25–27 (353–355).

[25 continued] For hunting[1] tigers, two carriages[2] form a squad.[3] When the tiger has not yet crossed the ....[4] and they pursue[5] him and the tiger turns back,[6] they are fined one suit of armour. [26] When the tiger escapes[7] and they do not catch it, (the occupants of) the carriages are fined one suit of armour. When the tiger is about to attack, the foot-soldiers[8] come out[9] and shoot at it; if they do not catch it, they are fined one suit of armour.

When a leopard escapes[10] and it is not caught, the fine is one shield. ○ The Major of Government Carriages' [27] Statutes of Hunting.[11]

1 *She* 射, lit. "shooting". — Professor Hervouet, *Poète*, pp. 215–236, provides a survey of the royal hunts in ancient China; he notes that the Han histories mention a "tiger enclosure", *hu ch'üan* 虎圈 (*SC* 102.4, Watson, *Records* I, p. 534; *HSPC* 50.1b) in the Shang-lin park.
2 SS translates "two tiger-hunt carriages", referring to *San-kuo chih*, *Wu chih* 7.3a (T'ung-wen edition); there, however, we learn that the emperor of Wu, Sun Ch'üan, had this carriage expecially made so as to enable him to enjoy his favourite sport in comparative safety. I therefore believe that the SS translation is not correct.
3 *Ts'ao* 曹.
4 The text reads *hu wei yüeh* "*chih*" *hsien* 虎未越泛蘚. "*Chih*" 泛 is unknown; the editors suggest that this should be *fan* 泛, "to float", which is an attested loan for *fan* 覂, "to overturn", i.a. in *SC* 9.6 (*Mh* II. p. 411) and *HSPC* 6.30b (*HFHD* II, p. 97). *Hsien* 蘚 is "moss"; SS thinks it is used as a loan for *hsien* 鮮 "fresh or raw meat". The binome—if it is a binome—is unknown, and the editors of S frankly say so; in view of the context, it might indicate some kind of enclosure or obstacle. The editors of SS, however, present the following fallacious solution: 1) *yüeh* 越 would be "to run away", which is nowhere attested; they base this on the meaning "far away" which they found in the (inaccessible) *Hsiao Erh-ya* 小爾雅, but which actually occurs in an untraced passage in the *Kuo yü* (see GSR, p. 92, no. 303); 2) *Fan* 泛 is a loan for *fan* 覂 (accepted, see above), and for the latter word the *Kuang ya* (inaccessible) indicates the meaning *ch'i* 棄, "to discard"; 3) *hsien* 鮮 is "raw meat", but now explained as "bait". With these elements they arrive at the rendering "Before the tiger has thrown away the bait and run away ...", which is unacceptable
5 One of the meanings of *ts'ung* 從 is "to pursue"; I follow SS.
6 *Huan* 環 is an accepted loan for *huan* 還.
7 *Shih* 失 for *i* 佚.
8 *T'u* 徒: the *SW* explanation is "to go on foot".
9 Evidently with the special "tigerhunt carriage" (see note 2 above) in mind, SS has the footsoldiers *ch'u* 出 "come out" of the carriage, although the normal expression for leaving a vehicle is *hsia* 下; moreover, this special carriage had only two occupants, viz. the emperor of Wu and the coachman. It is, of course, impossible to say where the footsoldiers came from; they may have been standing by in an enclosure.
10 According to the editors'decipherment, the text reads *sui* 旞, a kind of banner, decorated with feathers (see Hayashi, "Hata", p. 77 f.), which they take to be a loan for *sui* 遂, explained as "to escape" in *SW*.
11 The Major of Government Carriages, *kung chü ssu-ma* 公車司馬, is mentioned in the commentary to *HSPC* 19A.11b, referring to the (lost) *Han kuan i*; this says that the Major was in charge of the Major's Gate of the palace, that he patrolled the palace grounds at night, and that he took charge of all persons who came to report matters to the throne or who had been summoned.

C 17 W 7.10a–b; SII.29a–b; S V.92a–b; SS 140–141; str. 27–29 (355–357).

[27 continued] When wounding horses of the ruler's carriage,[1] a tear in the skin is fined one shield, for two inches the fine is two shields, for over two inches the fine is one suit of armour. ○ When grading coursers,[2] if after a full year [28][3] from six heads down to one head, the fine is one shield. ○ Stallions[4] are lodged[5] behind the carriage horses; one should not venture to whip[6] them. Transgression of (this) Ordinance is fined one shield. Not to unharness horses that have been running [29] is fined one shield.

1 *Sheng-yü* 乘輿 is a current expression for the ruler. As indicated in SS, the commentator Yen Shih-ku (581–145) explains *sheng-yü ma* as horses of the emperor's carriage (*HSPC* 7.7b, *HFHD* II, p. 167).
2 *K'uai* (or *chüeh*)*-t'i* 駃騠. This binome seems to be late; it is not found in GSR. Its earliest occurrence in literature seems to be in Li Ssu's letter protesting against the expulsion of

aliens from Ch'in, probably written in 237 B.C. (*SC* 87.9; Bodde, *Unifier*, p. 19; for the date see p. 59). Professor Egami sees reasons to identify the *k'uai-t'i* (perhaps *kiwat-*d'ieg, in view of GSR p. 93, no. 312, and p. 228, no. 866) with the so-called Aryan horse from Central Asia, the "blood sweating horse" (see Egami, p. 102); it is not impossible that such horses had been brought to China earlier than 115 B.C. (cf. *CICA*, p. 132 f.). Only one instance of the importation of Hsiung-nu horses seems to be known (*HSPC* 91.5b–6a; Swann, p. 430), but there might easily have been more cases, and the editors of SS may therefore be justified in assuming that the Ch'in used such horses. However, *SW* unexpectedly defines *k'uai-t'i* as "a mule, the offspring of a stallion and a she-ass"; this explanation has been adopted by S.

3 Here either the copyist omitted part of the text, or, what seems more likely, a whole strip is missing. The explanations proffered by the editors are forced and unacceptable; S suggests that the rule concerns insufficient offspring, whereas SS makes it refer to poor training.

4 The expression *chih ma* 志馬 (quite clear on the strip) is unknown. It remains unexplained in S, but SS suggests that *chih* is a loan for *t'e* 特, "stallion", referring to the commentary to the *Chou-li* by Cheng Chung (A.D. 5–85) (*Chou-li chu-su* 33.2b (1180); *Chou-li* 18/62.46; Biot II, p. 256), which is of no help. Karlgren, "Loan characters I", p. 48, nos. 128–131, quotes passages in classical literature where Chinese scholars have suggested that *chih* *t̑i̯əg was used as a loan for words pronounced *śiək, *t̑iək, *tiəg and *dz'iəg, but *t'e* *d'ək is not among these; its pronunciation seems far more different from that of *chih* than the other proposed loans. To me, the expression *chih ma* remains incomprehensible; it could hardly be a scribal error for *mu ma* 牡馬, "male horse".

5 *She* 舍 will have to be taken as a verb, "to lodge".

6 All editions read two hardly legible characters as *ch'ui ch'ih* 炊飭. S leaves *ch'ih* unexplained and takes *ch'ui* literally as "to cook" suggesting that this means that grooms living behind the carriage horses should not cook. SS considers *ch'ui* to be a loan for *chui* 箠, "to whip". For want of a better solution I have followed the translation in SS.

C 18 W 7.10b; S II.29b; S V.93a–b; SS 142; str. 29–30 (357–358).

[29 continued] When the horses of carriages for officials are measured[1] and they (are found to be) morbidly thin,[2] as well as (when the officials concerned) do not meet at the date[3] of the measuring, the fine in both cases is one shield. When the performance[4] of the horses is rated as inferior, the Overseer of the Stables is fined one suit of armour; [30] the Prefect,[5] his Assistant and the assistants and clerks are each fined one shield. When the performance of the horses is rated as inferior, the Overseer of the Corrals is fined one shield.[6]

1 See note 1 to A 7 above.

2 The editors of both S and SS consider *tu* 篤 and *tzu* 犨 as two separate words, and they therefore translate *tu* as "slow moving", following the explanation of *tu* in *SW*, overlooking the fact that the horses upon being *measured* are found to be *tu tzu*. Now *tzu* meaning "emaciated" (see note 5 to A 74 above) fits the verb "to measure", but "slow moving" does not, nor does the usual meaning of *tu*, namely "solid". However, *tu* is also frequently used as a qualification of sickness. In several edicts of emperor Kuang-wu (reigned A.D. 25–57) we find the expression *tu lung* 癃 (*HHSCC* Ann. 1B.1a, 20a, 20b); in the biography of the first empress *née* Teng there is *tu chi* 疾 (*HHSCC* Ann. 10A.16a) and in that of the later empress *née* Teng there occurs *ping chien tu* 病漸篤 (*HHSCC*, Ann. 10A.21b), and finally, in the 4th chapter of the *Shen chien* (p. 20; Ch'en Ch'i-yün, p. 166) we have *tu huan* 患, which Professor Ch'en renders loosely as "chronic diseases". *Tu* can therefore be rendered as "serious(ly); morbid(ly)", qualifying a disease or, as in this case, its symptoms.

3 *Ch'i hui* 期會 are meetings or interviews for which a date has been set; see Lao Kan, *K'ao shih, k'ao cheng*, p. 18; cf. D 143 below.

4 This is a tentative rendering of *lao* 勞.

5 Or the Director; see note 2 to C 13 above.

6 More than half of this strip has been left blank.

C 19 W 7.10b; S II.29b; S V.93b; SS 142–143; str. 31 (359).

[31] When of ten full-grown[1] cows six have no offspring, the Overseer and the Assistant are each fined one shield. ○ When of ten ewes[2] four have no offspring, the Overseer and the assistants are each fined one shield. ○ When cows and sheep are rated. . .[3]

1 *Ta* 大, lit. "big", i.e. "adult".

2 *Yang* 羊, "sheep or goats". *Yang* is more likely to mean sheep than goats, because, as far as I am aware, it is mainly pottery tomb figures of sheep that have been found; see e.g. "Han An-ling", fig. 6 and plate IX. Still, in a late Later Han tomb mural painting, representing a lively kitchen scene, beside an ox and a pig, there is an unmistakable picture of a horned goat; see "Chu-ch'eng", p. 19, ill. 7.

3 I believe that the strip which contained the continuation of the text is missing. There is a black dot before the last words and the editors therefore consider these as a title, "The rating of cows and sheep", but that would be a curious exception, because all other titles contain the word *lü* 律, "statute".

C 20 W 7.10b; S II.29b; S V.93b–94a; SS 143–144; str. 32–33 (360–361).

[32] When they fail to report[1] stalwart youths,[2] as well as when they are careless in registering[3] the disabled,[4] the (village) chief[5] and the elders[6] (are condemned to) redeem (the punishment of) shaving off the beard.[7] ○ When commoners are not warranted to be considered as old,[8] or when they have reached old age not to put in a request,[9] those who venture to engage in deceit[10] [33] will be fined two suits of armour. The (village) chief and the elders who do not denounce this will each be fined one suit of armour, and the members of the group of five[11] (will be fined) one shield per household. All are to be banished. ○ Statutes concerning Enrolment.[12]

1 *Ni* 匿, lit. "to hide".

2 The text has *ao t'ung* 敖童, "loafing youths", evidently young men of service age, whom S wants to identify with the "bad young men", *o shao nien* 惡少年, mentioned in *HSPC* 61.10b (*CICA*, p. 230) as being called up for military service in 102 B.C. The editors also suggest that *ao* might stand for *hao* 勢, "healthy", which is the *SW* explanation; I have adopted this rendering. SS indicates that the term *ao t'ung* is found in Chia I's *Hsin shu* (not accessible), ch. "Ch'un-ch'iu". SS also remarks that in view of the "Chronicle" (SS, p. 6, under *chin yüan nien* 今元年) young men were registered or enrolled at seventeen years of age, but Kao Min, *Ch'u t'an*, pp. 18–24, has demonstrated that this was done at the age of fifteen; see also Kao Heng.

3 *Chan* 占, "to declare", usually for purposes of taxation, as in *HSPC*, 24B.13b, Swann, p. 282.

4 *Lung* 癃, i.e. 癃, "ill; weak". This will be the same as *p'i-lung* 罷癃, used in D 111 below and also found in *HSPC* 24A.21a (Swann, p. 209); this is a general term for "handicapped, disabled", as shown by Hiranaka, "Kō-fu".

5 *Tien* 典 for *li* 里 *tien*; see note 11 to A 7 above.

6 Elders were the traditional leaders of the village and possessed a considerable measure of authority and control; see Moriya, "Furō".

7 Cf. note 6 to C 5 above.

8 In Han times, commoners were freed from conscript duties at the age of sixty (see Kao Min, *Ch'u t'an*, p. 24 f.). The rule evidently means that persons had been removed from the duty roster before they had reached the age of retirement.

9 This seems to indicate that for persons liable for service a request had to be made to remove their name from the rolls when they had reached the required age.

10 The organization of the population in groups of five households is ascribed to Shang Yang; see *SC* 68.7; Duyvendak, *Lord Shang*, p. 14 and cf. p. 58 f. In D 82 below, the "four neighbours" are identified with the members of the group of five, *wu jen* 伍人.

[11] See note 2 to A 100 above.
[12] Cf. note 1 to A 13 above.

C 21 W 7.10b; S II.29b; S V.94b; SS 144–145; str. 34 (362).

[34] When infantry conscripts do not mount guard and the Master of the detail,[1] the corporals and sergeants do not denounce this, they are each fined one shield. When the guards have already gone up to guard the steps,[2] to go down without authorization is fined two suits of armour per person.[3]

[1] For *shu* 署, "a post; to post; to be assigned to a post", see note 1 to A 15 above; in a military sense, *shu* is "a detail; to detail". The present *shu chün-tzu* 署君子 is therefore the Master (for this rendering of *chün-tzu* see note 11 to A 64 above) of the "detail" or squad or group of soldiers. However, in their note to A 64 above the editors of SS state, without any textual basis, that "anciently" a section of the defences was called a *shu*, perhaps inspired by ch. 70 of the *Mo-tzu*, p. 351, which states that a man who unauthorizedly left his *shu* (hence his assigned post) was punished (an actual example is found in *HSPC* 76.21b, where we find an officer being punished for "unauthorizedly leaving his post", *shan li pu shu* 擅離部署). SS therefore concludes that the *shu chün-tzu* was the person responsible for such a section.
[2] According to *SW*, *ch'u* 除 is "the stairway of a palace-hall", *tien pi* 殿陛.
[3] The editors of SS remark that the title of the statute is missing.

C 22 W 7.10b; S II.29b; S V.94b–95a; SS 145–146; str. 35–36 (363–364).

[35] When those assigned for a levy[1] return and the statement[2] is made; "The (number of) days[3] has been[4] completed", whereas the documents[5] have not yet come, (or)[6] these do not agree with the statement, the fine is per day[7] four months[8] station at the frontier. ○ When in the army (rewards) have just been decided[9] concerning an attack on a walled town, and the town has fallen, (but) there still are stragglers[10] [36] who have not arrived at the scene of the fighting, (and who then) report: "I was surrounded in battle, but I broke through[11] and escaped"—if this is false, (they will be punished by) shaving off the beard.[12] If the corporal and the (members of his) squad[13] know this and do not denounce it, they will be fined one suit of armour; the group of five[14] (will be fined) two suits of armour. ○ Statutes for. . . .[15]

[1] *Jung mu* 宂募; for *jung* see note 6 to A 7 above. *Mu* cannot mean "to call up volunteers" as the editors of SS seem to suggest by referring to *HSPC* 69.11a, where *ying* 應 *mu*, "to answer the call for volunteers" occurs.
[2] For *tz'u* 辭, "oral statement", see *RHL*, p. 77.
[3] The editors have corrected *ch'iu* 囚 in *Wenwu* to *jih* 日 (twice).
[4] I have used the perfect because of *i* 已, "already".
[5] Here the editors again take *chih* 致 to mean "document(s)" (cf. note 4 to A 5 above), and again I have followed them for want of a better solution.
[6] The word "or" is necessary, because documents that have not arrived cannot be said to conflict with an oral statement. SS glosses over this difficulty by translating "these circumstances do not agree with the statement by the persons concerned."
[7] The translation in SS neglects the word "day".
[8] *Ssu yüeh* 四月 is written as a single character 胃.
[9] For *lun* 論 see note 5 to E 4 below.
[10] The editors consider *hsi* 棲, lit. "to roost" as a loan for *ch'ih* 遲, "to be slow or late". Although not attested elsewhere, this loan is phonetically possible; see *GSR* p. 158, no. 592 l and p. 160, no. 596d.
[11] All editions read *che* 折, "to break", but I suspect that the characted is *hsi* 析, "to split"; in this connection it is curious, that *SW* does not contain the character 折 but 斨 (see *SWKL*,

p. 445b f.). I take the word literally, in the sense that the man "cut his way out". The editors of SS neglect the difficulties presented by the word order and by *i* 以, translating: "a report says that he was killed in the fighting when the town was surrounded, whereas this was a lie".

12 As in the preceding cases, the hard labour punishment is not mentioned.

13 This must be a group of ten men, *shih wu* 什伍; see Lo K'ai-yu, "Shih-wu", p. 87.

14 *Wu* 伍. I assume that the men of the small group to which the guilty man belonged were punished more heavily than the other group of five which together formed the squad.

15 I do not understand this title. A *t'un* 屯 seems to be another term for a group of five soldiers (see note 7 to C 1 above), but the meaning of *piao* 表 in this context is unclear; in the military organization *piao* were striped sails, used for signalling on the watchtowers (see *RHA* I, p. 86 f., and Hsieh Ying-ch'ün, p. 362).

C 23a W 7.10b; S II.30a; S V.95b; SS 136–147; str. 37–38 (365–366).

[37][1] When someone has died in battle for the service without surrendering,[2] a decision[3] is taken (to reward) his successor.[4] When again later it is shown that he did not die, the successor is divested of the aristocratic rank. The men of his group of five are freed (of punishment).[5] The man who had not died is made a bond-servant on his return.[6]

C 23b

[38] Enemies[7] who surrender are made bond-servants.[8]

1 *Wenwu* has combined strips 37 and 38 to form one article, but S and SS have split the text into two independent articles. Because I follow the arrangement in *Wenwu* I have used the numbering 23a and 23b.

2 *Ssu shih* 死事, "to die in or for the service", viz. of the ruler or of the state; see the commentary by Cheng Hsüan (A.D. 127–200) on this expression in the *Yüeh-ling* chapter of the *Li chi*: *i kuo shih ssu che* 以國事死者 (*Li-chi chu-su* 17.6a (0815); Couvreur, *Li ki* I, p. 392; Legge, *Li ki* 27, p. 298), and the commentary to ch. 24 of the *Kuan-tzu*, p. 146 (this commentary is wrongly attributed to Yin Chih-chang (c. 655–718); see van der Loon, p. 370): *ssu wang shih* 死王事.—The text reads *ch'u* 出 (*t̂'i̯wət); SS suggests that this "should be read *ch'ü* 屈" (*k'i̯wət; see GSR, p. 135, no. 496a and w). This substitution as a loan is not attested; it might simply be a scribal error.

3 For *lun* 論 see note 5 to E 4 below.

4 *Hou* 後, the eldest son of the chief wife.

5 *Ch'u* 除; see note 3 to B 7 above. According to ch. 19 of the *Shang-chün shu*, p. 72 (Duyvendak, *Lord Shang*, p. 296), the four remaining members of a squad of five suffered a mutilating punishment when one of the squad was killed; in the present instance the punishment is evidently not to be carried out. However, SS wants *ch'u* to mean "to punish", but this meaning is nowhere attested; the basic meaning of *ch'u* is "to remove". *Ch'u* is only translated as "to punish" in a commentator's paraphrase of the words *ch'u t'e* 除慝 "to remove evil" in the *Chou-li* (*Chou-li chu-su* 41.2b (1496); *Chou-li* 38/80.32; Biot II, p. 522).

6 The lightest but one of the hard labour punishments in Han times, with a term of three years (*RHL*, p. 130), but see the introduction, p. 15 and note 8.

7 *K'ou* 寇, lit. "invader; robber".

8 This stipulation signifies that enemies who surrendered were enslaved or condemned to several years' hard labour; in view of the continual wars, this must have meant a constant supply of unfree labour. Professor Wilbur has discussed the question whether in the Han period prisoners of war were enslaved, tentatively concluding that *some* captives may have been made slaves (Wilbur, pp. 98–117); he rightly stresses (p. 102 f.) the difference between prisoners of war and troops who surrendered voluntarily like the Hsiung-nu king of Hun-yeh and his tribe in 121 B.C. Here it should be noted that under the Han, enemies were practically without exception alien tribes, whereas the Ch'in wars were mainly fought against Chinese. We ignore the further fate of the men who surrendered to the Ch'in; it is hardly to be expected that they were eventually sent home. The editors of SS adduce the passage

in *SC* 120.10 (rather freely translated in Watson, *Records* II, p. 350; *HSPC* 50.12a, Wilbur, pp. 220–222) about Chi Yen's suggestion that the surrendered horde of the Hun-yeh should be enslaved.

C 24 W 7.10b; S II.30a; S V.95b; SS 147; str. 38–39 (366–367).

[38 continued] The Statute concerning the Arrest of Robbers says: "Those who transfer arrested persons to another in order to receive aristocratic rank[1] (are condemned to) shaving off the beard.[2] ○ Thief-catchers must not be ordered (to act as escorts for) seeing off or welcoming (important visitors) or to perform other (tasks)[3]; those who order them to see off or welcome (visitors) or to perform other [39] tasks will be fined two suits of armour.

1 This must be distinct from the practice of rewarding the capture of enemies by the bestowal of aristocratic rank. For rewards in money see D 112–119 below.
2 The essential hard labour punishment is not specified. In D 117 below a rank-holding official and his partner who had committed this offence are fined two suits of armour.
3 Whereas the preceding five words are accompanied by the repetition marker, the scribe forgot to add this sign to the word *shih* 事 which stands at the beginning of a new strip.

C 25 W 7.10b; S II.30a; S V.96a; SS 147–148; str. 39 continued (367).

[39 continued] The Statute concerning Military Service says: "Members of the same household[1] are not to be levied simultaneously. When the Prefectural Overseer,[2] the Commandant as well as the sergeant major make levies for military service not in accordance with the Statutes, they are fined two suits of armour."

1 Cf. note 15 to A 41 above.
2 See note 5 to A 19 above.

C 26 W 7.10b; S II.30a; S V.96b; SS 148; str. 40–42 (368–370).

[40] When men in military service build as well as repair walls, they are made to guarantee[1] the sections (of wall)[2] for one year. If parts of the walls they have built collapse, the Masters[3] of the Prefectural Controller of Works who have been detailed[4] to lead (these men) are each fined one suit of armour; the Prefectural Controller of Works' [41] Assistant in charge of the leaders[5] is fined one shield. The men in military service should be ordered to exert themselves in repairing the walls; when detailing them they must not be ordered to perform other tasks. When the repairs are finished, they must be ordered to heighten the defences[6] and to reinforce[7] the defences. The Prefectural [42] Commandant constantly goes around to inspect their work[8] as well as what they are doing. When somebody ventures to order them to perform other tasks,[9] the person who has made them do so[10] is fined two suits of armour.

1 See note 8 to A 64 above; the two rules are partly parallel.
2 See note 9 to A 64 above.
3 See note 11 to A 64 above.
4 See note 2 to C 21 above.
5 As indicated in note 4 to A 15 above, *chu* 主 is "to be in charge of work", whereas *chiang* 將 is "to be in charge of men". In the present case, the meaning of the combination of the two terms seems to be that given in the translation.

[6] For *sai* 塞 meaning "(border) defence works" see Lao Kan, "T'ing chang", pp. 510–512.

[7] I have followed the explanation in SS for *tseng* 增 as "to increase in height" and *p'i* 埤 as "to increase in thickness" (the *Erh-ya* says that *p'i* is *hou* 厚); in *HSPC* 36.23b the two words are combined: *tseng p'i wei kao* 增埤爲高, leading to a different translation: "to increase what is low to make it high" (namely emperor Ch'eng's Chang-ling tomb), where Yen Shih-ku (581–645) explains *p'i* as *hsia* 下.

[8] The text has *kung* 攻 for *kung* 功.

[9] Cf. Kao Heng, p. 534.

[10] *Shih* 使, "to cause to do"; see *RHL*, pp. 268–270.

GROUP D

The texts belonging to the fourth group of strips, called by the editors *Ch'in lü ta wen* 秦律答問, "Answers to questions about the Ch'in Statutes", consist of 190 articles (D1–D190) in the division adopted in *Wenwu* 1976/8 and followed here. The 210 strips have a length of c. 25.3 cm. or 1 foot 1 inch Ch'in-Han measure; they were held together by three sets of strings: at the top, in the middle and at the bottom. Each article starts on a new strip, with the result that many strips are only partly inscribed; strips fully covered with writing contain forty characters or a few more. The end of a sentence is sometimes marked by a black dot, signalized in the translation by a small circle. The handwriting is small and crabbed, most characters being 0.3–0.4 cm. high; little space has been left between the signs. According to CM, p. 74, the strips had been placed to the right of the thorax.

D 1 W 8.27a; S II.32a; S V.98a; SS 150–151; str. 1–2 (371–372).

[1][1] When wardens[2] go by different paths[3] to steal, their punishment is increased.[4] What[5] is the meaning of "the punishment is increased?" ○ When five[6] men commit robbery and the illicit profit[7] is one cash or more, amputate their left foot[8] and tattoo them and make them *ch'eng-tan*. When they are not fully five men and what they rob exceeds 660[9] cash, [2] tattoo them, slice off their nose[10] and make them *ch'eng-tan*. (In case the illicit profit is) not fully 660 cash, down to 220 cash, tattoo them and make them *ch'eng-tan*; (if it is) not fully 220 cash, banish them. Thief-catchers[11] are assimilated[12] to this rule.

1 This article, as well as many of the following ones, starts with a quotation from a statute. The title of the statute is sometimes mentioned, sometimes the single word *lü* 律, "the Statute (says)" is used, but in most cases it is the context which shows that the text contains a quotation. This context consists of one or more questions concerning the meaning of the quotation, followed by one or more replies.

2 The editors are right in reading the first, badly preserved character on the strip as *hai* 害; here, as well as on strip 3, *hai* is written 𡧢, a form which also occurs in Han inscriptions; see *HLTY*, *ch'ü-sheng* 25b. However, this *hai tao* 盜 is not an "evil robber" (note that *tao* is used both for theft and for robbery, "despoiling a person of property by violence" according to *The Concise Oxford Dictionary*), comparable to the *ch'iang tao* 彊盜 in *HHSCC*, Mem. 36.11b (cf. *HLCI* 2.8b) or the *ch'iang tsei* 强賊 in *CS* 30.11a (Uchida, p. 107 and note 8), but he is identical with the *hsien* 憲 *tao* mentioned in A 103 above; this is also clear from the last line of this article and from D 2 below, where the (*hai*, correctly) *hsien tao* is assimilated to the well-known *ch'iu tao*, "thief catcher". The substitution of *hai* for *hsien* must be sought in an ideosyncracy or a mistake of the scribe; it is not a phonetic loan, as suggested by the editors of SS in their note to A 103 above (SS, p. 107). That *hai* is not the phonetic element of *hsien* had been indicated by Chinese scholars several centuries ago (see *SWKL* 4662a–b); the impossibility of such a loan is shown by the ancient pronunciation of the two words: *hai* was *g'ad, whereas *hsien* was *χi̯an (GSR, p. 80, no. 250a, and p. 94, no. 314a).

3 The text reads *pieh chiao* 別徼. SS says that *pieh* is "to be read as" *pei* 背, "the back; to turn the back on". Phonetically this is impossible, for *pieh* was *b'i̯at or *b'i̯ät, whereas *pei* was *pwəg or *b'wəg (GSR, p. 89, no. 292a, and p. 241, no. 909e). Such a loan is

nowhere attested. Only in *SWKL* 1725a I found that the *SWTHTS* quotes a commentary to the *Li sao* in the "Elegies of Ch'u", the *Ch'u tz'u* (inaccessible), where *pieh,* evidently meaning "to part from", is said to be "like (*yu* 猶) *pei.*" But this seems absurd here. For the contrary suggestion that *pei* should stand for *pieh* see note 1 to D 154 below.—*Chiao* the editors of SS consider to be an abbreviation of *yu* 游 *chiao,* "rural constable" (see *HSPC* 19A.30a; Bielenstein, *Bureaucracy,* p. 100, "patrol leader"), because in *SC* 30.37 the commentator Ju Shun explains the single word *chiao* in this manner (*Mh* III, p. 590, "patrouille"; *HSPC* 24B.17b, Swann, p. 303, "patrol service"). In their translation the editors of SS therefore render *pieh chiao* by "they turn their back on the rural constables". Still, in a further note they say that another possibility would be to explain *pieh* as "separate" and *chiao* as "to patrol". To me this seems to be the correct interpretation, with one possible modification: *chiao* can also mean "path, road" according to some scholars, refuted by others (see Morohashi, vol. 4, p. 933, no. 10261, *sub* 5).

4 *Chia* 駕 is used for *chia* 加.

5 Here, as well as in numerous other passages, the text reads *k'o* 可 for *ho* 何.

6 It is not known, how many persons constituted a band. Perhaps already three men were a band, in view of *Han Fai-zu,* ch. 30, p. 162 (Liao I, p. 287): *san jen tsu i wei chung i* 三人足以爲衆矣. Many centuries later, in the new Chin laws of A.D. 234, it was also three men (*CS* 30.15b; Uchida, p. 129); according to the Han statute quoted in note 2 to A 6 above, three persons already constituted a crowd. However, the number five mentioned here may indicate that in Ch'in law a band consisted of five persons; in E 12 below the band of robbers described there also had five members.

7 *Tsang* 臧 stands for *tsang* 贓, the profit obtained from any illegal act: theft, robbery, extortion, embezzlement, fraud, bribery. The term occurs frequently in the following articles; it is also found in the Edsin-gol documents, e.g. *tsang erh pai wu shih i shang* 臧二百五十以上 (Lao Kan, *K'ao shih,* p. 148, no. 7222 (434) 229.1 and 2).

8 *Chan tso chih* 斬左止 (for 趾). Until the middle of the 2nd century B.C. the so-called mutilating punishments included amputation of the left foot, and amputation of the right foot, i.e. both the left and the right. Hu Hou-hsüan has devoted an article to the historical development of this punishment since high antiquity; see also *RHL,* p. 125. The texts uniformly write *chih* 止, i.e. *chih* 趾, "foot". It is unknown how this cruel punishment was applied. I have at least never seen archaeological reports mentioning the discovery of skeletons showing this kind of mutilation, and so I do not know whether the foot was cut off above the ankle or whether the forepart was hacked off near the instep. I have no taste for grisly details, but the question is of some importance, because the victims who survived had to perform hard labour as *ch'eng-tan.* A few passages in early literature give the impression that it was the front part of the foot which was severed, because they mention special foot-wear for amputated men, *yung* 踴 or 踊 (*Chuang-tzu,* p. 33; Legge, *Chuang-tzu* 39, p. 228; *Han Fei-tzu* 15/37, p. 273; Liao II, p. 157; *Tso chuan* Duke Chao 3, with Tu Yü's commentary, 42.6a (1685); Couvreur, *Tch'ouen-ts'iou* III, p. 57).

9 In the present rule as well as in some of the following articles, values are expressed in multiples of eleven; see note 1 to A 44 above.

10 For this punishment see *RHL,* p. 125.

11 *Ch'iu tao* 求盜; see *HSPC* 1A.6a, *HFHD* I, p. 33 and note 2.

12 *Pi* 比, lit. "to compare", are "comparable cases"; cf. *RHL,* p. 48, no. 3.

D 2 W 8.27a; S II.32a; S V.98b; SS 151–152; str. 3 (373).

[3] When thief-catchers rob, they warrant a mutilating punishment[1] and being made *ch'eng-tan.* Question: does (their) punishment warrant increasing, as for wardens,[2] or does it not warrant this? It is warranted.[3]

1 Cf. note 11 to A 68 above.

2 Explained in D 1 above.

3 Cf. the last sentence in D 1.

D 3 W 8.27a; S II.32a; S V.99a; SS 152; str. 4 (374).

[4] A plots to send[1] B out to steal. One day, B is about to go and steal, but

before he arrives, he is caught. Both (A and B) are to redeem[2] tattooing.[3]

[1] *Ch'ien* 遣; cf. the Han time expressions *shih* 使, "to cause" and *chiao* 教 *shih*, "to instruct and to cause"; see *RHL*, p. 265.
[2] It deserves notice that persons could be condemned to redemption; cf. my "Legalists", p. 15, and p. 18 of the introduction.
[3] Namely tattooing and being made a *ch'eng-tan*. As in the many cases where the punishment mentioned is "shaving off the beard", the hard-labour punishment is omitted, as being understood.

D 4 W 8.27a; S II.32a; S V.99a; SS 152–153; str. 5 (375).

[5] Somebody's slave[1] A plots to send this person's[2] female slave[3] to steal (their) master's ox; they sell[4] (it) and, taking[5] the money, together they flee the country. When leaving the border they are caught. How should each of them be sentenced? They warrant (the hard-labour punishment) *ch'eng-tan*; tattoo them. Each is to be given back[6] to their master.

[1] *Jen ch'en* 人臣. For *ch'en* and *ch'ieh* 妾 being slaves see note 6 to A 65 above.
[2] Again *jen* 人.
[3] See note 1.
[4] *Mai* 買 for *mai* 賣.
[5] The use of *pa* 把 deserves notice.
[6] Presumably on the completion of their term of hard labour.—In these texts, *pi* 畀 is not simply "to give, to bestow", but "to give back; to return", viz. to the original owner of goods or slaves; see D 20, 59, 62, 147, 172.

D 5 W 8.27a; S II.32a; S V.99b; SS 153–154; str. 6 (376).

[6] A steals an ox; at the time he stole the ox he was 6 feet[1] tall. Having been held in detention[2] for one year, he was measured[3] again; he was 6 ft. 7 in.[4] tall. Question: how is A to be sentenced? He warrants being made an intact *ch'eng-tan*.[5]

[1] About 1 m. 40.
[2] The text writes *ch'i* 毄 for *chi* 繫; this implies detention in gaol, see *RHL*, p. 74.
[3] *Chang* 丈, a length of ten feet; the word is also used for measuring land, but here it is evidently used for measuring the height of a person.
[4] C. 1 m. 57. According to A 12 above, bond-servants and *ch'eng-tan* whose height was not fully 6 ft. 5 in. (slightly over 1 m. 50) were considered "small", i.e. below the qualification for enrolment as adults. "A" was evidently a youth.
[5] As he did not suffer a mutilating punishment—unlike the persons mentioned in D 4 above—A's size, i.e. his age, at the time of the theft were taken into consideration. This shows that the Ch'in already had a rule similar to that of the T'ang and later dynasties, which stipulated that "when at the time of the transgression (the culprit) was young and small, and at the time of the discovery he is an adult, he is to be condemned according to (the provisions for) the young and small"; see *RHL*, p. 62 and note 83.

D 6 W 8.27a; S II.32a; S V.100a; SS 154; str. 7 (377).

[7] Someone stealthily picks another's mulberry leaves; the illicit profit is not fully one cash. How is he to be sentenced? He is to be fined three decades' statute labour.

D 7 W 8.27a; S II.32a; S V.100a; SS 154; str. 8 (378).

[8] A robber-guard[1] steals 110 cash, (but) previous (to being discovered) he

voluntarily[2] denounces himself. How is he to be sentenced? He is warranted to have his beard shaved off and to be made a bond-servant[3]; another opinion is[4]: he is to be fined two suits of armour.[5]

[1] In Han times, robber-guards were persons condemned to two years' hard labour. They must have had a special status, for A 65 above shows that they could be placed in charge of twenty *ch'eng-tan*, whereas A 71 forbids their use as cooks or menials. Still, they also had to perform hard labour as is shown by A 15, where we observe them building pisé walls together with *ch'eng-tan*, and by the Later Han brick markers, placed on the graves of convict labourers who had died on the work site (see Wu Jung-tsung).

[2] *Tzu* 自; not so much "personally" as "of his own accord; spontaneously".

[3] In Han times: three years' hard labour.

[4] *Huo yüeh* 或曰, "some say".

[5] The relation between the two punishments is not clear. For persons who performed labour in order to pay off a fine, the value of one day's work was 8 cash, or, in case they received rations, 6 cash (see A 68 above). If the Ch'in bond-servant also had to perform hard labour for three years (see note 3), this would be equivalent to c. 1100 days at 6 cash, or 6600 cash. But this sum cannot be equivalent to the value of two suits of armour, if the value of one single shield was already 5000 cash, as suggested in my "Ch'in documents", p. 211.

D 8 W 8.27a–b; S II.32a; S V.100a; SS 154–155; str. 9 (379).

[9] A steals; the illicit profit is worth[1] one thousand cash.[2] B, knowing that he had stolen, accepts part of the illicit profit (worth) not fully one cash. Question: how is B to be sentenced? He is to be sentenced in the same way as A[3].

[1] *Chih* 直 for *chih* 值.

[2] The text clearly reads *ch'ien* 千; confusion with *shih* 十, "ten", is excluded.

[3] Here the circumstance that B had not denounced A as a thief will have been of importance; cf. D 9.

D 9 W 8.27b; S II.32b; S V.100b; SS 155; str. 10 (380).

[10] A steals (to the value of) not fully one cash. He goes to B's house; B is not aware of it (viz. the theft). Question: how is B to be sentenced? Do not sentence him. In case he has observed and known it, but he has not arrested him, he is warranted to be fined one shield.

D 10 W 8.27b; S II.32b; S V. 100b; SS 155–156; str. 11 (381).

[11] A steals money and uses it to buy silk. He entrusts this to B, and B accepts it, not knowing that it was stolen. How is B to be sentenced? Do not sentence him.

D 11 W 8.27b; S II.32b; S V.100b; SS 156; str. 12 (382).

[12] A and B never[1] knew[2] each other. A goes to rob C. When he has just[3] arrived, B also comes to rob C. He talks with A and thereupon both steal. The illicit profit is worth[4] 400 (cash) for each. When they have already left, they are both arrested. If they had plotted beforehand, they are warranted to be sentenced for the combined illicit profit;[5] if they had not plotted, each is to be adjudicated for the illicit profit (he had personally acquired).[6]

1 *Ya pu* 雅不.
2 *Chih* 智 for *chih* 知.
3 The editors decipher this character—illegible to me—as *ch'an* 毚 which they identify with *ts'ai* 纔, of which *ch'an* forms the "phonetic element"; although the loan is not attested, it is undoubtedly correct, because it exactly fits the context.
4 *Chih* 直 for *chih* 值.
5 *Tsang* 臧 for *tsang* 贓.
6 It seems to me that the scribe omitted *ch'i* 其, "his", before *tsang*.

D 12 W 8.27b; S II.32b; S V.101a; SS 156; str. 13 (383).

[13] An artisan steals, taking (the stolen goods) out; the illicit profit is not fully one cash. Are the men of his group[1] warranted to be bastinadoed[2] or are they not warranted? They are not warranted to be bastinadoed.

1 *Ts'ao* 曹; cf. note 4 to C 11 above.
2 *Chih* 治 for *ch'ih* 笞; *chih* may mean "to try", but then its object is always a lawsuit, a case, and not a person.

D 13 W 8.27b; S II.32b; S V.101a–b; SS 157; str. 14 (384).

[14] A husband steals one thousand cash and hides three hundred in his wife's place.[1] How is the wife to be sentenced? In case the wife hid them, knowing[2] that her husband had stolen them, she is warranted to be sentenced for the three hundred;[3] it is a case[4] of theft. If she did not know it, it is a case of "holding".[5]

1 *Suo* 所, "place", indicating the wife's quarters, is used in a similar way on strips 14 and 25 of a lawsuit of A.D. 28; see my "Lawsuit", pp. 27 and 28.
2 *Chih* 智 for *chih* 知.
3 And not for the full thousand. The stipulations of D 1 above show clearly that the gravity of the punishment depended on the amount of the illicit profit.
4 For this rendering of *wei* 爲 see note 5.
5 The text reads *wei shou* 爲收. Because *shou* often means "to arrest" (it is e.g. the only meaning indicated in *SW*), the editors of S explain *shou* as "to be 'confiscated' as a member of the offender's family and to be made a government slave". But this explanation disregards several points. In the first place, the woman is not to be co-adjudicated (*lien tso* 連坐 as the editors put it) for her husband's crime, but on her own account. Secondly, the editors neglect the word *wei* 爲. And thirdly, the same construction is found in this very article (*wei tao* 爲盜 above) and in the next, D 14 (not explained in S). In D 14 it is said of the wife who ignored that her husband was a thief: *wei shou tsang* 爲守臧, and to me this can only mean "this is (a case of) guarding (or keeping or preserving) illicit profit". In none of these cases a verdict is mentioned; perhaps it can be assumed that the code contained stipulations on these points, which both appear to deal with receiving stolen goods, The difference between *shou* 收, "holding", and *shou* 守, "guarding" stolen property is not clear to me. I was glad to see that the editors of SS had arrived at a similar conclusion.—For the different aspects of meaning of *shou* 收 see note 10 to A 41 above.

D 14 W 8.27b; S II.32b; S V.101b; SS 157–158; str. 15–16 (385–386).

[15] A husband steals 300 cash. He informs his wife, and his wife together with him drinks and eats it.[1] How is the wife to be sentenced? If there had been no previous plotting,[2] this is to be considered as a case of "holding".[3] If they had previously plotted, (she is to receive) the same punishment[4] (as her husband). A husband steals 200 cash and hides 110 cash in his wife's place. How is the wife to be sentenced? If she knew that her husband [16] had stolen them

this is to be considered as a case of theft.[5] If she did not know it, is a case of "guarding illicit profit."[6]

[1] I.e. they spend the money on food and drink.
[2] *Ch'ien mou* 前謀; cf. *RHL*, p. 265: "the accent is on the planning, not on the undertaking." See also D 60 below.
[3] See note 3 to D 13 above.
[4] Cf. D 18 below.
[5] See note 3 to D 13 above.
[6] See note 3 to D 13 above. SS suggests that, because the share kept by the wife is proportionately larger, this might be considered *shou* 守 and punished more severely than *shou* 收.

D 15 W 8.27b; S II.32b; S V.101b–102a; SS 158; str. 17 (387).

[17] On an earlier occasion[1] (somebody) stole (goods, where) the illicit profit had a value[2] of 110 cash. His wife and children, knowing this, ate meat together with him; they are warranted (to suffer) the same punishment.[3]

[1] The editors of S say that they do not understand *ch'ien tao* 前盜, which recurs in D 16 below. To me, the meaning is doubtful; does it imply that the thief proved to be a recidivist? SS and CM, however, read the hardly legible first character as *hsiao* 削; SS takes it as a loan for *hsiao* 宵, "night", which is possible (see GSR, p. 296, no. 1149; both *siog). But it is to be noted that in E 22 and 23 below *hsiao* 宵 is used for "night".
[2] *Chih* 直 for *chih* 值.
[3] Cf. D 18 below.

D 16 W 8.27b–28a; SII.32b; S V.102a; SS 158–159; str. 18 (388).

[18] On an earlier occasion[1] (somebody) stole (goods, where) the illicit profit had a value of 150 cash. He informed A, and A together with his wife and children, knowing[2] (that the other man was a thief) together (with the thief)[3] ate meat. A's wife and children (are to suffer) the same punishment as A.[4]

[1] See note 1 to D 15 above.
[2] *Chih* 智 for *chih* 知.
[3] *Kung* 共, "in common with".
[4] Cf. D 18 below. The punishment is not indicated. A will have been punished because he had not informed the authorities that the other man was a thief, and because he had received a share of the thief's booty.

D 17 W 8.28a; S II.33a; S V.102a; SS 159; str. 19 (389).

[19] A father stealing from his children is not a case of theft. ○ Now a foster father steals from his foster children. How is he to be sentenced? It is warranted to be considered a case of theft.

D 18 W 8.28a; S II.33a; S V.102a–b; SS 159–160; str. 20–21 (390–391).

[20] The Statutes say "the same rules as for theft"; they also say "the same punishment as". These are two (different) things.[1] When his (i.e. the culprit's) household members,[2] the (village) chief[3] and (the members of his) group of five are warranted to be adjudicated for his (crime), this is called "the same punishment as". When (the Statutes) say: "reverse the punishment,"[4] they are not warranted to be adjudicated.[5] ○ When a person's slave or slave-woman rob their master's father [21] or mother, is this 'robbing one's master',

or is it not? If they (i.e. the parents) are household members, it is 'robbing one's master'; if they are not household members, it is not 'robbing one's master'.

[1] The text reads *wu* 物; cf. note 2 to A 52 above. SS translates similarly "two types of crimes". For a similar use of *wu* see the chapter *Wen wang shih-tzu* 文王世子 in the *Li-chi* (*Li-chi chu-su* 20.9a (0949); Couvreur, *Li-ki* I, p. 477; Legge, *Li-ki* 27, p. 352).
[2] See note 15 to A 41 above.
[3] See note 5 to C 20 above.
[4] To reverse the punishment means that the accuser receives the punishment laid down for the crime of which he had falsely accused another person; see my "Lawsuit", p. 25.
[5] This must mean that in case of false accusation of a crime resulting in the co-adjudication of the culprit's household, the members of the false accuser's household were not to be co-adjudicated.

D 19 W 8.28a; S II.33a; S V.103a; SS 160; str. 22 (392).

[22] (The Statutes say)[1] "Robbery and all[2] other crimes where 'those who dwell together'[3] are warranted to be adjudicated". What is the meaning of 'those who dwell together?' The household is (meant by) 'those who dwell together'. Servants[4] are (co-)adjudicated, (but) for servants' (crimes) the household is not (co-)adjudicated;[5] that is the meaning.

[1] The following sentence is a quotation, which has to be explained; it is evidently a passage in a statute.
[2] *Che* 者 for *chu* 諸.
[3] *T'ung chü* 同居. In the forgoing articles I have translated this term as "household members", but in consideration of the following question I have rendered it literally.
[4] *Li* 隸, "dependents". This is a general term which will have included unfree personnel, and perhaps persons of commoner status.
[5] The editors of both S and SS maintain the very opposite, namely that "anciently" servants were not adjudicated for their masters' crimes, whereas masters had to suffer for their servants! To support this weird contention (easily refuted, if merely by a reference to Ch'u Shih-pin, briefiy noted in my "Rebels", p. 318), the editors of SS refer to *HSPC* 92.14b (Watson, *Courtier*, pp. 243–244; Wilbur, pp. 458–459). There we do find that a master was arrested in connection with a crime committed by his slave, who had run away. The context clearly shows that this was a pretext used to get rid of a notorious trouble maker; moreover, the prefect who had the master arrested, released him after he had apologized for his slave's crime—a procedure which would have been impossible, if the master had been legally responsible.

D 20 W 8.28a; S II.33a; S V.103a; SS 160–161; str. 23–24 (393–394).

[23] (The Statutes say)[1] "When a robber robs somebody and he sells[2] what he has robbed, thereby buying other things, all are given back to the owner (of the stolen goods)". Now a robber steals A's clothes; he sells these, and thereby buys cloth,[3] and he is caught. Is it warranted to take the clothes as well as the cloth and give these back (to A), or is this not warranted? It is warranted to take the cloth as well as other things which he has bought and [24] give these back to A; the clothes are not warranted (to be returned).[4]

[1] See note 1 to D 19 above.
[2] *Mai* 買 for *mai* 賣.
[3] In view of the following sentence, the editors are right in considering the following *i* 衣 to be an intrusion.
[4] This exegesis seems to protect the unsuspecting buyer of A's clothes.

D 21 W 8.28a; S II.33a; S V.103b; SS 161–162; str. 25–26 (395–396).

[25] "When the official[1] sacrifice[2] is not yet over,[3] stealing the preparations[4] warrants a fine. . . .[5], having the beard shaved off and being made a bond servant."[6] Now somebody steals[7]; he steals a kidney, and the illegal profit[8] of one kidney is not fully one cash. How is he to be sentenced? In sacrifices one uses, of course[9], hearts and kidneys as well as other joints[10]; all these are each one preparation. When the illegal profit of one preparation is not [26] fully one cash, stealing it warrants shaving off the beard.[11] It may have a value[12] of twenty cash, but it is only partly[13] stolen, and so it is not completely one preparation; (for such a theft) as well as for stealing "incorrect"[14] ones, one is condemned according to the Statutes.[15]

1 In these texts *kung* 公 mostly means "official; government . ."; it does not seem to refer to the duke of Ch'in, except in D 109 below, where the tombs of two former dukes are mentioned. However, because in D 23 below the expression "sacrifices of the Royal House", *wang shih ssu* 王室祠, is found, the editors of SS and Professor Li Hsüeh-ch'in, "Mo-tzu", p. 334, suggest that the present article D 21 might be early, belonging to a time when the Ch'in rulers had not yet adopted the title of *wang* 王, "king". According to *SC* 5.58 (as corrected by the great pre-modern *SC* specialist Liang Yü-sheng (1745–1819); not utilized in *Mh* II, p. 70) the change in title took place in 325 B.C.

2 *Ssu* 祠. SS refers to *SC* 28.21f. (*Mh* III, p. 432 f.; *HSPC* 25A. 10b f.) for an enumeration of Ch'in sacrifices.

3 The fourth character on strip 25 (which recurs in D 22, strip 27 below), the editors, rather surprisingly, decipher as *ch'iao* 闕, which, according to the *Kuang yün* (inaccessible), means "wide open doors." This the editors brilliantly take to be a mistake for *ch'üeh* 闋. *SW* explains this word as "to close the doors when the affair (i.e. sacrifice) is finished"; it is used in the chapter *Wen-wang shih tzu* 文王世子 in the *Li chi* in the sentence "(the music) is finished" (*Li-chi chu-su* 20.15b (0962); Couvreur, *Li ki* I, p. 492; Legge, *Li ki* 27, p. 361). In D 22 below the significance of *ch'üeh* is explained in detail.

4 *Chü* 具 is explained in *SW* as *kung chih* 共 (i.e. 供) 置, "to set down as an offering", and in the commentary by Cheng Hsüan (A.D. 127–200) as *suo kung chung wu* 所共 (i.e. 供) 衆物, "all objects that are offered" (*Li-chi chu-su* 49.2a (1987); Couvreur, *Li-ki* II, p. 321, wrongly "ustensiles"; Legge, *Li-ki* 28, p. 238, "things necessary for the service"). With this specific meaning of "sacrificial item", *chü* occurs frequently in the *Han shu* treatise on sacrifices; see *HSPC* 25A.14a, 15a, 17a, 19a–b, 25a, 27a, 32b, 33b, and 25B.1b, 2a, 5b, 14a. Both *HSPC* 68.6a and 86.10b show that during the Han these items were furnished by the Ch'ang-an Kitchen (for this office see *HSPC* 19a.21a and Bielenstein, *Bureaucracy*, p. 88). The Edsin-gol strips furnish a concrete example; under the caption *tui ssu chü* 對祠具 there are listed: 1 chicken, two *tou* of wine, 1 *tou* of barley, 1 *tou* of millet and 1/3 *sheng* of salt (see Lao Kan, *K'ao shih*, p. 13, no. 586 (29) 10.39; *Chia pien*, no. 99). *Chü* occurs frequently in the lists of funerary goods, *ch'ien ts'e* 遣策, but there it has the usual meaning of "a set" (*Ma-wang tui* I, p. 148, no. 236; Ch'en Chen-yü, p. 37 f.). Even the special tomb-chamber, the outer wall of piled up timber (*huang ch'ang t'i-ts'ou* 黃腸題湊, for which see Lu Ch'i, "Ta-pao-t'ai") and the cedar beams used for the burial of the regent Huo Kuang in 68 B.C. were all called *chü* (*HSPC* 68.11b).

5 I suspect that the scribe has omitted several characters, because *tzu i hsia* 貲以下 makes no sense; the amount of the fine is missing. *I hsia* may have been preceded by the indication of a certain rank. The editors do not remark on this; SS translates "if it is a crime to be punished by a fine or less", which makes no sense either.

6 This first sentence doubtless is a quotation from the statutes concerning the theft of sacrificial meat.

7 I fully agree with the editors that *i* 益, clearly legible on the strip, is a copyist's mistake for *tao* 盜. A similar mistake is found in *SC* 123.36; see my "Authenticity", pp. 115 and 120.

8 *Tsang* 臧 for *tsang* 贜.

9 *Ku* 固; perhaps better "always"?

10 *Chih* 支 for *chih* 肢, "limbs, members".

11 The accompanying hard labour punishment is not mentioned, but SS suggests that this was "being made a bond-servant", as mentioned in the first sentence of this article.

12 *Chih* 直 for *chih* 值.

13 Cf. note 29 to A 19 above.

14 The text writes *pu chih* 不直. The editors of SS assume that the scribe has used *chih* 直 and *chih* 置 indiscriminately, with the meaning of the latter character, viz. "to place", and more specifically "to place sacrifices before the spirits or gods", as is made clear in D 22 below. They translate *wei chih chi pu chih che* 未置及不直者 as "objects that have not yet been set out as well as objects that have not been prepared for setting out.". However, the ritual handbooks show that the animals and the pieces of meat were inspected before being offered in sacrifice; cf. *I-li*, ch. *t'e sheng* 特牲 (*I-li chu-su* 44.5b (1280); Steele II, p. 131), *Li-chi*, *Yüeh-ling*, *chung ch'iu* (*Li-chi chu-su* 16.12b (0774), Couvreur, *Li-ki* I, p. 380 f.; Legge, *Li-ki* 27, p. 288; and *Chou-li*, *t'ien kuan*, *nei yung* 內饔 (*Chou-li chu-su* 4.6b (0140); Biot I, p. 131). I suppose that during this inspection certain pieces were rejected as being "incorrect". *Pu chih* meaning "incorrect" in a general sense occurs in an edict of emperor Wu of c. 134 B.C. (*HSPC* 56.3a).

15 The punishments were graded according to the value of the "illicit profit."

D 22 W 8.28a; S II.33a; S V.104a; SS 162; str. 27 (397).

[27] What is the meaning of "the sacrifice is not yet over?"[1] When the beakers and stands that have been placed before the spirits have not yet been removed—that is "(the sacrifice) is not yet over". (Sacrifices) not yet placed (before the spirits) as well as those that are "incorrect"[2] do not constitute a "preparation"; they must already have been placed (before the spirits) and only then they are preparations.

1 See note 3 to D 21 above.

2 Cf. note 14 to D 21 above.

D 23 W 8.28a; S II.33b; S V.104a; SS 163; str. 28 (398).

[29] What is the meaning of "thievishly digging in a pit?"[1] At the sacrifices of the Royal House, the preparations[2] are buried; this is meant by "pit".

1 Neither 埾 nor 𢈈 is to be found in the dictionaries, but *ch'u* 埱 and *ya* or *yai* 厓, often written 涯 or 崖, are. According to *SW*, the former is "vapours arising from the soil", whereas the latter is a river edge or a cliff. The editors believe, that *ch'u* must mean "to dig", for that is the meaning of the same character in E 22 below. S states that *yai* is "a square pit", but this is not supported. SS suggests that 𢈈 *yai* might stand for *kui* 圭. Besides "jade sceptre" *kui* can mean "pure" (see Karlgren, "Glosses Siao-ya", p. 36. no. 426); with this meaning *kui* is found in the *I li* (34.6b (1252); Steele II, p. 125). Having stated this, the editors of of SS then say "therefore, in the present article the buried offerings are called *kui*" (which is wrong, for *kui* is "pure" and not "offerings"), but they translate "they bury the offerings; this is called *kui*", which is neither logical nor correct. It is also possible to refer to *kui* or *wa* 窐, "a hole", although the meaning "pit" is not attested.

2 See note 3 to D 21 above.

D 24 W 8.28a; S I.33b; S V.104b; SS 163–164; str. 29 (399).

[29] A commoner[1] A steals a goat[2]; on the neck of the goat there is a rope, and the value[3] of the rope is one cash. Question: how is he to be sentenced? A's attention was on the goat he stole, whereas the rope was attached to the goat. As A led the goat away, the deliberations should not go beyond the goat.[4]

1 Cf. note 2 to A 100 above.
2 Because the animal is attached to a rope, it is more likely to be a goat than a sheep; cf. note 2 to C 19 above.
3 *Chih* 直 *for chih* 値.
4 I.e. in determining the punishment, based on the value of the stolen goods, the value of the rope should not be taken into consideration. The text writes *pu wei kuo yang* 不爲過羊, where one would expect *wu* 勿 *kuo*.

D 25 W 8.28a; S II.33b; S V.104b; SS 164; str. 30–31 (400–401).

[30] "Forcing[1] a lock[2] (is punished by) redemption[3] of tattooing"[4]. What is the meaning of "forcing a lock"? When the person who forced the lock has already forced it open, then this is (a case of) "forcing". Furthermore,[5] when it has not yet been opened, is this also "forcing"? If by forcing one is unable to open it and leaves, to be caught some other time,[6] how are both (these cases) to be sentenced? If one forces it with the desire to steal, (but) one is unable [31] to open it, or[7] one is caught before[8] having opened it, this warrants (the punishment of) redemption of tattooing. If one forces it without desiring to steal: if it has already been opened, then this is (a case of) forcing[9]; if it has not yet been opened, this warrants a fine of two suits of armour.

1 *Yüeh* 抉, lit. "to pull up; to gouge".
2 *Yüeh* 籥, lit. "flute", is used also for both "key" and "lock". Here it surely means "lock" (and so it does in the *Chin t'eng*, "The metal-bound casket", in the Book of Documents, in spite of Karlgren's remarks in "Glosses, Documents I", p. 254, no. 1574).
3 See my "Legalists", p. 15, and p. 18 of the introduction.
4 This first sentence is evidently a quotation from some unnamed statute. The hard labour punishment accompanying tattooing is not mentioned.
5 This is another question.
6 *I jih* 一日; I believe that this is equivalent here to *i tan* 一旦, but SS translates "on the same day", which seems to be the accepted meaning of *i jih*.
7 *Jo* 若.
8 *Wei ch'i* 未啓, lit. "not yet opened".
9 Punishable by tattooing, as stated in the first sentence.

D26 W 8.28a; S II.33b; S V.105a; SS 165; str. 32 (402).

[32] "Stealthily[1] to borrow[2] government[3] money in a storehouse[4] and to use it is (subject to the) same rules as theft".[5] What is the meaning of "in a storehouse"? Only the prefectural Treasury[6] is "in a storehouse"; the others[7] are not.

1 *Ssu* 私, "stealthily" or "privately".
2 *T'e* 貣 for *t'ai* 貸, which means both "to borrow" and "to lend"; cf. note 6 to A 31 above.
3 *Kung* 公.
4 In spite of the explanation of *fu chung* 府中 in this article, I fail to understand the real meaning of this term.
5 See D 18 above. — This first sentence is obviously a quotation from some unnamed statute.
6 For this rendering of *shao nei* 少內 see my "Ch'in documents", p. 195 f.
7 Perhaps treasuries belonging to other organs.

D 27 W 8.28a–b; S II.33b; S V.105a–b; SS 165–166; str. 33–34 (403–404).

[33] The commoner A commits a theft. "At the moment of capture, the illegal profit is evaluated".[1] The value of the illegal profit was more than

660[2] cash, (but) the officials did not evaluate it. Only[3] when the case was tried[4] they evaluated the illegal profit. The value of the illegal profit was 110[5] cash and therefore (A) was sentenced to shaving off the beard.[6] Question: how are A as well as the officials to be sentenced? A warrants tattooing and being made a *ch'eng-tan*. As regards the officials, it is (a case of) making a mistake in punishing a crime.[7] [34] If perhaps[8] they did it on purpose,[9] it is (a case of) "being untruthful".[10]

[1] This seems to be a quotation from an unnamed statute; the same sentence recurs in D 28 below. The text has *tsang chih* 臧直 for 贓值.
[2] This is the sum when punishments become heavier, as shown below.
[3] *Nai* 乃 in the second half of the sentence.
[4] *Yü chü* 獄鞫; see *RHL*, p. 79.
[5] That is to say: the estimate made at the time of the trial was 110 cash, whereas it should have been "more than 660 cash", as stated above.
[6] The editors of SS suggest that, in view of D 28 below, this would have been "shaving off the beard and being made a bond-servant."
[7] The text reads *shih hsing tsui* 失刑罪. *Shih* can mean "(to make a) mistake" (see *RHL*, p. 262) and in view of D 28 below that is the meaning here. *Shih* here is not equivalent to *tsung* 縱, which in Han times had the technical meaning of "to pronounce too light a sentence"; see *RHL*, p. 252.
[8] I do not understand the real meaning of *huo* 或 here.
[9] The editors of S explain *tuan* 端 as *chuan* 專; for this meaning Morohashi, vol. 8, p. 722, refers to an undefined passage in the *CKT*, where the commentators provide this equation, and it is evidently the same passage where Karlgren renders *tuan* by "to take the initiative" in GSR, p. 65, no. 168f. SS, however, refers to the *Mo-tzu*, ch. 70, where Pi Yüan (1730–1797) explains *tuan* as "on purpose, intentionally" (followed by Forke, *Mê Ti*, p. 620, "absichtlich", whereas Sun I-jang, *Mo-tzu*, p. 350, wants *tuan* to mean "start"). In view of the context I have rendered *tuan* as "on purpose", which is also the only way to translate *tuan* in D 30 and D 77 below.
[10] See *RHL*, p. 258, for Han time cases of "being untruthful", i.a. when trying criminal cases; cf. p. 252. In D 77 below *pu chih* 不直 is explained as intentionally punishing too lightly or too severely; the editors indicate that the expression occurs in *SC* 6.49, rendered in *Mh* II, p. 169, as "pas intègre".

D 28 W 8.28b; S II.33b; S V.105b–106a; SS 166; str. 35–36 (405–406).

[35][1] The commoner A commits a theft. Evaluating the illegal profit at the moment of his capture, the value of the illegal profit was more than 110 (cash), (but) the officials did not evaluate it. Only when the case was tried the illegal profit was evaluated; the value of the illegal profit was more than 660 (cash). A was tattooed and made a *ch'eng-tan*. Question: how are A and the officials to be sentenced? A is warranted to have his beard shaved off and to be made a bond-servant. As regards the officials, it is (a case of) making a mistake in punishing [36] crime. A has committed a crime. . . .[2] When the officials were aware[3] of this and purposely (punished it) too heavily or too lightly,[4] how are they to be sentenced? These are (cases of) "being untruthful".[5]

[1] This article is the reverse of the preceding; the vocabulary is practically identical.
[2] Here strip 36 has a blank space of the size of three or four characters, where the pale photograph shows no trace of writing; this is indicated in SS, but neglected by *Wenwu* and S.
[3] *Chih* 智 for *chih* 知.
[4] Cf. *RHL*, p. 253.

5 See note 10 to D 27 above.

D 29 W 8.28b; S II.34a; S V.106a; SS 167; str. 37 (407).

[37] Somebody steals 1000 cash before an amnesty.[1] After the amnesty, when he has completely spent it, he is caught. How is he to be sentenced? Do not sentence him.

1 For amnesties see McKnight, pp. 22–36, and *RHL*, p. 225 ff.

D 30 W 8.28b; S II.34a; S V.106a–b; SS 167–168; str. 38–39 (408–409).

[38] A person is denounced for having stolen 110 (cash); the interrogation (shows) that he stole 100 cash. How is the denouncer to be sentenced? He is warranted to be fined two suits of armour. The theft was 100 (cash). If this is purposely increased[1] by adding 10 cash, the question is: how is the denouncer to be sentenced? He is warranted to be fined one shield; the fine of one shield corresponds to the Statutes. However, according to the practice[2] of the court[3] he is sentenced for [39] carelessness[4] and fined two suits of armour.

1 The text clearly reads *chi tuan tao chia shih ch'ien* 即端盜駕十錢, where *tao* is rather surprising (for *tuan* see note 9 to D 27 above). SS explains *tao* as "stealthily", but I believe that the copyist made a mistake, either by writing *tao* for *i* 益 (see note 7 to D 21 above) or by inverting *chia* and *tao*.

2 *Hsing shih* 行事 is a precedent. The editors of SS refer to *HSPC* 84.2a, where *hsing shih* is explained as *ch'eng shih* 成事, and more pertinently to Wang Nien-sun, *Tu-shu tsa-chih* IV, 12 (inaccessible), where Wang notes that both expressions mean "ancient precedents that have become law"; the editors add, that *hsing shih* must be equivalent to the Han expression *ku shih* 故事, mentioned in *RHL*, p. 48, no. 2.

3 *T'ing* 廷. In pre-modern times, a law court was not referred to as *t'ing*. As shown by D 79 below, *t'ing* may indicate the office of the Commandery Administrator, but in *HSPC* 92.14a (Watson, *Courtier*, p. 244) it unambiguously refers to the Prefect's yamen. Ch'ien Chien-fu, p. 140, note 2, shows that also during the Later Han the offices of both Grand Administrators and Prefects were called *t'ing* (see e.g. *HHSCC* Mem. 57.10a and 19a) and even *ch'ao* 朝 (ibid. 15a).

4 *Pu shen* 不審; see note 41 to A 64 above.

D 31 W 8.28b; S II.34a; S V.106b; SS 168; str. 40 (410).

[40] A person is denounced for having stolen 1000 cash. The interrogation shows that he stole 670 (cash).[1] How is the denouncer to be sentenced? Do not sentence him.

1 That is to say: the sum exceeds the critical limit of 660 cash, mentioned several times in the preceding articles.

D 32 W 8.28b; S II.34a; S V.106b; SS 168; str. 41 (411).

[41] Somebody is falsely denounced of having stolen 1000 cash. The interrogation shows that he stole 670 (cash). How is the false accuser to be sentenced? Do not sentence him.[2]

1 *Wu* 誣 is "to slander", but because this "slander" results in a judicial action, it is in fact "to lodge a false accusation". The technical term for this is *wu kao* 告, which is used in D 89,

91 and 92 below. It should be remembered that *kao* is used for private individuals who "denounce" a person to the authorities, whereas officials *ho* 劾 "accuse" (cf. *RHL*, p. 74).

2 Whereas a false accusation might result in "reversing the punishment", this is not done here, because both 1000 and 670 cash exceed the critical limit of 660 cash; for "reversing the punishment" see note 4 to D 18 above.

D 33 W 8.28b; S II.34a; S V.106b–107a; SS 168–169; str. 42 (412).

[42] A denounces B for having stolen to the value of. . . .[1] The interrogation shows that B had stolen (to the value of) 30 (cash); A slanderously added[2] 50 (cash) to B's (theft), being careless[3] about the 30 (cash). Question: is A warranted to be sentenced or is he not warranted? According to the practice of the court A is to be fined two suits of armour.[4]

1 Several characters on the strip are illegible, but in view of the following, the text must have read *pa shih* 八十, "eighty".

2 This is how I understand *chia i wu shih* 駕乙五十; the translation in SS is of no help, because it simply repeats these words.

3 The clearly legible words *ch'i sa pu shen* 其卅不審 are curious; I have followed the translation in SS.

4 Cf. D 30 above.

D 34 W 8.28b; S II.34b; S V.108a; SS 172; str. 49 (419).

[49] A person is falsely accused of stealing to the value of 20 (cash). Before a verdict has been pronounced, he[1] also commits another theft to the value of 100 (cash), and only then it[2] is discovered. Is it warranted to combine (the value of the two) illicit profits, or are we to act on the actual crime and also[3] sentence him for falsely accusing another person? He is warranted to be fined two suits of armour and one shield.[4]

1 From what follows it is clear that this is the person who laid the false accusation.

2 Namely, that he had falsely accused the other person.

3 *Yu* 有 for *yu* 又.

4 The reply does not explain the composition of this fine. It is curious to observe that the theft of 100 cash—or of 120, if the two "illegal profits" are combined—is being punished by a fine, whereas in other cases the punishment is hard labour; this may be the result of the offender's status, although this is not mentioned.

D 35 W 8.28b; S II.34a; S V.107a; SS 169; str. 43 (413).

[41] A denounces B for having stolen an ox or for having intentionally[1] wounded a person. Now B did not steal an ox, nor has he wounded a person. Question: how is A to be sentenced? If he did it on purpose,[2] this is (a case of) falsely accusing another person; if it was unintentional, it is (a case of) carelessness in denouncing.

1 For *tsei* 賊, "murderously", i.e. with malice aforethought, intentionally, wounding or killing people, see the discussion in *RHL*, pp. 253–257. *Tsei* is used in contrast to *tou* 鬭, a sudden, unpremeditated fight; see *RHL*, p. 254, and cf. D 71 below. Yates, p. 140, note 92, argues in favour of rendering *tsei* by "wantonly", and on p. 154 translates *tsei ssu* 死 as "death by wanton violence'.

2 See note 9 to D 27 above.

D 36 W 8.28b; S II.34a; S V.107a; SS 169–170; str. 44 (414).

[44] A denounces B for having stolen an ox. Now B (proves) to have inten-

tionally[1] wounded a person; it is not that he had stolen an ox. Question: is A warranted to be sentenced, or is he not warranted? He is not warranted to be sentenced; he is likewise not warranted to be rewarded.[2] Another opinion: this is (a case of) carelessness in denouncing.

[1] See note 1 to D 35 above.
[2] For having led to the discovery of a murderous attack. — *Kou* 購 is explained in *SW* as "to try to obtain by means of money". It is the technical term for the reward, promised for the capture of a person, like e.g. in *HSPC* 31.24b, where Hsiang Yü says: "I have heard that Han has promised a reward for my head, *kou wo t'ou* 購我頭, for a thousand catties of gold and a fief of tenthousand families" (*SC* 7.73, *Mh* II, p. 320, Watson, *Records* I, p. 73). SS refers to an Edsin-gol strip, where a reward of 100,000 cash is promised for the capture or killing of the leaders (probably of a band of robbers), and of 50,000 cash for that of their followers (Lao Kan, *K'ao-shih*, pp. 31–32, no. 1545 (77) 503.17 and 8; *Chia pien*, p. 80, no. 1933; see also Lao Kan, *K'ao shih k'ao-cheng*, p. 13). See also D 112–119 below.

D 37 W 8.28b; S II.34b; S V.107b; SS 171; str. 47 (417).

[47] A denounces B for having stolen an ox. Now B had stolen a sheep; he had not stolen an ox. Question: how is A to be sentenced? This is (a case of) carelessness in denouncing. ○ When (the imposition of) a fine of (one)[1] shield is "untruthful",[2] how is this to be sentenced? This[3] is fined one shield.

[1] The text does not indicate a number; I agree with SS that "one" will have been intended.
[2] See note 10 to D 27 above.
[3] Referring to the official who had been "untruthful".

D 38 W 8.28b; S II.34a; S V.107a; SS 170; str. 45 (415).

[45] A stole a sheep. B, being aware of this, intentionally denounces him, saying: "A has stolen an ox." Question: is B (a case of) "falsely accusing another", or is it (a case of) "carelessness in denouncing"? This is warranted to be considered (as a case of) "denouncing theft and increasing the (amount of the) illegal profit".[1]

[1] *Chia tsang* 駕贓 for *chia tsang* 加贓.

D 39 W 8.29a; S II. 34b; S V.107b; SS 170–171; str. 46 (416).

[46] A stole sheep. B knows[1] that he stole sheep, whereas he does not know the number of sheep. He then denounces him to the officials, saying: "He has stolen three sheep." Question: how is B to be sentenced? This is (case of) "denouncing a thief, increasing (the amount of) the illegal profit."[2]

[1] *Chih* 智 *for* chih 知.
[2] *Chia tsang* 駕贓 for *chia tsang* 加贓.

D 40 W 8.29a; S II.34b; S V.108b; SS 173; str. 50 (420).

[50] A, holder of the aristocratic rank of *shang tsao*,[1] stole a sheep. Before the case has been judged, he falsely accuses another person, saying: "He has stolen a pig".[2] How is he to be sentenced? This warrants (the punishment of) being left intact and being made a *ch'eng-tan*.[3]

1 This was the second lowest of these ranks.
2 From the context one would expect a pig to be more expensive than a sheep, but in the only sum in the *CCSS* where the price of a sheep and of a pig are mentioned together, the value of the sheep is 500 cash, but that of the pig only 300 (*CCSS*, p. 133; Vogel, p. 85, no. 8).
3 In Han times four years' hard labour; see *RHL*, p. 130.

D 41 W 8.29a; S II.34b; S V.108b; SS 173; str. 51 (421).

[51] "Those who praise the enemy[1] in order to frighten the mind of the population will be dishonoured[2]".[3] What is "to dishonour"? To dishonour him when alive, and when the dishonouring is over, to cut him asunder[4]—that is what is meant.

1 *Shih* 適 for *ti* 敵.
2 *Lu* 翏 for *lu* 戮. *Lu* often means "to kill, to execute", e.g. in the chapter *Kan shih* in the Book of Documents (see Karlgren, "Glosses, Documents I", p. 170, no. 1403), but in view of the combination *sheng* 生 *lu* used here and of the fact that the culprit is cut asunder afterwards, *lu* must mean "to dishonour". It is unknown which form this dishonouring took. See *SC* 10.29, *Mh* II, p. 475, and *HSPC* 23.13a, *RHL*, p. 334 and p. 379, note 161. A similar use of *lu* is found in the *Shuo-wen* dictionary (SWKL, p. 6632b, as noted by Wang Jen-chün II, p. 7). Here the author explains *ju* 辱, "to shame", by writing *shih keng shih yü feng chiang shang lu chih* 失耕時於封畺上戮之, "When one has missed the season for ploughing, one is dishonoured on the border marks (between the fields)". In his commentary to this passage Kuei Fu 桂馥 (1736–1805) in his *Shuo-wen chieh-tzu i-cheng* 義證 (included in SWKL, p. 6633a) quotes the *Wu pen lun* 務本論, "on devoting all energy to the principal (i.e. agriculture)", by Wang Ts'an 王粲 (A.D. 177–217. — Text in Yen K'o-chün, *Ch'üan Hou-Han wen* 91.5a), who states that men who had been remiss in ploughing and weeding were punished.
3 This quotation of an unnamed statute agrees with a sentence in the 70th chapter of the *Mo-tzu* (*Mo-tzu*, p. 357; Forke, *Mê Ti*, p. 625): "Those who praise the enemy, saying that there are many when there are few, that they are in good order when they are in disorder, that the enemy attack was skilful when it was clumsy, are cut down."
4 I believe that here *chan* 斬 means *yao* 要 *chan*, "to cut in two at the waist"; this was a frequently used form of capital punishment, especially during the Former Han (see *RHL*, p. 111), but is only rarely alluded to in pre-Han sources (*SC* 68.8, Duyvendak, *Lord Shang*, p. 14; SC 87.43, Bodde, *Unifier*, p. 52). It is to be noted that Cheng Hsüan (127–200) explains *chan* in the very first sentence of the article *chang lu* 掌戮 in the autumn section of the *Chou-li* as "to cut in two at the waist" (*Chou-li chu-su* 36.7b (1292); *Chou-li* 20/69.16; overlooked in Biot II, p. 368).

D 42 W 8.29a; S II.24b; S V.109a; SS 173–174; str. 52 (422).

[52] "Those who stimulate[1] the mind of the population, (so that) fame is spread right and left[2] are rewarded". The general deliberates[3] whether to reward them with cash or with gold; there is no fixed[4] amount.

1 The editors take *kuang* 廣 for *k'uo* 擴; they refer to *Sun Pin*, p. 32, where the expression *k'uo chih* 志 occurs.
2 I fail to understand the meaning of this phrase. The editors think *tso yu* 左右 refers to the general's suite and therefore indirectly to the general himself. And whose is the fame? That of the men who stimulate the masses?
3 *Ts'ai* 材 for *ts'ai* 裁.
4 *Heng* 恆, lit. "constant, permanent".

D 43 W 8.29a; S II.34b; S V.109a; SS 174–175; str. 53–54 (423–424).

[53] "When there are 'thrown letters,'[1] these are not to be opened; as soon as they are discovered, they are to be burned. Persons who are able to arrest

(the person who threw the letter) are rewarded with two slaves.[2] Detain the person who threw the letter, question him and report."[3] (What the statute) means is: when the letter is discovered, whereas the person who threw it is not caught, the letter is to be burned; it must not be opened. When the person who threw it is caught, [54] the letter is not burned; he is to be questioned and reported—that is what is meant.

[1] *T'ou shu* 投書. The editors believe this to mean "to lodge an anonymous accusation", but I fail to see why this would have been forbidden. In the History of the Han dynasty we even hear of an official who had special receptacles made for such letters (*HSPC* 76.2a). I am inclined to think that secret communications with the enemy are meant, because of a sentence in one of the military chapters of the *Mo-tzu* (*Mo-tzu*, p. 357; Forke, *Mê Ti*, p. 625): *k'o she i shu pu te chü* 客射以書不得擧, "letters shot in by the enemy must not be picked up", and again: *chin wu te chü shih shu* 禁無得擧矢書, "It is forbidden to pick up 'arrow letters' ". On the other hand, persons who shot letters to the enemy were to be executed together with their parents. Professor Koga adopts the editors' explanation and establishes a link with false accusations (Koga, *Chō-an*, p. 301 f.), which seems needlessly complicated.

[2] *Ch'en ch'ieh erh jen* 臣妾二人; for slaves see note 6 to A 65 above.

[3] The editors adopt the *SW* explanation of *yeh* 讞, i.e. 讞, namely *i tsui* 議罪, "to discuss the punishment", but from the context it seems evident that the matter had "to be reported to higher authority"; cf. *HSPC* 5.8b, *HFHD* I, p. 326, and *RHL*, p. 339 and p. 390, note 211.

D 44 W 8.29a; S II.35a; S V.109b; SS 175; str. 55 (425).

[55] What is "to forge[1] an order of the Assistant (Prefect)?" This is (a case of)[2] a Rank-holder[3] counterfeiting his seal to be (that of) a Great Overseer.[4]

[1] The editors read the first character *ch'iao* 僑, but I think it is *chiao* 撟, which is an accepted loan for *chiao* 矯 (see *SWKL*, p. 5449a), the usual word for "to forge", which is used *passim* in the Han histories in the expression *chiao chih* 制, "to forge an imperial decree."

[2] The editors consider *wei* 爲 to be equivalent to *ju* 如, "as; as if", which is an accepted commentator's explanation.

[3] See note 3 to A 22 above.

[4] See note 5 to A 19 above.

D 45 W 8.29a; S II.35a; S V.110a; SS 175–176; str. 56 (426).

[56] How is "thievishly to seal (as) an Overseer"[1] to be sentenced? (According to) the practice of the court[2] this is considered as "counterfeiting a seal."

[1] *Tao feng se-fu* 盗封嗇夫. SS suggests that this means "to seal pretending to be an Overseer".

[2] See notes 2 and 3 to D 30 above.

D 46 W 8.29a; S II.35a; S V.110a; SS 176; str. 57–58 (427–428).

[57] "To open[1] a counterfeit document and not to become aware[2] (that it is counterfeit) is fined two suits of armour". Now in Hsien-yang they open a counterfeit passport[3]; not becoming aware (that it is counterfeit), they immediately seal it and transmit it to another prefecture, and this other prefecture also transmits it to the prefectures in succession. When (he[4]) arrives at a pass[5] he is caught. Now, is only (the authority in) Hsien-yang warranted to be adjudicated and fined for this, or are the other [58] prefectures warranted to be all[6] fined? Those in Hsien-yang as well as in the other prefectures

who opened (the document) without becoming aware (that it was counterfeit) are all warranted to be fined.

[1] *Fa* 發. In view of D 43 above, which stipulates that a "thrown letter" should not be *fa*, but had to be burned, *fa* can only mean "to open" and not "to despatch", for A 95 above shows that this is *hsing* 行.
[2] *Chih* 智 for *chih* 知.
[3] See note 6 to A 32 above.
[4] As it is only a person who can be *te* 得, "caught" (i.e. arrested), the bearer of the passport is meant.
[5] *Kuan* 關, "passes" or control points, situated on the borders between the states and on the frontier between the Chinese and the alien tribes; here travellers were checked and duties were levied. *CCSS*, p. 109 (Vogel, p. 69), mentions a traveller passing through five such stations; the same mathematical handbook also mentions custom duties—curiously enough only for gold and cash—on pp. 38, 99 and 109 (Vogel, pp. 28, 63, 69). More interesting are the reports on travellers who had gone through the pass, included in the Edsin-gol documents (see *RHA* I, pp. 108–114). The Commandants of the Passes were probably in charge of several of such control stations, but their main responsibility will have been to keep a check on travellers; late in 99 B.C., when there was large-scale social unrest in Shantung, they were ordered to be especially vigilant (*HSPC* 6.34b; *HFHD* II, p. 106). A curious light is thrown on the custom duties, when we read that, at least in one case, these served to provide food for the officers and conscripts stationed at the pass (*HSPC* 6.33a; *HFHD* II, p. 103). The office of Commandant of the Passes is said to have been created by the Ch'in (*HSPC* 19A.29b; cf. *RHA* I, pp. 61 and 107).—A cursory reading of the chapter on the administrative geography in the History of the Han dynasty (*HSPC* 28) leads to the discovery of the names of a number of passes, both in the interior and on the borders. As regards the latter, there are the famous Yü-men 玉門 kuan and the Yang 陽 kuan in the Tun-huang area (see *CICA*, p. 71, note 7), and the (Ch'ien-shui) Chin (肩水) 金 kuan and the So 索 kuan in the Edsin-gol defence lines (see *RHA* I, pp. 110–111); in the North-East there was the Chü-yung 居庸 kuan in Shang-ku 上谷 Commandery (*HSPC* 28Bi. 44b). In the South the nameless pass in Chin-sang 進桑 Prefecture in Yang-k'o Commandery led into Vietnam (*HSPC* 28Aiii.-94b), whereas the Mei-ling 梅嶺 kuan led into Kuang-tung (*HSPC* 95.17a). In the interior, the most famous pass was the Hsien-ku 函谷 kuan on the Yellow River, which blocked the entrance into Ch'in (*HSPC* 28Ai.39b; it was shifted further East in 115 B.C.; see *HSPC* 6.18b; *HFHD* II, p. 73). North-west of Lo-yang was the Huan-yüan 轘轅 kuan (*HSPC* 1A.16a; *HFHD* I, p. 52), and south-west of this city the I-chüeh 伊闕 pass (*HSPC* 28Ai.44a). In Shang-tang Commandery there were the passes of Shang-tang 上黨, Hu 壺, Shih-yen 石研 and T'ien-ching 天井 (*HSPC* 28Ai.59a–b). The Ching-hsing 井陘 pass led from the Great Plain through the T'ai-hang mountains towards T'ai-yüan (*HSPC* 1A.35a, *HFHD* I, p. 83; *HSPC* 28Aii.55a). Passes leading from Ch'in to the South were the Wu 武 pass (*HSPC* 1A.16a, *HFHD* I, p. 54; *HSPC* 28Ai.45b) and the Yao 嶢 pass (*HSPC* 1A.18b, *HFHD* I, p. 55).

D 47 W 8.29a; SII.35a; S V.110b; SS 176–177; str. 59 (429).

[59] It is a Precedent of the Court that, when an official has been engaged in deceit[1] and counterfeiting, and the fine is [one][2] shield or more, once the sentence has been executed, he is also to be (permanently)[3] dismissed.

[1] The text reads *tsi* 詛, "to utter imprecations". The editors suggest that it should be read *cha* 詐, "to deceive". This reading confirms the suggestion by the ancient commentators that *tso* 作 was used as a loan for *tsu* 詛 in Ode 255; Karlgren's refutation of this suggestion is therefore unjustified (see his "Glosses Ta Ya and Sung", p. 96, gloss 937, repeated in "Loan characters IV", p. 50, no. 1881). The editors note that the expression *cha wei* 僞 occurs in the abecedarium of the 1st century B.C. *Chi-chiu p'ien*, p. 300; the passages collected in Morohashi, vol. 10, p. 428, 35373, no. 6, show that this binome occurs frequently in texts of the Warring States period.
[2] This figure is missing in the text.
[3] See note 5 to A 90.

D 48 W 8.29a; S II.35a; S V.110b; SS 177; str. 60 (430).

[60] It is a Precedent of the Court that, when a person has committed a crime warranting banishment and judgment has already been pronounced and orders have been given,[1] but before he has been (made to) go[2] he dies or absconds,[3] the persons he had guaranteed[4] are (still) warranted to proceed to the place of banishment.

[1] The text reads *i tuan i ling* 已斷已令, clearly referring to two separate actions. I believe that the orders are those given to the officials to execute the sentence, hence, in this case, to despatch the condemned man to the place of banishment; cf. note 4 to A 88 above.

[2] *Hsing* 行.

[3] Cf. note 4 to A 39 above.

[4] The text reads *ch'i suo pao* 其所包, "those he had *pao*". I have followed the editors' explanation; they suggest that *pao* 包 is a loan for *pao* 保; the latter word is used for "to guarantee" in an edict of 44 B.C. (*HSPC* 9.6b; *HFHD* II, p. 316). This edict abolished an ordinance which stipulated that several kinds of court officials *pao fu mu t'ung ch'an* 保父母同產, "guaranteed their parents and their brothers and sisters"; according to the commentators, these officials were held responsible for the actions of their relatives. The loan is not attested, but it is phonetically possible (*pao* 包 = *pộg and *pao* 保 = *pôg, see GSR p. 285, no. 1113a, and p. 273, no. 1057a). Professor Koga provides no reason for his rendering of *pao* 包 by "to transfer the wife and children of an exile to the place of banishment" (Koga, *Chō-an*, p. 171, note 68), and SS avoids all difficulties by translating "his relatives who have to leave". The long note 141 on this subject in Yates, p. 149, is of little help, i.a. because of the surprising rendering of *ch'i suo pao* by "those who have guaranteed him"; see also note 11 to E 17 below.

D 49 W 8.29a; S II.35a; S V.111a; SS 177; str. 61 (431).

[61] How is an Overseer to be sentenced who does not apply himself to the business of his office, but to evil things? He is warranted to be banished. Is the wife of the exile warranted to be considered as "guaranteed",[1] or is she not warranted? She is not warranted to be considered as "guaranteed".

[1] In view of the preceding article D 48 I maintain this clumsy rendering; the implication is, of course, that she is not to be banished. SS believes that this is due to the position of her husband, because normally she would have had to follow him into exile, as is clear from D 50 below.

D 50 W 8.29a; S II.35a; S V.111a; SS 178; str. 62 (432).

[62] (A person) is warranted to be banished. His wife has of her own accord denounced him earlier. She is (nevertheless) warranted to be considered as "guaranteed."

D 51 W 8.29a; S II.35a; S V.111a; SS 178; str. 63 (433).

[63] Somebody leading a person who had been unpleasant[1] in his village,[2] to a superior,[3] lets him go; how is he to be sentenced? He is warranted to be detained and to be put to work like the person whom he let go, pending the latter's arrest; in case he possesses aristocratic rank, he is to work in a government storehouse.

[1] *Pu jen* 不仁; see note 9 to A 50 above. SS renders this by "to do evil".

[2] *I-li* 邑里.

[3] *Chiang shang* 將上, "to lead.... to a superior".

D 52 W 8.29a; S II.35b; S V.111b; SS 179; str. 65 (435).

[65] To admit. . . . .[1] (is punished by) redemption of shaving off the beard. Now one admits a person, but before this person has. . . .,[2] he is caught. How is he to be sentenced? He is to be excused.[3]

1 The text reads *nei chien* 內奸, where the editors take *nei* as *na* 納, which is common. The expression is unknown. The editors suggest that it means "to let bad men enter", but this seems improbable, in view of the relative lightness of the punishment. *Chien*, besides being a general term for "evil", can mean "fornication"; see note 3 below.

2 The text reads *shih chien* 飾奸, where the editors equate the first character with *shih* 蝕 (correctly so, in view of *SWKL* 5999b f.) which they take as a loan for *shih* 食. This is phonetically possible, both being *d̂'i̯ək (*GSR* p. 243, no. 921a and d) and it has been suggested in another context (see Karlgren, "Loan characters III", p. 108, no. 1524). All this is in order and acceptable, but the explanation of *shih* 食 is unexpected: the editors believe *shih* to mean "to accept", because in *HSPC* 85.8a Yen Shih-ku in his commentary says that *shih* "is like *shou na* 受納", i.e. "to accept, to obtain"; Yang Shu-ta, p. 515, points out that this meaning for *shih* is required in *YTL* 20, p. 23. However, in their translation the editors of SS render this sentence as "before he has realized his evil plots he is arrested", without a trace of their learned speculations.

3 I fail to understand the key phrases of this article. Does it perhaps concern sexual matters? *Shih* 食 can mean "sexual intercourse" (see Wilbur, p. 431, note 10), whereas *chien* 奸 can mean "to fornicate", also in the Ch'in texts, as is shown by D 151–153 below.

D 53 W 8.29b; S II.35b; S V.112a; SS 179–180; str. 66(436).

[66] When a thief-catcher pursues and arrests a malefactor, the malefactor beats the thief-catcher and kills him. Question: is the killer to be considered as having killed a person with murderous (intent) or as having killed him in a fight[1]? It is killing a person in a fight, but the Precedents of the Court consider it as murderous (intent).

1 See note 1 to D 35 above. On the strip *tou*, "fight" is written 斲.

D 54 W 8.29b; S II.35b; S V.112a; SS 180; str. 67 (437).

[67] A plots[1] to send B to rob and kill a person; as his share he receives ten cash. Question: B is not yet six feet tall[2]; how is A to be sentenced? He is warranted to be executed and exposed.[3]

1 I do not understand the value of *mou* 謀, "to plot", because from the context it is clear that the murder actually took place.

2 I.e. B was still young and not considered as an adult; see above, A 12 and D 5.

3 For *che* 磔 see *RHL*, p. 110 f.; it does not seem to mean "quartering", nor "to be torn apart by carriages", as suggested by SS.

D 55 W 8.29b; S II.35b; S V.112a; SS 180–181; str. 68 (438).

[68] A kills a person, but this is not discovered. Now, only when A has died of an illness and has already been buried, somebody belatedly denounces A. That A had killed a person is shown to be true. Question: is A warranted to be sentenced and are (the persons to be co-adjudicated)[1] to be confiscated,[2] or is this not warranted? The denunciation is not to be accepted.[3]

1 I agree with the editors of SS that this addition is implied by the single word *shou* 收.

[2] For *shou* see note 10 to A 41 above; in view of the context here it means "to be confiscated and made a government slave".
[3] *T'ing* 聽, lit. "to listen".

D 56 W 8.29b; S II.35b; S V.112b; SS 181; str. 69–70 (439–440).

[69] Unauthorizedly to kill a child (is punished by) tattooing and being made a *ch'eng-tan* or a grain-pounder.[1] When the child is newly born and has strange things on its body, as well when it is deformed,[2] to kill it is not to be considered a crime. Now, when a child is born and the child's body is whole and there are no strange things—merely[3] for the reason that one has (too) many children and does not wish that it should live, and consequently not [70] to lift it up,[4] but to kill it, how is this to be sentenced? This is (a case of) killing a child.

[1] *Ch'ung* 舂, "to pound grain"; this was the punishment for women equivalent to *ch'eng-tan* for men; see *RHL*, p. 128 f.
[2] *Pu ch'üan* 不全, lit. "not whole, incomplete".
[3] *Chih* 直.
[4] *Chü* 擧. To lift up the new-born child signified its acceptance; see *HSPC* 97B.9b, Watson, *Courtier*, p. 265 and note 1, and Maspero, *Chine*, p. 107, note 3.

D 57 W 8.29b; S II.35b; S V.113a; SS 181–182; str. 71 (441).

[71] The commoner A has no sons; he makes his younger brother's son his successor.[1] Living together[2] with him, he unauthorizedly kills him. This warrants beheading.[3]

[1] *Hou* 後. This means that A adopted the boy who would eventually perform the ancestral sacrifices for his foster-father.
[2] *T'ung chü* 同居; see note 15 to A 41 above, and D 181 below.
[3] D 56 shows that the unauthorized killing of one's children (irrespective of age!) was punished by tattooing and hard labour. That capital punishment is demanded here is doubtless because the victim was not his foster-father's own child, *ch'in tzu* 親子 (a term used in E 18 below); see further note 4 to D 85 below.

D 58 W 8.29b; S II.35b; S V.113a–b; SS 182; str. 72 (442).

[72] "When somebody unauthorizedly kills or mutilates[1] or shaves[2] his successor-son, this is to be reported."[3] What is the meaning of "successor-son"? . . . .[4] his son, making him successor to the aristocratic rank,[5] as well as the heirs-apparent established as successors by the princes or chiefs[6] of states that are subject (of Ch'in), are all successor-sons.

[1] *Hsing* 刑.
[2] *K'un* 髡, "shaving off the hair and whiskers" was part of the hard labour punishment *ch'eng-tan*. It should be remembered that before the compulsory introduction of the queue during the Manchu dynasty, Chinese men wore their full hair long and bound up in a topknot.
[3] This is a quotation from an unnamed statute. See note 3 to D 43 above; also in the present context which deals with noblemen and foreign princes, the translation of *yeh* 瀗 (i.e. 讞) as "to report to a higher authority" is to be preferred to the rendering "to sentence", adopted by SS.
[4] The nearly illegible character is read *kuan* 官 by the editors, who explain the word as "officially approved", as they do in D 145 below, where a woman who had deserted her husband

is only to be condemned if *i kuan* 已官, "(the marriage) had been officially approved"; it is a possibility.

5 *Chiao* 爵. It is unknown, which ranks could be inherited under the Ch'in; in the Han period only nobles, *hou* 侯, and perhaps also *kuan-nei hou* 關內侯 (on this point see Makino, p. 261, note 2) could pass their rank to the eldest son of their chief wife.

6 *Chün chang* 君長. This binome is used for the chiefs of alien tribes, and the editors of SS therefore explain the term as "the leaders of minority peoples subject to Ch'in". In my rendering I have steered a middle course, for it is not to be excluded that also Chinese states were concerned, as is also assumed by the editors of S, who explain the term as "lesser states dependent on Ch'in as well as 'minorities' " (S V.113b, note 3).

D 59 W 8.29b; S II.36a; S V.113b; SS 183; str. 73 (443).

[73] When a person's slave unauthorizedly kills (his) child, he is to be made a *ch'eng-tan* and to be tattooed,[1] (eventually) to be given (back) to his master.

1 In view of D 56 above, this was the normal punishment for this crime. It is to be noted that in this case the offender's slave status did not result in a heavier punishment.

D 60 W 8.29b; S II.36a; S V.114a; SS 184; str. 76 (446).

[76] "Slaves plot[1] to kill their master"[2]; what is the meaning of "to plot"? ○ Wishing murderously[3] to kill their master, but before having killed him they are caught, is (a case of) "to plot."[4]

1 It is clear from the context that *mu* 牧, lit. "to herd" (GSR p. 270, no. 1037a, *mi̯ôk) is a loan for *mou* 謀, "to plot" (GSR, p. 250, no. 948f, *mi̯ug), although the loan is not attested.

2 This is a quotation from an unnamed statute.

3 See note 1 to D 35 above.

4 For "to plot" see *RHL*, p. 265.

D 61 W 8.29b; S II.36a; S V.114b; SS 184; str. 77 (447).

[77] Somebody kills himself. The inmates of his house[1] do not report[2] this to the officials, (but) immediately bury him. Question: the deceased has a wife and children; are they warranted to be arrested?[3] To bury without reporting warrants a fine of one suit of armour.

1 Cf. D 181 and E 23 below; in D 181 *shih jen* 室人 is explained as "the whole household".

2 In official parlance *yen* 言 means "to report"; the Edsin-gol documents furnish hundreds of instances where a subordinate ends a letter to his superior with *kan yen chih* 敢言之, "I beg to report this".

3 The editors of both S and SS do not take this sentence as a question. To them, *shou* 收 means *shou lien* 殮 or *shou shih* 尸, "to encoffin", and SS therefore translates "Upon enquiry it becomes known that the deceased had a wife and children who were warranted to encoffin him"; I do not think that this is correct, considering the many cases that *wen* 問 means "question" in these texts.

D 62 W 8.29b; S II.36a; S V.114a–b; SS 183; str. 74 (444).

[74] When a person's male or female slave[1] beats[2] a child and the child therefore sickens[3] and dies, (the offender) is to be tattooed on the forehead and the cheekbones[4] and to be given back to the master. ○ When people fight and wound each other, are they both to be sentenced or not? They are both[5] to be sentenced.

1 Because in E 16 below a slave woman is simply called *ch'ieh* 妾, I assume that the expression *nu* 奴 *ch'ieh* indicates a male and a female slave.
2 *Chih* 治 for *ch'ih* 笞, lit. "to bastinado".
3 The word 肓 is unknown; *ku* 胋 is "to dry; to expose". SS suggests that is to be taken as *ku* 枯, lit. "to wither", which, according to the commentary to *Huai-nan-tzu*, ch. 1, p. 17, last line, can also mean "to sicken".
4 In contrast to D 59 above, no hard labour punishment is mentioned, but cf. D 154 below.
5 For this use of *chiao* 交 SS refers to the *Mencius* IA.i.4 (*Meng-tzu chu-su* 1.1b (0022)), where the commentary says *chiao wei chü yeh* 交爲俱也; Morohashi, vol. 1, p. 534, adduces several more examples of this usage.

D 63 W 8.29b; S II.36a; S V.114b; SS 184; str. 78 (448).

[78] "Beating one's grand-parents (is punished by) tattooing and being made a *ch'eng-tan* or a grain-pounder".[1] Now (someone) beats his great-grand-parents; how is this to be sentenced? Comparable to (beating) one's grand-parents.

1 This is a quotation from an unnamed statute.—For "grain-pounder" see note 1 to D 56 above.

D 64 W. 8.29b; S II. 36a; S VI. 115a; SS 185; str. 79 (449).

[79] His wife being obstreperous, the husband beats and bastinadoes[1] her, tearing an ear or breaking a limb[2] or fingers, or dislocating a joint.[3] Question: how is the husband to be sentenced? He warrants shaving off the beard.

1 The text reads *ou chih* 毆治 (for *ch'ih* 笞), whereas other texts, like D 63 above, only have *ou*. I have therefore rendered *chih/ch'ih* separately.
2 *Chih* 支 for *chih* 肢.
3 *Tieh t'i* 胅膿. *SW* explains *tieh* as "to dislocate"; 膿 is an unknown variant of 體 or 軆.

D 65 W 8.29b; S II. 36a; S VI.115a; SS 185–186; str. 80 (450).

[80] The Statute says: "When fighting to tear a person's ear (is punished by) shaving off the beard". Now tearing the ear, this was never[1] pierced[2] and what was torn was not the place where an ear-pendant is inserted; how is (the offender) to be sentenced? What the Statute says is not that it must be the place where an ear-pendant is inserted (that has to be torn) for it to be considered "tearing". To tear a man's or a woman's ear is both warranted (to be punished by) shaving off the beard.

1 *Ku* 故, "as of old"; *ku pu* 不 is therefore "never".
2 *Ch'uan* 穿, viz. for the insertion of an ornament.

D 66 W 8.29b; S II.36a; S VI.115b; SS 186; str. 81 (451).

[81] Someone fights with another person; he binds him and completely pulls out his beard and his eyebrows.[1] How is he to be sentenced? He warrants to be made an intact *ch'eng-tan*.

1 *Hsü mi* 須麋 for 鬚眉. *Mi* is a loan for *mei* (*GSR*, p. 184, no. 598f *mi̯ər for GSR, p. 151, no. 567a *mi̯ər); the same expression is found in the *Hsün-tzu*, ch. 5, p. 47(Dubs, *Hsün-tze*, p. 70).

D 67 W 8.29b; S II.36b; S VI.115b; SS 186; str. 82 (452).

[82] When pulling out a person's hair, how large is a *t'i*? A *t'i* is more than a *chih*.[1]

[1] *Chih i shang wei t'i* 智以上爲提. This is apparently a simple equation with both factors unknown, for it is evident that two quantities are meant, although the dictionaries do not say so. SS refers to the chapter *Shao i* of the *Li chi* (*Li-chi chu-su* 35.12b (1518); Couvreur, *Li-ki* II, p. 22; Legge, *Li-ki* 28, p. 79), where the commentator says *t'i yu chüeh yeh* 提猶絕也, "*t'i* is like severing"; here SS adds "the meaning is that the hair is pulled out"! SS translates the second sentence as "when it goes beyond the feelings of the man whose hair is pulled out, this is called *t'i*", which is unacceptable.

D 68 W 8.30a; S II.36b; S VI.115b; SS 186–187; str. 83 (453).

[83] When during a fight someone bites off another person's nose or ear or finger or lip, how is each (of these actions) to be sentenced? It is suggested[1] that these all warrant shaving off the beard.

[1] The text reads *i* 議, which SS translates by the modern term *i-ch'u* 議處, i.e. "to pass a resolution; to take a decision". However, as far as I am aware, in early Chinese texts *i* never means "to decide", but always "to propose; to suggest" or "to deliberate"; hence my translation.

D 69 W 8.30a; S II.36b; S VI.115b; SS 187; str. 84 (454).

[84] The commoner A in a fight drew his sword and struck, cutting off the other man's (hair) topknot.[1] How is A to be sentenced? He is warranted to be left intact and to be made a *ch'eng-tan*.

[1] The text reads *chieh* 結, which the editors rightly take to be a loan for *chi* 髻.

D 70 W 8.30a; S II.36b; S VI.116a; SS 187–188; str. 85 (455).

[85] When spears,[1] halberds and lances (which all) have a sheath are drawn for fighting, without causing wounds, this is to be sentenced comparable to (drawing) a sword.[2]

[1] The *p'i* 鈹 is a spear with a straight blade, like a sword (to which *SW* compares it), in contrast to the *mao* 矛, "lance", where the tip first broadens, to narrow down again towards the haft; see Hayashi, *Buki*, pp. 121 and 127 f., and ills. nos. 156, 157, 159–161, and Liu Chan-ch'eng, "T'ung p'i". The *p'i* must have been a weapon not unlike the 17th century partizan.

[2] See D 69 above, where drawing a sword during a fight without causing wounds is punished by being left intact and being made a *ch'eng-tan*.

D 71 W 8.30a; S II.36b; S VI.116a; SS 188; str. 86 (456).

[86] In a fight one uses a needle, a long needle[1] (or) an awl; if the needle, the long needle (or) the awl wound people, how is each (of these cases) to be sentenced? (When this was done during an un-premeditated) fight,[2] this warrants a fine of two suits of armour; when (with) murderous (intent),[3] it warrants tattooing and being made a *ch'eng-tan*.

[1] *Shu* 鉥 is explained in the commentary to ch. 81 of the *Kuan-tzu*, p. 81, as "a long needle" (perhaps for stitching soles? see *SWKL*, p. 6279b).

[2] and [3] See note 1 to D 35 above.

D 72 W 8.30a; S II.36b; S VI.116b; SS 188; str. 87 (457).

[87] Someone fights with another person and tears his lip. How is he to be sentenced? Comparable to (causing) welts or bruises.[1]

1 According to the commentary of Ying Shao (fl. 140–206) to *HSPC* 83.7b, the expression *chih wei* 疻痏 occurred in the Han statutes; it is also mentioned in the abecedarium *Chi-chiu p'ien*, p. 310. Ying Shao explains *chih-wei* as "hitting or beating a person with a stick or the hands, scraping his skin so that it swells and becomes black and blue, but without the traces of a wound." The Ch'in texts do not indicate the punishment for causing welts or bruises.

D 73 W 8.30a; S II.36b; S VI.116b; SS 189; str. 88 (458).

[88] Someone in a fight bites the other person's cheekbone or face; the size (of the wound) is a square inch; its depth half an inch. How is he to be sentenced? Comparable to (causing) welts or bruises.[1]

1 Cf. note 1 to D 72 above.

D 74 W 8.30a; S II.36b; S VI.116b; SS 189; str. 89 (459).

[89] In a fight (someone) is beaten by another person; there are no welts nor bruises, but the attacker[1] on the contrary[2] broke his teeth. How are they to be sentenced? Each one is to be sentenced according to the statutes concerned.[3]

1 Lit. "the beater".
2 *Ku* 顧.
3 The Ch'in texts do not indicate the punishment for breaking a tooth.

D 75 W 8.30a; S II.36b; S VI.117a; SS 189–190; str. 90 (460).

[90] "When foreigners[1] and people from Ch'in[2] fight, using[3] sharp weapons,[4] quarterstaffs,[5] sticks[6] or fists,[7] and they wound people,[8] this is wiped off[9] by means of (a payment in) cloth".[10] What is the meaning of "wiped off"? The wiping-off-cloth is paid to the authorities,[11] like cloth (for the payment of) fines; when paying, one provides[12] cash in accordance with the Statutes.[13]

1 *Pang k'o* 邦客. Like in D 58, *pang* is used for states outside Ch'in; *k'o* is frequently used for "strangers".
2 Whereas the stranger is the guest, the inhabitants of Ch'in are the "hosts", *chu-jen* 主人.
3 The editors of SS assume that it is the foreigners who use weapons; although grammatically possible, this assumption seems unwarranted.
4 *Ping jen* 兵刃, lit. "the cutting edge of weapons".
5 I follow the editors who believe that *t'ou* 投 is a mistake for *shu* 殳; for *shu* see note 1 to B 21 above.
6 D 76 defines *t'ing* 梃 as "(pieces of) wood that can be used to strike".
7 *Ch'üan chih* 拳指, lit. " 'fisted' fingers".
8 *Jen* 人; this general term would seem to include not only the persons engaged in the fight, but also bystanders.
9 I prefer this literal rendering of *min* 擎 (or 播) to the version in SS where the word is assumed to mean "to console".
10 The value of the "cloth" medium of exchange was eleven cash; see A 43 above.
11 *Ju kung* 入公.
12 Cf. note 6 to A 56 above.

13 It is also possible to translate *ju chi ch'ien ju lü* 入齎錢如律 by "one pays the 'provisioning value' according to the Statute", where the statute would refer to the *Chi lü* 齎律, which seems to have determined the value of certain goods, as suggested in note 6 to A 56 above.

D 76 W 8.30a; S II.37a; S VI.117a; SS 190; str. 91 (461).

[91] "To use a stick to wound people with murderous (intent)".[1] ○ What is the meaning of "stick"?[2] A stick is (a piece of) wood that can be used to strike.

1 See note 1 to D 35 above.
2 *T'ing* 梃; this is a quotation from an unnamed statute.

D 77 W 8.30a; S II.37a; S VI.117b; SS 191; str. 93 (463).

[93] In pronouncing judgment in criminal cases, [what is meant by][1] "not straight"? What is meant by "to let go an incarcerated person?"[2] When a crime warrants a heavy (punishment) and purposely[3] to lighten it, or when it warrants a light (punishment) and purposely to make it heavy, that is the meaning of "not straight".[4] When a sentence is warranted, purposely not to sentence it, as well as to make light[5] of the case, purposely making it not come up to[6] (a crime) and pronouncing a sentence which acquits[7] him—this is what is meant by "letting go an incarcerated person".

1 (*K'o* =) *ho wei* (可=) 何謂; these words are missing in the original but they have been rightly restored by the editors.
2 *Ch'iu* 囚; pending trial all accused persons were held in gaol.
3 *Tuan* 端; see note 9 to D 27 above.
4 *Pu chih* 不直; see note 41 to A 64 and note 10 to D 27 above, and cf. *RHL*, p. 258. SS translates *pu chih* by *pu kung-cheng*, "unjust".
5 *I* 傷, explained as "light" in *SW*.
6 *Pu chih* 不致, which the editors explain as *pu chih* 不至, "not to come up to the standard", but cf. *RHL*, p. 418 f., note 340.
7 *Ch'u chih* 出之; cf. the Exegesis of the Statutes quoted by Chin Cho (fl. c. A.D. 218) in his commentary to *HSPC* 17.22b: *Lü-shuo ch'u tsui wei ku tsung* 律說出罪為故縱, "The Exegesis of the Statutes (says) 'to let out of punishment' (i.e. to acquit) is intentionally to let go (scot-free)"; cf. *RHL*, p. 253.

D 78 W 8.30a; S II.37a; S VI.118a; SS 191–192; str. 94 (464).

[94] When (the allocation for) the redemption of a punishment[1] has been untruthful,[2] and the Clerk disagrees[3] with the Overseer, it is asked how the Clerk should be sentenced. He is warranted to be fined one shield.

1 See *RHL*, p. 205 f.
2 See note 4 to D 77 above.
3 This is a tentative translation of *pu ho* 不和, lit. "not in harmony". SS, however, believes that the Clerk had not *ho mou* 合謀 with the Overseer; I do not know the meaning of *ho mou*, which can hardly mean "to conspire", Could it mean "to take counsel with"? Whatever rendering one takes, the statement about these two men and the resulting condemnation of the Clerk remain inexplicable.

D 79 W 8.30a; S II.37a; S VI.118a–b; SS 192; str. 95 (465).

[95] "The person who makes a statement,[1] makes this statement in the

court". ○ Now, is the Commandery Administrator the court, or is he not? He is. ○ "The person who makes a statement does not first make this statement to Office Chiefs or Overseers". ○ What is the meaning of Office Chiefs? What is the meaning of Overseers? (Officials in charge of) General Offices[2] are called[3] (Office) Chiefs; (officials in charge of offices) in the prefectures are called Overseers.

1 *Tz'u* 辭 is a statement made by a defendant; see *RHL*, p. 77. It is not an accusation, *su-sung* 訴訟, as SS translates *tz'u*, because an accusation brought forward by private individuals was a denunciation, *kao* 告, or, if pronounced by an official, *ho* 劾.

2 See note 19 to A 9 above. In actual fact, the term *tu kuan* 都官 refers to offices in the prefecture, directly subordinate to the central government, whereas *se-fu* 嗇夫, Overseers, were local appointments, made by the prefect; see A 9, note 19, above, and esp. Ch'iu Hsi-kuei, "Se-fu", p. 231.

3 Like the editors I take *ming* 命 for *ming* 名, which is quite common.

D 80 W 8.30a; S II.37a; S VI. 118b; SS 192–193; str. 96–97 (466–467).

[96] "When a member of a group of five[1] denounces another member,[2] hoping thereby to escape[3] punishment, (and the denunciation is) careless,[4] (the denunciator) is to be punished with the punishment he had hoped to escape".[5] (The Statute) also[6] says: "When one is unable to determine the criminal and denounces another person, this is (a case of) being careless in denouncing". Now A says: "The member of my group of five (called) B has killed a person with murderous (intent)".[7] B is immediately arrested, but questioning (shows) that he did not [97] kill a person. What A reported[8] was careless. Is he warranted to be sentenced for carelessness in denouncing, or for what he (had hoped) to escape? To sentence him for what he (had hoped) to escape is fitting.

1 *Wu-jen* 伍人, Following Shang Yang's suggestion, the population was organized in groups of five families with the express purpose that they should denounce each others' misdeeds, on pain of being co-adjudicated; see *SC* 68.7–8; Duyvendak, *Lord Shang*, p. 14. SS refers to the abecedarium *Chi-chiu p'ien*, p. 301, which says: "For incidents, fighting, wounding and killing, the neighbours in the group of five are arrested". See also Lo K'ai-yü, "Shih-wu".

2 Taking *hsiang* 相 not as "mutually", but as indicating the object of the following verb.

3 The text reads *pi* 辟, which both *Wenwu* and S explain as *p'i* 避, "to avoid, to escape". SS, however, though noting this as a possible explanation, prefers another, frequent, meaning of *pi*, namely "punishment", and translates "charges (him) with a crime". This is unacceptable, because a) this neglects the words *ch'ieh i* 且以, "hoping thereby", and b) it gives *pi* a verbal meaning, which, in view of the occurrence of *pi* in other passages, it does not seem to possess. The article presupposes that A was aware of a crime committed by some member of the group of five to which he belonged, and denounced it in order to escape being co-adjudicated, denouncing, however, the wrong person. It seems rather unlikely that A himself was the culprit, for in that case the statutes would have mentioned this.

4 For "carelessness" see note 41 to A 64 above.

5 This is a quotation from an unnamed statute.

6 *Yu* 有 for *yu* 又.

7 See note 1 to D 35 above.

8 For *yen* 言 meaning "to report" see note 2 to D 61 above.

D 81 W 8.30a; S II.37a; S VI.118b–119a; SS 193–194; str. 98 (468).

[98] A murderer[1] enters into A's house and murderously wounds A. A cries

out: "Robbers!",[2] (but) his four neighbours,[3] the (village) chief[4] and the (village) elders[5] have all gone out and are absent,[6] and they do not hear A crying "Robbers!" Question: are they warranted to be sentenced or are they not warranted? If the investigation shows that (his four neighbours)[7] were absent, they are not warranted to be sentenced, (but) the (village) chief and the elders, although they were absent, are warranted to be sentenced.

1 For *tsei* 賊 see note 1 to D 35 above; a thief is a *tao* 盜, like in E 7 and E 25 below.
2 *K'ou* 寇.
3 As explained in D 82 below, the four neighbours are the four households, who together with the household of A formed a group of five, for which see note 1 to D 80 above.
4 For (*li*) *tien* (里) 典 see note 11 to A 7 above.
5 See note 6 to C 20 above.
6 Cf. note 1 to A 81 above.
7 Because three groups have been mentioned before, and because of these three groups the last line mentions two, viz. the village chief and the elders, only the neighbours can be intended here.

D 82 W 8.30b; S II.37a; S VI.119a; SS 194; str. 99 (469).

[99] What is the meaning of "four neighbours"? The four neighbours mean the people of the group of five.[1]

1 See note 1 to D 80 and note 3 to D 81 above.

D 83 W 8.30b; S II.37b; S VI.119b; SS 194–195; str. 101 (471).

[101] It happens that a person is murderously killed or wounded on the road,[1] (but) the bystanders[2] do not help him. If (they are) within one hundred paces,[3] this comparable to the suburbs[4] and warrants a fine of two suits of armour.[5]

1 *Ch'ung-shu* 衝術; both words mean "road". As noted by the editors, the binome occurs in ch. 70 of the *Mo-tzu*, p. 348, where it indicates the main thoroughfares in a city. I should add that the first word is rather vague on the strip and looks more like *chung* 重; such a loan does not seem to be attested.
2 *Chieh p'ang-jen* 偕旁人. *P'ang-jen* by itself means "bystanders" and occasionally "witnesses" (see my "Contracts", pp. 24–27). *Chieh* is "companion". One could therefore also translate "(his) companions and the bystanders."
3 I *pu* equalled six feet or c. 1 m. 40; 100 *pu* is therefore c. 140 m.
4 *Yeh* 壄 is the old form of *yeh* 野 according to *SW*. *Yeh*, meaning "wild" is also used to indicate the outskirts of a city.
5 Although the purport of this article is clear enough, the meaning of the details escapes me.

D 84 W 8.30b; S II.37b; S VI.119a; SS 194; str. 100 (470).

[100] What is the meaning of "repeated[1] denunciations"? A person who repeatedly makes denunciations denounces a criminal, yet[2] in his denunciation he is careless.[3] Then again[4] he denounces him for another matter. (These denunciations) are not to be accepted,[5] but (the denouncer) is to be sentenced for his carelessness.[6]

1 *Chou kao* 州告. The editors take *chou* to be a loan for *chou* 周, "to eircle", hence "coming round again and again", i.e. "repeatedly". As both words had the same pronunciation *t̂i̯ôg (GSR, p. 280, no. 1086a, and p. 279, no. 1083a), the loan is quite acceptable. In this

connection it should be noted that a word containing 州 as the phonetic element, viz. *ch'ou* 酬 (GSR, p. 280, no. 1086e) means "to pledge (with wine) *for the second time*". Karlgren, "Loan characters I", p. 52, no. 154, rejects that *chou* 周 could be a loan for *ch'ou* 酬 in Ode 153, but now it remains a possibility. Ch'en Chih, "Shu wen", p. 71, insists that in ancient texts 周, 州 and 舟 are frequently used as substitutes for each other.

2 The text reads *ch'ieh* 且, which SS explains as *shang ch'ieh* 尚且, "still, yet", but translates as "already"! It might perhaps be rendered as "all the same ; nevertheless".

3 I.e. it is untrue; see note 41 to A 64 above.

4 *Yu* 有 for *yu* 又.

5 Lit. "not to be listened to", *pu t'ing* 不聽.

6 *Ch'i pu shen* 其不審. He is not to be sentenced for the crime of which he had wrongly accused another person (*wu kao* 誣告), because D 35–38 show that a clear distinction was made between false accusation and "carelessness in denouncing".

D 85 W 8.30b; S II.37b; S VI.119b; SS 195; str. 102 (472).

[102] (A man) relieved (from statutory duties because of) age[1] denounces another person because of[2] unfilial behaviour[3] and requests that he be killed.[4] Is he warranted to be three times. . . .[5] or not? He is not warranted to be. . .[5] He is to be quickly seized[6] and not to be lost.[7]

1 Depending on their status, men were excused further statutory service at 56 when they possessed one of the aristocratic ranks and at 60 when they were commoners without rank; see my "Statute labour".

2 The text reads *i wei pu hsiao* 以爲不孝, which would mean "considering (him) to be unfilial", but in this context this is strange. Perhaps a copyist inserted *wei* by mistake. The translation in SS disregards this curious construction.

3 In Han times unfilial behaviour was sometimes characterized as *ta ni pu tao* 大逆不道, "greatly refractory and impious" (see *RHL*, p. 156 f.). According to the canonical Book of Filial Piety, *Hsiao-ching*, unfilial behaviour was the most serious of all crimes.

4 The text merely says *yeh sha* 謁殺, which leaves the question open, whether it was the father or the authorities who were to kill the unfilial person. But, whatever the solution of this question, the procedure indicated here presupposes that a father was not entitled to kill or otherwise punish his children without more ado, but had to obtain official permission; actual examples of this procedure are provided by E 15–18 below. In this connection it should be recalled that also infanticide was prohibited (see D 56 above). This is in sharp contrast to the rules given in D 86 and 87, which stipulate that children were punished when they denounced their father for these very acts, and that denunciations by outsiders were not to be accepted. Do we have to assume that D 86 and 87 were ancient rules, supeerseded by later ones, i.e. D 56 and 85? A surprising aspect of the present article is that the denunciation does not seem to have been directed against the accuser's own child, but against "another person", *jen* 人.

5 The editors read this character with the "jade radical" *huan* 環, "a ring; to encircle", and consider it as a loan for *yüan* 原. This loan is not attested, but it does not seem impossible in view of the ancient pronunciation, *huan* being *g'wan, and *yüan* being *ngi̯wăn (GSR, p. 82, no. 256n, and p. 83, no. 258a). The editors explain *yüan* as "to forgive; to treat leniently". On the one hand they refer to *San-kuo chih*, *Wei chih* 8.22b (T'ung-wen ed.), which reads *fan fa che san yüan jan hou nai hsing hsing* 犯法者三原然後乃行刑, "Those who transgress the laws are three times *yüan*, and only then the punishment is executed." On the other hand, they refer to the *Chou-li*, *ssu-tz'u* 司刺 (*Chou-li chu-su* 36.2a (1281); *Chou-li* 19/68.91; Biot II, p. 35), which mentions the *san yu* 三宥, "the three indulgences", namely for cases of ignorance, involuntary mistakes, or negligence (cf. *RHL*, p. 262 f.). SS therefore translates: "Should the procedure of three times forgiving (*yüan yu* 原宥) be applied or not?". To me, this seems very doubtful. In the first place, *yüan* meaning "to forgive" appears only in Later Han texts, e.g. in *HHSCC* Mem. 21.14a (c. A.D. 180; rebels are *yüan* and made commoners) and Mem. 71.18b (also c. 180; the person in question was "especially *yüan* and not tried"), and in the *San-kuo chih* passage quoted above. — Huang Chan-yüeh, p. 3, writes: "The Ch'in statutes stipulate that in general—the present case being an exception—for death

sentences the system of 'three investigations and the final investigation', *san shen chung shen* 三審終審, was applied". Now *chung shen* seems to be Ch'ing law, involving high ministers, in view of Morohashi, vol. 8, p. 1028, no. 55, which seems hardly applicable here. *San shen* was T'ang law; it meant that the accused had to be questioned three times on three different days, under threat that in case he made a false accusation, he himself would suffer the punishment for the crime he had wished to foist on another person; see *TLSI*, vol. 2, 4.1, *TLT* 6.34b, and *T'ung-tien* 165.17a, all conveniently assembled in Niida, *Tōrei*, p. 778. Then Huang Chan-yüeh adopts virtually the same attitude as the editors of S and SS, writing: "The origins of the system of the 'three investigations' is very early". He then refers to the chapter *Wang-chih* of the *Li-chi* (*Li-chi chu-su* 13.5b (0616); Couvreur, *Li-ki* I, p. 307; Legge, *Li-ki* 27, p. 237), which says that when the complete case, i.e. all the records, had at last been presented to the king, *wang san yu* 王三又 (for *yu* 宥 as all authorities agree). However, as Legge translates, in agreement with Couvreur, "the king . . . considered it with the three mitigating conditions", and in view of the *Chou-li* quoted above, these were the cases of ignorance etc., which have nothing to do with "the three investigations" (or "three hearings"). Moreover, the very text of the *Wang chih* (*Li-chi chu-su* 13.5a (0615); Couvreur, *Li-ki* I, p. 305; Legge, *Li-ki* 27, p. 236) a few lines earlier uses the word *yüan* 原—which S and SS want to substitute for *huan* in the Ch'in text—in a completely different manner. Not for "to forgive", as the editors think, but for "to enquire into" (or, as Couvreur and Legge translate more freely, "tenir compte", resp. "to have respect for"), namely to enquire into the possible implications of the relation between father and son or between prince and subject, in case of a lawsuit. — Finally it seems odd, if not downright impossible, to forgive or treat with indulgence a person who had not even been arrested. As a result of all these considerations I must confess that the meaning of *san huan* remains unclear to me.

6 *Chih* 執. This is a third term for "to arrest", beside *pu* 捕, the formal word for "to arrest", and *te* 得, "to catch", which seems to be reserved for an arrest by people who were not officials.

7 *Shih* 失, "to lose", but also "to let slip; to allow to escape".

D 86 W 8.30b; S II.37b; S VI.119b–120a; SS 195–196; str. 103 (473).

[103] [What][1] is "official[2] denunciation"? What is "unofficial denunciation"? To kill or wound with murderous intent (or) to rob other people are (cases of)[3] official [denunciation].[4] When a child robs his father or mother, or when a father or mother unauthorizedly kill, mutilate or shave their children as well as their male or female slaves,[5] these are not cases of official denunciation.[6]

1 The word "what" (*k'o* 可 for *ho* 何), omitted in the text, has been rightly supplied by the editors.

2 *Kung shih* 公室 in ancient texts designates the ruling house or clan. In the Ch'in texts, however, *kung* 公 prefixed to other words, like *ma* 馬 or *niu* 牛, means "official", or rather "government", horses or cattle. In the present context, *kung shih* in the same way will mean "government" or "official", without the connotation of "ruling house". It is understood here that it is not the government which denounces, but private individuals who denounce a crime or a suspect *to* the government authorities.

3 Cf. note 5 to D 13 above.

4 In view of the context, this word has to be supplied.

5 Cf. note 1 to D 62 above.

6 D 56 and 57 above clearly show that the unauthorized killing of one's children was a punishable offence. The fuller text of D 87 below shows that denunciations by inmates of the culprit's household with an inferior status (children, slaves) were not to be heeded, but the same text also shows that denunciations of "other persons" were not to be received. If these "other persons" were complete outsiders, the only people left who could possibly denounce the crime must have been senior members of the culprit's family; otherwise the prohibition contained in D 56 above would have remained inapplicable to free persons.

D 87 W 8.30b; S II.37b; S VI.120a–b; SS 196; str. 104–105 (474–475).

[104] "Children denouncing their father or mother (and) male and female

slaves denouncing their master are unofficial denunciations; they are not to be accepted".[1] ○ What is the meaning of "unofficial denunciation"? ○ When a master unauthorizedly kills, mutilates or shaves his children or his male or female slaves, this is "unofficial denunciation". When (although) it is not accepted, one (still) lodges[2] a denunciation, the denouncer is punished.[3] When the punishment has already been carried out and another person[4] [105] in succession[5] denounces it,[6] this is likewise not warranted to be accepted.

1 This is a quotation from an unnamed statute.
2 *Hsing* 行, "to enact".
3 In view of the following sentence, *tsui* 罪 here does not mean "crime" but "punishment."
4 This appears to be an outsider, not related to the culprit; cf. note 6 to D 86 above.
5 *Hsi* 襲.
6 *Chih* 之; it is, of course, also possible to translate this ambiguous word by "him".

D 88 W 8.30b; S II.37b; S VI.120b; SS 197; str. 106 (476).

[106] "As regards sentencing members of the household,[1] this concerns 'household crimes' (committed) at the time of the father's (life); if these are only[2] denounced when the father has died, this is not to be accepted".[3] What is the meaning of "household crimes"? "Household crimes" are the father killing persons as well as slaves[4] and denouncing this when the father has died; this is not to be tried.[5]

1 Because slaves are involved, it seems better to translate *chia tsui* 家罪 by "household crimes" than by "family crimes".
2 *P'u* 誧, lit. "to brag", is used here and in D 89 below for *fu* 甫, "to begin; only then". The loan seems unattested, but it is quite possible.
3 This is a quotation from an unnamed statute.
4 *Jen* 人 in its usual meaning of "other people" probably refers to people who are not members of the culprit's household; the slaves, however, will have belonged to his household.
5 *Chih* 治 is the normal term for "to try"; see *RHL*, p. 74, as well as E 1 below. Here it must imply that members of the household were not to be co-adjudicated.

D 89 W 8.30b; S II.37b; S VI.121a; SS 197–198; str. 108 (478).

[108] What is meant by "household crimes"? When father and son live together and (the son)[1] kills or wounds his father's slaves or cattle, or he steals them, and someone denounces this when the father has already died, this is not to be accepted; this is called "household crimes"[2] ○[3] [109 continued] When persons with the status of *pao-tzu*[4] [or higher, whose case][5] has not yet been decided [110] falsely accuse people and the crime warrants mutilation and being made a *ch'eng-tan*, they should have their beard shaved off and be made a *kui-hsin*,[6] however shackling their legs.[7] This is what is meant by ....[8] the *pao-tzu*.

1 Evidently, only the son and not the father could kill or steal his father's slaves or cattle.
2 This is a quotation from an unnamed statute.
3 The editors of S and SS are undoubtedly correct in assuming that the ancient scribe made a mistake when copying these rules; he may have been confronted with broken strips which he arranged to the best of his understanding; cf. *CICA*, pp. 14–15. They have therefore exchanged a passage found here with a passage in D 92. I have followed their example.

[4] For *pao-tzu* see note 19 to A 68 above.
[5] The strip is badly preserved; *pao-tzu* can still be identified, but then there follow some effaced characters. Considering the text in A 68 and in D 90, the illegible passage may have contained the words *i shang yü* 以上獄, "or higher, whose case"; I have therefore placed these words between square brackets.
[6] In Han times, *kui hsin* meant three years' hard labour; see *RHL*, p. 130.
[7] The text reads *wu* 鋈, which means "to plate", In their notes, the editors of SS first suggest that *wu* should be taken as *yao* 夭, which, according to the *Kuang ya* (inaccessible) meant "to break", *che* 折. From this, the editors deduce that *wu* should mean "to amputate", and it is this meaning which they use in their translation. Still, they note another possibility, namely, that *wu* might mean "to attach fetters to the leg(s)". It is the latter meaning which had been adopted in S, and this is undoubtedly correct; it has also been adopted by Liu Hai-nien, "Hsing-fa", p. 178. According to the process of "reversing the punishment" in cases of false accusation (see note 4 to D 18 above), the *pao-tzu* should have suffered a mutilating punishment and should have served a long term as a hard-labour convict, but he is actually condemned to the lighter punishment of *kui hsin*. This means that he was not to suffer mutilation—the parallels in D 91 and 92 say so literally: *wu hsing* 勿刑—so that amputation of a foot is out of the question.
[8] The editors decipher the fragmentary character on the strip as *chieh* 耤, "sacred field", which they wish to read as *cho* 斮, "to hack; to cut off"; the loan is not attested, but possible (*chieh* = *dz'i̯ăk, and *cho* = *ts̯i̯ak; see GSR, p. 210, nos. 797i and 798o). They refer to a line in the poem *yüan shih* 怨世 in the *Ch'u tz'u*, reading *tsu. . . cho* 足 . . . 斮. But, because amputation is out of the question, as explained in note 7, the fragmentary character must have another meaning. I can only suggest that it might mean "to fetter", e.g. *t'a* 錔; leg-irons were called *ti* 釱, defined in *SWKL*, p. 6294a, as *ching ch'ien* 脛鉗, "lower leg ring" (as corrected by Tuan Yü-ts'ai).

D 90 W 8.30b; S II.37b; S VI.121a; SS 197; str. 107 (477).

[107] When (persons with the status of) *pao-tzu*[1] and higher die or they have already been buried before a case (has been made against them) and they are denounced only then,[2] this is likewise not warranted to be accepted for trial, nor should (persons to be co-adjudicated) be arrested;[3] procedure in all these cases should be as in the case of family crimes.[4]

[1] See note 19 to A 68 above.
[2] See note 1 to D 88 above.
[3] Cf. note 10 to A 41 above.
[4] See D 89 above.

D 91 W 8.30b; S II.38a; S VI.122a; SS 199; str. 111–112 (481–482).

[111] Before a decision has been taken in a criminal suit against a *pao-tzu*,[1] [he falsely accuses another person; the[2] crime][3] warrants a mutiliating punishment and being made a *kuei-hsin*.[4] Do not mutilate him, but execute the shaving of the beard; moreover, detain him among the *ch'eng-tan* for six years.[5] What is the meaning of "warrants a mutilating punishment and being made a *kuei-hsin*"? ○ Warranting to have his beard shaved and being made a *kuei-hsin*, before a decision has been taken, he falsely accuses persons[6] (of crimes) warranting a mutilating punishment and being made a *li-ch'en*, as well as [112] remaining intact and being made a *ch'eng-tan*. This is the meaning of "warrants a mutilating punishment and being made a *kuei-hsin*".

[1] See note 19 to A 68 above.
[2] The word *ch'i* 其 is ambiguous, for it may refer either to the *pao-tzu* or to the victim of the false accusation.

3 The text consists of two fragments which the editors have combined but together these fragments do not form a complete strip. The editors have filled the remaining lacuna by means of the words between square brackets, undoubtedly inspired by the similar text of D 92.
4 In Han times three years had labour.
5 The fact that the number of years is explicitly mentioned is an indication that the normal length of the period of hard labour for a *ch'eng-tan* was less. It may have been four years for an "intact" (non-mutilated) *ch'eng-tan* and five years for a *ch'eng-tan* wearing an iron collar and leg-irons (or, more likely, having had a foot amputated), as in the Han period; cf. *RHL*, p. 129 f.
6 The plural is indicated, because in the next part of this sentence two punishments are mentioned.

D 92 W 8.30b; S II.38a; S VI. 121b; SS 199; str. 109–110 (479–480).

[109] "Before a decision has been taken in a criminal suit against a *pao-tzu*,[1] he falsely accuses another person; the[2] crime warrants a mutilating punishment and being made a *li-ch'en*. Do not mutilate him, but execute the shaving of the beard; moreover, detain him among the *ch'eng-tan* for six years."[3] ○ What is the meaning of "warrants a mutilating punishment and being made a *li-ch'en*"?[4] ○ [108 continued] He is held[5] and warrants shaving off the beard, (but) before a decision has been taken, he falsely accuses a person of a crime warranting mutilation and being made a *li-ch'en*. This is the meaning of "warrants a mutilating punishment and being made a *li-ch'en*."

1 See note 19 to A 68 above.
2 See note 2 to D 91 above.
3 See note 5 to D 91 above.
4 Here the passage from D 89 starts; see note 3 to D 89.
5 *Shou* 收, i.e. held in custody; see the discussion in note 10 to A 41 above. The function of *yu* 有 in *yu shou* is unclear; SS translates *yu shou* in the passive, "he is arrested", without further explanation.

D 93 W 8.30b–31a; S II.34b; S VI.107b–108a; SS 171–172; str. 48 (418).

[48] (A person) is warranted to be fined one shield; (the official concerned)[1] confiscates[2] 5,000 cash and loses these.[3] How should he be sentenced? He is to be reprimanded. ○ To denounce a person, saying that he has absconded from the state, when (in fact) he did not go outside the border and did not abscond without permission,[4] constitutes carelessness[5] in denouncing. How should he be sentenced? This is a case of carelessness in denouncing (a crime punishable by) being tattooed and made a *ch'eng-tan*.[6]

1 In view of the context, only an official can be intended.
2 This character the editors read *mo* 没; considering the forms signalized in *HLTY*, *ju sheng*, 19b, this reading must be correct. Normally, *mo* means "to confiscate", but it is hard to see how a fine could be confiscated.
3 *Shih* 失. This word has two meanings, viz. "to lose" and "to loose", the former being the technical term for letting a culprit go unpunished (see *RHL*, p. 252). The editors have adopted the second solution but this cannot be correct, because an official who had first embezzled money and then had let a culprit go scotfree surely would have been punished more severely than by a mere reprimand.
4 *Lan* 闌 is "to trespass; to enter or leave without permission"; see e.g. *HSPC* 10.4a, *HFHD* II, p. 381, note 4.2. The Edsin-gol strips contain many negative reports about nomads "unauthorizedly entering" the defence lines; see *RHA* II, p. 143.

[5] See note 36 to A 64 above.
[6] This shows that leaving the Ch'in state without permission was heavily punished.

D 94 W 8.31a; S II.38a; S VI.122a; SS 200; str. 113–114 (483–484).

[113] What is meant by "redeeming (the hard-labour punishment called) *kuei-hsin* with the feet shackled"?[1] What is meant by "redeeming castration"?[2] When princes and chiefs of genuine Jung (barbarians)[3] who are vassal states,[4] whose rank is equivalent to (the Ch'in aristocratic rank of) *shang tsao*[5] or higher, have committed crimes that are warranted to be redeemed,[6] (then), if it is a case of robbery in a band,[7] they should be made to redeem (the punishment of being made a) *kuei-hsin* with the feet shackled; if they have committed a crime (warranting) castration,[8] they redeem castration. For other crimes which are comparable to robbery in a band, this rule is likewise to be followed.[9]

[1] Cf. note 8 to D 89 above.
[2] For castration see Introduction, p. 17; for the Han time punishment see *RHL*, p. 127.
[3] *Jung* 戎 is the general name for the tribes which had not yet adopted the Chinese civilization; as shown by Průšek, *Statelets*, p. 210 f., these tribes were not fundamentally different from the Chinese. — *Chen* 眞, "genuine, true", is explained in D 157 below as "children born of a vassal-state father and mother, as well as those born in another state"; these children are contrasted to *hsia-tzu* 夏子 who had a vassal-state father and a Ch'in mother.
[4] *Ch'en pang* 臣邦. For the Han concepts of *nei ch'en* 內臣, "inner vassals", i.e. the kings within the empire, and *wai ch'en* 外臣, "outer vassals", i.e. the rulers of foreign states which maintained relations with China, see Kurihara, pp. 229–282. Whereas for the Han period something is known about these relations (see Kurihara, *loc. cit.*, and cf. Hulsewé, "Rebels"), material on the Ch'in is lacking so far. It is therefore unknown whether the vassal states maintained their own institutions. The editors of SS (p. 200, note 5) refer to a passage in *HHSCC*, Mem. 76.9b, showing, as they phrase it, "the preferential treatment of the minorities" (this term nowadays replaces the traditional epithet "barbarians"). The passage reads: "When King Hui of Ch'in had incorporated Pa-chung (see *SC* 5.59, *Mh* II, p. 72 and note 2; the date 316 B.C. is contested), he made the Pa clan the rulers of the barbarians, generation after generation these married women of Ch'in. The aristocratic ranks of their people were assimilated to (the Ch'in rank) *pu-keng* (the 4th rank), and when they committed crimes, they were allowed to have their punishment remitted by means of these ranks". However, this passage is late and therefore perhaps not reliable. — The difference between vassal states and dependent states is not clear (see note 7 to A 110 above).
[5] *Shang tsao* was the second lowest of the Ch'in ranks.
[6] Cf. D 157.
[7] For robbery in a band see above, note 6 to D 1.
[8] The normal term for castration is *kung* 宫; "rottenness", *fu* 腐, is an alternative expression, see *HSPC* 5.7a, *HFHD* I, p. 321 f.
[9] The text simply reads *i ju tz'u* 亦如此, "also like this".

D 95 W 8.31a; S II.38a; S VI.122b; SS 200–201; str. 115 (485).

[115] Is[1] 'to beg[2] for an enquiry'[3] as well as 'to beg for an enquiry on behalf of another person' only accepted when the case has been decided, or is it accepted when the case has not yet been decided? It is only accepted when the case has been decided. How[4] is the failure[5] (to punish a culprit with) fettering the leg[6] sentenced? Like the failure to punish with a mutilating punishment.

[1] I cannot read the first character on the strip. The editors interpret it as *i* 以, but this is un-

likely, considering the form which this sign usually has on these strips, as e.g. in the centre of strip 113 or the sixth character on strip 117. The editors then wish to explain this as a loan for *i* 已 and they translate it as "already". However, there are three reasons which militate against this. In the first place, the eleventh character on this very strip is a clearly legible 已, meaning "already". In the second place, the meaning "already" does not fit the context. And in the third place, the confusion between 以 and 已 is brought about by the misreading of 目, an alternative form of 以, as 已, and not by a confusion between 以 and 已; this misreading is usually found in later texts.

2 *Ch'i* 气 is used for *ch'i* 乞, "to beg, to request" (*GSR*, p. 140, no. 517a and f).

3 For this procedure see *RHL*, p. 79 f. (where two misprints occur on p. 80: in line 21 from above read "abolished" for "altered", and in line 22 read "*Chin shu* 30.12b" for "7b"). This procedure was *tu chü* 讀鞫, "reading out (the result of) the enquiry (to the defendant)", as stated in the commentary to the *Chou li* article *hsiao ssu-k'ou* (*Chou-li chu-su* 35.1b (1244); *Chou-li* 19/66.39; Biot II, p. 319). In his commentary to *SC* 95.19 (not in *HSPC* 41.9a) Chin Cho (3rd century) says: "When the lawsuit has been wound up, the words of the incarcerated person during the enquiry and the circumstances of the crime were read out. If the prisoner stated that he had been unjustly treated and he begged for another enquiry, this was granted". There was a time limit to such a request: "When a convict has been condemned fully three months (ago), he can no longer beg for an enquiry" (commentary to *Chou-li chu-su* 35.12b (1266), *Chou-li* 19/68.80; Biot II, p. 350, note 2). Family members of the defendant could also beg for another enquiry in case the punishment was two years' hard labour or more (*Chin-shu* 30.12b; Uchida, p. 111).

4 This is an independent article, written on the strip without a break.

5 See note 3 to D 93 above.

6 See note 7 to D 89 above.

D 96 W 8.31a; S II.38a; S VI.123a; SS 201–202; str. 116 (486).

[116] When a *li-ch'en* leads[1] *ch'eng-tan* and lets him (or them) abscond, he is made an intact *ch'eng-tan*, and his wife (living) outside and his children are confiscated.[2] When the children are small and cannot yet be separated from (their mother), let them join their mother when confiscated. ○ What is the meaning of "joining their mother when confiscated"? People will surely buy[3] them, but the children, being small, cannot be separated (from her); the mother of the children must not be sold[4] (separately)—that is the meaning.

1 *Chiang* 將, "to lead, to escort". For *li-ch'en* being placed in charge of *ch'eng-tan* see A 69 above; a group of *ch'eng-tan* consisted of twenty men.

2 *Shou* 收; see the discussion in note 10 to A 41 above.

3 These texts write *mai* 買 for both *mai* 買, "to buy", and *mai* 賣, "to sell". The word occurs twice in this strip; whereas it is clear that on its second occurrence it means "to sell", it surely means "to buy" in the first instance, for otherwise the mention of *jen* 人, "(other) people", would be inexplicable. The editors, however, take it to mean "to sell".

4 See note 3.

D 97 W 8.31a; S II.38a; S VI.123b; SS 202; str. 117 (487).

[117] (A person) warranted to have his beard shaved off and being made a *ssu-k'ou* falsely accuses another person (of a crime warranting) to have his beard shaved off and being made a *li-ch'en*. How is he to be sentenced? He is warranted to have his beard shaved off and being made a *li-ch'en*. ○ (A person) warranted to have his beard shaved off and being made a *hou*[1] . . . .[2] crime falsely accuses another. How is he to be sentenced? He is warranted to have his beard shaved off and being made a *ssu-k'ou*.[3]

[1] For *hou* 候 see note 1 to A 103 above.
[2] The editors correctly remark that the scribe must have omitted a passage after the word *hou*. Considering thc reply and judging from similar cases, the text should have contained the words "warranting shaving off the beard and being made a *ssu-k'ou*".
[3] These are evidently cases where the accuser receives the punishment set for the crime of which he falsely accused another person.

D 98 W 8.31a; S II.38b; S VI.123b; SS 202; str. 118 (488).

[118] (A person) warranting to have his beard shaved off and being made a *li-ch'en* fasely accuses another (of a crime warranting) to be made a *ssu-k'ou*. How is he to be sentenced? He is warranted to have his beard shaved off and being made a *li-ch'en*; moreover, he is to be detained among the *ch'eng-tan* for six years.[1]

[1] Hence, he is condemned to his original punishment, but, because of his false accusation, he is to be detained for six years (during the early Han period the term was three years). His detention among the *ch'eng-tan* may have meant that he had to perform the same type of heavy labour.

D 99 W 8.31a; S II.38b; S VI.123b; SS 203; str. 119 (489).

[119] An[1] intact *ch'eng-tan* falsely accuses another person (of a crime warranting) tattooing and being made a *ch'eng-tan*. How is he to be sentenced? He is warranted to be tattooed. ○ A[2] wounds another person with murderous intent.[3] The official sentences him for wounding another person in an (unpremeditated) fight.[4] Is the official warranted to be sentenced or is he not warranted? He is warranted to be berated.

[1] Because the preceding articles start with *tang*, "warranted to", the editors of SS translate the sentence as if *tang* was found in the text.
[2] *Chia* 甲.
[3] and [4] See note 1 to D 35 above.

D 100 W 8.31a; S II.38b; S VI.124a; SS 203; str. 120 (490).

[120] (A person) warranted to be tattooed and to be made a *ch'eng-tan* falsely accuses another of (a crime warranting) to be left intact and made a *ch'eng-tan*. How is he to be sentenced? He is warranted to be tattooed and to have his nose cut off.[1]

[1] The same combination of punishments is found in D 1 above. For amputation of the nose see *RHL*, p. 125. Because the punishment for the crime mentioned in the false accusation is lighter than the punishment to which the false accuser had been condemned in the first place, his original punishment is aggravated.

D 101 W 8.31a; S II.38b; S VI.124a; SS 203–204; str. 121 (491).

[121] (The statute says): "When a leper[1] commits a crime, he is to be... killed".[2] What is "...killing"? Alive, he is to be... killed in the water; that is what is meant. Some say[3] that he is to be buried alive, (but) to bury him alive is another matter.[4]

[1] For a diagnosis of leprosy see E 19 below.
[2] The text reads *ting sha* 定殺. The editors of SS suggest that *ting* is a loan for *t'ing* 渟, "stagnant

water", but this can hardly be correct, because in the explanation *ting sha* is followed by *shui chung* 水中, "in the water". It is therefore clear that the leper is to be drowned, but the significance of *ting* remains unclear. Bodde, "Medicine", p. 11, takes *t'ing* to mean "shore" and translates the next sentence as "alive on shore, executed in the water", but this is unsatisfactory. To assume that *ting* 定 is a mistake for *tien* 淀, "dregs; mud", hardly provides a better solution.

3 The formula *huo yüeh* 或曰 is often used, e.g. in the *SW* dictionary, with the meaning "another opinion is. . ."

4 *I shih* 異事. To express the same idea, D 147 writes *i shih* 是; the latter might be a loan for the former, or a mistake based on the identity of the pronunciation of the two words (GSR, p. 256, 971a: *dz'i̯əg; p. 228, 866a: *d'i̯əg).

D 102 W 8.31a; S II.38b; S VI.124a–b; SS 204; str. 122 (492).

[122] A has committed a crime punishable by remaining intact and being made a *ch'eng-tan*. Before his case has been decided, A (proves to be) a leper.[1] Question: how is A to be sentenced? He is warranted to be banished[2] to the lepers' place and made to live there. Some say: he is warranted to be banished to the lepers' place to be killed by drowning.[3]

1 Cf. D 101 above.

2 *Ch'ien* 遷 is the current term for "to banish".

3 The text again uses the unknown expression *ting sha*, for which see note 2 to D 101 above.

D 103 W 8.31a; S II.38b; S VI.124b; SS 204; str. 123 (493).

[123] When *ch'eng-tan* and *kuei-hsin* are lepers,[1] how are they to be sentenced? They are warranted to be banished to the lepers' place of banishment.

1 The meaning of this brief phrase is, of course, "when it is discovered that persons who have committed crimes, punishable by being made *ch'eng-tan* or *kuei-hsin*, are lepers".

D 104 W 8.31a; S II.38b; S VI.124b; SS 204–205; str. 124 (494).

[124] When arresting (a person guilty of) a crime (warranting) a fine, one stabs and kills him on purpose[1] with a sword or[2] with a sharp weapon.[3] How is be to be sentenced? If he killed him, he is to be left intact and made a *ch'eng-tan*; if he wounded[4] him, he is to have his beard shaved off and made a *li-ch'en*.

1 See note 7 to D 27 above.

2 Actually, the text reads *chi* 及, "as well as".

3 *Ping jen* 兵刃, literally "the cutting edge of a weapon".

4 The question does not mention wounding.

D 105 W 8.31a–b; S II.38b; S VI.124b–125a; SS 205; str. 125–126 (495–496).

[125] (A person)[1] leads and supervises[2] (incarcerated[3]) people, and they abscond. If he personally is able to arrest them, as well as if his relatives (or) his friends[4] arrest them for him, he is let off[5] and not punished; those already mutilated[6] are placed in the Hidden Office.[7] For which punishments is it allowed to place (people) in the Hidden Office? ○ When robbers in a band,[8] who have been amnestied and made commoners,[9] lead manacled[10] incarcerated convicts who have been robbers and [126] who have been (pun-

ished by) mutilation[11] or more, and these abscond, (the men who lead them) are sentenced for their former crime: they have their left foot cut off and are made *ch'eng-tan*. Later, they personally arrest[12] those whom they had let escape.[13] This is meant by "being placed in the Hidden Offices". ○ Other crimes, comparable to "robbery in a band" are all (treated) like this.

1 The subject of this sentence is not indicated. The following reply shows that this is an amnestied robber who has become a commoner, but it does not explain his function.
2 The same term *chiang ssu* occurs in A 69 above. There we find that a group of twenty *ch'eng-tan* was "led" by a *ch'eng-tan* robberguard, i.e., according to Han practice (cf. *RHL*, p. 336), a *ch'eng-tan*, who after having served a term of three years, had been made a *ssu-k'ou* 司寇, robberguard. However, in the present instance the guard is a commoner.
3 *Jen* 人 is occasionally used for convicts; cf. C 12 above. It is also possible that the copyist, perhaps faced with a deteriorated text, mistook *ch'iu* 囚, "incarcerated convict", for 人.
4 *Chin* 智 read as *chih* 知; *so* 所 *chih*, "those whom he knows" are "friends, acquaintances".
5 *Ch'u* 除; cf. note 3 to B 7 above.
6 *Hsing* 刑. Hori, "Keimei", p. 119, finds reasons to assume that, when *hsing* is used alone, it indicates the lightest of the mutilating punishments, namely tattooing. However, this does not hold good in the present case, because the following sentence shows that the delinquent guard had his left foot amputated.
7 See note 1 to A 91 above.
8 See note 6 to D 1 above.
9 See note 37 to A 68 above.
10 *Chieh* 戒 is used for *chieh* 械; see *RHL*, p. 74.
11 See note 6 above.
12 It is difficult to imagine how hard-labour convicts with a foot amputated would be able to arrest fugitives from justice.
13 *So wang* 所亡.

D 106 W 8.31b; S II.39a; S VI.125a–b; SS 206; str. 127–128 (497–498).

[127] The Grandee[1] A leads[2] *kuei-hsin*, and the *kuei-hsin* abscond. Question: how is A to be sentenced? He is warranted (to be made) to work[3] in a government storehouse until[4] those who had absconded have been caught. ○ Now A is working (in a government storehouse) and again[5] (they[6]) leave and abscond, to be caught within a month; how is he to be sentenced? He is warranted to be fined one shield, and (to be made) again to work (in a government storehouse). He is working (in a government storehouse) and again they abscond, to be caught within a year. [128] How is he to be sentenced? He is warranted to have his beard shaved off.

1 The fifth of the Ch'in aristocratic ranks was the plain *ta fu* 大夫, and it is probably this rank that is meant here, but it is to be noted that the sixth and seventh rank also contained the term *ta fu* in their title, namely *kuan* 官 *ta fu* and *kung* 公 *ta fu*; see Loewe, "Rank", p. 99.
2 The text clearly writes *chien* 堅, "hard". S suggests that this should be *ch'ien* 擊, "to knock, to beat", but SS believes that it is a loan for *hsien* 礥, which, according to the *Kuang yün* (inaccessible) means "to whip". I would suggest that *ch'ien* 掔 is meant, which is used as a loan for the homophonous *ch'ien* 牽, "to pull, to lead" (see GSR, p. 106, 368d).
3 *Ts'ung shih* 從事; see note 1 to A 12 above.
4 *Hsu* 須, lit. "waiting".
5 SS believes that the following refers to the grandee, but this seems contradicted by the word *yu* 有 (i.e. 又), "again", which in my opinion can only refer to the *kuei-hsin*, who had already escaped once.
6 No further punishment is mentioned, but it will have been hard labour.

D 107 W 8.31b; S II.39a; S VI.125b; SS 206–207; str. 129 (499).

[129] When transporting food,[1] one loses[2] more than one *kuei-hsin* outside.[3] How is this to be sentenced? Do not sentence this.

[1] *Kuei* 餽 is "to present or send food"; *SW* equates it with *shang* 饟. The combination *kuei-shang* occurs in *HSPC* 24B.7a (Swann, p. 247); here the commentator Yen Shih-ku (581–645) remarks that *shang* is the same as *kuei* 饋, which again means 'to present food."

[2] *Wang* 亡 is "to abscond"; in English, this cannot be used in the passive voice.

[3] SS also presents an alternative rendering, viz. that the whole phrase would mean "to present food on more than one occasion to absconded *kuei-hsin* who are outside". However, SS does not adopt this version in the translation, because the refusal to have the responsible person punished shows that the event was not considered serious, whereas aiding fugitives from justice was a crime. In Han times this was *t'ung hsing yin shih* 通行飲食, "to allow to pass and to provide with food and drink", but the texts (*HSPC* 98.1b and 18b; *HHSCC* Mem. 36.11b) do not mention the punishment. The early commentators have no remarks on this point, but Yen Shin-ku suggests that the crime was the same as that indicated in the T'ang code: *kuo chih tzu chi* 過致資給 (*TLSI*, vol. 4, p. 69), explained in the commentary as "to indicate roads and paths, to help through dangerous passages, to assist in transport, and to provide with clothes and provisions". The T'ang punishment for this crime was one degree lighter than that of the fugitive criminal.

D 108 W 8.31b; S II.39a; S VI.126a; SS 207; str. 130 (500).

[130] "When arresting persons who have absconded and these persons carry money, (the men who) make the arrest are allowed to take the money."[1] They are allowed to take the money, if the arrested persons are warranted to be punished by shaving off the beard and more severely.

[1] In view of the following explanation, this may be a quotation from a statute.

D 109 W 8.31b; S II.39a; S VI. 126a; SS 207; str. 131 (501).

[131] When (persons) abscond carrying (the tools or arms) that had been lent (to them),[1] and they are caught, as well when they give themselves up, (is their crime) warranted to be considered as robbery, or is it not warranted? If they give themselves up, they are to be sentenced for absconding.[2] If they are caught, they are to be adjudicated for the illegal profit; it is a case of robbery.[3] In case the punishment for robbery would be lighter than that for absconding, they are to be sentenced for absconding.

[1] For tools loaned see A 8, 39 and 57 above; for arms loaned see A 71.

[2] To judge from E 6 below, the length of absence determined the punishment; cf. also D 144 below.

[3] The height of the value of the stolen goods—for that is the meaning of *tsang* 臧, i.e. 贓 (see note 6 to D 1 above)—determined the punishment, see e.g. D 27 above.

D 110 W 8.31b; S II.39a; S VI.126a; SS 208; str. 132 (502).

[132] *Li-ch'en* and *li-ch'ieh*, detained among the *ch'eng-tan* and the grain-pounders,[1] who abscond and who have already run away,[2] but who give themselves up[3] before having been sentenced, are warranted to be bastinadoed with fifty strokes; they have to fulfil their days of detention.

[1] For a case of a bond-servant, detained among the *ch'eng-tan* as an aggravation of his punishment, see D 98 above.
[2] This addition may be an explanation of "to abscond".
[3] For such a case see E 6 below.

D 111 W 8.31b; S II.39a; S VI.126b; SS 208; str. 133 (503).

[133] When disabled persons[1] who guard a government storehouse abscond and are caught, is it allowed (to punish them in a manner) comparable to persons disabled in the government service[2] or is it not allowed? It is allowed (to punish them) comparably to these.

[1] See note 4 to C 20 above.
[2] Kung lung 公㾩. I have followed the suggestion of the editors of SS.

D 112 W 8.31b; S II.39a; S VI.126b; SS 208; str. 134 (504).

[134] A denounces B for having wounded a person with murderous intent; the interrogation (shows) that B killed a person with murderous intent; it was not so that he wounded him. A warrants a reward;[1] how large should the reward be? He is warranted to be rewarded with two ounces.[2]

[1] Cf. note 2 to D 36 above.
[2] The editors of SS believe that this refers to ounces of gold. In Han times, the catty of 16 ounces was reckoned theoretically at 10.000 cash; two ounces would therefore be equivalent to $2/16 \times 10.000 = 1250$ cash.

D 113 W 8.31b; S II.39a; S VI.126b; SS 209; str. 135 (505).

[135] How large is the reward for arresting an intact *ch'eng-tan* who had absconded? This warrants a reward of two ounces.[1]

[1] Or 1250 cash; cf. note 2 to D 112 above.

D 114 W 8.31b; S II.39b; S VI.127a; SS 209; str. 136 (506).

[136] A husband, his wife and his children, (in all) five persons, together commit robbery; they are warranted to suffer mutilation[1] and be made *ch'eng-tan*. Now A[2] arrests them all[3] and denounces them. Question: with how much is A warranted to be rewarded? Per person a reward of two ounces.[4]

[1] See note 6 to D 105 above.
[2] The text clearly writes *chung* 中, an evident mistake for *chia* 甲.
[3] *Chin* 盡, lit. "exhaustively, completely".
[4] Or 6250 cash; cf. note 2 to D 112 above.

D 115 W 8.31b; S II.39b; S VI.127a; SS 209; str. 137 (507).

[137] A husband, his wife and his children, (in all) ten persons, together commit robbery; they are warranted to suffer mutilation and be made *ch'eng tan*, (but) they abscond. Now A arrests and catches eight of them. Question: with how much is A warranted to be rewarded? He is warranted to be rewarded with two ounces per person.[1]

1 Or 10.000 cash.

D 116 W 8.31b; S II.39b; S VI.127a; SS 209–210; str. 138 (508).

[138] A arrests B and denounces him for having fraudulently copied[1] the seal of an Assistant (Prefect) and having absconded with it. The interrogation (shows) different dates[2] for the abscondence; the rest was as A (had said). B has already been sentenced to have his beard shaved off. Question: is A warranted to be rewarded or is he not warranted? He is not warranted (to be rewarded).

1 Cf. D 44 and D 45 above.
2 The text clearly reads *wang erh jih* 亡二日. Because this statement is unfavourable for A, who is not rewarded, this cannot mean "he had absconded for two days". The editors of SS therefore suggest that *erh* should mean "not one", i.e. "not identical; different", referring to ch. 30 of the *Li-chi* (*Li-chi chu-su* 55.3b–4a (2116–2117); Couvreur, *Li-ki* II, p. 519; Legge, *Li-ki* 28, p. 355). This text mentions leaders of the people who *pu erh* their clothes, and the commentators explain *erh* as *pu i* 不壹, "not unified". Couvreur therefore renders *pu erh* as "ne changent pas la forme", and Legge translates "use no (improper) variations". The editors of SS conclude that *wang erh jih* implies that the actual time of B's absence as established during questioning did not agree with A's statement.

D 117 W 8.31b; S II.39b; S VI.127a; SS 210; str. 139 (509).

[139] A rank-holding official[1] arrests (a) person(s) who had unauthorizedly absconded; he presents him (them) to B, ordering him to proceed (to a government office) and agreeing with him to divide the reward. Question: how are the official and B to be sentenced? They are warranted to be fined two suits of armour each; they are not to be rewarded.[2]

1 See note 1 to A 22 above.
2 Cf. C 24 above for a similar rule.

D 118 W 8.31b; S II.39b; S VI.127a–b; SS 211; str. 140 (510).

[140] "(When persons have been arrested)[1] for thievishly taking pearls[2] and jade outside the passes[3] of the state as well as selling these to strangers[4] the pearls and jade are sent to the Minister of Finance; the Minister of Finance deliberates[5] on the bestowal[6] of a reward." ○ By what means are (the persons who made the arrest) to be rewarded? If a crime punishable by shaving off the beard is concerned, the reward is like that for arresting men guilty of other crimes[7]; if the punishment is a fine, there is no reward.

1 Because in the following question an arrest is mentioned, I have added the words between brackets. — This is evidently a quotation, perhaps taken from a statute.
2 The text writes *chu* 朱, "cinnabar", for *chu* 珠, "pearls".
3 Cf. note 4 to D 46 above.
4 *K'o* 客.
5 Cf. note 3 to D 42 above.
6 For *shu* 鼠 used for *yü* 與 see note 20 to A 30 above.
7 In view of D 112–115 above, this reward will have been two ounces of gold per person.

D 119 W 8.31b–32a; S II.39b; S VI.127b; SS 211; str. 141 (511).

[141] Somebody arrests a slave-woman (belonging to) another person, and

denounces her for having stolen 110 cash. Question: does the owner reward him or does the government reward him? The government rewards him.[1]

[1] As remarked by the editors, the second character *chih* 之 is superfluous.

D 120 W 8.32a; S II.39b; S VI.128a; SS 211–212; str. 142 (512).

[142] What[1] is "to transgress the Ordinances"[2] and "to set aside[3] the Ordinances"? What the Statute means is that when an Ordinance says "do no do this" and yet to do it—that is what is meant by "to transgress the Ordinances". When an Ordinance says "do this", then not to do it—this is what is meant by "to set aside the Ordinances". It is the practice of the court[4] that both are sentenced as "transgressing the Ordinances".

[1] Differing from other articles, the text writes *ho ju* 可（=何）如 instead of simply *ho*.
[2] *Ling* 令. It is not clear from these texts whether the Ch'in had Ordinances, like the Han; for the latter see *RHL*, pp. 31 f. and 47 f. It is also possible to translate *ling* literally as "order".
[3] For *fa* 灋 used for *fei* 廢 see note 5 to A 90 above. For *fei* meaning "to set or to lay aside" see the constantly recurring phrase in *SC*, where Ssu-ma Ch'ien exclaims *fei shu t'an yüeh* 廢書嘆曰, "I laid the text aside and said with a sigh. . ."
[4] See notes 2 and 3 to D 30 above.

D 121 W 8.32a; S II.39b; S VI.128a; SS 212; str. 143 (513).

[143] Are (officials), who have been dismissed or transferred, pursued[1] for having set aside or transgressed the Ordinances? Pursue them.

[1] *Ta* 逻, GSR, p. 180, no. 678e:*d'əp, meaning "to reach, to overtake", is used for *tai* 逮, GSR, p. 139, no. 509c:*d'əd, which also means "to reach"; see *SWKL* pp. 747a–b and 763b–764b. Both words, and especially *tai*, have come to mean "to overtake a criminal", i.e. "to arrest", e.g. in *HSPC* 23.12b (*RHL*, p. 343 and p. 378, end of note 158) and in *HSPC* 53.19a (*SC* 59.17–18; Watson, *Records* I, p. 460; *RHL*, p. 78). This meaning is closely connected with that of *chi* 及, likewise "to reach, to overtake", which has the technical meaning of "to implicate", viz. to implicate other persons in a crime (see *RHL*, pp. 397–398, the second part of note 239). In the present case I prefer to translate *ta* as "to pursue", since the delinquent officials are in a place different from that where they committed their misdemeanours. — For *ta* used in a temporal sense, viz. "until", see note 7 to A 57 above.

D 122 W 8.32a; S II.39b; S VI.128a; SS 212; str. 144 (514).

[144] How are (clerical) Assistants who have been appointed by a Commandery or a Prefecture and who serve in another Commandery or Prefecture, but who do not perform their tasks,[1] to be sentenced? They are to be sentenced for minor transgressions of the Ordinances.[2]

[1] *Shih shih* 視事; see note 2 to A 80 above.
[2] See D 120 above for "transgressing the Ordinances"; the scope of *hsiao* 小, "minor", is unknown.

D 123 W 8.32a; S II.40a; S VI.128b; SS 212–213; str. 145 (515).

[145] (An official) recommends and guarantees[1] a person (to be appointed) as Assistant (Prefect). Later, when (this) Assistant (Prefect) has been dismissed, (the official)[2] becomes Prefect. Now the person he had orginally re-

commended and guaranteed commits a crime. Is the Prefect warranted to be dismissed or is he not warranted? He is not warranted to be dismissed.[3]

[1] For this rendering of *jen* 任 see note 1 to C 1 above. The editors of SS add a reference to *SC* 79.33 (not in Watson, *Records*), which reads: "According to the laws of Ch'in, when one recommends and guarantees a person and the recommended person is not good, one is punished with his punishment".

[2] This solution, which is clear from the context, has also been adopted by the editors of SS. However, Kao Heng, "Chih-kuan", p. 211, presents a completely different solution, in view of his remark that the present rule "shows that not only the guarantor was co-adjudicated when the person for whom he had stood surety had committed a crime (i.e. the case presented in "the laws of Ch'in" quoted in note 1 above, also quoted by Kao Heng), but that also the person guaranteed was co-adjudicated when his guarantor had committed a crime". Kao Heng must therefore have understood the present rule to mean: "Somebody guarantees another (to be appointed) as Assistant (Prefact). The Assistant (Prefect) is dismissed, but later he becomes Prefect. Now the person who had originally recommended him commits a crime. Is the Prefect warranted to be dismissed or not? He is not." Although I do not think that this meaning is intended here, this rendering is also possible; the Han histories show cases of both types, see *RHL*, p. 272 f.

[3] This does not contradict "the laws of Ch'in" mentioned in note 1, because the culprit was no longer an Assistant Prefect and therefore no longer guaranteed by the other man.

D 124 W 8.32a; S II.40a; S VI.128b; SS 213; str. 146 (516).

[146] When (an official[1]) loses documents,[2] tallies,[3] official seals or balance weights,[4] and he has already been adjudicated and sentenced, but later he personally finds what he has lost—is the sentence warranted to be repealed[5] or is it not warranted? It is not warranted.

[1] The subject is not mentioned, but considering the lost objects, it must have been a government servant.

[2] As remarked in note 3 to A 47 above, *chiu* 久 as a loan for *chi* 記 is quite acceptable, though not attested; as a matter of fact, I do not think that *chi* is found in the legal texts translated here. For *chi* used in isolation, SS refers to *HSPC* 76.18b, where the T'ang commentator explains the word as "notifications to subordinate officials". Taken together, *chi-shu* 記書 appears to be a general term for "documents".

[3] See Ōba, "Dōkofu".

[4] A 104 above shows that many offices possessed weights and measures, whereas A 54 shows that these were annually checked.

[5] *Ch'u* 除, lit. "to remove"; cf. note 3 to B 7 above.

D 125 W 8.32a; S II.40a; S VI.128b; SS 213–214; str. 147 (517).

[147] A moves his residence.[1] He requests the official to transfer[2] the (population) register,[3] but the official refuses[4] and does not change[5] the register for him. Now A commits a crime (punishable by) shaving off the beard or[6] by a fine. Question: how is the official to be sentenced? (For a crime punished by) shaving off the beard or more heavily, he is warranted to be fined two suits of armour.

[1] *Hsi chü* 徙居. Because in this case the population register has to be transferred, A evidently moved to another locality. It is, of course, unknown, whether A was at liberty to do so, or whether he was ordered to move.

[2] Also *hsi* 徙.

[3] *Shu* 數; cf. note 6 to A 35 above.

[4] The editors refer to a phrase in the *Chou-li*, *hsia kuan*, where *huan* 環, normally "a ring; to

encircle", is explained as *ch'üeh* 郤, "to drive back; to refuse" (*Chou-li chu-su* 30.8b (1091); *Chou-li* 17/58.4; Biot II, p. 200).

5 *Keng* 更.

6 "Or" is necessary here, because there exists no relation between these two types of punishment.

D 126 W 8.32a; S II.40a; S VI.129a; SS 214; str. 148 (518).

[148] "When the common people have debts, one should not venture unauthorizedly to extort pledges.[1] The unauthorized extortion of pledges, as well as accepting pledges with mutual consent[2] are both fined with two suits of armour".[3] It is the practice of the court that he who extorts a pledge from another person is sentenced; he who gives[4] the pledge is not sentenced. In case of accepting a pledge with mutual consent, the person who gives the pledge is (also)[5] sentenced.

1 *Ch'iang chih* 强質, "by force to (take a) pledge".

2 *Ho* 和; both parties being "in harmony".

3 The foregoing seems to be a quotation of the code.

4 Cf. note 9 to A 37 above.

5 The editors leave a blank space for an illegible character; in view of the context, this may be a word meaning "likewise".

D 127 W 8.32a; S II.40a; S VI.129a; SS 215; str. 149 (519).

[149] When in offices (concerned with grain) storage the door-bar[1] is not tight, admitting fingers or a scoop,[2] it is the practice of the court that this is fined with one suit of armour.

1 According to SW, *kuan* 關 is a horizontal bar for closing the two wings of a door.

2 *Yüeh* 抉 is "to scoop out; to gouge". SS believes it was some kind of crow-bar.

D 128 W 8.32a; S II.40a; S VI.129b; SS 215; str. 150 (520).

[150] When the wings of the door(s) of an office (concerned with grain) storage are not tight, so that the grain can escape,[1] it is the practice of the court that this is fined with one suit of armour.

1 *Ch'u* 出. The phrase might also be translated "so that it is possible to take out grain".

D 129 W 8.32a; S II.40a; S VI.129b; SS 215–216; str. 151 (521).

[151] In an empty granary there is matting[1]; when underneath the matting there is one bushel or more of grain, it is the practice of the court[2] that this is fined with one suit of armour, and that the Prefectural Clerk who supervises (this granary is fined) one shield.

1 *Chien* 薦; see note 2 to A 4 above.

2 In the expression *t'ing hsing shih* 廷行事 the word *shih* has been omitted.

D 130 W 8.32a; S II.40a; S VI.129b; SS 216; str. 152 (522).

[152] How many rat holes in a granary warrant sentencing or[1] berating? It is the practice of the court that for three or more rat holes the fine is one

shield and that for two or less (the responsible official) is berated. Three mouse[2] holes are equivalent to one rat hole.

[1] The text has *chi* 及, "as well as".
[2] *Hsi* 鼷. According to the dictionaries, this is the smallest of the rat family; hence my translation.

D 131 W 8.32a; S II.40a; S VI.129b–130a; SS 216–217; str. 153 (523).

[153] Certain[1] issues are to be made in beans[2] or barley; although warranted to be issued, they are not[3] issued, but grain is issued as an equivalent of beans or barley. The price[4] of beans and barley is low and that of grain is high; how is this to be sentenced? This warrants a fine of one suit of armour.[5]

When[6] there happens to be an amnesty and (a culprit), not yet sentenced, escapes, to be caught six months after the expiration of the amnesty,[7] he is warranted to have his beard shaved off.[8]

[1] The text reads *yu* 有, "there are".
[2] The text has *shu* 叔 for *shu* 菽.
[3] The use of the perfective negative *wei* 未 is striking.
[4] The text has *chia* 賈 for *chia* 價.
[5] Compare D 132 below, where the issuing of excess rations is punished as theft.
[6] This is an independent article.
[7] This shows that the validity of an amnesty was limited, but it is unknown, how this worked in practice. For Ch'in amnesties see *Ch'in hui-yao*, p. 347 f.
[8] As no crime nor a punishment are mentioned, the only possible conclusion seems to be that the amnesty had relieved the man of the punishment for his criminal act, and that it was the escape which was punished by shaving off the beard, i.e. hard labour.

D 132 W 8.32a; S II.40b; S VI.130a; SS 217; str. 154 (524).

[154] When for officials there exist reasons[1] why their food (rations) should be stopped, but these are not stopped, and the full rations are issued[2] — how is this to be sentenced? (The official)[3] is warranted to be adjudicated for what was issued in excess, as being a case of theft.[4]

[1] These reasons are not specified. Officials might be sent on a mission, whereupon their home issues were stopped; see A 31 above.
[2] Cf. A 33 above.
[3] It is unclear who is to be punished. It could be the official who accepted these extra rations, or the man who issued them without passing them on but appropriating them for his own benefit.
[4] In that case the value of the stolen goods determined the punishment.

D 133 W 8.32a; S II.40b; S VI.130a; SS 217; str. 155 (525).

[155] When an official works in a government storehouse, is he warranted to be co-adjudicated for (crimes committed by) members of his group of five?[1] He is not warranted (to be co-adjudicated).

[1] For the organization of the population into groups of five families whose members were held accountable for each other's misdeeds see note 1 to D 80 above, as well as D 81 and 82.

D 134 W 8.32a; S II.40b; S VI.130b; SS 217; str. 156 (526).

[156] Are Grandees,[1] being few,[2] warranted to be incorporated into a group

of five[3] . . . .[4] other people, or are they not warranted? They are not warranted.

[1] Cf note 1 to D 106 above.
[2] *Kua* 寡.
[3] See note 1 to D 80 above. as well as D 81 and 82. It is unclear whether they should form a group of five together with other families of Grandees, or with their less elevated neighbours.
[4] The writing on the strip clearly reads *chi* 及, which in these texts usually means "as well as", although sometimes it has to be rendered by "or"; however, neither meaning makes sense in this context. *Chi* does not mean "like". A complicated solution could be to give *chi* the meaning "to be attained by, i.e. to be implicated in" a lawsuit against another person (cf. note 1 to D 121 above). This would lead to the translation "are they warranted . . . . to be implicated (in crimes committed by) other people?", namely by other members of the group of five.

D 135 W 8.32a–b; S II.40b; S VI.130b; SS 218; str. 157 (527).

[157] When a Section[1] Assistant "hides"[2] fields of commoners,[3] and the commoners are not aware[4] of this, are they warranted to be sentenced?[5] When a Section Assistant commits "hiding fields", what does he commit? When he has already taxed the people, (but) he does not report this, that is a case of "hiding fields". When he has not levied the tax, he is not sentenced . . . .[6] is a case of "hiding fields".

[1] For *pu* 部 see note 4 to A 6 and note 7 to C 8 above. SS idetifies the Section Assistant with the *hsiang* 鄉 or Commune Assistant, of whom *HHSCC* Tr. 28.8a says that he was "in charge of the people and collected the different taxes".
[2] *Ni* 匿, "to hide", i.e." to suppress, to conceal, to fail to report"; cf. D 175 below.
[3] The text reads *che* 者 for *chu* 諸. *Chu min* 民 seems to be unknown, although the meaning is clear. Also, the use of *chu* for *shu* 庶 is attested in antiquity, e.g. in the *Li-chi*, ch. *Ch'ü li* (Li-chi *chu-su* 2.7b–8a (0082–83); Couvreur, *Li-ki* I, p. 29; Legge, *Li-ki* 27, p. 77), so that *chu min* is evidently equivalent to *shu min*, for which see note 37 to A 68 above.
[4] *Chih* 智 for *chih* 知.
[5] The questioner's doubt appears justified when it is observed that in D 81 above the Village Chief and the Elders were still punished, although they had been absent when a villager had cried for help when attacked by robbers in his house.
[6] Here two or three characters are effaced, but in the SS translation no notice is taken of this fact.

D 136 W 8.32b; S II.35b; S V.111b; SS 178; str. 64 (434).

[64] "Thievishly to shift border marks[1] (is punished by) redemption of shaving off the beard." What are border marks? Border marks are the field paths.[2] Are the borders[3] between *ch'ing*[4] border marks or are they not? Why is the punishment for shifting these as heavy as redemption of shaving off the beard?[5] They are (border marks). It is not heavy.

[1] *Feng* 封 are border marks between fields in the form of small mounds of earth; according to the isolated article from the Ch'in Statutes on Agriculture, translated in G below, such a mound was four feet or not quite one meter high, with sides of the same length.
[2] *Ch'ien-mo* 阡陌, written here as 千佰, traditionally explained as running North—South, c.q. East—West (or E—W and N—S! Yang K'uan, "Ch'ing-ch'uan", p. 84, believes that the different explanations depended on the course of the rivers in the different areas).
[3] *P'an* 畔, here written *pan* 半, explained in SW as "borders of fields", *t'ien chieh* 田界.
[4] A *ch'ing* 頃 was a plot of 100 *mu* or c. 4.57 hectare.

5 This translation follows the rendering in SS, taking the text beginning with "Are the borders..." to consist of two consecutive questions, followed by two answers. The version presented in Koga, *Chōan*, p. 105, is unacceptable.

D 137 W 8.32b; S II.37a; S VI.117b; SS 190; str. 92 (462).

[92] Small cattle[1] having entered a person's house, the inmates of the house[2] take quarterstaffs[3] or sticks[4] and beat[5] and kill them. Those killed have a value of 250 cash; how are they to be sentenced? This warrants a fine of two suits of armour.

1 Probably sheep (see C 19 above) or pigs (see A 34 above).
2 *Shih jen* 室人; cf. D 61 above.
3 For *shu* 殳 (here written *t'ou* 投), "quarterstaffs", see note 1 to B 21 above.
4 *T'ing* 梃; see D 76 above.
5 *Fa* 伐; see D 76 above.

D 138 W 8.32b; S II.40b; S VI.131a; SS 218; str. 158 (528).

[158] A is small and not fully six feet (tall).[1] He has one horse which he personally takes to graze. Now the horse is. . .[2] by another person and eats one bushel of another's grain. Question: is he warranted to be sentenced or is he not warranted? He is not warranted to be sentenced nor to repay the grain.

1 Cf. A 12 above.
2 The strip clearly reads *pai* 敗, "to defeat, to spoil". The editors of SS suggest that here it should mean "to frighten".

D 139 W 8.32b; S II.40b; S VI.131a; SS 219; str. 159 (529).

[159] When lodging in a government residence,[1] one causes a fire[2] which burns down the lodge; although it contains government tools, these must not be charged.[3] ○ Now, when lodging in a government residence, one causes a fire which burns the carriage(s) and horses that had been borrowed;[4] are these warranted to be charged,[5] or are they not warranted? They are not warranted; cancel[6] them.

1 The text reads *kung kuan* 公官; the editors take *kuan* 官 as a loan for *kuan* 館, which is possible in view of *SWKL*, p. 6473a-b. The term *kung kuan* 公館 is found in the *Li-chi* chapter *Tseng-tzu wen* (*Li-chi chu-su* 19.11b (0916); Couvreur, *Li-ki* I, p. 459; Legge, *Li-ki* 27, p. 340), where Cheng Hsüan explains it as the *kuan she* 官舍, "government lodges" (according to the *chiao-k'an chi* 19.17b (0928), most versions of this commentary read *kuan kung* 官宮) in the prefectures.
2 The text is transcribed in all editions as *sui huo* 旞火. The SW says that *sui* is the same as *i* 𣄰, (*SWKL*, p. 2963b–64b); the SW commentators refer to Ode 223, *Hsiao ya*, *Chüeh kung* 角弓, which in verse 7 reads *hsia i* 下遺, whereas the *Hsün-tzu*, ch. *fei hsiang* 非相, p. 49 (not in Dubs, *Hsüntze*) reads *hsia sui* 下隧. This leads SS to the suggestion that *sui huo* should be read *i huo* 遺火, which is a known expression for "to cause a fire"; however, the earliest example quoted in Morohashi, vol. 11, p. 182, only occurs in *HHSCC* Mem 73.8a, in a story set in the 1st century A.D. It should not be overlooked that, according to GSR, p. 142, no. 526m, *sui* 旞 was *dzi̯wəd, whereas GSR, p. 144, no. 540m, *i* 遺 (𣄰 not in GSR) was *gi̯wɛd. Karlgren, "Glosses Siao-ya", p. 156, no. 724, rightly warns against taking *i* 遺 and *sui* 隧 in Ode 223 and in its quotation in the *Hsün-tzu* as loan words; they are textual variants in two different versions of the Odes, where *sui* 隧 in the *Hsün-tzu* is to be taken

as *chui* 墜, "to fall". In stead of the very complicated argument of the editors—which also seems quite uncertain—I would suggest that in the present instance *sui* 燧 stands for *chui* 墜. PWYF, p. 2012, column 3, actually includes the term *chui huo* 墜火, though it is to be noted that this term only occurs in a work that seems to be late, viz. the *Shu min chui t'u tan chuan* 書民墜塗炭傳, about which I lack further information.

3 *Tse* 責.

4 An official would be travelling in a government carriage, which he evidently is assumed to have "borrowed" for the occasion.

5 *Fu* 負, "to (be made to) bear".

6 *Ch'u* 出; see note 18 to A 9 above. On the strip the word *ch'u* is provided with the repetition marker =, but, as remarked by the editors, this is a mistake.

D 140 W 8.32b; S II.40b; S VI.131b; SS 219; str. 160 (530).

[160] Causing a fire which spreads and burns the gate of the ward,[1] warrants a fine of one shield; when it is the gate of a city,[2] the fine is one suit of armour.

1 In view of the context, *li* 里 seems more likely to be a city ward (cf. Miyazaki, p. 378) than a village.

2 The expression *i-pang* 邑邦 appears to be unknown.

D 141 W 8.32b; S II.40b; S VI.131b; SS 219–220; str. 161 (531).

[161] "Unauthorizedly to perform irregular sacrifices is fined two suits of armour".[1] What is "irregular"[2]? There exist, of course, sacrifices which the royal clan is warranted to perform, (but) unauthorizedly to possess altars for spirits[3] is "irregular"; others[4] are not.

1 This is evidently a quotation from a statute.

2 The meanings of *chi/ch'i* 奇 agree with those of the English word "odd"; *chi* are "odd numbers", whereas *ch'i* is "strange, queer, extraordinary". *Ch'i ssu* 奇祠 are therefore "irregular religious practices".

3 *Kuei* (*li* for) *wei* 鬼 (立 for) 位. The editors of SS believe that these *kuei wei* are the same as the *shen wei* 神位 mentioned in the *Kuan-tzu* chapter 40, "The Four Seasons", *ssu shih*, p. 239. This term is not explained there, but the text-critical remarks, *chiao-cheng*, on p. 248 refer to a similar expression in the comparable and partly parallel chapter 5 of the *Huai-nan-tzu*, "Rules for the Seasons", *Shih tse p'ien*, p. 70. This expression is *ssu wei* 祠位, explained in the commentary as "altars".

4 It remains unclear, what these "others" are.

D 142 W 8.32b; S II.40b; S VI.132a; SS 220; str. 162 (532).

[162] "One must not venture to wear brocade shoes".[1] What is the form of brocade shoes? What the Statute means are shoes made of silk woven in different colours, (so that) the shoes are patterned; then they are "brocade shoes". Shoes with brocade side-pieces[2] are not, but in the practice (of the courts)[3] they are assimilated[4] to them.[5]

1 This is clearly a quotation from a statute.

2 The strip reads *man* 縵, but because this word means "plain, unpatterned silk", the editors of SS are undoubtedly right in suggesting that this is a loan (or a mistake?) for *man* 鞔, "the two sides or halves of a shoe". The two words are homophones, both *mwân (GSR, p. 74, no. 222f, and p. 85, no. 266k), which explains the confusion. SW explains it as "the throat of a shoe", which Tuan Yü-ts'ai explains further as *hsieh pang* 鞋幫, "the halves of a shoe".

3 From the standing expression *t'ing hsing shih* 廷行事 (for which see note 1 to D 30 above), the word *shih* has been omitted here.

4 *Pi* 比, "to compare", in Chinese legal parlance "to be treated like, i.e. in analogy with".

5 In a note, the editors of SS refer to an interesting passage from the *Chung-hua ku-chin chu* 中華古今注 (p. 7b in the *HWTS* edition), where the early 10th (!) century author says about hempen shoes: "At the time of the Ch'in they were made of silk and courtiers were ordered to wear these; commoners were not permitted to do so"; I do not know whether this passage is based on an older source. — Hayashi, *Bunbutsu*, p. 29 f. and ills. I.49–66, contain a wealth of information on Han foot wear.

D 143 W 8.32b; S II.41a; S VI.132a; SS 220–221; str. 163 (533).

[163] "For not coming to the assembly[1] one is bastinadoed. If arrested before a full year is over, the bastinado is again applied for vagrancy".[2] Now the commoner A has not come to the assembly and (should be) given fifty strokes. He is caught before the year is over. Is it warranted to increase[3] the bastinado or is it not warranted? It is warranted.

1 *Pu hui* 不會, namely, of statute labourers; see D 144 below.
2 The editors of SS refer to *SWTHTS*, quoted in *SWKL* p. 1311a, where *chiang-yang* 將陽 is explained as *hsiang yang* 相羊, "to wander".
3 The text writes *chia* 駕 for *chia* 加. For "increasing" see note 3 to D 1 above.

D 144 W 8.32b; S II.41a; S VI.132b; SS 221–222; str. 164 (534).

[164] What is the meaning of "to evade service"[1] as well as of "to fail in statutory labour"[2]? What the statute means is, that when one is warranted (to perform) statutory labour, and the officials and the (Village) Chief have already ordered it, then to abscond and not to come to the assembly—that is "to evade service". When the inspection has been held and when also the carts and food have been assembled,[3] or when (the labourers are) on the march to the site of the statute labour—then to abscond are all cases of "failing in statutory labour".

1 *Pu shih* 逋事. SW explains *pu* as *wang* 亡, "to abscond". However, in many Han decrees *pu* means "to evade", namely the payment of taxes, i.e. "to default". See e.g. *HSPC* 6.10a; 6.26a; 7.8b–9a; 10.10b; *HFHD* II, pp. 49, 88–89, 170, 380, 394, 400; *HHSCC* Ann. A1.4b.
2 *Fa yao* 乏徭.
3 This is a tentative translation. *Tun* 敦 often means "to bring together", especially soldiers. In the present rule I believe the word is applied to the carts needed for the work and to the food for the conscript laborers. To me this seems a logical solution: a roll-call has been held, the train has been assembled, and the workers are ready to start or they are already on the march. However, the editors of SS suggest that *tun* 敦, *twən, stands for *t'un* 屯, *d'wən (see GSR, p. 128, no. 464 p, and p. 118, no. 427a). This is possible (cf. *SWKL*, p. 1352b), and Karlgren states that the two words are "closely cognate" ("Glosses Kuo-feng", p. 126, gloss 112, and "Loan characters IV", p. 20, no. 1730). Now the editors need the equation of *tun* and *t'un* for a particular reason: they want to go one step further and equate *t'un* with *t'ung* 同, "together", because the practically parallel sentence in C 8 above reads *t'ung chü shih* 同車食! Their justification for this unwarranted equation they find in a sentence in the 35th chapter of the *Hsün-tzu*, p. 253: ...... *t'un erh chia* 屯二甲, "(the Village Chief and the Elders are fined) two suits of armour *together* (as they believe, but actually "per village", *t'un* being used for *t'un* 邨, as rightly indicated by Wang Hsien-sheng). Still, in spite of their reference to C 8, where they translate *t'ung chü shih* by "belonging to the same carriage and eating together", they now translate *tun* = *t'un* = *t'ung chü shih* by "together they mount the carriage and eat the provisions". All this is unacceptable.

D 145 W 8.32b; S II.41a; S VI.133a; SS 222; str. 166 (536).

[166] The woman A is somebody's wife; she leaves him and absconds. When

she is caught as well as when she gives herself up, she is small,[1] being not fully six feet (tall). Is she warranted to be sentenced or is she not warranted? In case ....,[2] she is warranted to be sentenced; in case not. ..., she is not warranted to be sentenced.

[1] See A 12 above.
[2] Like in D 58 above, the editors explain *kuan* 官 as "officially approved or recognized", translating "in case the marriage had been officially recognized."

D 146 W 8.32b; S II.41a; S VI.133a; SS 223; str. 167 (537).

[167] The woman A leaves her husband and absconds; the man B also unauthorizedly absconds. They become man and wife. A does not inform him of the circumstances;[1] only after two years, when she has born children, she informs him of the circumstances. B thereupon does not repudiate her. They are caught. How are they to be sentenced? They warrant tattooing and being made a *ch'eng-tan* and a grain-pounder (respectively).

[1] The text clearly reads *ch'ing* 請, but the editors are certainly right in wishing to read this as *ch'ing* 情.

D 147 W 8.32b–33a; S II.41a; S VI.133b; SS 223; str. 168 (538).

[168] A marries[1] a wife who had run away from another man, and makes her his wife; he is not aware that she had run away. He has children by her. Now she[2] is caught. Question: where are their children to be placed? Are they warranted to be given back[3] or to be confiscated by the government?[4] Confiscation by the government is another matter.[5]

[1] The use of *ch'ü* 取 (for *ch'ü* 娶) and *ch'i* 妻 is to be noted, because these terms seem to imply a regular marriage.
[2] It is also possible to translate "they are caught".
[3] For the same usage of *pi* 畀 see note 5 to D 4 above.
[4] As the husband did not know that ths wife had run away from a former husband, it is likely that he was not punished and that the children were returned to him; they could hardly have been given back to the woman's former husband. As regards the woman, D 145 above shows that the run-away wife was only punished in case the marriage had been officially registered—at least, if that is the correct interpretation of *kuan* 官 in D 145. On the other hand, D 146 shows that she might be condemned to tattooing and hard labour.
[5] Cf. note 4 to D 101 above.

D 148 W 8.33a; S II.41a; S VI.133b; SS 224; str. 169 (539).

[169] "Repudiating one's wife and not reporting this in writing is fined two suits of armour."[1] Is the repudiated wife also warranted to be sentenced or is she not warranted? She is fined two suits of armour.

[1] This is evidently a quotation from the statutes.

D 149 W 8.33a; S II.41a; S VI.133b–134a; SS 224; str. 170 (540).

[170] "When the husband has committed a crime and his wife first[1] denounces him, she is not to be confiscated."[2] Are the slaves, clothes and vessels[3] of her dowry[4] warranted to be confiscated or are they not warranted? They are not warranted to be confiscated.

[1] *Hsien* 先, i.e. before someone else had reported the crime to the authorities.
[2] For *shou* 收 see the discussion in note 10 to A 41 above; here, as well as in the following lines, *shou* surely means "to be confiscated". — This is evidently a quotation from the statutes.
[3] *Ch'i* 器; presumably this term also covers other goods.
[4] *Ying* 賸, "to increase", but according to SW also "to present", can be used for *yimg* 媵, which also means "to present", specifically to present servants or slaves to accompany the bride. For simplicity's sake I have rendered the word by "dowry".

D 150 W 8.33a; S II.41a; S VI.134a; SS 224; str. 171 (541).

[171] If a wife has committed a crime, for which she is arrested,[1] are the slaves, clothes and vessels of her dowry[2] warranted to be confiscated,[3] or are these returned to her husband? To be returned to her husband.

[1] Here *shou* 收 can only mean "to be arrested"; cf. note 10 to A 41 above.
[2] See note 4 to D 149 above.
[3] Here *shou* must mean "to confiscate"; see note 1.

D 151 W 8.33a; S II.41b; S VI.134a; SS 225; str. 172 (542).

Incest
Beheading

[172] When (children of) the same mother (but) of different fathers fornicate with each other, how are they to be sentenced? By beheading.[1]

[1] Lit. "to be cast away in the market place"; cf. *RHL*, p. 110.

D 152 W 8.33a; S II.41b; S VI.134a; SS 225; str. 173 (543).

[173] A and B fornicate with the woman C; for this reason A and B stab and wound each other, (but) C is not aware[1] of this. How is C to be sentenced? Do not sentence her.[2]

[1] *Chih* 智 for *chih* 知.
[2] The men were of course sentenced for fighting.

D 153 W 8.33a; S II.36a; S V.114a; SS 183–184; str. 75 (445).

[75] When a slave rapes[1] his owner, how is this to be sentenced? Comparable to beating one's owner.[2] ○ When in a fight one breaks the spine or the neck,[3] how is this sentenced? Comparable to breaking a limb.[4]

[1] Literally "by force committing fornication with one's owner".
[2] The punishment for a slave who beat his owner is unknown. As for commoners the punishments for beating one's grand-parents was tattooing and the heaviest hard labour punishment (see D 63 above), the slave will surely have suffered the death penalty.
[3] The text reads *chi hsiang ku* 脊項骨, which is repeated as such in the translation in SS, without further explanation; the dictionaries do not contain the expression—if it is an expression. Because the injury is "comparable to breaking a limb", the victim must have stayed alive.
[4] D 64 above shows that a husband who broke his wife's limbs was condemned to hard labour; the punishment for persons who did not stand in an hierarchical relation to each other like husband and wife will have been heavier.

D 154 W 8.33a; S II.41b; S VI.134a–b; SS 225; str. 174 (544).

[174] A woman is the wife of a bond-servant[1]; she has children by him. Now the bond-servant dies. The woman turns her back[2] on the children and

considers them as not being the children of the bond-servant. Question: how is the woman to be sentenced? Some say she is to be tattooed on the forehead and the cheekbones[3] and to be made a bond-woman; some (others) say that she is to be left intact.[4] To leave her intact is fitting.[5]

[1] I.e. a man condemned to this type of hard labour.

[2] The character on the strip is *pei* 北, which the editors of the *Wenwu* and the folio text correctly interpret as *pei* 背, without, however, providing any further explanation. It is, in fact, very difficult to establish the true meaning of this sentence. Does it mean that the woman repudiates the children and leaves them to their fate? It can hardly mean that she "takes them on her back" and runs away. I do not know the correct answer. The editors of SS have opted for another—and untenable—solution. They believe that *pei* 北 stands for *pieh* 別, and their translation then runs, most unexpectedly, "she removes the children from the house", whatever that may mean. The reading of *pieh* for *pei* they base on a passage in a *San-kuo chih* biography (*Wu chih* 12.6a; T'ung-wen edition), where a learned Confucian during a discussion of difficult passages in the classics remarks that "*pei* is the ancient form of *pieh*". This curious suggestion has been thrashed out by numerous scholars in *SWKL* 498b–503a; there it is shown that not 北 but 八 was meant, making the identification of 北 and 別 baseless. Also the ancient pronunciation of the two words was widely different, *pei* being *pək, whereas *pieh* was *b'i̯at (see GSR, p. 240, no. 909a, and p. 89, no. 292a); see also Karlgren, "Glosses Documents", p. 92, gloss 1272. For the contrary suggestion that *pieh* should stand for *pei* see note 3 to D 1 above. For note 3, 4 and 5 see the Addenda et corrigenda.

D 155 W 8.33a; S II.41b; S VI.134b; SS 226; str. 175 (545).

[175] Carrying women in one's official carriage[1]—how is this sentenced? The fine is two suits of armour. To harness official horses[2] to one's private carriage and to ride in it is not to be sentenced.

[1] *Sheng-chü* 乘車. In the *Li-chi*, ch. *Ch'ü-li* I (*Li-chi chu-su* 3.3a (0145); Couvreur, *Li-ki* I, p. 66; Legge, *Li-ki* 27, p. 96) this indicates the ruler's carriage, but because here this is contrasted to *ssu* 私 *chü*, "private carriage", *sheng chü* will mean the carriage which an official used for official functions. The expression is found in *SC* 37.23, where Chavannes translates it as "char ordinaire" (*Mh* IV, p. 208), but the present text shows that this is too general. The editors of SS refer to a sentence in the *Shang-shu ta chuan*, where *sheng-chü* is explained as *an-chü* 安車, an "easy carriage", but I see no reason to adopt this explanation.

[2] *Sheng-ma* 乘馬 will similarly mean "official horses".

D 156 W 8.33a; S II.41b; S VI.134b; SS 226–227; str. 176 (546).

[176] "When persons of vassal states[1] are not satisfied with[2] their lords and chiefs[3] and wish to leave Hsia[4] this is not to be permitted".[5] ○ What is the meaning of "(to leave)[6] Hsia"? Wishing to leave the Ch'in dependencies,[7] that is the meaning of "(to leave)[8] Hsia".

[1] See note 4 to D 94 above.

[2] *Pu an* 不安, lit. "not at peace with"; note that the following "lords and chiefs" are the grammatical object of *pu an*.

[3] *Chu chang* 主長; in D 58 above the text reads *chün chang* 君長.

[4] Hsia 夏, the Chinese oikoumenè, to which the Ch'in considered themselves to belong, as pointed out by the editors of SS.

[5] It is noteworthy that these persons "wish" to leave and that this is not "permitted", which shows that the movement of persons was not free.

[6] As pointed out by the editors of SS, the copyist seems to have omitted the word *ch'ü* 去.

[7] Cf. note 7 to A 110 above.

[8] See note 6.

D 157 W 8.33a; S II.41b; S VI.135a; SS 227; str. 177–178 (547–548).

[177] When princes and leaders[1] of genuine vassal states[2] commit crimes that go so far as (warranting) shaving off the beard and higher, they must be made to redeem these.[3] What is the meaning of "genuine"? Children born of a vassal state father and mother, as well as born in another state, these are called "genuine". What is the meaning of "Hsia[4] child"? ○ (Children born of) a vassal state [178] father and a Ch'in mother are meant.

[1] *Chün kung* 君公; cf. note 3 to D 156 above. *Chün kung* occurs in the *Mo-tzu* 3/12.52 (Forke, *Mê Ti*, p. 226) and in the spurious *Yüeh ming* chapter of the Book of Documents (*Shang-shu chu-su* 10/13.2b (0336)), explained by the T'ang commentator as "feudal lords".
[2] See note 4 to D 94 above.
[3] Cf. D 94.
[4] See note 4 to D 156 above.

D 158 W 8.33a; S II.41b; S VI.135b; SS 227–228; str. 179 (549).

[179] When strangers from the feudal lords come, the transverse bar[1] and the yokes[2] (of their carriages) must be singed[3] with fire.[4] Why are they singed? If[5] the feudal lords do not treat the gadflies,[6] the gadflies all attach[7] themselves to the transverse bar and the yokes, to the neck-straps,[8] the girth,[9] the shafts[10] (and[11]) the belt;[12] therefore they are singed. ○ What is the meaning of "losing a tally[13] with evil consequences"?[14] ○ To lose the right-hand part of a tally used for checking is "with evil consequences".

[1] In the following notes, grateful use has been made of Professor M. Hayashi's *Bunbutsu*.— When pulling carriages with a single ridge-pole as well as those with two shafts, the horses went under a transverse bar, *heng* 衡, tied to the pole or the shafts; *Bunbutsu*, p. 316.
[2] The horses' necks were caught in a yoke, shaped like an inverted V: *e* 厄 (軛, 軶), the top of which was tied to the transverse bar; *Bunbutsu*, p. 316.
[3] *Yen* 炎, "flames".
[4] This may be a quotation from a statute.
[5] *Tang* 當 is sometimes used for *t'ang* 儻.
[6] *Sao ma ch'ung* 騷馬蟲, "insects which make horses restless". This term is not found in the dictionaries and my rendering is therefore provisional; it may well have designated maggots living in wounds caused by the chafing of the harness.
[7] One of the meanings of *li* 麗 is "to attach".
[8] According to SW, *yang* 鞅 is a "throat-strap", *ching ta* 頸靼; Hayashi, *Bunbutsu*, p. 338, describes it as an ornamental collar. However, Sun Chi, "Chü chih", p. 451, identifies *yang* as the breast-strap, to which the pulling ropes were attached; the SW "throat strap" Sun believes to have kept the yoke down.
[9] To translate *hsien* 韅 as "girth" is a makeshift solution; in fact, it was a strap passing underneath the horse's chest behind the forelegs. According to Hayashi, *Bunbutsu*, p. 320, it was tied to the ends of the shafts, so as to keep the yoke down, but Sun Chi, "Chü chih", p. 450, believes that the function of this girth was to keep the breaststrap and the attached pulling ropes in place.
[10] *Yüan* 轅, "shaft", but also used for "ridgepole", originally *chou* 輈, with which SW identifies it.
[11] From the point of syntax, one could also translate "the belt of the shafts", but this seems unsuitable because of the existence of the *hsien*, for which see note 9.
[12] The text reads *shen* (?) 軷, which Morohashi, vol. 12, p. 157, identifies with *shen* 紳, "belt, girdle"; the word is not found in SW nor in Hayashi, *Bunbutsu*, and its function is unknown. The editors of S explain *shen* as "leather on the shafts of a carriage", which is too vague, though it might be correct in principle. The editors of SS believe that *shen* should be read as *yin* 靷, presumably because it is this word which occurs together with *hsien* (see note 9)

and *yang* (see note 8) in a passage in the *Tso chuan*, duke Hsi 28 (*Tso chuan* 16.12a (0643); Couvreur, *Tch'ouen-ts'iou* I, p. 396), where the commentator Tu Yü (222–284) merely says that the *yin* was "on the chest" of the horse. However, SW, Hayashi, *Bunbutsu*, p. 320, and Sun Chi, "Chü-chih", p. 450, explain *yin* as pulling ropes, forming the prolongation of the breast piece and attached to the axle tree.

13 *Ch'üan* 券; as it is divided into a right hand and a left hand part, it may designate here a bronze or a bamboo tally; cf. note 3 to C 3 above.

14 *Hai* 害. According to the Han statutes, "forging a decree with greatly evil consequences (was punished by) cutting in two at the waist (cf. *RHL*, p. 111)", *chiao chao ta hai yao chan* 矯詔大害要斬. Ju Shun (fl. 221–265) quotes this law in his commentary to *HSPC* 17.21b (*SC* 20.35; *Mh* III, p. 161, no. 8) and adds that there also existed cases of forging a decree with simply "evil consequences" and "without (*wu* 無) evil consequences". From the cases recorded it is clear that forging a decree with evil consequences was punished at least by beheading (*HSPC* 52.12b (not in *SC* 107.26); *HSPC* 64B.6b; *HHSCC* Mem. 36. 1b). The punishment for doing so "without evil consequences" is unknown, because in the single recorded case the guilty nobleman was simply deprived of his nobility (*HSPC* 18.8a; *SC* 20.14, *Mh* III, p. 163, no. 19). Now the present strip shows that not only forging a decree, but also losing a tally could be considered *hai*; perhaps also other actions could be qualified in this manner.

D 159 W 8.33a; S II.41b; S VI.136a; SS 229; str. 180 (550).

[180][1] When on a mission to the feudal lords or to the outer vassal states[2] the state's men[3] and the assisting officials[4] do not come,[5] . . . .[6] not to be adjudicated. ○ What is the meaning of "the state's men" and "the assistant envoys"?[7] Men and officials[8] who accompany[9] the mission and who are not private retainers,[10] these are meant by "the state's men" and "the assisting envoys".[11]

1 This article is incomprehensible to me. Nevertheless, I have tried to translate it word by word, only in one case following a suggestion by the editors of SS (see note 4), and explaining my difficulties in the following notes.

2 See note 4 to D 94 above.

3 *Ch'i pang t'u* 其邦徒. At first sight, it would seem logical to render this by "those states' men", namely those of the feudal lords or the outer vassal states. However, *ch'i* is ambiguous, because it may also refer to the Ch'in mission. The reply in the second half of the text is of no help, because the persons "who accompany the mission" can likewise be either Ch'in men or people from the state visited. *Pang* just means "state" and it may refer either to the foreign states or to Ch'in; examples of this double usage are frequent in these texts. And, finally, *t'u* is unclear. In these texts *t'u* generally seems to denote persons in a subordinate position, like labour or military conscripts (A 64; C 8, 11, 16, 21), servants (? A 55), convicts (? SS, p. 286, *t'u li* 隸, for which see *RHL*, p. 130). SS explains *t'u* as "followers, suite", referring to *Tso-chuan*, duke Chao 4 (*Tso-chuan* 42.16b (1706); Couvreur, *Tch'ouen-ts'iou* III, p. 90), where the commentator Tu Yü explains *t'u* as *ts'ung-che* 從者. As a result, SS translates "the envoy's followers of his own country", whereas Professor Koga on the contrary adopts the rendering "the clansmen of the rulers of the foreign states" (Koga, *Chōan*, p. 341).

4 The text clearly writes *wei li* 僞吏 here, and again below, at the beginning of the reply, as noted in note 8, but both the question and the reply also write *wei shih* 使! Could this be a copyist's mistake? As regards *wei* 僞, this normally means "false, counterfeit, artificial". In later times *wei* is used in a derogatory sense for states considered to have arrogated imperial prerogatives; this usage is found especially during periods of division or when foreign rulers had established themselves on Chinese soil. Hence, for instance in Sung times, *wei li* or *wei shih* could mean an official or an envoy of the Chin or the Hsi-Hsia. But here there is no cause for referring to a foreign state's institutions as "counterfeit", all the less when in D 184 below a foreign envoy is called a *k'o shih* 客使. Nevertheless, Professor Koga believes that *wei* indicates the foreign states (Koga, *Chōan*, p. 341). Another solution is offered by SS in their notes: *wei* 僞 should be understood as *wei* 爲, with the rather un-

expected meaning "to assist", for this is the explanation of the latter given in the commentary to Ode 248, *Fu-i* 鳧鷖, verse 3 (*Shih ching* 17/2.10a (1467)), which says that *wei* 爲 is "like *chu* = to assist", *yu chu* 猶助; Karlgren, "Glosses to the Ta Ya and Sung", p. 74, gloss 892, agrees. But this explanation is not used in the SS translation, which merely repeats the term used in the Ch'in text.

5 The text reads *lai* 來, "to come", but because SS assumes that the *t'u* and the *shih/li* belong to the envoy's retinue, they feel obliged to render *lai* by "to return".

6 The person who is not to be adjudicated might be the envoy.

7 Here the strip reads *shih* 使.

8 Here the strip reads *li* 吏.

9 *Yü chieh* 與偕, "to accompany". The expression occurs in D 184 and E 13 below as *yü chieh che* 者. In A 26 above and in *HSPC* 6.6b (*HFHD* II, p. 42) the person accompanied is mentioned between *yü* and *chieh*, whereas on the strip under discussion the word "mission" is placed after *yü chieh*.

10 *She jen* 舍人.

11 Here the strip reads *shih* 使.

D 160 W 8.33a; S II.42a; S VI.136b; SS 229–230; str. 181 (551).

[181] (A person or persons) who had absconded from the state (of Ch'in) come(s)[1] to pass money,[2] over ten thousand (cash). When it has already been returned,[3] he (or they) come(s) later to commit robbery and is (or are) caught. For what is he (or are they) to be sentenced? For passing money.

1 This seems to imply that the fugitive(s) returned to Ch'in.

2 *T'ung ch'ien* 通錢; the expression is also found in D 161 and 162 below, but its meaning remains unclear. The editors of both S and SS suggest that *t'ung ch'ien* might mean "to bribe", but from the passage they quote to support this, this does not seem likely. They refer to *HSPC* 59.5a (*SC* 122.20; Watson, *Records* II, p. 432), which describes how an official had financial dealings with a merchant, *yü ch'ien t'ung* 與錢通, but because the integrity of the merchant is especially praised, *t'ung ch'ien* cannot mean "to bribe". From D 162 it is clear that it was a punishable offence. As further examples are lacking (the expression is not found in the thesaurus *PWYF*, Morohashi or Fujita), the exact meaning of the expression cannot be elucidated for the present.

3 *Fu* 復. This word often means "to return, to repay, to restore"; it also has the technical meaning of "to exempt", viz. of taxes and statutory services (frequent in the Han histories). The editors of both S and SS translate *fu* as "to forgive", *k'uan mien* 寬免. They base this explanation on a passage in *HHSCC* Mem. 21.3b, but there *fu* is explained as *yu k'uan* 優寬, "to treat with great liberality", as is also quite clear from the main text. But how and why the money had first been "passed" and then "returned" remains unclear.

D 161 W 8.33a; S II.42a; S VI.136b; SS 230; str. 182 (552).

[182] Being aware[1] that somebody had been passing money, one hides[2] it for him. When its owner has already fetched it, somebody afterwards denounces the person who had hidden it. Is the person who had hidden it to be sentenced or is he not to be sentenced? He is to be sentenced.[3]

1 *Chih* 智 for *chih* 知.

2 *Ts'ang* 臧 for *ts'ang* 藏. This appears to be a third way of "receiving", besides *shou* 收 (D 13, note 3) and *shou* 守 (D 14, note 4).

3 In view of the severity of the punishment for passing money (see D 162 below), and also in view of the fact that the persons who were aware of a theft, but still accepted to hide part of the booty, were punished according to the value of that part (D 13 and 14 above), it seems certain that the person who hid the money in the present instance would have been punished. However, the text on the strip is curious, for there we find *lun pu lun pu lun* 論不論不論, with a repetition marker after the last word. This can only be a copyist's

mistake, but it leaves the reader in a quandary: if the repetition marker was added by mistake, the text plainly says that the man is not to be prosecuted, but if the copyist mistakenly repeated the words *pu lun*, he was to be sentenced! I agree with the editors that the latter possibility is correct.

D 162 W 8.33a; S II.42a; S VI.136b–137a; SS 230; str. 183 (553).

[183] A falsely denounces B for having passed one[1] cash, a crime (punishable by) being tattooed and made a *ch'eng-tan*. Question: are the members of A's household,[2] the Chief and the Elders (of his village) warranted to be co-adjudicated or are they not warranted? They are not warranted.

[1] The text clearly reads *i* 一, "one"; it is not a partly effaced character for "ten", *shih* 十, or "thousand", *ch'ien* 千.
[2] *T'ung chü* 同居; see note 15 to A 41 above.

D 163 W 8.33b; S II.42a; S VI.137a; SS 230–231; str. 184 (554).

[184] When a stranger,[1] before he has made a statement[2] to the officials, trades with them,[3] this is fined one suit of armour.[4] What is the meaning of "making a statement to the officials"? ○ To take one's credentials[5] to the officials—that is meant by "making a statement to the officials".

[1] *K'o* 客.
[2] *Pu* 布, "to lay out; to expose".
[3] *Yü ku* 與賈. The omitted object of *yü* can only be the officials; this rendering has also been adopted in SS.
[4] This leaves the question unanswered as to who was to pay the fine. One might expect this to have been the officials who did not ask for the stranger's travel documents. Still, if the word *yü* 與 is taken to mean "to take part in" and *yü ku* to mean "to take part in trading", the fine would have been paid by the foreign merchant.
[5] See note 3 to C 3 above.

D 164 W 8.33b; S II.42a; S VI.137a; SS 231; str. 185 (555).

[185] When a descendant of the ruling house[1] who does not possess aristocratic rank[2] is warranted to redeem a mutilating punishment—is it allowed to assimilate[3] (his case) to that of a *kung shih*[4] redeeming shaving off the beard? It is allowed to assimilate this thereto.[5]

[1] As indicated in SS, Ying Shao (fl. 140–206). in his commentary to *HSPC* 2.3a (*HFHD* I, p. 176) explains *nei wai kung sun* 內外公孫 as descendants of kings and nobles in the male and female lines.
[2] Shang Yang had even said that members of the ruling house who had no military merit should be struck off the clan register (*SC* 68.9; Duyvendak, *Lord Shang*, p. 15).
[3] *Pi* 比; cf. note 3 to D 142 above.
[4] The lowest of the aristocratic ranks.
[5] *Yen* 焉.

D 165 W 8.33b; S II.42a; S VI.136b; SS 231; str. 186 (556).

[186] Crossing the wall which forms the border between one ward and another ward—is this wall a *yüan*[1] or is it not? Where lanes are confronted,[2] that is a *yüan*; where houses[3] are confronted, this is not a *yüan*.

[1] *SW* explains *yüan* 院 as an encircling wall. As remarked by SS, some statute must have

made crossing, c.q. climbing over, such a wall a punishable offence; the questioner wants to know whether the wall separating two city-wards was such a wall.

2 *Chih* 直, "to face, to confront", like e.g. in *HSPC* 94A.7a and 22b (*SC* 110.21 and 61; de Groot, *Urkunden* I, pp. 58 and 151; cf. *CICA*, p. 215, note 803). *Chih* with this very meaning is also found in E 20 below.

3 *Yü* 宇 is also used for "house" in E 3 below.

D 166 W 8.33b; S II.42a; S VI.137b; SS 232; str. 187 (557).

[187] What is the meaning of "Palace Inspector"?[1] He is the person in charge of the watchmen inside the palaces.

1 *Kung chün jen* 宮均人. The editors of both S and SS suggest that *chün* 均 should be read 徇, and the latter is a variant of *hsün* 徇, which in its turn is another form of *hsün* 循, "to go around, to inspect". As indicated by the editors, 徇 occurs in the second part of the *T'ai shih* chapter (of dubious authenticity) of the Book of Documents (*Shu ching* 11.4b (0368)), where the pseudo-K'ung An-kuo commentary explains it as 循. The question remains, why the title of the chief differed from that of his subordinates; was it perhaps more archaic?

D 167 W 8.33b; S II.42a; S VI.138a; SS 232; str. 188 (558).

[188] What is the meaning of "Palace watchmen"?[1] Palace servants[2] who have suffered a mutilating punishment[3]—that is the meaning of Palace watchmen.

1 *Kung keng-jen* 宮更人. One might speculate on the word *keng* 更, which is nowhere explained. I would suggest that the early forms of this character show a hand, striking an object (see GSR, p. 198, no. 745b, and the examples taken from the *Chin wen pien* 金文編 included in *SWKL*, p. 1339a); could this be the nightwatch man's rattle or rather its Chinese equivalent, still seen—and heard in the stillness of the night—in Peking fifty years ago? Or was it a drum? The 3rd century commentator Hsieh Tsung in *Wen-hsüan* 2.3b explains *yen keng* 嚴更 as *tu hsing yeh ku* 督行夜鼓, "to go on inspection with the night drum". *Keng-jen* 更人 would then be the Chinese counterpart of the Dutch "klepperman" and the German "Klappermann" or "Rasselmann", i.e. clapper-man or rattle-man. This might explain why *keng* indicates the five watches, into which the night was divided. Whether these night-watchmen were relieved regularly, so that *keng* came to mean "turn of duty" is a question I cannot answer, and even less whether this eventually led to the meaning "change".

2 *Li* 隸. SS translates *li* by "slaves", but this is uncertain. The idealizing *Chou-li* mentions several types of *li*; one group consisted of criminals, other groups were formed by "barbarians". In view of the present text it is striking to observe that the latter were supposed to be armed, guarding the palace! (*Chou-li chu-su* 36.9a (1295); *Chou-li* 20/69.21 f.; Biot II, p. 370 f.).

3 *Hsing* 刑. For mutilated men working out of sight see A 91 and D 105 above.

D 168 W 8.33b; S II.42a; S VI.138a; SS 233; str. 189 (559).

[189] What is the meaning of "Palace Hounds'[1] Constable"[2] and "Outside Hounds' Constable"? Both are persons in charge of the king's dogs.

1 *Chiao* 狡. SS refers to the chapter *Wang hui* 王會 of the *I Chou shu* (inaccessible), which says that *chiao* were large dogs of the Hsiung-nu, but SW defines *chiao* as a small or a young dog and then quotes the information from the *I Chou shu*.

2 *Shih* 士.

D 169 W 8.33b; S II.42b; S VI.138a; SS 233; str. 190 (560).

[190] What is the meaning of "Field men"?[1] Field men are the persons who guard the tombs of Duke Hsiao and Duke Hsien.[2]

1 *Tien jen* 甸人. As noted by the editors of SS, these *tien jen* cannot be identical with the *tien jen* mentioned in the *Li-chi* or the *tien shih* 師 of the *Chou-li* who were concerned with agriculture.

2 Two Ch'in rulers who reigned between 384 and 362, and 361–338 B.C. This indicates that the explanation will have to be dated after 338 B.C.

D 170 W 8.33b; S II.42b; S VI.138b; SS 233; str. 191 (561).

[191] What is the meaning of "illustrious counsellors[1] who serve"?[2] Those who in serving arrive at[3] being known[4] to the king, as well as officials (with a salary of) six hundred bushels and higher[5] are all illustrious counsellors.

1 *Ta-fu* 大夫, "counsellor"; see *CICA*, p. 153, note 441.

2 As duly noted in SS, *huan-che* 宦者 here means "persons who serve", i.e. officials, and not eunuchs.

3 *Chi* 及.

4 *Chih* 智 for *chih* 知.

5 SS rightly refers to the paraphrase of an edict of emperor Hui of 195 B.C. (*HSPC* 2.2b, *HFHD* I, pp. 175–176; not in *SC*), where the same terminology is found: "... officials (ranking at) six hundred bushels and above, as well as those who serve (*huan*) the emperor so that he knows their names".

D 171 W 8.33b; S II.42b; S VI.138b; SS 234; str. 192 (562).

[192] ......[1] ○ What is the meaning of "furnace man"? Anciently, it was the person in charge of furnaces and stoves.[2]

1 Judging by the photographs, the first part of the strip shows faint traces of writing, which may have been scraped off. S and SS indicate eleven missing characters.

2 The difference between *ts'uan* 爨 and *tsao* 竈 escapes me; to the Han commentators of the ritual handbooks both were stoves. Perhaps *ts'uan* was the older term; cf. the article *heng jen* 享人 in the *Chou-li* (*Chou-li chu-su* 4.8b (0144); *Chou-li* 3/8.10; Biot I, p. 83). These stoves are discussed in Hayashi, *Bunbutsu*, p. 168 f., and illustrated on pl. 64, nos. 26 and 27. *Ts'uan* is also used as a verb, "to cook", i.a. in the *Mencius* IIIA, iv, 4.

D 172 W 8.33b; S II.42b; S VI.138b; SS 234; str. 193 (563).

[193] What is the meaning of "Collector"? Anciently, it was the person in charge of gathering firewood.[1]

1 Chang Cheng-lang, "Chi-jen", tries to prove that *chi* 集, *dzi̯əp (GSR, p. 182, no. 691a) originally meant "firewood", *ch'iao* 樵, *dz'i̯og (GSR, p. 296, no. 1148i).

D 173 W 8.33b; S II.42b; S VI.138b; SS 234–235; str. 194 (564).

[194] What is the meaning of "diviners' servants[1] with their beard shaved off and astrologers'[2] servants with their beard shaved off"? Diviners and astrologers warranted to have their beard shaved off have their beard shaved off and are made diviners' and astrologers' servants.[3] ○ Later, this statute was changed (and their punishment was) like that of other people.[4]

1 *Li* 隸. It is clear from the context that this is a punishment; it is uncertain that it was equivalent to *li ch'en* 臣, "bond-servants"; cf. note 2 to D 167 above.

2 These diviners and astrologers are mentioned in A 94 above.

3 In stead of being made convict labourers, they became "servants" in their former office.

4 This implies that they became normal hard labour convicts.

D 174 W 8.33b; S II.42b; S VI.139a; SS 235; str. 195 (565).

[195] What is the meaning of "man marmot"?[1] What is meant by "man marmot" is that his children go[2] to take care of their master.[3] If they do not go to take care of their master, they are warranted to be confiscated.[4] Although they do not take care of their master, but they bring in food,[5] they are not confiscated; they are given back to their master.[6]

[1] I fail to understand the meaning of this rule. The text clearly reads *ho* 貉, "marmot". Karlgren, GSR, p. 202, no. 766h, notes that this word is confused with *mo* 貊, a tribe of the North mentioned in the *Chou-li* (*Chou-li chu-su* 36.9b (1296); *Chou-li* 20/69.23; Biot II, p. 373) and in *Lun yü* XV, v, 2. SS therefore assumes that these persons might be men from the North, overlooking the fact that the text reads *jen ho* and not *ho jen*. *SWKL*, p. 4262b, does not mention any likely loans.

[2] *Ju* 入, "to go in; to enter"; the children evidently enter the other's household.

[3] The function of the master, or owner, *chu* 主, is not clear.

[4] *Shou* 收; see note 10 to A 41 above.

[5] SS is surely right in explaining *liang* 量 in the text as *liang* 糧.

[6] Cf. note 2.

D 175 W 8.33b; S II.41a; S VI.132b; SS 222; str. 165 (535).

[165] What is the meaning of "hiding[1] households", as well as of "not enrolling stalwart youths"?[2] To hide households, not making them perform statute labour and work,[3] and not ordering them to produce the household tax[4]—that is the meaning.[5]

[1] Cf. D 135 above.

[2] See C 20 above.

[3] The word *shih* 使 here is rather strange and the editors have obviously been puzzled, considering the difference in interpunction in the three editions. It is neglected in the SS translation.

[4] In D 135 above it is the land tax that is embezzled.

[5] There is no reply to the question about the "stalwart youths".

D 176 W 8.33b; S II.42b; S VI.139a; SS 235–236; str. 196 (566).

[196] What is the meaning of "posted[1] men" and "watch[2] men"? Suppose[3] a gaol has six posts. . . .[4] are called "posted men"; the others are all called "watch men". Some say that (those who) guard incarcerated convicts are watchmen; originally[5] they were posted men.

[1] For *shu* 署, "to post", see note 1 to A 15 and note 1 to C 21 above.

[2] See note 1 to D 167 above.

[3] The text writes *chi* 耤, which SS explains as *chieh* 籍, often used for "supposing, assuming".

[4] The text reads *ch'iu tao i shu sui, suo tao sui che* 囚道一署旞所道旞者. I fail to understand this. SS suggests two solutions, both based on explaining *tao* 道 as *yu* 由, "to go via or by way of", and *sui* 旞 as *sui* 遂, meaning *hsing* 行, "to go", or, in the second version, as a loan for *shu* 述 (for the possibility of such a loan see Karlgren, "Loan characters III", p. 114, no. 1551). Now, in the commentary to Ode 29, *Jih-yüeh*, *shu* is explained as *hsün* 循, which the editors wish to understand as "to patrol, to inspect"! This is certainly wrong, because *hsün* means "to follow"; see Karlgren, "Glosses Kuofeng", p. 111, gloss 78A, as well as Morohashi, vol. 4, p. 908, which furnishes dozens of examples of this primary meaning of *hsün*. The two solutions suggested by SS are: "the convicts pass a stretch guarded by a post, and this post is called 'posted men' ", or "in the gaol there are six posts which the convicts pass (?); one post inspects (*sic*) those who pass; the persons who inspect are called 'posted men' ". All this passes my understanding.

[5] The text reads *yüan* 原. The editors of SS translate *yüan* by *tu ch'a* 督察, "to supervise; to inspect", basing themselves on the T'ang commentary on a passage in the *Kuan-tzu* 10/26.155, which explains *yüan* as *ch'a* 察. However, they overlook that there, as well as in similar passages in ancient literature, *yüan* does not mean "to inspect" but "to search for the origin of". I have taken *yüan* literally, in spite of the following *che* 者.

D 177 W 8.33b; S II.42b; S VI.139b; SS 237; str. 198 (568).

[198] What is the meaning of "leaders[1] and stalwarts"?[2] Leaders and stalwarts are (men) fit[3] for (the post of) Village Chief;[4] that is what is meant.

[1] The text reads *shuai* 衛, identical with *shuai* 率, "to lead; to be in charge; to command".
[2] See note 2 to C 20 above.
[3] *Tang* 當, "equivalent to; capable of coping with".
[4] See note 11 to A 7 and note 5 to C 20 above.

D 178 W 8.33b; S II.43a; S VI.140a; SS 237–238; str. 199 (569).

[199] What is the meaning of "highway crowds"?[1] When there is a great (levy of) statute labour[2] and the labour gangs[3] fight and rush at each other, that is the meaning of "highway crowds".

[1] *K'uei* 逵 is a wide road, hence "highway". *Tsu* 卒 is a conscript, but here it seems to be a loan for another word. The editors prefer *ts'u* 猝, because this is the reading provided for *tsu* 卒 by the commentator in *HSPC* 69.18a (not in *SC*) to the sentence *wang i ying tsu* 亡以應卒, "(if no preparations are made in advance) one has no means to react to a sudden/unexpected event". The commentator then explains *ts'u* as *pao* 暴, which likewise means "suddenly". But the editors, who do not seem to have checked the context, adopt the other meaning of *pao*, viz. "violent", and explain *pao* as *pao-tung* 動, "riot, insurrection", which is wrong. For my part I prefer to take *tsu* 卒 as a loan for *ts'ui* 萃, which can mean "a crowd".
[2] SS refers to a similar expression, *ta yao i* 大徭役, in *SC* 7.4 (*Mh* II, p. 249; Watson, *Records* I, p. 37 f.; *HSPC* 31.9a).
[3] *Ts'ao* 曹, "a group or a squad (of labourers)"; cf. C. 11, 12, 13 and D 12 above.

D 179 W 8.33b; S II.43a; S VI.139b; SS 236–237; str. 197 (567).

[197] What is the meaning "to...[1] one's post"?[2] Is "to ... one's post" to leave one's post, or is it not? It is. How is this to be sentenced? Hence (like) leaving one's post.[3]

[1] The text reads *tou* 竇, which SW explains as *k'ung* 空. The editors of S and SS merely quote SW, apparently believing that *k'ung* means "empty". However, the commentators to SW indicate that *k'ung* is a synonym of *k'ung* 孔, "hole", and in the classics *tou* invariably means "hole" or "drainage". I therefore suggest that *tou* has been used for another sign with the same phonetic element. Of these, there are several with an unfavourable meaning, like *tu* 遺, "careless", or *tu* 嬻, "over-familiar", or *tu* 黷, "to besmirch"; all three can form the second element in the binome *hsieh* 媟 *tu* (see *Tz'u-t'ung* II, p. 2231). Here *tou/tu* will mean "to neglect" or something similar.
[2] See note 2 to A 15 and note 2 to C 21 above.
[3] The question concerning the punishment is not answered, but cf. C 21.

D 180 W 8.33b; S II.43a; S VI.140a; SS 238; str. 200 (570).

[200] What is the meaning of "travellers"? ○ Lodgers[1] as well as strangers[2]—that is the meaning of "travellers".

[1] *Chi* 寄, "to dwell temporarily; to lodge"; cf. Duyvendak, *Lord Shang*, p. 220 and note 5: "temporary sojourners".

[2] *K'o* 客.

D 181 W 8.33b; S II.43a; S VI.140a; SS 238–239; str. 201 (571).

[201] What is the meaning of "the people of the house"?[1] What is the meaning of "dwelling together"?[2] "Dwelling together" means "only the mother of the household".[3] ○ "People of the house" means "the whole house", all those who are warranted to be co-adjudicated with a criminal.

[1] *Shih jen* 室人. In view of the following statement, *shih jen* would seem to include also non-relatives, like servants and slaves; however, Satake, "Kazoku", p. 14, suggests that *shih* indicates the clan. The editors of SS refer to the *Hun-i* chapter of the *Li-chi* (*Li-chi chu-su* 61/44.5a (2387); Couvreur, *Li-ki* II, p. 647; Legge, *Li-ki* 28, p. 431), where the commentator Cheng Hsüan (127–200) gives a completely different explanation, namely *nü ku nü shu chu fu* 女姑女叔諸婦, i.e. the elder and younger sisters of a husband! This is certainly not applicable here.

[2] See note 15 to A 41 above.

[3] The transcription reads *tu hu mu* 獨戶母. If this is correct, it could be brought more or less in agreement with Cheng Hsüan's commentary, quoted in note 1, by rendering *mu* in the plural, meaning the mother and the aunts. Taken literally, however, the statement makes no sense, nor does the translation in SS: "persons in a household who have the same mother"; furthermore, it is in flagrant contrast with D 19 above. Satake, "Kazoku", p. 13, assumes that the transcription *mu* 母 is wrong, and he suggests that the character on the strip is actually *kuan* 毌, identical with *kuan* 貫 (see *SWKL* 3026b f.). Satake believes that the sentence means " 'those who dwell together' solely indicates (the persons inscribed on) the household-register, *hu-kuan* 戶貫". This is a tempting solution, but if the thesaurus *P'ei-wen yün-fu* is right, the earliest example of the binome *hu-kuan* only occurs in a memorial of A.D. 487 (*PWYF* refers to *Pei shih* 40.2b; the parallel is found in *Wei shu* 60.3a, both according to the T'ung-wen edition), i.e. more than seven centuries after the Yün-meng strips. An argument from silence against *hu-kuan* being a Ch'in-Han expression is its absence in Fujita, a meticulous and exhaustive compilation.

D 182 W 8.34a; S II.43a; S VI.140a–b; SS 239; str. 202 (572).

[202] What is the meaning of "...."?[1] A ... is a label[2] for jade. Once[3] the jade is lost, or somebody has displaced[4] it, by looking at the label one may know[5] its size[6] and thereby pronounce sentence as well as impose a charge according to (the Statute on) Equipment.[7]

[1] The editors transcribe the character on the strip as 琼, which is the simplified modern form of *ch'iung* 瓊. This is another word for "jade", according to SW (cf. *Tso-chuan*, duke Hsi 28, *Tso-chuan* 15.14a (0647); Couvreur, *Tch'ouen-ts'iou* I, p. 398).

[2] *Chien* 檢; for examples of such labels see Hayashi, *Bunbutsu*, ills. 11–23, 24, 25, and Ōba, *Mokkan*, p. 27 f.

[3] *Chieh* 莭 for *chi* 即.

[4] *Mao-i* 貿傷 (=易); as indicated in SS, this term is found in *HSPC* 75.32b, where it is said that "high and low *mao-i*, change places."

[5] *Chih* 智 for *chih* 知.

[6] *Hsiao-ta* 小大.

[7] I assume that *i chi fu chih* 以齎負之 has the same meaning as *i chi lü* 律 *tse* 責 *chih* in A 56 above; cf. also A 88 above, which mentions objects that have no *chi*, *wu* 毋 *chi*, hence objects that are "not listed, or considered, as equipment", so that their value was unknown.

D 183 W 8.34a; S II.43a; S VI.140b; SS 239–240; str. 203 (573).

[203] What is the meaning of "to *hsün*[1] jade"? As regards "to *hsün* jade", when strangers[2] from the feudal lords come on a mission and enter Ch'in,

it is apropriate[3] that they take jade to enquire[4] after the king. This is meant by "to *hsün* jade".

[1] The character on the strip is unknown; it consists of *hsün* 熏 over *pei* 貝. In view of the context, it evidently means "to present".
[2] *K'o* 客.
[3] *Tang* 當.
[4] *Wen* 問. SS refers to a passage in the *Ch'ü-li* chapter of the *Li-chi* (*Li-chi chu-su* 2.17a (0101); Couvreur, *Li-ki* I, p. 45; Legge, *Li-ki* 27, p. 86), where the commentator Cheng Hsüan (127–200) explains *wen* as *i* 遺, "to give". Accordingly, SS translates *i yü wen wang* 以玉問王 as "to present jade to the king". However, Couvreur and Legge, inspired by the more detailed explanations of the later commentators, write "un message avec des présents", c.q. "friendly messages, with the present of. . .". Similarly Karlgren in his translation of Ode 82, *Nü yüeh chi ming* (Karlgren, *Odes*, p. 55): "I (will make enquiries about =) attend upon you with" certain gifts.

D 184 W 8.34a; S II.43a; S VI.141a; SS 240; str. 204 (574).

[204] What is the meaning of *ch'ieh*[1] *mien*?[2] As regards *ch'ieh mien*, suppose[3] that persons from Ch'in go on a mission, and capable[4] officials of the other state and those who march as troops[5] accompany them, the foreign[6] officials are called *ch'ieh* and those who march as troops are called *mien*.

[1] The details of this paragraph are unclear. The text reads *ch'ieh* 匧, which SS explains as *ch'ieh* 篋, but as both mean "box", this gives no sense; the editors of SS provide no further explanation. I would suggest that *ch'ieh* stands for *hsieh* 挾, which can mean "to surround", e.g. in the *Hsün-tzu*, ch. 18, p. 223 (Dubs, *Hsüntze*, p. 201), where nobles "surround" the king's chariot. In this way, the foreign dignitaries "surround" the Ch'in envoy.
[2] The text reads 靣, an ancient form of *mien* 面, "face". The editors of S suggest that this means something like "vanguard" or "forerunners", but SS is silent on this point. The early commentators to the *Han shu* explain *mien* as "to turn one's back on" or "to look away" (*HSPC* 31.24a; *SC* 7.72, *Mh* II, p. 320; Watson, *Records* I, p. 72; *HSPC* 46.9b; *SC* 103.18; Watson, *Records* I, p. 554), but this view has been criticized by later scholars and Chavannes therefore translates "le dévisagea" and Watson (I, p. 72) "eyed him carefully". However, it seems impossible to render *mien* in either way when referring to troops who serve as an escort.
[3] Cf. note 3 to D 176 above.
[4] *Nai li* 耐吏, where the editors assume that *nai* stands for *neng* 能, which is quite common.
[5] *Sui* 旞. S takes the word literally as meaning some kind of streamers or pennants made of feathers (see Hayashi, *Bunbutsu*, p. 478), but SS believes it to be a loan for *tui* 隊, "a body of troops", which is quite acceptable.
[6] Literally "guest officials", *k'o li* 客吏.

D 185 W 8.34a; S II.43a; S VI.141a; SS 240; str. 205 (575).

[205] What is the meaning of "(to involve) people (by) concealing"?[1] (To involve) people (by) concealing is when A takes along[2] his clothes and hides[3] these in B's house, whereupon he announces[4] that these are lost, wishing to cause that B will be considered as having stolen them, whereas in fact he did not steal them—that is meant.

[1] The text reads *ts'ang* 臧, "to conceal"; it is not necessary to take *ts'ang* as *tsang* 贓, "illegal profit" (cf. note 6 to D 1 above), as is done by the editors of all editions.
[2] For a similar use of *pa* 把 see D 4 and D 109 above.
[3] "To hide" is expressed here by a binome, *ni ts'ang* 匿臧.
[4] *Kao* 告, currently rendered in the present translation as "to denounce."

D 186 W 8.34a; S II.43a; S VI.141b; SS 241; str. 206 (576).

[206] "To give loans[1] to people in excess of the Statutes,[2] as well as giving[3] to people". ○ What is the meaning of "giving to people"?[4] When it is not warranted to give a loan (and yet) to give them a loan—that is meant by "giving to people".

1 *T'e* 貣 for *tai* 貸; see note 6 to A 31 above.
2 See note 8 to C 4 above.
3 The text reads *chieh* 介, "scale (of scale armour)", but the editors suggest that *chieh*, *kad (GSR, p. 97, no. 327a) is a loan for *kai* 匄, *kâd (GSR, p. 93, no. 313a), which can mean both "to beg" and "to give, to present"; with the latter meaning it occurs i.a. in *HSPC* 96B.18a (*CICA*, p. 169). The editors' solution is undoubtedly correct, in spite of Karlgren's objections in "Loan characters I", p. 90, no. 337.
4 This is evidently a quotation of a passage (or two?) of a statute.

D 187 W 8.34a; S II.43a; S VI.141b; SS 241; str. 207 (577).

[207] "To give supplies[1] to people in excess of the Statutes[2] as well as giving to[3] people".[4] ○ What is the meaning of "giving to people"? When it is not warranted to give supplies, and yet by mistake to give them supplies—that is meant by "giving to people."

1 For this rendering of *ch'i* 氣 see note 9 to A 19 above.
2 See note 8 to C 4 above.
3 See note 3 to D 186 above.
4 This is evidently a quotation of a passage (or two?) of a statute.

D 188 W 8.34a; S II.43b; S VI.141b; SS 241–242; str. 208 (578).

[208] What is a "serious wound"?[1] A serious wound is when a limb[2] has perhaps not been completely severed,[3] (but the injury) goes so far[4] that the leader[5] or the chief[6] has to order two men to support him out[7]—that is a serious wound.

1 *Ta i* 大痍; SW explains *i* as "wound".
2 *Chih* 支 for *chih* 肢.
3 *Wei tuan* 未斷, literally "not yet cut off".
4 I follow SS for this rendering of *chi* 及.
5 *Chiang* 將; according to *Shang-chün shu*, p. 72 (Duyvendak, *Lord Shang*, p. 296) a *chiang* was in charge of one hundred men.
6 *Chang* 長, probably in charge of a squad of five men, *t'un-chang* 屯長 (*Lord Shang*, loc. cit.).
7 *Ch'u* 出, viz. out of the fray.

D 189 W 8.34a; S II.43b; S VI.142a; SS 242; str. 209 (579).

[209] What are "serious mistakes"? (Mistakes in the number of) households,[1] horses, cattle, as well as all[2] goods[3] whose value[4] exceeds 660 cash are serious mistakes; the others are small (mistakes).[5]

1 See note 1 to B 28 above.
2 *Che* 者 for *chu* 諸.
3 *Huo-ts'ai* 貨材 (for *ts'ai* 財).
4 *Chih* 直 for *chih* 值.
5 Practically the same rule is found in B 29 above.

D 190 W 8.34a; S II.43b; S VI.142a; SS 242; str. 210 (580).

[210] What is the meaning of "sheep's eyes"?[1] "Sheep's eyes" is a herb with edible seeds.

[1] *Wenwu* and S VI print *k'ou* 瞘, "sunken eyes" (only found in late dictionaries; no text examples); SS and CM print 𦗖, which SS explains as a varient of *chü* 軀, "body". Judging by the photograph, the form with the "eye radical" is correct; the form with the "ear radical" seems to be unknown. The term is not found in the dictionaries I possess.

GROUP E

The texts belonging to the fifth group were first called provisionally "Models for trying cases", *chih yü ch'eng-shih* 治獄程式, but in fact, as discovered later (see SS, introduction, p. 2, note 1), they are entitled "Models for sealing and investigating", *feng chen shih* 封診式. They consist of twenty five *yüan shu* 爰書, "reports" (E 1–E 25). The following translation follows the order in which these texts were published in *Wenwu* 1976/8. The 98 strips have a length of c. 25 cm. or 1 foot 1 inch Ch'in-Han measure; they were held together by three sets of strings: at the top, in the middle and at the bottom. Each report is started on a new strip, with the result that quite a few strips are left partly blank. Strips completely covered with writing contain thirty characters, or a few more, rather closely spaced. The title of each "model" is written close to the top of the strip and the text then follows; the text on the following strips starts at the same level at the text on the first strip, leaving the top blank.

These "models" have been translated by Katrina C.D. McLeod and Robin D.S. Yates under the title "Forms of Ch'in law; an annotated translation of the *Feng-chen shih*", in *HJAS* 41 (1981), pp. 111–163, referred to in the following pages as "Yates". There are several reasons why, in spite of the existence of this translation, I venture to present a rendering of my own. In the first place, I believe it to be useful that the complete information concerning the Ch'in laws should be available in one volume. Secondly, the existence of several annotated translations will, I hope, enable the serious student to draw his own conclusions concerning certain passages; du choc des opinions jaillit la vérité. Finally, I may have profited from Chinese and Japanese studies which only appeared when the Yates-McLeod translation had already been sent to the printers. Professor Derk Bodde extensively discusses several of the following cases in his "Forensic medicine in pre-imperial China", in the *Journal of the American Oriental Society* 102 (1982), pp. 1–15.

E 1 W 8.34a; S II.45a; S VII.144a; SS 245–246; str. 1 (581); Yates, no. 5.1, pp. 130–131.

[1] Trying lawsuits—If in trying lawsuits it is possible by means of documents to track down[1] his (or their[2]) words, obtaining the facts[3] of the person[4] without using the bastinado[5] is the best[6]; applying the bastinado is inferior, (for) when there is fear, (everything) is spoiled.[7]

[1] This article is also translated in Vandermeersch, "Procédure", p. 17.—*Ts'ung* (for *tsung*) *chi* 從 (for 蹤) 迹, "foot-prints, tracts", also used verbally "to follow, to track down; to lead to".

[2] As rightly observed by Dr. Yates, apart from the main suspect, also witnesses were questioned.

[3] The text reads *ch'ing* 請, which is either a mistake or a loan for *ch'ing* 情.

[4] Or "the persons concerned"; cf. note 2.

[5] *Ch'ih lüeh* 治 (for 笞) 諒 (for 掠).

[6] *Shang* 上.
[7] *Pai* 敗; cf. my "Ch'in documents", p. 193.

E 2 W 8.34a; S II.45a; S VII.144b; SS 246–247; str. 2–5 (582–585); Yates, no. 5.2, pp. 131–133.

[2] Interrogating[1] in a lawsuit.—In all cases of interrogating in a lawsuit one should first listen fully to his (or their)[2] words and note these down, (letting)[3] each (of the persons questioned) set out his statement.[4] Although (the investigator) knows that he is lying, there is no need to insist[5] every time. When his statement has been completely noted down, and [3] it cannot be understood, then insist on the points (which need) insisting. When, having insisted, one has again fully listened and noted down the explanatory statements, one looks again at other unexplained points and insists again on these. When one has insisted to the limit,[6] but he has repeatedly [4] lied, changing his words and not submitting,[7] then, for those persons whom the Statutes warrant to be bastinadoed, bastinado them. When bastinadoing him, be sure to note down: "Report.[8]—Because X[9] repeatedly changed his words and made no explanatory statement, [5] X has been interrogated with the bastinado."

[1] This article is also translated in Vandermeersch, "Procédure", p. 17.—*Hsün* 訊 is a technical term for "to interrogate"; see *RHL*, p. 79.
[2] Dr. Yates is right when he remarks that also witnesses were interrogated.
[3] Following the translation in SS.
[4] *Tz'u* 辭; see *RHL*, p. 77.
[5] *Ch'ieh* 詰, "to question urgently; to reprove"; I prefer "to insist". Another possible rendering would have been "to press"; *HHSCC*, Mem. 67.2a, mentions an imperial messenger who *ch'ieh* a Grand Administrator, accused of having killed innocent persons.
[6] *Chi* 極.
[7] *Fu* 服, "to submit", i.e. to admit the truth of the accusation; see *RHL*, p. 77.
[8] *Yüan shu* 爰書 originally was a "transposed writing", or "transcript", i.e. the written form of an oral statement; see Ōba, "Ensho kō". (The suggestion in *RHL*, p. 72 and p. 95, note 3, that a *yüan shu* was "a document written in the style of the *yüan li*", is wrong.). In other words, *yüan shu* is the equivalent of the French "procès verbal". This type of "transcript" is found in the present Ch'in texts and in many of the Edsin-gol strips (see e.g. my "Lawsuit"). However, the Edsin-gol strips also show, that *yüan-shu* eventually came to mean simply "report", without the connotation of an originally oral statement. Examples of this type are "one report about sick conscripts", *chi tsu yüan-shu i pien* 疾卒爰書一編 (Lao Kan, *K'ao-shih*, p. 118, no. 5654 (350) 42.11a), or a *yüan-shu* about the repayment of a dead horse, with dates equivalent to 15 and 14 B.C. (*ibid.*, p. 148, no. 7222 (443) 229.1 and 2). Dr. Loewe is quite justified in calling a *yüan-shu* a "formal report" (*RHA* II, p. 59, no. 28, and p. 60, nos. 30 and 34).

E 3 W 8.34a–b; S II.45a–b; S VII.146a–b; SS 249–250; str. 8–12 (588–592); Yates, no. 5.4, pp. 137–139.

[8] Sealing and guarding.[1]—Report from (authority) X of a district[2]: Because of the letter from Assistant (Prefect) X of X Prefecture, (I) have sealed the house, the wife and children, slaves, clothing, tools and cattle of A, a commoner of X ward[3] who is under investigation.[4] ◯ As regards A's house and the people: one house [9] with two rooms, each with a door; the inner dwellings are all covered with tiles;[5] a large wooden post[6] at the gate; ten mulberry trees.[7] ◯ The wife is called X; she had absconded and did not

attend the sealing. ○ A child: an adult daughter[8] X, who does not yet have a husband. ○ [10] A child: a minor boy X, 6 ft. 5 in. tall.[9] ○ A slave X. A slave woman: a minor girl X. ○ One male dog. ○ (I) questioned[10] the (Village) Chief[11] XX[12], the member of A's group of five[13] with the aristocratic rank of *kung shih*, XX, (saying): "If[14] A has [other][15] (property) [11] warranted to be sealed and guarded, which (you) XX[16] have omitted and not listed[17] in writing, you will have committed a crime." XX all stated: "A's property that had to be sealed is all this; there is nothing else that warrants sealing". Thereupon (I) handed A's sealed (property) over to X [12] X, to be guarded in turns (of duty) together with people of the village, awaiting[18] (further) orders.

1 This article is also translated in Vandermeersch, "Procédure", p. 18.—*Feng shou* 封守. These are evidently two separate actions, viz. to put the property under seal, in the same manner as the fixing of seals to grain-stores, mentioned i.a. in A 19 above, and to guard or keep under surveillance persons and animals; this is also the opinion expressed in SS, p. 248, note 6.

2 The text reads *hsiang mou* 鄉某, "a certain person (or rather authority) of the district"—a district which is not further indicated. As noted in SS, a district had several functionaries: a Rank-holder, *yu ch'ih* 有秩, a Thrice Venerable, *san lao* 三老, an Overseer, *se-fu* 嗇夫, and Constables, *yu chiao* 游徼, according to *HSPC* 19A.30a (see Bielenstein, *Bureaucracy*, pp. 103–104).

3 *Li* 里, a village or a town-ward.

4 *Yu chü* 有鞫, cf. *RHL*, pp. 79–80.

5 Tiles in contrast to straw; a tile roof indicates a certain degree of wealth, an impression which is reinforced by the mention of two slaves.

6 The text is transcribed as *chü* 具; SS suggests that this should stand for *chü* 椇, "like in the expression *chü wu* 屋", but I cannot understand this, because this binome is not to be found in the dictionaries available to me; the only meaning I could fined for *chü* is "hand-barrow", used for transporting dishes or earth. I would like to suggest another solution. To me, the character on the strip seems more complicated than *chü* 具; could it be *nieh* 臬, i.e. *nieh* 闑? This is a short but heavy wooden post, sometimes decorated, standing in the centre of the doorway; see Hayashi, *Bunbutsu*, p. 194 f. and ills. 4–38, 59 and 61; the word occurs i.a. in the *Ch'ü-li* chapter of the *Li-chi* (*Li-chi chu-su* 2.2a (0071); Couvreur, *Li-ki* I, p. 17; Legge, *Li-ki* 27, p. 71).

7 Reading *chu* 朱 (i.e. *chu* 株, numerical term for trees) instead of *mu* 木.

8 *Ta nü-tzu* 大女子; cf. note 2 to A 13 above.

9 Cf. A 12 above, where persons with a height of less than 6 ft. 5 in. are classified as "small" and therefore not liable to perform labour.

10 *Chi hsün* 幾 (for 譏) 訊, evidently a binome, "to question; to interrogate".

11 *Tien* 典, i.e. *li* 里 *tien*, Village Chief; see note 11 to A 7 above.

12 I do not understand why *mou* 某 is reduplicated here; is this a copyist's mistake, induced by the following *mou mou* which indicates the members of the group of five?

13 See note 1 to D 80 above.

14 The text reads *tang* 黨, which the editors consider to stand for *t'ang* 儻, "if".

15 The editors are justified in inserting this word here, because it occurs in the man's answer.

16 Note the mark of the plural, *teng* 等.

17 *Chan* 占, "to report for insertion in the registers".

18 *Shih* 侍 for *tai* 待.

E 4 W 8.34b; S II.45a; S VII.145a–b; SS 247–249; str. 6–7 (586–587); Yates, no. 5.3, pp. 133–137.

[6] Under interrogation.[1]—I beg to report[2] to the Head[3] of X Prefecture: the man X is under interrogation. In his statement he said: "I am a com-

moner; I live in X village (or ward)". You should[4] determine his name, status and village (or ward); for which crimes he has been adjudicated and sentenced;[5] which crimes have been amnestied; [7] whether he has perhaps[6] been re-interrogated or not.[7] Despatch persons who know[8] to seal and guard (his property etc.[9]) according to the Statutes. (These persons) warrant the use of post-horses;[10] for post-horses every case is to be reported. Of this I beg to inform the Head (of the Prefecture).[11]

1 See note 4 to E 3 above.

2 *Kao* 告 here has the normal meaning of "to report, to inform", and not "to denounce".

3 *Chu* 主 is often used verbally, "to be in charge of", and this is probably the reason why SS renders *chu* by "the official responsible for the prefecture". In any case, *chu* is not a normal title. As indicated in Yates, p. 133, note 62, *chu* refers perhaps to the Assistant Prefect.

4 For *ting ming shih li* 定名事里 see note 27 to A 19 above. As also indicated by Dr. Yates, SS has not substituted *ho* 何 for *k'o* 可.

5 In their article Dr. Yates and Miss McLeod propose other translations for *tso* 坐 and *lun* 論, rendered above as "adjudicated" and "sentenced". In the following lines I explain my reasons for maintaining my terminology. *Tso* 坐, lit. "to sit", is derived from the ancient expression *tso yü* 獄, the two contending parties in a suit "sitting" and arguing their case in the presence of an arbiter or judge, like in *Tso chuan*, duke Hsiang 11 (*Tso chuan* 31.6b (1270); Couvreur, *Tch'ouen-ts'iou* II, p. 265); see Maspero, "Serment", p. 270. Eventually *tso* comes to mean "to sit in the judge's court to be tried and sentenced", the fixed terminology in historical texts being "the subject A *tso* the crime X". I have consistently rendered *tso* as "to be adjudicated for"; when *tso* is followed by a noun—often a name—I have rendered it as "to be adjudicated in connection with". The arguments in Yates, p. 134, note 65, in favour of translating *tso* as "to be liable" have not convinced me of the superiority of such a rendering. See further *RHL*, p. 397, note 239.—*Lun* 論, lit. "to discuss", has come to mean "to judge, to decide, to sentence" in legal parlance (see *RHL*, p. 80). Yates, p. 134, note 66, is in favour of retaining "to discuss", but then two points are overlooked. In the first place, the ancient Chinese law-court had one single judge, and no lawyers to plead for the defendant, so that there was no place for any discussion. And secondly, the contents of the *lun* was the verdict or judgment. In A 90 above, *lun* is used in a similar way; in that case it is not a verdict in the legal sense, but a decision, namely a decision to grant a reward. All dictionaries have a separate entry where *lun* is explained as "to sentence; to condemn". Rendering *lun* by "to discuss" moreover has the disadvantage of misleading the uninitiated reader, who will be led to think that in ancient China criminal suits were subject to discussion, which, of course, they were not.

6 This is a tentative rendering of *huo* 或; Yates, p. 134, translates "someone".

7 Yates, *l.c.*, also translates "reinterrogated", but SS renders *fu wen* 覆問 by "furthermore investigate whether there still are other points".

8 *Shih che* 識者. I expect these "persons who know" to be members of the local administration who knew the procedure to be followed; SS renders the term in a similar fashion by "persons who know the situation". Less acceptable seems Koga, *Chōan*, p. 157, "persons who know him (scl. the person under interrogation) by sight", because there *chih* 知 is used (see *RHL*, p. 78). The complicated argument in Yates, p. 136, note 68, in favour of the rendering "recorders", has not convinced me.

9 See note 1 to E 3 above.

10 The editors read this sign as *t'eng* 騰, "to rear; to prance; to rise", which does not make sense here. The editors, followed in Yates, believe this word to be a loan for *t'eng* 謄, "to copy"; the fact that this loan is not attested, neither in Karlgren, "Loan characters III", p. 136, nos. 1634, 1635, nor in Morohashi, is theoretically no obstacle. Furthermore, the preceding *tang* 當 the editors render by "correct; definite", translating *tang t'eng* as "make definite copies"; in Yates this is rendered by "should make copies". However, the only explanation of *t'eng* provided by SW is *chuan* 傳 (leaving aside the contested "other opinion" that it would mean "gelding"; see *SWKL*, p. 4339b f.), i.e. "post-horse" of the courier service. I have adopted the latter rendering, as has also been done in Koga, *Chōan*, p. 157.

11 This article seems to be a mixture of a model-report and of directions for the points to be entered in such a report.

E 5 W 8.34b; S II.45b; S VII.147a; SS 250–251; str. 13–14 (593–594); Yates, no. 5.5, p. 139.

[13] Re-interrogation.—I beg to report to the Head of X Prefecture:[1] a man X made the statement: "(I am) a commoner, living in X village of X Prefecture; I went away and absconded". You should determine his name, status and village; for which crimes he has been adjudicated and sentenced; which crimes have been amnestied; [14] whether he has (perhaps)[2] been re-interrogated or not[3]; inspect whether he has been registered as absconding;[4] when he absconded as well when he evaded service,[5] this was each time during how many days? Despatch[6] persons who know; they warrant the use of post-horses; for post-horses every case is to be reported. Of this I beg to inform the Head (of the Prefecture).

1 See note 3 to E 4 above.
2 The editors have rightly added *huo* 或 to the text, in conformity with E 4.
3 See note 7 to E 4 above.
4 *Chi chi wang* 幾籍亡. *Chi* 幾 can mean "how many", but it can also be used for *chi* 譏, "to examine; to inspect". In view of the series of commands in this text ("determine!", "despatch!"), I have opted for the second meaning; SS and Dr. Yates have adopted the first, rendering the phrase as "how many times he has been registered as absconding?"
5 *Pu shih* 逋事; see D 144 above.
6 From here on, the text is practically identical with that of E 4.

E 6 W 8.34b; S II.45b; S VII.147b; SS 278–279; str. 15–17 (676–678); Yates, no. 5.25, pp. 162–163.

[15] An absconder comes forward voluntarily.—Report from (authority) X of the District:[1] the man A came here[2] of his own accord. His statement is: "(I am) a commoner; I live in X village. In the past[3] second month, on a unknown day, I left and absconded. I have not been adjudicated for other (misdeeds). Now I have come forward voluntarily." ○ He was asked [16] ...[4] name and status. It was established[5] that on the day *ping-tzu* of the second month he wandered about[6] and absconded; in the course of the third month he evaded service for building a palace[7] during twenty days. For the fourth year, the third month, the day *ting-wei*,[8] it is registered that on the whole he absconded during five months and ten days. He has not been adjudicated for other (misdeeds). Nobody[9] [17] has reinterrogated him. I have handed A over[10] to the (Village) Chief B for investigation. Now I have ordered B to escort him to proceed to be sentenced.[11] I beg to report this.

Models for sealing and investigating.[12]

1 See note 2 to E 3 above.
2 *I* 詣, "to proceed", i.e. to go to a superior.
3 *Nai* 迺 is frequently used to indicate the recent past.
4 One character missing.
5 *Ting* 定. SS considers *ting* as the last word of the previous sentence and renders it by "certified".
6 See note 2 to D 143 above.
7 *Kung* 宮. As indicated by SS, *kung* does not necessarily signify a royal palace; it is rendered in Yates by "government building".

[8] As noted in Yates, p. 162, note 185, these indications fit the year 243 B.C., according to Huang, "Pien cheng", pp. 4–5.

[9] SS renders *mo* 莫 as a prohibitive, translating "it is not necessary to reinterrogate him", but this seems doubtful, because in the other parts of the Yün-meng strips the normal prohibitive is *wu* 勿 or 毋.

[10] *Hsien* 獻 normally means "to present to a superior"; in the present context, this is rather surprising, because the District was higher than the Village; moreover, in the next sentence the District authority gives orders to the Village Chief.

[11] *Chiang chih i lun* 將之詣論.

[12] These words were only discovered when the Yün-meng texts had already been published in the journal *Wenwu* and in S. They occur on the back of the strip, which must therefore have been the first or the last strip of the fascicle; SS accordingly places this article at the end of this group.

E 7 W 8.34b; S II.45b–46a; S VII.148a; SS 251; str. 18–19 (595–596); Yates, no. 5.6, pp. 139–140.

[18] A robber voluntarily denounces himself.—. . . .[1] report: A, with the aristocratic rank of *kung shih*,[2] of X village, voluntarily denounced himself, saying: "On the last day of the fifth month, together with the commoner C[3] of the same village, I robbed one thousand cash from the commoner D of X village. I have not been adjudicated [19] for other (misdeeds). I have come to denounce myself voluntarily and to denounce C." Immediately an order was given to the [Prefectural][4] Clerk to go and arrest[5] C.

[1] Three characters are missing.

[2] The first or lowest rank.

[3] The equivalent of B, *i* 乙, is not used.

[4] SS suggests that the reduplication sign has been inadvertantly omitted after *ling*; according to SS the text should read *ling ling shih* 令令史.

[5] *Chih* 執, explained in SW as *pu tsui-jen* 捕罪人, "to arrest criminals", appears to be a third term for "to arrest", besides *pu* 捕 and *te* 得, the latter rendered as "to catch" in the present translation.

E 8 W 8.34b; S II.46a; S VII.148b; SS 252–253; str. 20–21 (597–598); Yates, no. 5.7, pp. 140–141.

[20] . . . [arrest].[1]—Report. The man A bound and brought along the man C.[2] His statement is: "(I), A, am a former[3] commoner, living in X village. In the past[4] fourth month I stole an ox and absconded.[5] C has been adjudicated for murderously[6] . . .[7] a man, [21] (but) he absconded.[8] Yesterday in the day-time[9] (I), A, seeing C hiding[10] among the labourers[11] in the market, arrested him and came with him, coming forward voluntarily". A has not been adjudicated for other (misdeeds).

[1] The first character is illegible; the editors believe that the second sign might be *pu* 捕.

[2] See note 3 to E 7 above.

[3] *Ku* 故. It remains unexplained why A defines himself as a "*former* commoner"; cf. the similar use of *ku* in C 5 above.

[4] See note 3 to E 6 above.

[5] The text clearly reads *ch'ü wang i ming* 去亡以命. Whereas *wang ming* is common for "to abscond; to escape", the present construction is inexplicable; the interpretation of the commentaries quoted in Yates, viz. that the fugitive "erased his name from the population register", is unacceptable. *Ch'ü wang* occurs in D 145 above.

6 *Tsei* 賊, the technical term for "with murderous intent"; see note 1 to D 53 above, and cf. *RHL*, p. 253 f.
7 Here the copyist appears to have omitted either "to wound" or "to kill".
8 One character illegible; this could be *wang* 亡.
9 As explained by the editors of SS, *tzu chou* 自晝 must have this meaning, because in E 22 and E 23 below *tzu hsiao* 自宵 can only mean "yesterday night" in view of the context.
10 *Yin* 陰 for *yin* 隱.
11 *Yung* 庸, "hired labour".

E 9 W 8.34b; S II.46a; S VII.149a; SS 252–253; str. 22–23 (599–600); Yates, no. 5.8, p. 141.

[22] . . . Report:[1] the commoners A and B of X village bound and brought in the men C and D, as well as 110[2] new cash and two sets of cash-molds.[3] They denounced them, saying: "C surreptitiously[4] cast these cash; D helped in the casting. [23] (We), A and B, arrested them, and, searching[5] their house, we found these cash-molds. We have come to bring them in".[6]

1 The tip of the strip has been broken off and therefore both the title and the first character of the expression *yüan shu*, "report", are missing.
2 For this figure see note 9 to D 1 above.
3 *Ch'ien jung* 錢容 (for 鎔), Chinese cash were not struck but cast in molds, consisting of two parts, hence *ho* 合, "a combination".
4 *Tao* 盜, "in a thievish manner".
5 索 for *so* 索, like in A 15 above.
6 This case is of interest, because it tends to prove that coining was a government monopoly under the Ch'in, at least in the 3rd century B.C.—a hitherto debated point; cf. Sung Shee-wu, p. 6 f. However, the date of the introduction of this monopoly might have been rather late, because there exist coins datable in the years immediately preceding 235 B.C. On the one hand, coins have been found with the inscription Ch'ang-an 長安, which was the fief of the First Emperor's younger brother, who committed suicide in 239 B.C. (*SC* 6.6; *Mh* II, p. 106); other coins are inscribed Wen-hsin 文信, which was the name of the nobility conferred on the famous chancellor Lü Pu-wei, who committed suicide in 235 B.C. (*SC* 6.3 and 6.14; *Mh* II, pp. 101 and 116); see "Ku ch'ien".

E 10 W 8.34b–35a; S II.46a; S VII.149b; SS 252–254; str. 24–25 (601–602); Yates, no. 5.9, pp. 141–142.

[24] Stealing a horse.—Report. The thief-catcher of the post on the thoroughfare south of the market in[1] X ward, (called) A, bound and brought in a man C, as well as a horse, a piebald mare . . .[2] on the righthand side, an orange[3] lined gown [25] with silk lining, a large[4] bordered collar and sleeves, as well as shoes. In his denunciation he said: "C stole this horse and these clothes. To-day I saw him beside the post; I arrested him and came, bringing him in."

1 *Ts'ai* 才 for *tsai* 在.
2 The text has *p'iao* 剽, "to stab". The editors suggest that this is a loan for *p'iao* 瞟, "blind in one eye", but in Yates the word is taken literally and translated "with a stab wound". In *RHA* II, pp. 305 and 307 Dr. Loewe writes "cut", explaining on p. 302 that this might refer to the horns of cattle, but that is, of course, impossible in the present case. Mori, *Kankan*, pp. 47–48, does not offer a solution. There are too many examples of *p'iao* in the Edsin-gol strips to make the meaning "to stab" acceptable. For the time being the SS translation "with a sick eye" seems the least objectionable. Perhaps *p'iao* could mean "to mark", but not by branding, for that is *chiu* 久 (see note 2 to A 47 above), and on some Edsin-gol strips *p'iao*

and *chiu* are found together; similar difficulties arise in connection with *chan* 斬, which appears to be again another term for "to mark" (see note 2 to E 15 below).

3 *SW* explains *t'i* 緹 as "crimson-yellow".

4 *Mang* 莽 can mean "vast"; see *SWKL*, p. 486b.

E 11 W 8.35a; S II.46a; S VII.150a; SS 254–255; str. 26–27 (603–604); Yates, no. 5.10, p. 142.

[26] A dispute about a cow.—Report. The *kung shih*[1] A of X village and the commoner B brought in a cow, with a long halter[2] and with horns. They reported,[3] saying: "This is the cow of A and B;[4] it ran away.[5] We each recognize it.[6] Together bringing it in we have come [27] to dispute it." Thereupon I ordered the Prefectural Clerk X to estimate the cow's age;[7] the cow was already[8] six years old.

1 The first or lowest of the aristocratic ranks.

2 The editors transcribe the text as *man mi* 曼靡. One of the meanings of *man* is long. *Mi* is assumed to be a loan for *mi* 縻, "a halter".

3 *Kao* 告.

4 As noted by the editors, the statements of the two men have been combined, for each one will have said "this is my cow"; in Yates, however, they are supposed to have said "A or B's cow".

5 The word *erh* 而 before *wang* 亡 is puzzling.

6 *Erh wang ko shih* 而亡各識 is translated in Yates by "it lacks the brand-mark of each party". Although this rendering would explain the presence of *erh* (see note 5), it is impossible. In the first place, *wang*, which i.a. in historical texts is frequently synonymous with *wu* 無, does not have this meaning in the texts under survey. And in the second place, more seriously, *ko* 各, "each", never occurs in an attributive position. Hence, although *shih* 識 occasionally means "mark" in these texts (see A 47 and B 19 above), *wang ko shih* can never mean "it lacks, *wu*, each (party)'s, *ko*, mark, *shih*".

7 *Ch'ih* 齒, "tooth", is frequently used for "age". The age of stock animals is determined by inspecting their teeth; here, *ch'ih* is used as a verb, viz. "to establish or determine the age". The translation in Yates, "to age the cow", is more curious than correct.

8 Implied by the use of *i* 矣 at the end of the sentence.

E 12 W 8.35a; S II.46b; S VII.150b–151a; SS 255–256; str. 28–33 (605–610); Yates, no. 5.11, pp. 142–144.

[28] Gang robbery.[1]—Report. A, the *hsiao-chang*[2] of post X, and the thief-catchers B and C in[3] X village, bound and brought in the man D, one severed head, two complete[4] cross-bows and twenty bolts.[5] He reported,[6] saying: "D and [29] the man to whom this head belonged[7] forcefully attacked and in a gang robbed people. Yesterday,[8] when (I), A, leading B and others, on patrol came to Mount X, we saw D together with the man to whom this head belonged and arrested them. These crossbows and bolts are D's as well as the man's to whom this head belonged [30][9] crossbows and bolts. The man to whom this head belonged used this crossbow and bolts. . . .[10] B; so, with a sword he felled him and collected his head. As the mountain was rugged,[11] we were unable to take the body out of the mountain. [31] [On interrogation[12]] D in his statement said:" I am a commoner, living in X village. This head (belonged to) the commoner E of X village. Together with (me), D, and the commoners F, G and H of X village, we forcefully attacked and in a

gang [32] robbed the house of the *kung shih*[13] X of X village, and having stolen 10.000 cash, we left and absconded. F and the others were caught earlier. (I), D, together with E, having left and absconded, roamed about without a place to stay. Yesterday[14] we were staying at Mount X. A [33] and the others then[15] arrested (me), D, and E shot at B, (who) then felled and killed him and collected his head." None[16] have been adjudicated for other crimes. ○ To examine a head without examining the body is permissible.

1 See note 5 to D 1 above.

2 *Hsiao chang* 校長. The rendering in Yates as "subaltern" will be closer to the truth than "Chief of a regiment" in Bielenstein, *Bureaucracy*, p. 21, because a regiment, *hsiao* (containing 800 men according to *T'ung tien* 通典 148. 16a; *TT* quotes an unknown source which seems to provide correct information for the Han period; see Chu Kuo-chao, pp. 22–26) was commanded by a *hsiao wei* 尉, usually translated as "colonel". As noted in Yates, a *hsiao chang* is mentioned in *SC* 90.5 (Watson, *Records* I, p. 191, likewise "subaltern"; *HSPC* 34.13b); his rank cannot have been very high, because he was ordered to behead an offender. In the passage in *HHSCC* Tr. 25.3a, used by Professor Bielenstein, the *hsiao chang* appears as a subordinate of each of the Prefects in charge of the imperial mausolea, "in charge of military matters (to guard against) robbery".

3 *Ts'ai* 才 for *tsai* 在.

4 *Chü nu* 具弩, i.e. crossbows ready for immediate use; see Lao Kan, *K'ao-shih, k'ao-cheng*, p. 48.

5 I have used the word "bolts" because the arrows for the crossbow differed from those used for the long bow. Sung Chao-lin, p. 76, quotes the *Chou-li, ssu kung-shih* 司弓矢, where the commentator Cheng Hsüan (A.D. 127–200) notes that there were four types of arrows each for the crossbow and for the long bow (*Chou-li chu-su* 32.5a (1153); *Chou-li* 18/61.9–10; not in Biot II, p. 249), the author adding that short arrows, i.e. bolts or quarrels, were used for the crossbow. As a matter of fact, it is inconceivable that a crossbow with a stock of only c. 50 cm. would shoot arrows of c. 70 cm. To my regret, neither Professor Hayashi's *Buki*, nor his *Bunbutsu*, throw any light on this problem, in spite of the wealth of detail he provides, especially about the types of arrow-heads.

6 *Kao* 告.

7 The text simply says *shou jen* 首人, "the man of the head".

8 See note 9 to E 8 above.

9 In actual fact, the text runs *shou* [30] *jen nu shih*, 首 [30] 人弩矢.

10 Six characters missing.

11 I have gratefully adopted Dr. Yates' rendering of *hsien* 險.

12 This word has been added by the editors as a suggested substitute for the first, illegible character on strip no. 31.

13 The first and lowest of the aristocratic ranks.

14 See note 9 to E 8 above.

15 I follow SS for this rendering of *erh* 而.

16 Literally "all have not", *chieh wu* 皆毋.

E 13 W 8.35a; S II.46b; S VII.151b–152a; SS 256–257; str. 34–36 (611–613); Yates, no. 5.12, pp. 144–145.

[34] Snatching away a head.—Report from (authority) X at Headquarters:[1] A, a commoner of X Village, bound and brought in a man C, as well as one severed head; a man D accompanied them. ○ He reported,[2] saying: "(I), A, am a private functionary[3] of colonel[4] X, [35] taking part in the battle of Hsing-ch'iu city.[5] To-day I saw C at the headquarter's company[6] straightaway felling and wounding D with his sword and snatching away this head.[7] I then[8] arrested him and came, bringing him in". We have examined the

head and we have already examined D; we have also examined [36] the condition of his wounds.

1 *Hsi* 戲 can be explained in two ways: it is a flag, indicating the commander, or one can follow SW, where *hsi* is explained as *p'ien shih* 偏師, "a detached corps".
2 *Kao* 告.
3 *Ssu li* 私吏. The expression is unknown; it is also rather surprising, for all authorities agree that *li* "govern the people", so that it is difficult to see how a colonel could have "private officials." It should be noted, however, that recently the seal was found of a "Household Overseer, *chia se-fu* 家嗇夫 (*Kaogu* 1982/4, p. 363), which shows that at least this title was not only borne by officials (see my "Ch'in documents", p. 201 f.), but also by members of the staff of a private household. Such a private household was probably the household of a nobleman, as demonstrated by Fu Chü-yu, p. 168; he shows that Han nobles had *chia li* 家吏. The rendering in Yates, "batman", i.e. officer's servant, must remain tentative.
4 Because a battle is mentioned here, the *wei* 尉 is more likely to be a *hsiao* 校 *wei* (see note 2 to E 12 above) than a military commandant in a commandery or a prefecture.
5 The battle for Hsing-ch'iu 刑 (for 邢) 丘 was fought in 266 B.C., see *SC* 5.75, *Mh* II, p. 90. It is mentioned in the "Chronicle" (SS, p. 5), and in E 14 below.
6 *Sui* 旞, "plumes tied to a banner", is quite probably a loan. The editors suggest *sui* 遂, "road", and not *tui* 隊 as they do in D184 above. Dr. Yates, however, prefers *tui*, which he renders by "section (in the army)". According to the *T'ung tien* passage quoted in note 2 to E 12 above, a *tui* contained fifty men.
7 The head must have belonged to an enemy, for rewards were given for enemies killed; see *Shang-chün shu*, ch. 19, p. 71 f. (Duyvendak, *Lord Shang*, p. 296 f.); see also *HHSCC* Mem. 79.9a *chan shou huo sheng chi kung shou shang ju ch'ang ko* 斬首獲生計功受賞如常格, "the accounting of merit and the bestowal of rewards for heads cut off and for (enemies) captured alive is done according to the permanent rules." Such rules are found in fragmentary form on the Han strips of the middle of the 1st century B.C., discovered in a tomb c. 20 km. south of *Ta-t'ung* 大通 Prefecture in Ch'ing-hai Province; see *Wenwu* 1981/2, pp. 16–26, and Chu Kuo-chao.
8 See note 8 to E 12 above.

E 14 W 8.35a; S II.47a; S VII.152a–b; SS 257–258; str. 37–39 (614–616); Yates, no. 5.13, pp. 145–146.

[37] . . . .[1] X report: "A commoner A from X village and a *kung shih*[2] from Cheng[3] (living) in[4] X village, called C, together brought in one severed head. They reported, saying each:" (I), A, (resp. I) C, fought at the city of Hsing-ch'iu,[5] and this [38] is the head (I), A, (resp. I), C, took. (We), A and C quarrelled about this and we have come to bring it". ○ On examing the head (it was found that) . . . .[6] . . . .[7] hair. On the right temple there is a wound,[8] five inches long, and so deep that it enters into the bone, resembling the traces of a sword. The neck[9] region[10] is irregular and mangled.[11] By letter (I) enquired[12] about the head, saying: "If there are persons missing from their squad[13] as well as persons who have been delayed[14] and who have not come, send (someone) to come and recognize (the head) at the commander's camp[15]".[16]

1 The title of this report, as well as the first two characters of the contents are illegible.
2 The first and lowest of the aristocratic ranks.
3 *Cheng* 鄭. According to *SC* 5.17 (*Mh* II, pp. 20–21) Cheng was made a Ch'in prefecture in 687 B.C.; it continued as a prefecture in the Capital District under the Han, as noted in *HSPC* 28AI.22a.
4 *Ts'ai* 才 for *tsai* 在.

[5] See note 4 to E 13 above.

[6] One character is illegible.

[7] The character is composed of the "radical" 髟 over 舀, or, according to others, over 貴. The first is unknown; the editors suggest that it is used here for *ssu* 鬆, "short hair". The second seems to mean "bunched up hair". The type of hair-dress denoted here is unknown. For the different ways in which Ch'in men dressed their hair, as shown by the life-size pottery statutes of the soldiers who guarded the First Emperor's tomb, see *Wenwu* 1975/11, p. 16.

[8] *Wei* 痏 usually means "a bruise", e.g. in the expression *shih* 疻 *wei*, "weals and bruises", which occurs in D 72–75 above. Here it evidently means "wound".

[9] The severed heads mentioned here and in E 12 and 13 above are referred to as *shou* 首. The word *t'ou* 頭 used here can therefore not mean "head", but it is used for *tou* 脰, "neck".

[10] *So* 所; a similar use of *so* is found in A 16 *lin so* 稟所; A 74 *chia jen so* 段人所; E 18 *pu hsiao chia so* 不孝甲所.

[11] *Ts'an-ts'an* 賤賤. The binome is unknown, but according to SW, *ts'an*, written 歺, means "food left by wild animals". The term could therefore mean "chewed up; torn; ragged"; I have gratefully adopted Dr. Yates' rendering "mangled". The solution suggested in SS that *ts'an-ts'an* should mean "short" seems unacceptable.

[12] *Hsüan* 譞.

[13] *Wu* 伍, lit. "group of five."

[14] *Shih* 菌, "dung", also written 屎, or, in E 21 below and in the Edsin-gol strips, 矢. The editors suggest that this word should be a loan for *ch'ih* 遲, or rather, I suppose, for *shih* 屖, both meaning "to tarry". Although this loan is, as far as I am aware, not attested, it is phonetically quite possible, *shih*, "dung", as well as *shih*, "to tarry", both being *si̯ər (GSR, p. 149, no. 561d, and p. 159, no. 595a; note that *ch'ih* is *d'i̯ər).

[15] *Tz'u* 朿.

[16] This is a strange case. The enquiry among the Ch'in troops shows, that the head was believed to be that of a Ch'in soldier. Now A and C could hardly have taken the head of a Ch'in soldier, and then have the effrontery to present it, in order to claim a reward; if a reward would not have been at stake, the two men would not have quarrelled. On the other hand, for an enemy head the enquiry would have been pointless.

E 15 W 8.35a–b; S II.47a; S VII.153a–b; SS 259–260; str. 40–44 (617–621); Yates, no. 5.14, pp. 146–147.

[40] Denouncing a slave.[1]—The commoner A of X village bound and brought in a man C; in his denunciation he said: "C is (my), A's, slave. He is arrogant[2] and obstreperous, he does not work the fields, he does not obey (my), A's, orders. I wish to sell him to the government,[3] to be amputated[4] and to be made [41] a *ch'eng-tan*, and to receive the price".[5] ○ When C was interrogated, he said in his statement:" I am A's slave. I have been really obstreperous and have not obeyed A's orders. A has never[6] liberated[7] (me), C. I have no illness; I have not been adjudicated for other crimes." [42] An order was given to the Prefectural Clerk X to examine C; he has no illness. ○ An order was given to the Treasurer[8] X and the Assistant (Clerk) to price C by the correct market price[9] before the Assistant (Prefect) X. C is an average person;[10] the price[11] was so and so many cash. ○ The Assistant (Prefect) X [43] informs[12] the Head of X District: "The man C is under interrogation.[13] In his statement he said: 'I am a slave of commoner A of X village'. Establish his name, status and village, the crimes for which he has been adjudicated, which crimes have been amnestied, whether somebody[14] has reinterrogated him, whether A has ever liberated C and re-enslaved him or not. Seal and guard (his property and dependents) according

to the Statutes.[15] When (this communication) reaches you, report (its arrival) in writing.[16,17]

[1] *Ch'en* 臣, "slave"; see my "Supplementary note".
[2] *Ch'iao* 橋 for *ch'iao* 驕.
[3] *Mai* 買 (for *mai* 賣) *kung* 公.
[4] *Chan* 斬, lit. "to hack, to hew". The editors offer different explanations. One the one hand they suggest that *chan* refers to the amputation of one or both feet, because up to 167 B.C. the condemnation to *ch'eng-tan* could be accompanied by this supplementary punishment; that this was also Ch'in practice is shown by D 1 and D 105 above. On the other hand it is suggested that *chan* might be a loan for *chien* 漸 (lit. "gradually"), which in some ancient texts is explained as *chin* 進 (*Chou I chu-su* 9.8a (0465); Legge, *I-ching*, pp. 437–438). However, the editors overlook that in these texts *chin* means "to advance" and not "to bring forward; to present". With some hesitation I would like to present a third suggestion. Whereas in D 1 and D 105 above it is explicitly added that the left foot is to be amputated, in the present case we find the word *chan* alone; could this signify that *chan* here has a different meaning? In the Edsin-gol documents *chan* is repeatedly found in the description of cattle, where bulls, oxen and cows are noted as *chan* on either the right or the left; see *RHA* II, pp. 304–307. *Chan* cannot be a brand-mark, because that is *chiu* 久 (see note 2 to A 47 above), and in one case a cow is reported as having a brand-mark on the right and the left as well as *chan* on the left, whereas in another case a bull is said to be *chan* but not brand-marked, ... *chan wu chiu* .. 斬毋久 (*RHA*, *loc. cit.*, nos. 1 and 13). I therefore believe that *chan* meant marking an animal by cutting or clipping, just as even to-day the ears of stock animals are sometimes clipped in order to mark them; Dr. Loewe suggests that the animals' horns might have been cut (*RHA* II, p. 302). *Chan* in isolation could therefore perhaps mean marking a convict in a way different from tattooing. Still, the meaning "amputate" remains the most likely. Kao Heng, "Nu-pi", pp. 142–143, thinks that this was done in order to prevent that the man would run away; he bases this on a story in ch. 24 of the *Chuang-tzu*, where kidnappers cut off the foot of their victim in order to sell him more easily! (*Chuang-tzu*, p. 133; Legge, *Chuang-tzu* 40, p. 108).
[5] *Shou chia ch'ien* 受賈 (for 價) 錢.
[6] *Wei shang* (for *ch'ang*) 未賞 (for 嘗).
[7] *Shen mien* 身免; for manumission of slaves during the Han period see Wilbur, *Slavery*, pp. 229–239.
[8] See note 9 to A 40 above.
[9] *I shih cheng chia chia Ping* 以市正賈 (for 價) 賈丙.
[10] *Chung jen* 中人.
[11] *Chia* 賈 for *chia* 價.
[12] *Kao* 告.
[13] Cf. E 4 above.
[14] Or "perhaps"; see note 6 to E 4 above.
[15] The procedure is described in E 3 above.
[16] As remarked in Yates, p. 147, note 134, this order is found in many Edsin-gol documents.
[17] Like E 4 above, this article appears to be a mixture of a model-report and directions for the compilation of such a report.

E 16 W 8.35b; S II.47a–b; S VII.154a–b; SS 260–261; str. 45–48 (622–625); Yates, no. 5.15, pp. 147–148.

[45] Tattooing a female slave.—The *kung shih*[1] A of X village bound and brought in an adult woman[2] C and reported,[3] saying; "(I am) am a household official[4] of the *wu ta-fu*[5] B of X Village. C is B's slave woman. B makes (me), A, say: 'C [46] is obstreperous. I request that C be tattooed and have her nose cut off.' ○ C, on being interrogated, said in her statement: '(I am) B's slave woman.' She has not been adjudicated for another (crime)." ○ The Assistant (Prefect) X informs the Head of X District: "A, a household

official of the *wu ta-fu* of X Village brought in B's [47] slave woman C, saying: 'B has ordered (me), A, to request that C be tattooed and have her nose cut off'. Enquire[6] whether (things are) as he says or not. Determine name, status and village, (the crimes) for which she has been adjudicated and sentenced, and whether she has perhaps been re-interrogated or [48] not. Report in writing."

[1] The first and lowest of the aristocratic ranks.
[2] *Ta nü-tzu* 大女子; see note 2 to A 13 above.
[3] *Kao* 告.
[4] *Chia li* 家吏; the editors refer to *HSPC* 97A.21b, where a certain person is described as a "household official" of the heir-apparent (Watson, *Courtier*, p. 256, writes "retainer"). See also note 3 to E 13 above.
[5] *Wu ta-fu* 五大夫 was the ninth of the aristocratic ranks.
[6] *Wen* 問.

E 17 W 8.35b; S II.47b; S VII.154b–155a; SS 261–262; str. 49–52 (626–629); Yates, no. 5.16, pp. 148–150.

[49] Banishing[1] a son.—Report: "A, a commoner of X Village, said in his denunciation[2]: 'I request to have the feet of my own[3] son, C, a commoner of the same village, fettered[4] and to have him banished to a border prefecture in Shu,[5] with the injunction[6] that he must not be allowed to leave the place of banishment. [50] This I beg to announce."[7] I inform the Head of Fei-ch'iu[8]: "The commoner from Hsien-yang, living in[9] X Village, called C, has been adjudicated because his father A requested to have his feet shackled and have him banished to a border prefecture in Shu, with the injunction that to the end of his life he be not allowed [51] to leave the place of banishment. We have sentenced[10] him and we banish C according to A's denunciation, to be guaranteed[11] according to the Statutes. Now we have fettered C's feet. An order has been given to (an) official(s) and conscripts[12] to lead and transfer[13] (him), as well as one. . . . letter[14] to be taken to the Prefectural Clerk,[15] so that he will receive[16] [52] and replace the official(s) and the conscripts. He is to be transferred through successive prefectures and to be taken to Ch'eng-tu.[17] In Ch'eng-tu the . . . letter[18] is to be presented at the place[19] of the Grand Administrator.[20] He is to be fed according to the Statutes.[21] When Fei-ch'iu has already transferred (him),[22] a report is to be made. This I beg to report to the Head."[23]

[1] For banishment see the introduction, p. 17, Ōba, "Shisen kei", and cf. *RHL*, p. 132 f.
[2] *Kao* 告.
[3] As rightly remarked in Yates, p. 148, note 139, *ch'in tzu* 親子 means a natural son, not an adopted child. Cf. also note 2 to A 91 above.
[4] See note 7 to D 89 above.
[5] *Shu* 蜀. Persons sentenced to exile were usually banished to the farthest limits of the state, often newly conquered territory; Shu was only conquered by Ch'in at the end of the 4th century B.C. and is frequently mentioned as a place of exile. During the Han period exiles were sent to the Canton area or to Tun-huang (except kings); see *RHL*, pp. 133–134.
[6] *Ling* 令, "order".
[7] The author of the report is not mentioned.
[8] Fei-ch'iu 廢丘 was a Ch'in prefecture on the Wei River, west of Hsien-yang (*HSPC* 28AI.

31a; see also *HFHD* I, map, square 3-C, and *Mh* II, p. 285). The editors of SS remark that Fei-ch'iu was the first station on the road to Ch'eng-tu.—*Chu* 主 can only refer to the Prefect.

9 *Ts'ai* 才 for *tsai* 在.

10 *Lun chih* 論之. Some kind of formal decision was evidently necessary in order to render the execution of the father's request possible. It is, however, unknown who it was that pronounced the sentence.

11 The technical meaning of *pao* 包, already discussed in note 4 to D 48 above, remains an enigma. The suggestion in Yates, p. 149, note 141, that *pao* should be interpreted as "a positive guarantee, specifically the "guaranteed [accompaniment]" of those sentenced to banishment whose family members stood as surety for their arrival" has no textual support. His translation of the phrase under discussion as "with guaranteed [accompaniment] in accordance with the law" is therefore unacceptable. Although it seems certain that *pao* concerns the exile's family, and especially his wife (see D 49 and 50 above), and that it likewise concerns the transfer of these family members to the place of exile, the exact technical meaning of *pao* remains unknown.

12 *Li t'u* 吏徒. For the uncertainty regarding the meaning of *t'u* see note 2 to D 159 above.

13 I take 傳 as *ch'uan*, "to transmit; to transfer", and so do the editors on the next occurrence of this word, but here they render it by "passport", i.e. *chuan*. An argument in their favour is the word *chi* 及, "as well as", which here connects *chiang chuan* 將傳 and *heng shu* 恒書 (see note 14), but in that case *chiang* has to be taken as "to take", which in literary Chinese precedes an object placed before the verb, and I do not think that this type of *chiang* construction is found in the Yün-meng texts. Still, SS translates: "they take the passport and the *heng-shu*, one letter, bringing these to the Prefectural Clerk"; this rendering has been adopted in Yates.

14 The term *heng shu* 恒書 is unknown; could it mean "the (constant =) routine documents"? The editors of SS suggest that this might refer to the escort papers. As in the Tun-huang and the Edsin-gol documents, letters are counted by *feng* 封, "sealed (documents)".

15 Presumably in each prefecture through which the escort passes.

16 *Shou* 受. The meaning of this word is unclear. Does it imply that the Prefectural Clerk would have to take care of the escort that was being relieved? It is neglected in the SS translation.

17 The capital of Shu commandery.

18 See note 14 above.

19 *Ch'u* 處. This might indicate the residence of the Great Administrator, like "Yeh's place" on pp. 27 and 28 of my "Lawsuit".

20 As rightly stressed in Yates, p. 150, note 143, it has always been assumed that the title *t'ai shou* 太守 had only been created by the Han emperor Ching in 155 B.C., and that before that time the governor of a commandery was simply *shou*; for the implications of the occurrence of the fuller title in the present text see Dr. Yates' note.

21 *I lü shih* 以律食; see A 92–94 above, and cf. A 31.

22 *I ch'uan* 已傳. I expect this to refer to the banished man alone.

23 See the end of note 8 above.

E 18 W 8.35b; S II.47b; S VII.155b; SS 263; str. 53–54 (630–631); Yates, no. 5.17, pp. 150–152.

[53] Denouncing a son.—The commoner A of X Village said in his denunciation: "(My), A's, own[1] son, the commoner C of the same village, is unfilial.[2] I request to have him killed."[3] This I beg to announce.[4] Forthwith the Prefectural Clerk E[5] was ordered to go and arrest[6] him. Prefectural Clerk E's [54] report: "Together with the Prison bond-servant[7] X I arrested C; we found him in the house of X." The Assistant (Prefect) X has interrogated C; in his statement he said:" (I am) A's own son; I have been truly unfilial towards A."[8] He has not been adjudicated for another crime.

1 Cf. note 3 to E 17 above.

2 Cf. D 85 above.

3 Cf. note 4 to D 85 above.
4 Because of the presence of the word *kan* 敢, the polite formula for "I venture to; I beg to", these words form the conclusion of the first report.
5 The equivalent of D, viz. *ting* 丁, is not used.
6 *Chih* 執; cf. note 5 to E 7 above.
7 *Lao li-ch'en* 牢隸臣. The position of the bond-servants in the Ch'in system of hard labour punishments remains unclear; see the discussion in note 146 on p. 151 of Yates. Here the prison bond-servant evidently functions as a warden or as some kind of police constable.
8 Here C's statement ends; the final sentence concludes the second report.—In C's statement the phrase *pu hsiao chia so* 不孝甲所 provides another example of the construction with *so*; see note 10 to E 14 above.

E 19 W 8.35b; S II.48a; S VII.156a; SS 263–264; str. 55–57 (632–634); Yates, no. 5.18. pp. 152–153.

[55] Leprosy.—Report. A, Chief of X Village,[1] brought in a commoner C from (his) village; in his report[2] he said: "I suspect he is a leper,[3] and so I came and brought him in." ○ On being interrogated, C said: "At the time I was three years old, I suffered from boils[4] and my eyebrows[5] fell out;[6] it was impossible to know[7] [56] what disease this was". He has not been adjudicated for another (crime). I ordered the physician[8] D to examine him. D reported[9] and said: "C has no eyebrows. The bridge of his nose[10] is severed. The nasal cavity has collapsed. When his nose is pricked, he does not sneeze.[11] Elbows and knees[12] [57] . . . .[13] attaining . . .[14] Both lower legs[15] are crippled.[16] (There is) one running sore.[17] His hands have no down.[18] When made to shout,[19] the breath of his voice gave out.[20] (This is) leprosy."[21]

1 *Li tien* 里典; see note 11 to A 7 above.
2 *Kao* 告.
3 For the following diagnosis of leprosy see the highly interesting information in Yates, p. 152, note 147, and the medical literature quoted there. See also Bodde, "Medicine", pp. 9–14.
4 *Pi* 疕, "boils; swellings".
5 For *mi* 麋 as a loan for *mei* 眉, see note 1 to D 66 above.
6 *T'u* 突. I have followed the editors' suggestion, but the translation in Yates is "swelled up."
7 *Chih* 智 for *chih* 知.
8 *I* 醫.
9 *Yen* 言.
10 The text has *ken pen* 艮本. The editors suggest in the first place that *ken* stands for *ken* 根, and secondly that *ken pen* is the same as *shan ken* 山根, "the bridge of the nose between the eyes". They also quote a second opinion, viz. that *ken pen* could refer to the roots of the hairs of the eyebrows.
11 *Chih* 疐 for *t'i* 嚏.
12 *Hsi* 厀 for *hsi* 膝, the former being the older form; see *SWKL*, p. 4024a–b.
13 Three characters illegible.
14 One character illegible.
15 *Tsu hsia* 足下. SS simply says "feet", Yates "the soles of the feet", Bodde ". .feet [are unequal] below".
16 *Ch'i* 踦; according to the 1st century *Fang yen* 方言, quoted in *SWKL*, p. 686a–b, "limbs that are incompete".
17 *Hui* 潰, "to leak".
18 *Po* 胈, small hair on the body.
19 The practically illegible character on the strip is transcribed as 濇, which I am unable to find in Morohashi, nor in SW; the editors identify it with *hao* 號, "to shout". See also note 41 to E 20.
20 *Ch'i yin ch'i pai* 其音氣敗; SS, followed by Yates, translates *pai* by "hoarse"; Bodde "feeble".

[21] D 101 above shows that for lepers the death penalty could be executed by drowning, and D 102 mentions places where lepers were moved to live.

E 20 W 8.35b–36a; S II.48a–b; S VII.156b–157b; SS 264–266; str. 58–65 (635–642); Yates, no. 5.19, pp. 154–155.

[58] Death by murderous intent.[1]—Thief-catcher A of post X in his announcement says: "At the place X within (the area of) my post[2] there is the corpse[3] of a murdered[4] (person), with bound-up hair, a man, (I) do not know who.[5] (I) have come to announce (this)". Forthwith an order was given to the Prefectural Clerk X to go [59] and investigate. Report of the Prefectural Clerk X: "Together with the Prison Bond-servant[6] X I went to[7] A to investigate. The corpse of the man lay South of X's house,[8] fully[9] on its back. On the left corner of his neck[10] there was a wound[11] made with a blade[12] [60] and on the back[13] two (wounds), all vertical[14] to the neck and the back, each four inches long, stuck together[15] and each one inch wide, all depressed,[16] resembling (wounds made by) an axe. The temples and cheek bones[17] had all bled, (the blood) covering and staining the neck, the back and the ground; of all these[18] [61] it was impossible to establish the width and the length. For the rest he was intact. He wore a hempen unlined skirt and jacket,[19] one piece each. The back of his jacket, facing[20] the wounds, had been torn with a blade in two places. Corresponding[21] to the wounds, the back of the jacket and the centre of the front-flap[22] [62] ...[23] were stained with blood. To the west of the man there was one pair[24] of Ch'in silk shoes,[25] one at over six paces, the other at ten paces;[26] shoeing him with the shoes, they fitted him.[27] The ground being hard, we were unable to recognize[28] the murderer's footsteps. The man is an adult,[29] of pale[30] colouring, his length is seven feet and one inch,[31] his hair is two feet long. On his belly there are two ancient moxa scars.[32] From the place of the man's corpse to the police-post X (the distance is) one hundred [64] paces,[33] to the farmhouse[34] of the commoner C of X Village two hundred paces.[35] ○ An order was given to the Prefectural Clerk A to bury[36] him, covered[37] by the hemp-cloth skirt, awaiting[38] (further) orders, and to take the jacket and the shoes and bring them to (Prefect's[39]) office. An interrogation was held of A, [65] the men of the police-post as well as C, (to ascertain) whether they knew[40] on which day the man had died, and whether they had heard him shout[41] "Robbers!"[42] or not.

[1] Yates: "death by wanton violence". See note note 1 to D 35 above.—This text is also analyzed in Bodde, "Medicine", pp. 5–6.

[2] *Shu chung* 署中; SS and Koga, p. 139, present a similar translation. For *shu* see note 1 to A 15 and note 1 to C 21 above.

[3] *Ssu* 死 for *shih* 尸 is common.

[4] *Tsei* 賊; see note 1 to D 35 above.

[5] *Chih* 智 for *chih* 知.—For *pu chih ho nan-tzu* 不知何男子 see Ch'ien P'an, *Ch'i chung*, p. 24b.

[6] See note 7 to E 18 above.

[7] *Chi* 即. SS renders *chi* by "to follow", because in his commentary to the Book of Changes Wang Pi (226–249) renders *chi* by *ts'ung* 從, probably inspired by the context (*Chou I chu-su* 1.18a (0061); Legge, *I ching*, p. 62). However, this is unnecessary, and K'ung Ying-ta (574–648) in his sub-commentary is fully justified when he explains *chi* quite normally as *chiu* 就, "to go to".

8 *Tsai mou shih nan shou* 在某室南首. The translation in SS agrees with mine. It would be possible to translate that the corpse "was in the house of X, with the head turned to the south" (and this has been done in Yates and Bodde), but this conflicts with the information that the corpse lay certain specified distances away from the police-post and a farm. *Nan shou* will therefore have to be taken as "in a southerly direction"; cf. *Li-chi*, ch. 11, *Yü tsao* (*Li-chi chu-su* 29.6b (1308); Couvreur, *Li-ki* I, p. 683; Legge, *Li-ki* 28, p. 5).

9 *Cheng yen* 正偃, translated in Yates as "straight on its back", but *cheng* will mean "exactly"; the corpse was not lying on its dide.

10 (*Mou*; correctly) *ch'i t'ou* (某, *recte*) 其頭. Both the transcription and the SS translation read *mou*, "a certain person; X", but I believe that the text on the strip simply has *ch'i* with a vertical smudge that has been misinterpreted as the vertical stroke of 木.—For *t'ou* 頭 used for *tou* 脰, "neck", see note 9 to E 14 above; with *shou* 首, "head" used on the same strip, it seems most unlikely that *t'ou* would mean "head", but that is the word used by SS, Yates and Bodde.

11 *Wei* 痏; see note 8 to E 14 above.

12 *Jen* 刃, "cutting edge".

13 *Pei* 北 for *pei* 背.

14 *Ts'ung* 從, taken as a loan for *tsung* 縱, "vertical", probably implying that the wounds had been caused by a downward blow of the axe and not by a sweeping stroke.

15 The text reads 耎, which the editors explain as *juan* 耎, suggesting that this is a loan for *ju* 濡, explained as "sticky".

16 *Hsüan* 臽, "pit".

17 *Nao chiao ch'u* 㞕, i.e. 腦角出. *Nao chiao*, "the corners of the skull", are the temples. *Ch'u*, in view of its position before *chieh* 皆, "all", must be a noun; the editors suggest *cho* 頔, "cheek-bones".

18 Presumably the places covered by the blood.

19 *Pu tan chün ju* 布禪帬襦. *Pu* is hemp cloth; *tan* (in the Edsingol documents often *tan* 單, "simple") is "unlined"; *chün* is a kind of skirt-like garment (see Hayashi, *Bunbutsu*, p. 20 and ill. 1–35); SW explains *ju* as "a short upper garment", hence a jacket.

20 *Chih* 直, "facing"; see note 2 to D 165 above.

21 *Ying* 瘫 for *ying* 應.

22 *Jen* 衽; see Hayashi, *Bunbutsu*, p. 19.

23 One character illegible.

24 *Liang* 兩. This word occurs frequently in the Tun-huang and the Edsingol documents, indicating pairs of shoes, socks or trousers; cf. my "Han documents", pp. 38–39.

25 *Ch'i* 綦, has two different meanings: 1) a colour; Morohashi, vol. 8, p. 1094: light green; Karlgren, GSR, p. 250, no. 952z: dappled grey, c.q. silk of that colour, and 2) laces, sewn to the back of a shoe and attached to the ankle (see Morohashi, *loc. cit.*, and Hayashi, *Bunbutsu*, p. 32, and ills. 1–51, 52). However, SS, disregarding the commentaries to the classics on which the above is based, prefers the explanation given by the 7th century commentator in *HHSCC*, Mem. 1.11a, viz. "embroidery on shoes". Here, in E 20, the exact meaning of *ch'i* is not important, but see note 24 to E 22 below. In Yates *ch'i li* is translated as "corded shoes", for which there is no evidence; the authors evidently think of Spanish or French "espadrilles", i.e. rope-soled sandals, but, as far as I know, these are unknown in China. Still, hemp and straw sandals existed; see Hayashi, *Bunbutsu*, p. 28 f., ill. 1–49f.

26 With six feet to the pace, and the Ch'in-Han foot at c. 23.1 cm., these distances correspond to c. 8½ and 14 m.

27 The word *li* 履 is first used as a verb, "to shoe", and then as a noun, "shoes; sandals"; cf. Hayashi, *Bunbutsu*, p. 30 f., from which it appears that *li* were mainly made of silk.—*Li* 利, lit. "advantageous".

28 *Chih* 智 for *chih* 知.

29 *Ting chuang* 丁壯.

30 *Hsi* 析, a loan for *hsi* 皙, which SW defines as "pale".

31 C. 1.7m.; the length of the hair is c. 0.45 m.

32 *Chiu* 久 for *chiu* 灸, but cf. note 3 to A 47 above.

33 C. 140 m.

34 *T'ien she* 田舍; see note 1 to A 6 above.

35 C. 280 m.

36 The text has *li* 貍, "wildcat", which is an accepted loan for *mai* 埋, "to bury".

37 This partly effaced character the editors decipher as 劉, which they assume to be a variant

of *yen* 剡, "sharp; to cut", taken to be a loan for *yen* 掩, "to cover". Phonetically, this seems not impossible—the loan is nowhere attested—*yen*, "sharp", being*di̯am/i̯äm, and *yen*, "to cover", *·i̯am/·i̯äm (GSR, p. 164, no. 617d, and 614b).

38 *Shih* 侍 for *tai* 待.

39 Cf. A 21 and note 29 to A 64 above.

40 *Chih* 智 for *chih* 知.

41 The text has 濐, which the editors explain as *hao* 號; for a similar character, likewise unknown and also explained as *hao*, see note 19 to E 19 above.

42 See D 81 and 83 above.

E 21 W 36a–b; S II.48b–49a; S VII.158a–159a; SS 267–270; str. 66–75 (643–652); Yates, no. 5.20, pp. 155–157.

[66] Death by hanging.[1]—A, Chief of X Village[2] says: "The commoncer C of (my) village has died by hanging in his house; I do not know[3] the reason. I have come to report."[4] ○ Forthwith the Prefectural Clerk X was ordered to go and investigate. ○ Report from Prefectural Clerk X: "Together with the Prison [67] Bondservant[5] X and[6] A, C's wife and daughter I investigated C. C's corpse[7] was hanging[8] on a rafter[9] of the north wall[10] of the east room[11] of his house, facing south.[12] He had used a hemp[13] rope, as thick as a thumb, and looped[14] it, tying [68] the neck,[15] with the loop-knot on the nape of his neck.[16] The upper end of the rope was knotted on the rafter, winding it around twice and tying the rope; the remainder was not quite two feet long. His head[17] was two feet distant from the rafter; his feet did not touch[18] the ground (but for) two inches. His head and back[19] [69] touched the wall. His tongue was level with his lips. Faeces[20] and urine[21] had been discharged, soiling both legs.[22] When the rope was untied, the air of his mouth and nose escaped like a sigh.[23] Along the trace of the rope there was congealed blood[24] around his neck except for two inches.[25] [70] Elsewhere[26] there were no traces of sharp weapons, wood or rope. The rafter was one span[27] thick and three feet long; to the west, it was two feet away from an earthen platform.[28] From the top of the platform it was possible to lead[29] and knot the rope. The soil was hard, so that it was not possible to recognize[30] people's [71] footsteps. The length of the rope was ten feet. He was dressed in an unbleached hemp[31] jacket and skirt,[32] one piece of each. He was barefoot[33] . . .[34] Immediately an order was given to A and the daughter[35] to transport C's corpse and take it to the (Prefect's) office.[36]

[37] When investigating, it is essential first carefully to examine and consider the traces. [72] One should go alone to the place where the corpse is and consider the knot of the rope. If[38] at the place of the knot there are traces of a noose, then observe whether the tongue protrudes or not, how far the head and the feet are distant from the place of the knot and the ground, and whether he had discharged faeces [73] and urine or not. Then untie the rope and observe whether mouth and nose emit a sigh or not. Then observe the condition of the blood-congealing along the trace of the rope. Try to free the head from the knot in the rope.[39] If you can free it, then [74] . . .[40] his clothes and completely observe his body, from inside the hair on his head[41] down to the perineum.[42] If the tongue does not protrude, if

mouth and nose do not emit a sigh, if there is no congealed blood along the trace of the rope, if the knot in the rope is so tight[43] that it cannot be slipped off, [75] . . .[44] Since[45] he has been dead for a long time, mouth and nose may perhaps not be able to produce a sigh. People who kill themselves must first have had reasons. Question the members of his household[46] in order to have them reply[47] concerning the reasons.

1 The meaning "hanging" for *ching* 經 is old; it is found i.a. in the *Kung Yang chuan*, duke Chao 13 (*Kung Yang chuan chu-su* 23.1a (0679)), and in *Lun yü* XIV, xviii, 3. — This text is also discussed in Bodde, "Medicine", pp. 6–8.

2 *Li tien* 里典; see note 11 to A 7 above.

3 *Chih* 智 for *chih* 知.

4 *Kao* 告.

5 See note 7 to E 18 above.

6 *Chi* 即. In spite of my argument in note 7 to E 20 above in favour of translating *chi* by "to go to", I now feel inclined to render it by "and", because the Village Chief A had "come to report" so that there was no need "to go to" him. Confusion between *chi* 即 and *chi* 及, "as well as", is impossible because of the difference in the ancient pronunciation (GSR, p. 113, no. 399a; *tsi̯ĕt, and p. 180, no. 681a: * g'i̯əp).

7 Cf. note 3 to E 20 above.

8 *Hsien* 縣 for *hsüan* 懸.

9 I suspect that the badly legible character on the strip is *shuai* 榱, which *SWKL* 2504b explains as "the Ch'in term for *ch'uan* 椽 "(see also "Ts'ang Chieh p'ien", p. 30, note 24). However, the editors, rather surprisingly, read the character as *ch'üan* 權, which they take to be a loan for *ch'uan* 椽, but this is phonetically impossible (*ch'üan* was *g'i̯wan, whereas *ch'uan* was *d'i̯wan, acc. to GSR, p. 62, no. 1580, and p. 66, no. 171e); needless to say, the loan is not attested.

10 *Pi* 廦, explained in SW as "wall" and therefore identical with *pi* 壁.

11 *Nei* 內 for "room".

12 *Hsiang* 鄕, i.e. *hsiang* 嚮. Note that E 20 writes *shou* 首; cf. note 8 to E 20.

13 *Hsi* 枲.

14 *Hsüan* 旋, "to turn around", which the editors believe to be a loan for *hsüan* 繯, which has the same meaning, "to encircle". This loan is impossible, for the first word was *dzi̯wan and the second *g'iwan (GSR, p. 77, no. 236a, and p. 82, no. 256q); it is, moreover, superfluous.

15 In this case *t'ou* 頭 could still be a loan for *tou* 脰 (see note 9 to E 14 above), but on its following occurrence (signalized by note 17) it surely means "head".

16 *Hsiang* 項.

17 See note 15.

18 *Tsu pu fu ti erh ts'un* 足不傅地二寸; *fu* for "to touch; to reach" is common.

19 *Pei* 北 for *pei* 背.

20 *Shih* 矢; see note 14 to E 14 above.

21 *Jo* 弱 for *niao* 溺.

22 *Ch'üeh* 郤 for *chüeh* (modern Pekinese *chiao*) 腳, "leg; foot" (usually written 脚).

23 *Wei* 渭 for *wei* 喟.

24 The text has 朹欝, which are variants of *chiao yü* 椒鬱 (modern simplified 郁!), where the first is taken as a loan for *tsu* 蹙 (not "*cu*" = *ts'u* as indicated in SS), hence *tsiôg for *tsiôk (see GSR, p. 269, nos. 1031q and t). Both words mean "(op)pressed". SS suggests that *yü hsüeh* 瘀血 is meant, viz. "congealing of the blood; haemorrage", which, as I learn from the excellent Aichi Sino-Japanese dictionary, is called *yü hsüeh* 鬱血 in Chinese medicine! It is to be noted that according to *SWKL*, 2659a, *yü* 鬱, *i̯wət, is used as a loan for *yü* 淤, *·i̯o (GSR, p. 135, no. 495a, and p. 36, no. 61); Karlgren's rejection of a similar loan ("Loan characters V", p. 32, no. 2186) is therefore to be reconsidered.

25 SS, p. 279, notes that the reverse of strip 68 shows traces of six characters, only three of which are legible .... *ko i ch'i* ? ? 各一其?, ". . .. one each; of this (or these). .".

26 The editors read the first three badly preserved characters as *t'o tu wu* 它度毋, where *tu*, lit. "to measure; to estimate", is inexplicable; SS translates it by "to inspect; to examine".

27 *Wei* 圍. Morohashi, vol. 3, p. 89, quotes several interpretations: three inches, five inches,

and even eight feet; SS suggests: the span of two hands, which would be roughly equal to 40 cm.

28 *K'an* 堪, explained in SW as *ti t'u* 地突, "earth protruding"; the editors render it by *t'u t'ai* 土台, "an earthen platform".

29 *Tao* 道, explained in SS as *yu* 由, and rightly taken as *tao* 導, "to lead", in Yates.

30 *Chih* 智 for *chih* 知.

31 *Lo* 絡, as explained in SW.

32 See note 19 to E 20 above.

33 The text reads *chien* 踐, "to tread on; to trample", but SS is surely right in referring to the remark by Meng K'ang (fi. 180–260) in his commentary to *HSPC* 4.19b, *HFHD* I, p. 269, note 1, saying that *chien* is *hsien* 跣, "barefoot" (although in the *HS* context this is wrong).

34 One character illegible.

35 *Nü* 女.

36 *T'ing* 廷; cf. A 21 and note 29 to A 64 above.

37 At this place the strip has the traditional phrase-marker ∠, which, as noted in my "Ch'in documents", p. 178, has been suppressed in all editions. Here it marks the end of the report by the Prefectural Clerk. The following lines contain directions for investigating cases of death by hanging, partly identical with the text of the report.

38 *Tang* 黨 for *t'ang* 儻.

39 I cannot understand the meaning of *tao* 道 here; it is neglected in the SS translation, but again rendered by "to lead" in Yates (see note 29 above).

40 One character illegible.

41 It should not be forgotten that men wore their hair long, usually done up in a top-knot, but also plaited in several strands, as is shown by the hair-dress of the pottery soldiers who guarded the First Emperor's tomb, illustrated in *Wenwu* 1975/11.

42 SS refers to the commentary to the *Huang-ti nei ching t'ai su* 黃帝內經太素 (inaccessible) which says that *tsuan* 篡 is to be read as *tu* 督, "where the two *yin* 陰 meet".

43 *Chi* 急.

44 The first few characters on this strip are badly effaced, but the editors only leave one sign unexplained and transcribe the following ones as *ssu* (probably for *shih*) *nan shen i* 死 (for 尸) 難審殹, "... corpse difficult to investigate."

45 *Chieh* 節 for *chi* 即.

46 *T'ung chü* 同居; see note 15 to A 41 above.

47 *Ho* 合 for *ta* 答.

E 22 W 8.36b; S II.49a–b; S VII.160a–161b; SS 270–274; str. 76–86 (653–663); Yates, no. 5.21, pp. 157–159.

[76] Robbery by tunnelling. — Report. The commoner B of X village reported[1] and said:" Yesterday night[2] I stored[3] (my), B's, lined[4] gown,[5] one (item), in (my), B's side room[6] and shut the door. (I), B, myself alone with my wife C in the night lay down in the main room.[7] When this morning I rose and opened the door [77] to fetch the gown, others had already tunnelled into the side room, penetrating into the room, and the gown was not to be found. I do not know[8] who the tunnelling robbers were, nor their number. No other things are missing. I have come to denounce[9] this." ○ Forthwith an order was given to the Prefectural Clerk X to go and investigate and to catch the thieves. Prefectural [78] Clerk X's report: "Together with the District ...[10] bond-servant X, B, and the (Village) Chief D, I went to investigate B's side-room. The side-room is to the east of the main room[11] and adjoining[12] it; it faces south and has a door and behind the room there is a small veranda.[13] In the centre of the room [79] there was a fresh hole; the hole penetrated[14] into the room. The lower edge of the hole was level with the small veranda. Above, it was two feet and three inches high, below, it was

2 ft. 3 in. wide.[15] Above, it had the shape of a pig 's hole.[16] The means whereby it was dug[17] resembled a broad[18] chisel; the traces had a width of [80] ... and two thirds of an inch.[19] The earth[20] from the hole was on top of the small veranda; facing the hole, the earth had been scattered and partly[21] introduced inside the room. Inside the room as well as inside and outside the hole, the earth's [81] surface[22] had traces of knees[23] and hands, six each. On the earth outside there were four places with traces of Ch'in silk[24] shoes, 1 ft. 2 in. long.[25] Their front, where the silk was dense,[26] had a length of 4 in., in the middle, where it was sparse, 5 in., and at the heel,[27] [82] where it was dense, 3 in. The traces of these shoes resembled old shoes. North of the room there was a wall; the height of the wall was 7 ft.[28] North of the wall there was an alley. From north of the wall it was a distance of 10 ft.[29] to the northern edge[30] of the small veranda; the eastern (end of the) wall was five paces[31] distant from the room. On its top there was [83] (some) fresh small damage, the damage facing outside from the centre, resembling traces of feet having crossed[32] it, but their size could not be measured. Because under the veranda and outside the wall the ground was hard, tracking was not possible. We do not know[33] the number of the robbers, nor where they went. [84] Inside the room there was a bamboo stand;[34] the stand was in the north-east (corner) of the room, 4 ft. each from the north and the east wall. It was 1 ft. high. B said:"...[35] gown was in the centre of the stand." ○ On being interrogated B and C both stated:[36] "B in the second month just past made[37] this garment, [85] (using) 50 ft.,[38] a silk lining with five catties[39] of floss stuffing,[40] and 5 ft. of ...[41] silk for the borders as well as for the edges.[42] We do not know[43] who the robbers were, nor the time[44] (of the robbery). We have no suspicions".[45] ○ On being interrogated, D and the member of B's group of five,[46] the commoner ...,[47] [87], said: "We have seen that B possessed a lined gown with ...[48] borders and edges; it was new. We do not know[49] of which material the lining ...[50] was, no the circumstances of its disappearance." ○ Based on this, we estimated[51] the price[52] of the gown.

[1] *Kao* 告.
[2] Cf. note 8 to E 8 above.
[3] *Tsang* 臧 for *ts'ang* 藏.
[4] *Fu* 復 for *fu* 複, "lined".
[5] The text reads *ku* 結, which, according to Morohashi, vol. 8, p. 1032, forms part of the name of a herb, and which is not found in SW. SS suggests that *chü* 裾, a long and wide gown, is meant; both characters have the same phonetic element, see GSR, p. 33, no. 49.
[6] *Fang nei chung* 房內中. *Fang* is explained as *p'ang* 旁, "side", in the *Shih ming* 釋名 (inaccessible).
[7] *T'ang shang* 堂上; the *t'ang* was built on a raised platform of pounded earth, see Hayashi, *Bunbutsu*, p. 178.
[8] *Chih* 智 for *chih* 知.
[9] *Kao* 告.
[10] In view of E 3 (note 2) and E 18, 20 and 21 above, the two illegible characters might be *mou* 某 and *lao* 牢.
[11] Here the main room is called *ta nei* 大內.
[12] *Pi* 比.
[13] Here *t'ang* 堂 seems to indicate a veranda or loggia; see Hayashi, *Bunbutsu*, p. 178.
[14] *Che* 徹, "to penetrate".

15 C. 0.53 and 0.58 m.
16 *Chu tou* 豬竇, "pig's hole or drain"; SS translates the term by "pig-sty".
17 See note 1 to D 23 above.
18 SS refers to the *Kuang ya* dictionary (inaccessible), which explains *p'ang* 旁 as "wide; broad".
19 The editors suggest that the missing character is *erh* =, "two"; 2 2/3 in. equals c. 6 cm.
20 *Hsiang* 壤 is "loose earth"; see *CCSS*, p. 65, Vogel, p. 43. Walls were not built of brick, but of pounded earth, which became of course loose when dug out.
21 For *p'i* 柀, "partly", see note 29 to A 19 above.
22 After "earth", strip 80 is completely blank, leaving a space for some fifteen or sixteen characters. The editors are surely justified in placing the next strip here, for it provides good sense.
23 *Hsi* 厀 is the old form of *hsi* 膝, "knee"; see SW.
24 See note be 25 to E 20 above.
25 C. 28 cm.
26 I am unable to read the vague photograph of this vague text. I also fail to understand how the print of a sole would show *ch'ou* 稠, "density", c.q. *hsi* 稀, "thinness; sparseness", of either shoe-laces or of patterned, c.q. embroidered silk (see note 25 to E 20 above), which one would expect on the upper part of a shoe and not on the sole. The translation in SS: "on the front of the shoe's imprint the pattern was tight, in the middle the pattern was sparse and at the heel it was dense", is inexplicable, unless one assumes that the soles had a pattern embroidered on them, like the hand-stitched cotton shoes of the present. In Yates, the translation is "cord [prints]"; on this minor point see note 25 to E 20 above.
27 *Chung* 歱, "heel", also *chung* 踵.
28 Slightly over 1.60 m.
29 C. 2. 30 cm.
30 *Ch'un* 脣, lit. "lip".
31 I.e. 30 ft. or c. 7 m.
32 According to SW, one of the meanings of *chü* 歫 is "to step over; to cross".
33 *Chih* 智 for *chih* 知.
34 *Shao* 柖, according to the *Kuang ya* dictionary (inaccessible) "a bath settee".
35 One character illegible.
36 *Yen* 言.
37 *Nai* 迺 indicating the recent past.
38 C. 11. 5 m.
39 C. 1.2 kg.
40 裝; the editors are certainly right in identifying this unknown word with *chuang* 裝, "to stuff; to fill".
41 *Miu tseng* 繆繒. The meaning of *miu*, "silk-like", in this context is unknown; *tseng* is a general name for silk tissues, for which see further note 158 on p. 171 in Yates.
42 The text has *tien* 殿, which the editors without further explanation equate with *ch'un* 純. As far as I am aware, this loan is nowhere attested, but it is quite feasible in view of the ancient pronunciation: *tien* = *tiən or *d'wən, whereas *ch'un* was *d̑i̯wən (GSR, p. 119, nos. 429c and 427n). As indicated by the editors of S, one of the meanings of *ch'un* is "ornamental edging or border", but that leaves the preceding *yüan* 緣, "edge; border" unaccounted for. The solution is found in Hayashi, *Bunbutsu*, pp. 22–23, which shows that the edges of Han clothes were decorated by several ornamental borders, stitched on to each other; perhaps *tien*, "bottom", was the outside border.
43 *Chih* 智 for *chih* 知.
44 *Tsao mo* 蚤莫 for *tsao mu* 早暮.
45 *I* 意 in the sense of "to suspect", i.e. *i* 疑, as in *HSPC* 47.3a (GSR, p. 252, no. 957a *·iəg, and 956a *ngiəg).
46 Cf. note 1 to D 80 above.
47 This illegible word must have been "X", *mou* 某.
48 See note 38 above.
49 *Chih* 智 for *chih* 知.
50 One character illegible.
51 *Chih* 直 for *chih* 值.
52 *Chia* 賈 for *chia* 價.

E 23 W 8.36b–37a; S II.49b–50a; S VII.162a–163a; SS 274–276; str. 87–93 (664–670); Yates, no. 5.22, pp. 159–160.

[87] A miscarriage.[1] — Report. A, the wife of a commoner of X village, made a denunciation,[2] saying: "(I), A, had been pregnant for six months. Yesterday, in the daytime,[3] I fought with the adult[4] woman C of the same village. (I), A, and C grabbed each other by the hair.[5] C threw (me), A, over and drove me back.[6] A fellow-villager, [88] the *kung shih*[7] D, came to the rescue and separated C and (me), A. As soon as (I), A, had reached my house, I felt ill and my belly[8] hurt; yesterday evening the child miscarried.[9] Now (I), A, have wrapped up the child and I have come to bring it, and to denounce myself[10] and to denounce C." Forthwith an order was given to the Prefectural Clerk X to go and arrest[11] C. [89] Immediately I inspected the baby (to see whether it was) male or female, whether it had grown hair, as well as the condition of the placenta.[12] Furthermore, an order was given to a bond-woman who had several times given birth to inspect the blood coming out of her front part[13] as well as the condition of her swellings.[14] I interrogated the members of A's household about A's situation[15] when she had reached her house [90], as well as the circumstances of the pain in her belly and of the child's coming forth. ○ Report of the Assistant (Prefect) B: Order was given to the Prefectural Clerk X and the bond-woman X to inspect the child which A had brought along. Before, it had been wrapped in a hemp cloth; it had the appearance of congealed blood,[16] as large as a hand;[17] it was not [91] recognizable[18] as a child. When it had been placed in a basin with water and shaken,[19] the clotted blood was a child. Its head, body, arms, fingers, and from the thighs down to its feet and toes, it resembled a human being, but it was not possible to recognize[20] the eyes, ears and nose, [92] or whether it was male or female. When taken out of the water, it again had the appearance of clotted blood. ○ Another model[21] says: An order was given to the bond-women XX who had several times given birth to inspect A. All said: "There is dried blood on the sides of her front part. At present still blood comes out, but (only) a little; it is not menstruation.[22] When X once[23] was pregnant and miscarried, her front part as well as the blood coming out were like A . . ."[24]

1 *Ch'u tzu* 出子. — This article is also analyzed in Bodde, "Medicine", pp. 8–9.

2 *Kao* 告.

3 Cf. note 8 to E 8 above.

4 See note 2 to A 13 above.

5 This is the SW explanation of *tso* 捽.

6 *Fen* 僨 is "to throw down; to fell", according to SW. 屏 is probably *ping* 屏, "to drive away".

7 The first or lowest of the aristocratic ranks.

8 *Fu* 復 for *fu* 腹, "belly",

9 *Pien ch'u* 變出. *Pien* is often used for untoward events. SS remarks that under *p'an* 姅, "menstruation", SW notes that the Han code prescribed: *chien p'an pien pu te shih tz'u* 見姅變不得侍祠, "having been in contact with menstruation, one is not allowed to attend a sacrifice". The dictionary *Yü tien* (inaccessible) repeats this, but adds "also 'harming the pregnancy' ", *yu shang yün* 又傷孕. The editors therefore suggest that in the present text *pien* by itself might mean "miscarriage".

10 *Tzu kao*, "to denounce oneself voluntarily"; cf. E 7 above. Would the woman have denounced herself because she had been engaged in a fight?

11 *Chih* 執.

12 *Pao* 保, * pôg (GSR, p. 273, no. 1057a) for *pao* 胞, *pọg (GSR, p. 285, no. 1113b).

13 Simply *ch'ien* 前, i.e. her private parts.

14 *Yung* 癰, lit. "ulcers", but, as indicated by the editors, *yung* here simply means "swellings or wounds".

15 *Chü ch'u* 居處, which SS renders by "living conditions"; the term occurs in *Lun yü* XIII, 19, where Legge renders it by "in retirement".

16 The text has a mutilated character, of which the remaining right-hand part is read *p'ou* 咅 by the editors. Because of the following word *hsüeh* 血, "blood", they believe that the full character must have been 䘲 (unknown), which they identify with *p'ei* 衃, explained in SW as "coagulated blood". In view of the virtual identity of 咅 and 否 (see GSR, p. 263, no. 999), this identification is undoubtedly correct.

17 SS refers to Chang Ping-lin, *Wen shih* 文史 (inaccessible), who says that "in general, when saying 'hand' or 'foot', the upper part, viz. the arm, is included"; they add that this would imply a length from the fingers to the elbow.

18 *Chih* 智 for *chih* 知.

19 *Yao* 榣, "the movement of a tree', for *yao* 搖, "to shake".

20 *Chih* 智 for *chih* 知.

21 *Ch'i i shih yüeh* 其一式曰. Here the compilers of these model reports introduce another example. The editors of SS, however, believe that the Assistant Prefect's report now turns to the bondwomen who had to inspect A's condition, but this seems unlikely, for the Assistant Prefect would hardly have called a report a "model".

22 The editors transcribe the hardly legible text as *fei shuo shih yeh* 非朔事殹, "this is not the affair of the first day (of the moon/month)", and they interpret *shuo shih* as "menstruation", indicating that a medical text, discovered at Ma-wang tui, has *yüeh shuo* 月朔. Morohashi, vol. 5, p. 1015, lists *yüeh shih* 月事, "the affair of the month", an expression which is found i.a. in *SC* 105.45, where Bridgman, p. 39, has no remarks.

23 *Shang* 賞 for *ch'ang* 嘗.

24 One character illegible.

E 24 W 8.37b; S II.50a; S VII. 163b–164a; SS 276–278; str. 94–97 (671–674); Yates, no. 5.23, pp. 160–162.

[94] Poisonous words. — A, a *kung shih*[1] of X Village, and others, (in all) twenty men, brought in their fellow-villager, the commoner C. All denounced[2] him, saying: "C has ...[3] poisonous words: (we), A and the others, object to drinking and eating with him. We have come to denounce him." Immediately a detailed note of A's and the others' names [95] and status was made on the back of a tablet.[4] ○ On being interrogated C said in his statement: "D, my maternal grandmother from the same village, was adjudicated for ...[5] poisonous words; when she was over thirty years old, she was banished. When[6] in (my), C's, household there are sacrifices, we invite A and the others, but A and the others are unwilling to come; [96] they also never invite (me), C, to drink. When[7] there are sacrifices in the village (I), C, together with the villagers as well as A, meet to drink and eat, but nobody[8] is willing to share a cup or a dish with (me), C. A and the others, as well as the brethren of the village, [97] as well as other people who know (me), C, all object to drinking and eating with me, but (I), C, do not carry[9] poison." C has not been adjudicated for any other (crime).

1 The first and lowest of the aristocratic ranks.

2 *Kao* 告.

3 Here, and at the place indicated by note 5, there occurs an expression transcribed by the

editors as *ning tu yen* 寧毒言. Although I am unable to suggest another character for the first, I doubt the correctness of the transcription *ning*, and I completely disagree with the editors of SS who assume that *ning* is a meaningless "particle". Still, whatever the meaning of this first word may be, it can only qualify *tu*, "poison"; because of the preceding *yu* 有, it can hardly be a verb. — *Tu yen*, "poisonous words", are known, because the expression is found in the *Lun heng*, ch. 23/66, p. 948. Forke, *Lun-heng* I, p. 298 (the reference in Yates, p. 161, note 180, mistakenly writes 198) translates the passage where *tu yen* is found as follows: "The fiery air of the sun regularly produces poison. This air is hot. The people living in the land of the sun are impetuous. The mouths and tongues of these impetuous people become venomous. Thus the inhabitants of Ch'u and Yüeh are impetuous and passionate. When they talk with others, and a drop of their saliva happens to fly against their interlocutors, the arteries of the latter begin to swell and ulcerate. The Southern Circuit is a very hot region. When the people there curse a tree, it withers, and when they spit upon a bird, it drops down". Contrary to Yates, p. 161, I do not think that "some concoction (was) slipped into the food and drink". I believe that we are faced here with a wide-spread superstition—of which Hang Hui in his commentary to *Lun-heng*, *loc. cit.*, gives other ancient examples—comparable e.g. to the belief in the evil eye.

4 *Su shu* (the personal data) *kuan tieh pei* 疏書 .... 關諜 (for 牒) 北 (for 背). *Su* will mean "to set out; to expatiate", and *su shu* "to write in detail"; a similar expression is found in *HSPC* 94A.12a, *su chi* 疏記, rendered in de Groot, *Urkunden* I, p. 81, rather freely, as "Buchführung". *Kuan tieh* is difficult to understand. Theoretically, the easiest solution would be to translate this binome as "a notification to (the official in charge of) a control post", but the editors of SS avoid this, evidently because the existence of such a control post inside a prefecture is unlikely. SS offers two suggestions: *kuan* could be a loan for *kuan* 貫, i.e. *kuan chi* 籍, "population register", or it could mean "a report to a superior". However, neither of these solutions is acceptable, because both terms are late. *Kuan*, "population register" occurs only in the 5th century (see note 3 to D 181 above), and *kuan*, "report", is even later, being a T'ang expression (see *Hsin T'ang shu* 46.4b and 15b; des Rotours, *Fonctionnaires* I, pp. 23 and 93). Likewise unclear is the reason, why these personal data were written on the back of a tablet.

5 See note 3.

6, 7 *Chieh* 節 for *chi* 即.

8 *Chieh mo* 皆莫.

9 *Pa* 把.

E 25 W 8.37b; S II.50a; S VII.164b; SS 278; str. 98 (675); Yates, no. 5.24, p. 162.

[98] Fornication. — Report. A, a commoner of X Village, brought in the man B and the woman C. In his denunciation[1] he said: "B and C fornicated together. Yesterday in the daytime[2] I saw them at the place X. I arrested and fettered[3] them and I have come to bring them in."[4]

1 *Kao* 告.

2 See note 8 to E 8 above.

3 *Chiao* 校 are "fetters" according to SW (see the discussion in *SWKL*, p. 1161a f.). But the text reads *pu chiao shang lai i chih* 捕校上來詣之, and in my translation the word *shang* has been neglected, as it has been in the versions in Yates and SS. Is *shang* a complement to the verb "fetter", or could *shang lai* possibly mean "to go up", viz. to a superior?

4 No reason is provided for the moral attitude of A. That certain types of sexual intercourse were punished is clear from D 151 and 153 above, but the present text does not provide any such indication, nor does it explain why the commoner A was entitled or authorized to arrest the couple. Could anyone interfere in case he knew that the woman was married, or that they were close kin?

GROUP F

This group, consisting of two articles from two different statutes of the state of Wei 魏 is not entered as a separate group in the Chinese publications, because these rules are found rather unexpectedly as an appendix to the collection of moralizing prose-pieces, which the editors have called "How to be a good official", *Wei li chih tao* 爲吏之道, this being the first phrase of the collection. These two laws are followed again by another appendix, viz. some proverbial sayings (see my "Ch'in documents", p. 185). The rules are written in the fifth or lowest register of strips 16–28 (for the organization of the writing on these strips see 'Ch'in documents", p. 183). The complete strips have a length of 27.5 cm. or 1 ft. 2 in. Ch'in—Han measure. From stains on most of the strips it is clear that they were held together by three sets of strings: close to the top and the bottom, and in the middle. Faint horizontal knife scratches over each of the five rubrics show, that the strips had been prepared before they received the writing. The whole set of fifty-one strips was found lying across the thighs of the corpse.

F 1 W 6.14b; S II.52b–53a; S VII.176b–177a; SS 292–293; str. 16–21 (694–699), 5th register.

[16] The 25th year, the intercalary doubled[1] 12th month whose first day was *ping-wu*, on the day *hsin-hai*[2] [3] announcement to [17] the Chancellor:[4] People[5] sometimes leave the settlements[6] (to go and) dwell in the countryside,[7] intruding among others' orphans and widows and demanding[8] [18] peoples' wives and daughters. This is against the ancient traditions[9] of the state. From now on, ...,[10] [19] inn-keepers,[11] debt slaves[12] and stepfathers[13] must not be made to form households[14] and must not be given[15] fields and houses.[16] [20] After three generations,[17] if they desire to serve,[18] make them serve, but still[19] note in their register:[20] "Formerly [21] debt-slave X of X Village,[21] the old man's[22] great-grandson."[23]

Wei Statute on Households.[24]

[1] *Tsai* 再. Perhaps this curious expression is related to the custom of "twice intercalating" in a period of five years, as stated in SW *sub voce jun*: *wu sui tsai jun* 五歲再閏.

[2] I.e. the sixth day. — The editors are agreed that this 25th year indicates the 25th year of king An-shi 安釐 of Wei, i.e. 252 B.C. However, the month and the cyclical dates do not correspond with those furnished by the chronological handbooks. According to Father Pierre Hoang, *Concordance des chronologies néoméniques chinoise et européenne*, Variétés sinologiques no. 29 (Zikawei, 1910; reprinted in Formosa), the Chinese year corresponding to 252 B.C. had no intercalary 12th month. The reason for this discrepancy must be that the state of Wei used a different calendar, the so-called Calendar of Hsia; see Huang, "Pien-nien chi", pp. 6 and 14, where he refers to an unpublished study on chronological problems by Yen Tun-chieh 嚴敦杰 (quoted in my "Ch'in documents", p. 177, note 9).

[3] There is a blank left above *kao* 告. The editors of SS suggest that, for reasons of respect the scribe omitted "the King", *wang* 王; in view of F 2 below this is not impossible, see note 8 to F 2.

[4] *Hsiang pang* 相邦, i.e. the *hsiang kuo* 國 known in historical literature. See Kamada, pp. 165–187, for the development of this institution in the different Warring States. *Hsiang kuo*

were only established exceptionally; mostly there were two chancellors, *hsiang*, of the Right and of the Left (it was only under the Han that the left took precedence over the right; see Kamada, p. 178).

5 The nearly illegible character which is transcribed *hsu* 壻 in *Wenwu* is interpreted as *min* 民 in the later editions.

6 *I* 邑.

7 *Yeh* 壄, i.e. 野.

8 *Chiao* 徼.

9 *Ku* 故; one might say "the antiquities".

10 The term *chia men* 叚 (= 假) 門 is unknown. The editors of SS suggest that *chia* 叚 is a loan for *chia* 賈. This would be theoretically possible, because both were *kå (GSR, p. 28, no. 33a, and p. 29, no. 38b). However, *chia* 賈 is consistently used in these texts for "price", whereas 賈 meaning both "trade" and "trader" is *ku* (*ko); this is confirmed by the word-play in ch. 25 of the *Po-hu t'ung* 白虎通, where *ku* 賈 is "explained" as *ku* 固 (see Tjan, *Po-hu t'ung* II, p. 537). In other words, the explanation of *chia men* in SS as "traders" in wrong. The rendering in Shin kan kōdoku kai 3, p. 81, note 57, as "persons given lodgings in an important family" is somewhat nearer to the truth, for *chia men* will probably have to be taken literally.

11 *Ni lü* 逆呂 (where 呂 is a loan for 旅; both were *gli̯o, according to GSR, p. 39, no. 76a and 77a); see *Shang-chün shu*, p. 6; Duyvendak, *Lord Shang*, p. 178.

12 *Chui hsü* 贅壻. As shown by Niida, pp. 94–101, these were indentured servants or bond-slaves, a debtor giving a son in pawn to a creditor; as creditors apparently sometimes gave one of their daughters in marriage to such a man, the term came to mean "a son-in-law living with his wife's family".

13 This is a tentative rendering of *hou fu* 後父. The term is unknown; the editors of SS suggest that they were men—evidently belonging to the proscribed outsiders—who had married a local widow with children, entering into her hosuehold.

14 *Hu* 戶, the formal unit.

15 For the use of *shu* 鼠 for *yü* 與 see note 22 to A 30 above.

16 *T'ien yu* 田宇; for the use of *yü*, "roof", for "house" cf. E 3.

17 The text has *yeh* 枼. Karlgren notes that this character with the meaning "generation" is found in a Chou inscription of the middle of the 1st millenium B.C.; see GSR, p. 169, no. 633a. *Yeh* 葉, "leaf", is used for "generation" in verse 7 of Ode 304, *Ch'ang fa* 長發 (*Shih ching* 20–4/70.5a (1939); Karlgren, *Odes*, p. 266).

18 *Shih* 士 for *shih* 仕.

19 The text has *nai* 乃, "thereupon". I have followed the suggestion in SS to read this character as *jeng* 仍, "as before; still".

20 *Chi* 籍, "population register"; see E 5 and 6 above.

21 The text reads *lü* 慮, *li̯o (GSR, p. 38, no. 69f), which the editors take as a loan for *lü* 閭, *gli̯o (GSR, p. 39, no. 76g). This loan, although not attested, is quite acceptable; cf. Karlgren, "Loan characters II", p. 101, no. 1021.

22 *Keng* 更 in the *Wenwu* transcription has been corrected to *sou* 叟, referring to the original settler.

23 *Nai sun* 乃孫 of the text corrected to *jeng* 仍 *sun* (for the same substitution see note 19 above). From the context it is clear that "great-grandson" is meant; see also Dubs' long note on this subject in *HFHD* I, p. 176, note 3, which surveys all the commentaries on the subject.

24 Except for the curious rule mentioned in *RHL*, p. 36, this appears the only Statute on Households, *hu lü* 戶律, we possess for the whole of the Ch'in-Han period, and even later. The Edsin-gol strip included in Lao Kan, *K'ao shih*, p. 81, no. 4024 (123, 202.10) does not indicate the contents of the *hu lü* to which it refers.

F 2 W 6.14b; S II.53a–b; S VII.177a–b; SS 294; str. 22–28 (700–706).

[22] The 25th year, the intercalary doubled 12th month whose first day was *ping-wu*, on the day *hsin-hai*.[1] [2] announcement to [23] the Generals:[3] . . . ., innkeepers, debt-slaves and stepfathers[4] sometimes induce[5] people [24] not to work[6] and not to take care of their houses.[7] (I), the Solitary Man,[8] do not wish this.[9] In case[10] they were to be killed, I cannot [25] bear this

(for the sake of) their clansmen.[11] Now despatch them to join the army. The generals [26] must not show pity. When beef is prepared[12] to feed the troops, grant them one third (of a peck)[13] of boiled grain, but [27] do not give[14] them meat.[15] When attacking walled towns, use them when there is an insufficiency;[16] let the generals use them to fill[17] the moats.[18]

[28] Wei Statute on Emergency Troops.[19]

[1] For the date see notes 1 and 2 to F 1 above.

[2] For this hiatus see note 3 to F 1 above and cf. note 8 below.

[3] It is, of course also possible to translate the term in the singular.

[4] For these people see notes 10–13 to F 1 above.

[5] *Shuai* 衛, i.e. 率, "to lead".

[6] I.e. to work their fields.

[7] *Shih-wu* 室屋.

[8] *Kua jen* 寡人, the term by which the heads of the states referred to themselves in the pre-imperial period.

[9] The editors translate *fou yü* 弗欲 by "do not like this."

[10] *Ch'ieh* 且 can mean "if".

[11] The clansmen, or, more literally, the clan brethren, *tsung-tsu k'un-ti* 宗族昆弟, are the object of *pu jen* 不忍, as in the famous passage in the *Mencius* IIA, 6, which speaks about "the mind which cannot bear [the suffering of] others", *pu jen jen chih hsin* 不忍人之心.

[12] The text reads *hsiang* 享, which the editors righlty take as a loan for *p'eng* 烹, see GSR, p. 189, no. 721.

[13] Cf. A 15 above.

[14] For *shu* 鼠 used for *yü* 與 see note 22 to A 30 above.

[15] *Yao* 殽, "meat with bones"; see *Li-chi*, ch. *Ch'ü-li* (*Li-chi chu-su* 2.10a (0087); Couvreur, *Li-ki* I, p. 33; Legge, *Li-ki* 27, p. 79).

[16] *Pu tsu* 不足; SS translates "use them wherever men are needed".

[17] *Yin* 堙.

[18] *Hao* 壕; this word can also mean a dry trench or ditch.

[19] For this rendering of *pen ming* 奔命 see the commentary in *HSPC* 7.2b, translated in *HFHD* II, p. 154, note 2.4.

GROUP G

In order to remain consistent, I have called also this last section a group, although it only consists of one single rule. Alerted by a chance discovery, during the years 1979–1980 three archaeological campaigns were devoted to the excavation of a Warring States cemetery, located c. 1 km. south of Ch'ing-ch'uan 青川 Prefecture in northern Ssu-ch'uan (close to the Kansu border at c. 32° 40′ N and 105° 10′ E). Here, tomb no. M 50 produced two strips, both 46 cm. long. One, 3.5 cm. wide, had become completely illegible, but the other, 2.5 cm. wide, proved to contain the clearly legible text—written in three columns—of a Ch'in Statute on Agriculture with a full date, equivalent to 27 September 309 B.C. The great length of the strips, namely two Ch'in-Han feet, shows that they contain commands of the ruler; the use of 2 ft. strips for similar purposes persisted during the Han, as witnessed by the *Tu tuan* 獨斷 and by the lost *Han chih-tu* 漢制度, quoted in the commentary to *HHSCC* Ann. A1.17a.

The text of the statute was published in facsimile and in modern transcription in "Ch'ing-ch'uan Report", p. 11, and in transcription only in Yü Hao-liang, "Ch'ing-ch'uan", p. 22, and in Li Hsüeh-ch'in, "Ch'ing-ch'uan", p. 68. Additional studies were written by Li Chao-ho, "Ch'ing-ch'uan", Yang K'uan, "Ch'ing-ch'uan", Huang Sheng-chang, "Ch'ing-ch'uan", and T'ien and Liu.

The following transcription is that of the "Ch'ing-ch'uan Report", to which have been added the emendations suggested by Yü Hao-liang (marked Yü), Li Chao-ho (marked LC), Huang Sheng-chang (marked Huang), Li Hsüeh-ch'in (marked LH), and T'ien and Liu (marked TL).

Because of a number of doubtful points, the translation presented here is tentative as regards details, but the general ideas are clear enough.

1* 二年十一月己酉朔=日王命丞相戊內史匽 a b 更脩[c]爲田律 田廣一步袤[d]八則爲畛畝二畛一百道百畝爲頃一

2 千道=廣三步封高四尺大稱其高捋[e]高尺下厚二尺以秋八月脩封捋正彊畔及癹千百之大草九月

3 大除道及除[f] 噲[g] 十月爲橋脩陂[h] 隄利津 i 鮮草雖[j] 非除道之時而有陷敗不可行相[k] 爲之 l m

*) The figures 1, 2 and 3 indicate the columns of writing on the strip.

a) Left blank in the Report; Yü and LH read *min* 民, LC and TL read *ch'ü* 取.

b) Left blank in the Report; Yü reads *yüan* 頟, i.e. 願 (cf. *HLTY*, *ch'ü sheng* 34a), LC and LH read *pi* 臂, TL reads *yü* (?), see note 6 below.

c) Considered implicitly by all authors as equivalent to *hsiu* 修.

d) Yü, LC and LH read *mou* 袤.

e) Considered by all authors as a loan or a mistake for *le* 埒.

f) Yü and LH read *pan* 阪; Huang reads *tsu* 阻.

g) Yü, Huang and LH read *hsien* 險, TL read *yin* 陰.

h) Yü and LH read *po* 波.

i) Left blank in the Report; Yü reads 梁, LC writes *shen* 深, Huang reads *i* 隘, LH reads *liang* 梁, TL read *k'ang* 康.

j) Yü and LH read *li* 離.

k) Yü and LH read *che* 輒.

l, m) Both the facsimile copy and the transcription in the Report end with two squares, indicating two illegible characters, but Yü, LC and LH do not refer to these. Huang believes they are merely smudges and not characters. TL think that they are illegible characters.

[1] In the second year, the eleventh month, the first day (of which is indicated by the cyclical signs) *chi yu*, on the first day,[1] the King[2] commands the Chancellor Mou[3] and the Minister of Finance[4] Yen[5] . . . .[6] again to prepare and make[7] a Statute on Agriculture. (The Statute reads): For a field, one pace wide and eight paces long make the paths;[8] one *mu* has two paths and one East-West road.[9] One hundred *mu* are one *ch'ing* with one [2] North-South road;[10] the road is three paces wide.[11] A border-mound[12] is four feet high; its size corresponds to its height.[13] A partition[14] is one foot high; at the bottom it is two feet thick. In autumn, in the eighth month, one repairs the border-mounds and the partitions and corrects the borders[15] and the field-limits,[16] as well as cutting[17] the tall grass on the East-West and the North-South roads. In the ninth month [3] there is a great clearing[18] of the roads as well as of the dangerous passages.[19] In the tenth month, bridges are made,[20] embankments and dikes are repaired, fords and bridges[21] are cleared,[22] and weeds are cut.[23] (Although) it is not the time for clearing the roads, whenever[24] there are holes and bad places, making it impossible to proceed, (clearing) is to be undertaken.[25,26]

1 This date is equivalent to 27th September 309 B.C.

2 This is king Wu of Ch'in; according to *SC* 6.52 and 64 (*Mh* II, pp. 75 and 76) he reigned between 310 and 307 B.C.

3 Kan Mou 甘戊 was chancellor of Ch'in between 309 and 306 B.C.; see *SC* 5.63 and 64; *Mh* II, pp. 75 and 77. Note that *SC* writes *Mao* 茂; Hervouet, "Valeur", pp. 73–75, discusses the peculiarity of *SC*, which consists in adding superfluous "radicals" to characters written without these in parallel texts.

4 For this rendering of *nei shih* 內史 see note 22 to A 9 above.

5 Yen 匽; this man is further unknown. Yen occurs both as a personal name (*SC* 35.54; *Mh* IV, p. 130) and as a surname (*HHSCC* Ann. 7.1a-b, and Ann. 10B. 5a).

6 Yü suggests reading *min yüan* 民願, "the people desire", which seems highly improbable. LC interprets the same mutilated characters as *ch'ü pi* 取臂 and assumes that *pi* is a loan for *p'i* 譬. Now, the expression *ch'ü p'i* occurs in the last verse of Ode 256, I 抑 (Karlgren, *Odes*, pp. 219, 221), and in *Lun yü* VI, xxviii, 3, meaning "to take as an example", and LC suggests that the example is the extant Statute on Agriculture, which, according to the following words, is to be revised. This seems an ingenious solution, but it then remains strange that this extant statute is not explicitly mentioned. Huang adopts LC's reading, but he thinks that Ch'ü-p'i is the personal name of the Minister of Finance, whose surname was Yen; he fails to explain why this man should be indicated by both his surname and his personal name, whereas the Chancellor is only referred to by his personal name. His suggestion that *yen* 匽 is used here as a loan for *yen* 燕 is unnecessary (see note 5 above), although it is possible in view of the ancient pronunciation: the former was *·i̯ăn (GSR, p. 81, no. 253d), whereas the latter was *·ian (GSR, p. 78, no. 243a); the loan is not attested. Still another solution is proposed by LH. He adopts the reading *min pi* 民臂, where he believes *pi* to be a loan for *p'i* 僻, "low, mean, wicked". He then translates *min p'i* as "the people are wicked *and do not uphold the laws*", adding the phrase in italics. He bases this

explanation on a passage in "Governor T'eng's written instructions", where the text, referring to the people, reads *hsieh pi* 邪避, taken as *hsieh p'i* 僻 and explained as "evil actions" (SS, p. 15 f.). T'ien and Liu read *ch'ü yü* 取髩. They believe that the unknown character *yü* (?) is used for *yü* 魚 which was the name of a statelet in Ssu-ch'uan province, mentioned in the *Tso chuan*, duke Wen 16 (611 B.C. — *Tso chuan* 20.2b (0822), Couvreur, *Tch'ouen-ts'iou* I, p. 535). The authors think that the king gave two orders to his ministers: to conquer Yü and to revise the statutes. This complicated solution seems unacceptable.

7 Two writers have tried to explain the sentence *keng hsiu wei t'ien lü* 更修爲田律 Huang, p. 72, and LH, p. 69. Huang insists that *keng hsiu* should not be taken as a binome, meaning "to revise", but that it should be considered as consisting of two separate words: *keng* as "again, anew", and *hsiu* as the equivalent of *chih* 治, "to practise, to apply". To him, the sentence means "anew to put into practice a Statute on Agriculture". However, the word *wei* 爲 is somehow neglected. LH, however, takes *keng hsiu* as "to revise", but he includes *wei* in the title of the statute, leading to the translation "to revise the Statute on the Making of Fields", which he believes to be quite distinct from the Statute on Agriculture. As shown by my rendering, I have taken a neutral position.

8 *Chen* 畛 is a field-path or track; SW explains it as "a path between fields", *ching t'ien chien* (*po* for) *mo* 井田間 (百 for) 陌. LH translates this sentence literally: "When a field is one pace wide and eight (paces) long, then one makes a path". He believes that this implies that even a small field of 1 × 8 paces should have a field-path. He accepts the traditional form of the *mu* as a long, narrow strip, 1 pace wide and 240 paces long, with narrow field-paths separating it from the next *mu*. Yang K'uan, "Ch'ing-ch'uan", p. 83, has a completely different suggestion, accepted by Huang, p. 72, which I have followed in my translation. The field-paths on either side of the *mu* having a length of 8 paces imply that the *mu*, instead of being a long strip, was 30 paces wide. That this surely is the correct solution is shown by the Early Han agricultural handbook *Fan Sheng chih shu*, p. 31, which indicates these very dimensions, expressed in the equivalent number of feet (48 × 180). The only drawback of this solution is the inordinate width of the field-paths of one pace of six feet or 6 × c.23cm. = c. 1.40 m., which is, however, confirmed by SWKL, p. 6197b. T'ien and Liu introduce a further refinement: the *mu* was divided into two halves by a *chen*, as is shown by the *Sun-tzu ping-fa*, ch. Wu wen 吳問, p. 94. These two halves were called *wan* 婉, a loan for 畹 (also anciently these two words had the same pronunciation *·i̯wăn according to GSR, p. 84, no. 260j and 261a).

9 For the East-West path see note 2 to D 136 above.

10 For the North-South road see note 2 to D 136 above.

11 The width of the road was therefore nearly 4.20 m.

12 *Feng* 封.

13 This passage shows that a *feng* was, theoretically, a pyramid with sides of four feet or c. 0.92 m., and not a low earth-wall.

14 *Le* 埒, a low earth-wall, which ran between the border-mounds; for examples see Yü, p. 23. The measurements indicated here are also found in SW, *s.v. le*.

15 *Ch'iang* 彊 for *chiang* 疆, also in the *Ts'ang Chieh p'ien*, see "Ts'ang Chieh p'ien", p. 29, fragment C 027, note 22.

16 *P'an* 畔, explained in SW as *t'ien chieh* 田界.

17 As indicated by Yü, p. 23 (followed by LH, p. 69), *p'o* 犮 is to be found in *SWKL*, p. 717a f., with the remark that this word occurred in "the Tradition of the *Ch'un-ch'iu*", where the present *Tso chuan*, Duke Yin 6 (*Tso chuan* 4.2a (0171); Couvreur, *Tch'ouen-ts'iou* I, p. 39) reads *shan* 芟, "to cut, to mow"; the *Tso chuan* commentator Tu Yü (222–284) refers to the *SW* variant. The commentators to SW indicate a few more passages in ancient literature where *p'o* must have been the original reading. SW explains *p'o* as "to trample down the grass", but the word must also have meant "to mow." For *ta* 大 T'ien and Liu read *liu* 六, which they believe to be a loan for *lu* 宍, "mushrooms". This emendation seems unnecessary.

18 *Ch'u* 除.

19 As indicated in notes *f* and *g* to the characters 除隋 in the transcription furnished by the Report, Yü and LH want to read these as *pan hsien* 阪險, "slopes and danger spots". This binome is found in *LSCC* 1/1.2 (Wilhelm, *Frühling*, p. 2). LC, however, retains *ch'u* 除, but he takes 隋 (unknown)as a variant of *k'uai* 澮, "ditch". Huang assumes that the first character is not *ch'u* 除, because it is unlike the preceding *ch'u*; the second character he takes to be *hsien* 險. He therefore suggests reading *tsu* 阻 *hsien*, or *o* 阨 *hsien*. *Tsu hsien* is found i.a. in *HSPC* 6.7a (*HFHD* II, p. 41, "narrow and dangerous places"), and in *SC* 92.14 =

HSPC 34.6b (Watson, *Records* I, p. 215· "difficulty of the position"). I have followed Yü and LH. T'ien and Liu read *ch'u yin* 除陰, where they believe *yin* to mean "low, marshy land", in view of the explanation of *yin* in the commentary to *LSCC* 26, p. 333 (Wilhelm, *Frühling*, p. 457). *Ta* is again read *liu* 六, but this is now taken literally, leading to the translation "in the ninth month the roads are cleared six times", which seems unacceptable.

20 Morohashi, vol. 6, p. 345, *s.v. liang* 梁, refers to a quotation of the Ordinances of Hsia, *ling* 夏令, in the *Kuo yü* (not further specified), reading *shih yüeh ch'eng liang* 十月成梁, "in the tenth month bridges are completed".

21 Yü interprets the damaged character on the strip as 𣷌 (unknown), which he identifies with *liang* 梁, "bridge", a reading also adopted by LH. LC, however, reads it as *shen* 深, "deep", but he fails to explain its meaning here. It is to be noted that the expression *chin liang* 津梁 is common; I have therefore adopted it. Finally, Huang (p. 75) suggests that the illegible character could be *i* 隘, in view of the seal-form of the latter reproduced in SW; he thinks that *chin* refers to waterways and *i* to overland routes. However, the context does not seem to permit this. T'ien and Liu read the disputed character *k'ang* 康, which, according to the *Shih ming*, ch. *shih ts'ao* 釋名, 釋草 (inaccessible), can mean "highroad".

22 *Li* 利. This word is found in the *Li-chi*, ch. *Yüeh ling*, 3rd month of spring: *hsiu li ti fang* 修利隄防 (*Li-chi chu-su* 15.7a (0719); Couvreur, *Li-ki* I, p. 349; Legge, *Li-ki* 27, p. 264)·, but the commentators are silent as regards the meaning of *li*. Morohashi, vol. 1, p. 311, says simply that 修利 is the same as *hsiu li* 修理, "to repair", without providing any proof. Equally without proof is the statement in Morohashi, vol. 2, p. 243, that *li* 利 should mean "to drain; to draw off". Perhaps a solution is provided by *SWKL*, p. 1828a, which quotes the *Erh shan lu* 兒笘錄 by Yü Yüeh 兪樾 (1821–1907) who suggests that *li* originally meant "to cut; to prune". Whatever the exact maning of *li* may be, the general sense is evidently "to clean" or "to clear" by some method. T'ien and Liu believe that *li* stands for *lin* 蹸, "to trample down", but this is an impossible loan.

23 *Hsien ts'ao sui* / *li* 鮮草雖 (Report)/離 (Yü). According to Yü *hsien* 鮮 *si̯an (GSR, p. 72, no. 209a), "fresh or raw meat", is a loan for *hsien* 獮 *sni̯an (GSR, p. 104, no. 3591), "autumn hunt". He bases this on the commentary by Hsü Kuang (352–425) to *SC* 33.20 (not included in *Mh* 4, p. 102, note 2), who says that *hsi* 肸 or 肹 (GSR, p. 318, nos. 1241d and h, *—/γiei) of the text, identified with Pi 費 in the title of the "Declaration at Pi" (cf. *Mh loc. cit.*) in the Book of Documents, in some texts was called the Declaration at Hsien 鮮 and in others the Declaration of Hsien 獮. Now this last word is said to be a synonym for "to kill" in the *Erh-ya* (*Erh-ya chu-su* 1.9a (0029)). Yü therefore translates *hsien ts'ao* as "to remove weeds". Yü considers *li* 離 (GSR, p. 26, no. 23f, *lia) to be a loan for *lai* 萊, "weeds" (GSR, p. 248, no. 944j, *ləg); Karlgren mentions several suggestions of the same type but refutes these ("Loan characters II", pp. 75–77, nos. 908–911); LH agrees with this solution. Both scholars have evidently overlooked that in the *Erh-ya* chapter *shih ts'ao* 釋草 (*Erh-ya chu-su* 8.5a (0329)) *li* 離 is said to to be a weed, as noted in *SWTHTS*, quoted in *SWKL*, p. 1528a. LC takes *hsien* 鮮 as "few", which is one of the usual meanings of this word, but he then gives a curious translation of *hsien ts'ao* as "when the weeds are comparatively few", which seems to run counter to normal grammar. In view of the context, I am ready to believe that *hsien* (always provided that the facsimile copy is correct in writing 鮮) will mean "to remove" or "to destroy". However, an easier way out would be to assume that it is not *hsien* 鮮 that is meant, but *su* 穌, which SW explains as "to gather", especially grass or weeds; cf. *SWKL*, p. 3125b, where Tuan Yü-ts'ai refers to *HSPC* 34.5b, the biography of Han Hsin (*SC* 92.12; Watson, *Records* I, p. 214), where *su* 蘇 is used for *su* 穌 in this very sense. — LC seems likewise to consider *li* 離 as "grasses" or "weeds", in view of his translation, but he does not explain himself on this point; his translation is such a free paraphrase that he might equally well have adopted the reading *sui* 雖 of the Report, because he was one of its authors (see the Report, p. 13). There are two reasons for preferring *li* 離 meaning "weeds" to *sui* 雖, "although". Firstly, the sentence contains several phrases consisting of three words; reading *sui* would result in a phrase of only two characters, *hsien ts'ao*. Secondly, in these legal texts conjunctions are rare (except *erh* 而), and the construction *fei...erh...*, 非...而 ..., is perfectly clear without *sui*. Huang (p. 75), however, reads *sui* because he thinks that the sign on the strip resembles the form of *sui* in certain inscriptions on bronzes. T'ien and Liu read *sui*. *Hsien ts'ao* they take literally: "(fresh) green grass."

24 For *hsiang* 相 in the Report, Yü and LH read *che* 輒, "then always" or "then immediately." This word always occurs in the second half of the sentence; it is best translated by "whenever" at the beginning of the statement. In view of his translation, LC also seems to consider

the character to be *che*. T'ien and Liu retain *hsiang* 相, but they explain it as *sui* 隨, "to follow", basing this rendering on the commentary to *Tso chuan*, duke Chao 3 (*Tso chuan* 42.6a (1685); Couvreur, *Tch'ouen-ts·iou* III, p. 257).

25 As already remarked in notes *l* and *m* above, the facsimile copy and the transcription in the Report end with two open squares, indicating two illegible or effaced characters, but these signs are not repeated in Yü's and LH's transcription, nor are they alluded to in LC's paraphrase; Huang Sheng-chang, "Ch'ing-ch'uan", p. 75, believes that they are merely smudges and not characters.

26 The reverse of the strip shows traces of writing in three clusters, but only the four columns of the upper cluster are partly legible. The first column reads *ssu* (Yü: *chiu*) *nien shih erh yüeh pu ch'u tao che* 四 (Yü 九) 年十二月不除道者 (where *che* could also be a figure, followed by *jih* 日), "Days during the 12th month of the 4th (Yü: ninth, but this seems less likely, because king Wu only reigned four years) year when the roads were not cleared". This is followed by eight days, indicated by single cyclical signs, taken from both the Heavenly Stems and the Earthly Branches, according to LC; Yü offers other readings. LH does not read *jih* 日, "day", but *t'ien* 田. "field", and he thinks that the preceding words are a name, followed by a number. Regardless of these details, this note shows that a record was kept of the work for clearing the roads.

ALPHABETICAL LIST OF THE CHINESE TITLES OF THE CH'IN STATUTES

Chi lü 齎律	A 88; reference only.
Chiao lü 校律	A 82–89; B 1–39.
Chih li lü 置吏律	A 79–81.
Chin-pu lü 金布律	A 36–50.
Chiu lü 廄律	A 100; reference only.
Chiu-yüan lü 廄苑律	A 7–9.
Ch'u li lü 除吏律	C 1.
Ch'u ti-tzu lü 除弟子律	C 4.
Chuan shih lü 傳食律	A 92–94.
Chung lao lü 中勞律	C 9.
Chün chüeh lü 軍爵律	A 90–91.
Chün kung lü 均工律	A 61–63.
Fan ling lü 犯令律	A 16; reference only.
Fu lü 傅律	C 30.
Hsing shu lü 行書律	A 95–96.
Hu lü (Wei) 戶律 (魏)	F 1.
Kuan shih lü 關市律	A 51
Kung lü 工律	A 52–57.
Kung-chü ssu-ma lieh lü 公車司馬獵律	C 16.
Kung jen ch'eng 工人程	A 58–60.
Nei-shih, tsa 內史雜	A 97–107.
Pen-ming lü (Wei) 奔命律 (魏)	F 2.
P'ing tsui-jen lü 平罪人律	A 87; reference only.
Pu tao lü 捕盜律	C 24.
Shu lü 戍律	C 25–26.
Shu-pang lü 屬邦律	A 110.
Ssu-k'ung lü 司空律	A 65–78.
T'ien lü 田律	A 1–6; G.
Tsang lü 臧律	C 10.
Ts'ang lü 倉律	A 10–35.
T'un piao lü 屯表律	C 21, 22.
Wei, tsa 尉雜	A 108–109.
Yao lü 傜律	A 64.
Yu-shih lü 游士律	C 3.

BIBLIOGRAPHY AND LIST OF ABBREVIATIONS

Amano	Amano Motonosuke, *Chūgoku nōgyō-shi kenkyū*, 天野元之助, 中國農業史研究 (Tōkyō, Nōgyō sōgō kenkyūjo, 1962).
An Tso-chang, "Nung-yeh"	An Tso-chang, "Ts'ung Shui-hu-ti Ch'in mu chu chien k'an Ch'in-tai ti nung-yeh ching-chi", 安作璋, 從睡虎地秦墓竹簡看秦代的農業經濟, in *CHSLT*, pp. 27–40.
Biot	E. Biot, *Le Tcheou-li*. 3 vols. (Paris, 1851; reprinted in Formosa).
Bodde, *Festivals*	Derk Bodde, *Festivals in classical China* (Princeton, N.J., Princeton University Press, 1975).
Bodde, "Medicine"	———, "Forensic medicine in pre-imperial China", in *Journal of the American Oriental Society* 102 (1982), pp. 1–15.
Bodde, *Unifier*	———, *China's first unifier* (Leiden, Brill, 1937; reprinted in Hongkong).
Bridgman	R.F. Bridgman, "Le chapitre 105 des *Mémoires historiques* de Sseu-ma Ts'ien", in *Mélanges chinois et bouddhiques* 10 (1952–1955), pp. 1–213.
Chang Chen-hsin	Chang Chen-hsin, "Han-tai ti niu-keng", 張振新, 漢代的牛耕, in *Wenwu* 1977/8, pp. 57–62.
Chang Cheng-lang, "Pao-tzu"	Chang Cheng-lang, "Ch'in lü 'pao-tzu' shih i", 張政烺, 秦律「葆子」釋義, in *Wen shih* 文史 9 (1980), pp. 1–5.
Chang Cheng-lang, "Chi-jen"	———, "Ch'in lü 'chi-jen' yin i", 秦律「集人」音義, in *YMYC*, pp. 346–350.
Chang Ming-hsin	Chang Ming-hsin, "Kuan-yü Ch'in lü chung ti 'chü' ", 張銘新, 關於秦律中的「居」, in *Kaogu* 1981/1, pp. 48–50.
Chavannes, *Stein*	Edouard Chavannes, *Les documents chinois découverts par Aurel Stein dans les sables du Turkestan oriental* (Oxford, 1913).
Chavannes	See *Mh*.
Ch'en Chen-yü	Ch'en Chen-yü, "Yün-meng hsi Han mu ch'u t'u mu fang ch'u shih", 陳振裕, 雲夢西漢墓出土木方初釋, in *Wenwu* 1973/9, pp. 37–39.
Ch'en Ch'i-yün	Ch'en Ch'i-yün, *Hsün Yüeh and the mind of Late Han China; a translation of the* Shen-chien (Princeton, N.J., Princeton University Press, 1980).
Ch'en Chih, *HSHC*	Ch'en Chih, *Han shu hsin cheng*, 陳直, 漢書新證 (Tientsin, Jenmin ch'u-pan-she, 1979).
Ch'en Chih, "Ku shu"	———, "Ku shu shu wen", 古書述聞, in *Wen shih* 文史 3 (1963), pp. 69–87.
Ch'en Chih, *Liang Han*	———, *Liang Han ching-chi shih-liao lun-ts'ung*, 兩漢經濟史料論叢 (Hsi-an, Shen-hsi jen-min ch'u-pan-she, 1958).
Ch'en Chiu-chin	Ch'en Chiu-chin and Ch'en Mei-tung, "Lin-i ch'u t'u Han ch'u ku li ch'u t'an", 陳久金, 陳美東, 臨沂出土漢初古曆初探, in *Wenwu* 1974/3, pp. 59–68.
Ch'en P'an I	Ch'en P'an, "Han Chin i chien ou shu", 陳槃, 漢晉遺簡偶述, in *CYYY* 16 (1947).
Ch'en P'an II	———, "Han Chin i chien ou shu chih hsü", ——— 之續, in *CYYY* 23/2 (1952).
Ch'en Pan, *Ch'i chung*	———, *Han Chin i chien shih hsiao ch'i chung*, 識小七種 (Taipei, Academia sinica, 1975).
Chi-chiu p'ien	Shih Yu, *Chi-chiu p'ien*, 史游, 急就篇. Ts'ung-shu chi-ch'eng vol. 1052 (Shanghai' Commercial Press, 1936).
Chia pien	*Chü-yen Han chien, chia pien* 居延漢簡, 甲編 (Peking, K'e-hsüeh ch'u-pan-she, 1959).
"Chiang-ling"	"Chiang-ling T'ien-hsing-kuan i hao Ch'u mu" 江陵天星觀一號楚

墓, in *Kaogu xuebao* 1982/1, pp. 71–106.

Ch'ien Chien-fu — Ch'ien Chien-fu, "Ch'in Han se-fu k'ao", 錢劍夫, 秦漢嗇夫考, in *Chung-kuo shih yen-chiu* 1980/1, pp. 131–142.

Ch'ien Ta-hsin — Ch'ien Ta-hsin, *Nien-erh shih k'ao i*, 錢大昕, 廿二史考異 (undated 19th century blockprint).

Ch'in Chung-hang — Ch'in Chung-hang, "Han Yang-ling fu-chin ch'ien-t'u mu ti fa-hsien", 秦中行, 漢陽陵附近鉗徒墓的發現, in *Wenwu* 1972/7, pp. 51–53.

Ch'in hui-yao — Sun K'ai, Ch'in hui-yao, 孤楷, 秦會要, revised by Hsü Fu 徐復 and republished as *Ch'in hui-yao ting-pu* 訂補 (Peking, Chung-hua shu chü, 1958).

"Ch'ing-ch'uan Report" — Ssu-ch'uan Provincial Museum a.o., "Ch'ing-ch'uan hsien ch'u t'u Ch'in keng-hsiu t'ien lü mu tu", 青川縣出土秦更修田律木牘, in *Wenwu* 1982/1, pp. 1–13.

Chiu chang suan shu — *Chiu chang suan shu* 九章算術. *Ts'ung-shu chi-ch'eng* vol. 1263 (Shanghai, Commercial Press, 1936).

Ch'iu Hsi-kuei, "Chü-yen" — Ch'iu Hsi-kuei, "Hsin fa-hsien ti Chü-yen Han chien ti chi-ko wen-t'i", 丘錫圭, 新發現的居延漢簡的幾個問題, in *Chung-kuo shih yen-chiu* 1979/4, pp. 103–110.

Ch'iu Hsi-kuei, "Hu-pei" — ———, "Hu-pei Chiang-ling Feng-huang-shan shih hao Han mu chien-tu k'ao-shih", 湖北江陵鳳凰山十號漢墓簡牘考釋, in *Wenwu* 1974/7, pp. 49–63.

Ch'iu Hsi-kuei, "Se-fu" — ———, "Se-fu ch'u t'an", 嗇夫初探. in *YMYC*, pp. 226–302.

Ch'iu Kuang-ming — Ch'iu Kuang-ming, "Shih lun Chan-kuo jung-liang chih-tu", 丘光明, 試論戰國容量制度, in *Wenwu* 1981/10, pp. 63–73.

Ch'iu Kuang-ming, "Heng chih" — ———, "Shih lun Chan-kuo heng chih", 試論戰國衡制, in *Kaogu* 1982/5, pp. 516–527.

Chou-li — Sun I-jang, *Chou-li cheng-i*, 孫詒讓, 周禮正義. Kuo-hsüeh chi-pen ts'ung-shu ed. (Shanghai, Commercial Press, 1937).

Chou-li chu-su — *Chou-li chu-su* 周禮注疏, in *Classics*.

Chou Shih-jung — Chou Shih-jung, "Yu kuan Ma-wang tui ku ti-t'u ti i hsieh tzu-liao ho chi fang Han yin", 周世榮, 有關馬王堆古地圖的一些資料和幾方漢印, in *Wenwu* 1976/1, pp. 28–32.

CHSLT — *Ch'in Han shih lun-ts'ung* 秦漢史論叢 (Hsi-an, Shen-hsi jen-min ch'u-pan-she, 1981).

"Chu-ch'eng" — "Shan-tung Chu-ch'eng Han mu hua-hsiang-shih" 山東諸城漢墓畫像石, in *Wenwu* 1981/80, pp. 14–21.

Chu Kuo-chao — Chu Kuo-chao, "Shang Sun-chia-chai mu chien ch'u t'an", 朱國炤, 上孫家寨木簡初探, in *Wenwu* 1981/2, pp. 27–34.

Ch'u Shih-pin — Ch'u Shih-pin, "Chü-yen chien-ts'e 'Kan-lu erh nien ch'eng-hsiang yü-shih lü-ling' k'ao shu", 初仕賓, 居延簡册「甘露二年丞相御史律令」考述, in *Kaogu* 1980/2, pp. 179–184

Chuang-tzu — Wang Hsien-ch'ien, *Chuang-tzu chi-chieh*, 王先謙, 莊子集解, in *CTCC*, vol. 3.

CICA — A.F.P. Hulsewé and M.A.N. Loewe, *China in Central Asia, the early stage: 125 B.C.-A.D. 23* (Leiden, Brill, 1979).

CKT — *Chan-kuo ts'e* 戰國策. Ts'ung-shu chi-ch'eng, vols. 3684–3687 (Shanghai, Commercial Press, 1937).

Classics — *Shih-san ching chu-su* 十三經注疏 (Ssu-pu ts'ung-k'an ed., reprinted Peking, Chung-hua shu-chü, 1957).

CM — *Yün-meng Shui-hu-ti Ch'in mu* 雲夢睡虎地秦墓 (Peking, Wen-wu ch'u-pan-she, 1981).

Couvreur, *Li-ki* — S. Couvreur, *Li-ki, Mémoires sur les bienséances et les cérémonies*, 2 vols. (Paris, Cathasia, 1950 reprint).

Couvreur, *Tch'ouen-ts'iou* — ———, *Tch'ouen-ts'iou et Tso-tchouan, la chronique de la principauté de Lou*, 3 vols. (Paris, Cathasia, 1951 reprint).

CS — *Chin shu* 晉書 (T'ung-wen 同文 ed.).

CTCC — *Chu-tzu chi-ch'eng* 諸子集成, 8 vols. (Peking, Chung-hua shu-chü, 1954).

de Groot, *Urkunden* — J.J.M. de Groot, *Chinesische Urkunden zur Geschichte Asiens*. vol. 1, *Die Hunnen der vorchristlichen Zeit*; vol. 2, *Die Westlande Chinas in der vorchristlichen Zeit* (Berlin, de Gruyter, 1921, 1926).

des Rotours, *Fonctionnaires* — R. des Rotours, *Traité des fonctionnaires et Traité de l'armée, traduits de la Nouvelle Histoire des T'ang (chap. XLVI-L)*, 2 vols. (Leiden, Brill, 1947).

Dubs, *Hsüntze* — H.H. Dubs, *The works of Hsüntze* (London, Probsthain, 1928).

Dubs — see *HFHD*.

Duyvendak, *Lord Shang* — J.J.L. Duyvendak, *The Book of Lord Shang* (London, Probsthain, 1928).

Egami — Egami Namio, "The t'ao-yü and the tan-hsi, the strange domestic animals of the Hsiung-nu", in *Memoirs of the Research Department of the Toyo Bunko* 13 (1951), pp. 87–123.

Emura — Emura Haruki, "Unmei Suikochi shutsudo Shin ritsu no seikaku wo megutte", 江村治樹, 雲夢睡虎地出土秦律の性格をめぐって, in *Tōyōshi kenkyū* 40 (1981), pp. 1–26.

Emura, "Sengoku" — ———, "Sengoku Shin Kan kandoku moji no hensen", 戰國秦漢簡牘文字の變遷, in *Tōhō gakuhō* 53 (1981), pp. 233–297.

Erh-ya — *Erh-ya chu-su* 爾雅注疏, in *Classics*.

Fan Sheng-chih shu — Shih Sheng-han [石聲漢], *On "Fan Sheng-chih shu" [氾勝之書], an agricultural book of China written by Fan Sheng-chih in the first century B.C.* (Peking, Science Press, 1959).

Fitzgerald — C.P. Fitzgerald, *Barbarian beds* (London, The Cresset Press, 1965).

Flessel, *Huang-ho* — Klaus Flessel, *Der Huang-ho und die historische Hydrotechnik in China* (Tübingen, 1974).

Forke, *Lun-heng* — Alfred Forke, *Lun-hêng; philosophical essays of Wang Ch'ung*. 2 vols. (London, 1907; Berlin, 1911; reprinted New York, Paragon, 1962).

Forke, *Mê Ti* — ———, *Mê Ti des Sozialethikers und seiner Schüler philosophische Werke* (Berlin, 1922).

Fu Chü-yu — Fu Chü-yu, "Kuan-yü Ch'ang-sha Ma-wang tui san hao Han mu ti mu-chu wen-t'i", 傅舉有, 關於長沙馬王堆三號漢墓的墓主問題, in *Kaogu* 1983/2, pp. 165–172.

Fujieda — Fujieda Akira, "Kan kan shokkan hyō", 藤枝晃, 漢簡職官表, in *Silver Jubilee Volume of the Zimbunkagaku Kenkyūsyo* (Kyoto, 1954), pp. 630–651.

Fujita — Fujita Shizen, *Go Kan sho goi shū sei*, 藤田至善, 後漢書語彙集成, 3 vols. (Kyoto, Jimbunkagaku kenkyūjo, 1962).

Gale — E.M. Gale, *The discourses on salt and iron* (Leiden, Brill, 1931).

GSR — Bernhard Karlgren, "Grammata serica recensa", in *BMFEA* 29 (1957), pp. 1–332.

Hamaguchi — Hamaguchi Shigekuni, "Kan-dai no teishi-kei to Sō-Gi no keimei", 濱口重國, 漢代の釱趾刑と曹魏の刑名, in *Tōyō gakuhō* 25 (1938), pp. 552–566; included in Hamaguchi, *Shin Kan* I, pp. 667–681.

Hamaguchi, *Shin Kan* — ———, *Shin Kan Sui Tō shi no kenkyū* 秦漢隋唐史の研究, 2 vols. (Tokyo, Tokyo University Press, 1966).

"Han An-ling" — "Han An-ling ti k'an-ch'a chi ch'i p'ei tsang mu chung ti ts'ai-hui t'ao yung", 漢安陵的勘査及其陪葬墓中的彩繪陶俑, in *Kaogu* 1981/5, pp. 422–425.

Han chiu i — Wei Hung (fl. A.D. 25–27), *Han chiu i*, 衛宏, 漢舊儀, in *HKCC*, pp. liii-xxxiv.

Han Fei-tzu — Wang Hsien-shen, *Han Fei-tzu chi chieh*, 王先愼, 韓非子集解, in *CTCC*.

Hayashi, *Buki* — Hayashi Minao, *Chūgoku In-Shū jidai no buki*, 林巳奈夫, 中國殷周時代の武器 (Kyoto, Jimbunkagaku kenkyūjo, 1972).

Hayashi, *Bunbutsu* — ———, *Kan-dai no bunbutsu* 漢代の文物 (Kyoto, Jimbunkagaku kenkyūjo, 1976).

Hayashi, "Hata" — ———, "Chūgoku zen Shin jidai no hata", 中國先秦時代の旗, in *Shirin* 49/2 (1966), pp. 64–94.

Hervouet, *Chapitre 117* — Yves Hervouet. *Le chapitre 117 du* Che-ki *(biographie de Sseu-ma*

Siang-jou). Bibliothèque de l'Institut des hautes études chinoises vol. XXIII (Paris, Presses universitaires de France, 1972).

Hervouet, *Poète* ———, *Un poète de cour sous les Han, Sseu-ma Siang-jou*. Bibliothèque de l'Institut des hautes études chinoises, vol. XIX (Paris, Presses universitaires de France, 1964).

Hervouet, "Valeur" ———, "La valeur relative des textes du Che-ki et du Han chou", in *Mélanges de sinologie offerts à Monsieur Paul Demiéville*, vol. II. Bibliothèque de l'Institut des hautes études chinoises, vol. XX (Paris, 1974), pp. 55–76.

HFHD H.H. Dubs a.o., *The History of the Former Han Dynasty*, 3 vols. (Baltimore, Waverly Press, 1938, 1944, 1955).

HHSCC Wang Hsien-ch'ien, *Hou-Han shu chi chieh*, 王先謙, 後漢書集解 (Ch'ang-sha, 1924; reduced facsimile reprint by the I-wen 藝文 Publishers in Formosa, 1965).

Hiranaka Hiranaka Reiji, *Chūgoku kodai no densei to zeihō*, 平中苓次, 中國古代の田制と稅法 (Kyoto, Tōyōshi kenkyūkai 1967).

Hiranaka, "Kōfu" ———, "Kansho shokka-shi ni mieru 'kōfu' ni tsuite" 漢書食貨志に見へる「更賦」について, in *Ritsumeikan Bungaku* 7 (1967), pp. 757–772.

Hisamura Hisamura Yukari, "Dō ni tsuite", 久村因, 道について, in Mikami Tsugio, ed., *Chūgoku kodaishi kenkyū*, 三上次男, 中國古代史硏究 (Tokyo, Yoshikawa Kobunkan, 1960), pp. 251–290.

HKCC Sun Hsing-yen, *Han kuan ch'i chung*, 孫星衍, 漢官七種, included in his *P'ing-chin-kuan ts'ung-shu* 平津館叢書 (1885), reproduced in Chen Tsu-lung, *Index du Han-kouan ts'i-tchong* (Paris, 1962).

HLCI Shen Chia-pen, *Han lü chih i*, 沈家本, 漢律摭遺 (preface 1912), included in *Shen Ch'i-i hsien-sheng i-shu* 沈寄簃先生遺書 (undated), reprinted as vols. *t'e* 特 451–453 in the *Jen-jen wen-k'u* 人人文庫 (Taipei, Commercial Press, 1976).

HLTY Lou Chi (1133–1211), *Han li tzu yüan*, 婁機, 漢隸字源 (preface 1197; undated early 19th century Japanese reprint of a Chi-ku ko 汲古閣 print of a Sung edition?).

Holzman Donald Holzman, "A propos de l'origine de la chaise en Chine", in *T'oung Pao* 53 (1967), pp. 279–292.

Hori, "Keimei" Hori Tsuyoshi, "Shin Kan keimei kō", 堀毅, 秦漢刑名考, in *Bulletin of the Graduate Division of Waseda University*, special issue 4 (1978), pp. 113–131.

Hori, "Yakuchū" ———, "Shin kan kōdoku-kai 'Kohoku Suikochi Shin bo chikkan yakuchū shokō" 秦簡講讀會「湖北睡虎地秦墓竹簡譯注初稿, in *Ronkyū* 論究 10/1 (Chūō University, March 1978), pp. 87–98.

"Hou-ma" "Hou-ma Chan-kuo nu-li hsün-tsang-mu ti fa-chüeh" 侯馬戰國奴隸殉葬墓的發掘, in *Wenwu* 1972/1, pp. 63–67.

Hsiang-ma ching "Ma-wang tui Han mu po shu 'Hsiang-ma ching' shih-wen", 馬王堆漢墓帛書「相馬經」釋文, in *Wenwu* 1977/8, pp. 17–22.

Hsieh Ch'eng-hsia Hsieh Ch'eng-hsia, "Ch'ang-sha Ma-wang tui Han mu po shu 'Hsiang-ma ching' ti ch'u t'an", 謝成俠, 長沙馬王堆漢墓帛書「相馬經」的初探 in *Wenwu* 1977/8, pp. 23–26.

Hsieh Ying-ch'ün Hsieh Ying-ch'ün, "Chü-yen 'Sai-shang feng-huo p'in-yüeh' ts'e", 薛英群, 居延「塞 上烽火品約」册, in *Kaogu* 1979/4, pp. 361–364.

"Hsing-t'u mu" Shih-huang ling yung-k'eng k'ao-ku fa-chüeh-tui, "Ch'in Shih-huang ling hsi-ts'e Chao-pei-hu ts'un Ch'in hsing-t'u mu", 始皇陵俑坑考古發掘隊, 秦始皇陵西側趙背戶村秦刑徒墓 in *Wenwu* 1982/3, pp. 1–11.

Hsiung, "Chün-shih" Hsiung T'ieh-chi, "Shih lun Ch'in-tai chün-shih chih-tu", 熊鐵基, 試論秦代軍事制度, in *CHSLT*, pp. 41–60.

Hsiung and Wang, "So-yu-chih" Hsiung T'ieh-chi and Wang Tuan-ming, "Ch'in-tai ti feng-chien t'u-ti so-yu-chih", 熊鐵基, 王端明, 秦代的封建土地所有制, in *YMYC*, pp. 67–78.

HSPC Wang Hsien-ch'ien, *Han-shu pu-chu*, 王先謙, 漢書補注 (Chang-sha,

	1900; reduced facsimile reprint by the I-wen 藝文 Publishers, Formosa, 1965).
Hsü Cho-yün	Cho-yun Hsu, *Han agriculture* (Seattle and London, The University of Washington Press, 1980).
Hsü P'ing-fang, "P'in-yüeh"	Hsü P'ing-fang, "Chü-yen Tun-huang fa-hsien ti 'Sai-shang feng-huo p'in-yüeh' ", 徐苹方, 居延敦煌發現「塞上烽火品約」, in *Kaogu* 1979/7, pp. 445–454.
Hsün-tzu	Wang Hsien-ch'ien, *Hsün-tzu chi-chieh*, 王先謙, 荀子集解, in *CTCC*, vol. 2.
Hu Hou-hsüan	Hu Hou-hsüan, "Yin-tai ti yüeh hsing", 胡厚宣, 殷代的刖刑, in *Kaogu* 1973/2, pp. 108–117.
Huai-nan-tzu	*Huai-nan-tzu* 淮南子, in *CTCC*, vol. 7.
Huang Chan-yüeh	Huang Chan-yüeh, "Yün-meng Ch'in lü chien-lun", 黃展岳, 雲夢秦律簡論, in *Kaogu xuebao* 1980/1, pp. 1–28.
Huang Chan-yüeh	———, "Chi Liang-t'ai Tung Han hua-hsiang shih shang ti 'K'un ch'ih t'u' ", 記凉台東漢畫像石上的「髡笞圖」, in *Wenwu* 1981/10, pp. 22–24.
Huang Chin-yen, "Tsu-fu"	Huang Chin-yen, "Ch'in-tai tsu-fu yao-i chih-tu ch'u t'an", 黃今言, 秦代租賦徭役制度初探, in *CHSLT*, pp. 61–82.
Huang Sheng-chang	Huang Sheng-chang, "Kuan-yü Chiang-ling Feng-huang-shan 168 hao Han mu ti chi-ke wen-t'i", 黃盛璋, 關於江陵鳳凰山 168 號漢墓的幾個問題, in *Kaogu* 1977/1, pp. 43–50.
Huang Sheng-chang, "Ch'ing-ch'uan"	———, "Ch'ing-ch'uan hsin ch'u-t'u Ch'in mu-tu chi ch'i hsiang-kuan wen-t'i", 青川新出土秦木牘及其相關問題, in *Wenwu* 1982/9, pp. 71–75.
Huang Sheng-chang "Pien-cheng"	———, "Yün-meng Ch'in chien pien-cheng", 雲夢秦簡辨正, in *Kaogu xuebao* 1979/1, pp. 1–24.
Huang Sheng-chang "Pien-nien chi"	———, "Yün-meng Ch'in chien 'Pien-nien chi' ch'u-pu yen-chiu," 雲夢秦簡「編年記」初步研究, in *Kaogu xuebao* 1977/1, pp. 1–21.
Huang Sheng-chang, "San Chin"	———, "Shih lun San Chin ping ch'i ti kuo-pieh yü nien-tai chi ch'i hsiang-kuan wen-t'i", 試論三晉兵器的國別與年代及其相關問題, in *Kaogu xuebao* 1974/1, pp. 33–44.
Hulsewé, "Authenticity"	A.F.P. Hulsewé, "The problem of the authenticity of *Shih-chi* 123, the memoir on Ta Yüan", in *T'oung Pao* 61 (1975), pp. 83–147.
Hulsewé, "Ch'in documents"	———, "The Ch'in documents discovered in Hu-pei in 1975", in *T'oung Pao* 64 (1978), pp. 175–217 and 338.
Hulsewé, "Comm. of Just."	———, "The functions of the Commandant of Justice in the Han period", in S. Blader and Ch. Le Blanc, eds., *Harmony and Conflict: A Festschrift in honor of Dr. Derk Bodde*. In the press.
Hulsewé, "Economy"	———, "The influence of the state of Qin on the economy as reflected in the texts discovered in Yunmeng Prefecture", in Stuart R. Schram, ed., *The Scope of State Power in China* (Hongkong, The Chinese University Press 1985.)
Hulsewé, "Han documents"	———, "Han time documents", in *T'oung Pao* 45 (1957), pp. 1–50.
Hulsewé, "Lawsuit"	———, "A lawsuit of A.D. 28", in W. Bauer, ed., *Studia sino-mongolica. Festschrift für Herbert Franke*. Münchener Ostasiatische Studien 25 (Wiesbaden, Franz Steiner Verlag, 1979), pp. 23–34.
Hulsewé, "Legalists"	———, "The Legalists and the laws of Ch'in", in W.L. Idema, ed., *Leyden Studies in Sinology* (Leiden, Brill, 1981), pp. 1–22.
Hulsewé, "Rebels"	———, "Royal rebels", in *Mélanges à la mémoire de Paul Demiéville*. Bulletin de l'Ecole française d'Extrême Orient 69 (Paris, 1981), pp. 315–325.
Hulsewé, "The Shuo-wen"	———, "The Shuo-wen dictionary as a source for ancient Chinese law", in Søren Egerod and Else Glahn, eds., *Studia serica Bernhard Karlgren dedicata* (Copenhaguen, Munksgaard, 1959), pp. 239–258.
Hulsewé, "Statute labour"	———, "Some remarks on statute labour during the Ch'in and Han period", in M. Sabattini, ed., *Orientalia Veneziana* I (Firenze, Olschki, 1984), pp. 195–204.

Hulsewé, "Supplementary note"	———, "Supplementary note on *li ch'en ch'ieh*", in *T'oung Pao* 67 (1981), p. 361.
Hulsewé, "Weights"	———, "Weights and measures in Ch'in law", in D. Eikemeier, ed., *State and law in East Asia. Festschrift Karl Bünger* (Wiesbaden, Harrassowitz, 1981), pp. 25–39.
Hulsewé	see also *CICA* and *RHL*.
HWTS	*Han Wei ts'ung-shu* 漢魏叢書 (lithographic edition of the Yü-wen shu-chü 育文書局, 1911; no place).
Iijima	Iijima Katsutoshi, " 'Bun mu gai'kō", 飯島和俊,「文無害」考 in *Chūō Daigaku Ajia-shi kenkyū* 3 (1979), pp. 54–73.
Ikeda	Ikeda Yūichi, " 'Kohoku Unmei Suikochi Shin bo kanken", 池田雄一, 湖北雲夢睡虎地秦墓管見, in *Chūō Daigaku Bungakubu Kiyō* 100 (1981), pp. 33–66.
I-li	*I-li chu-su* 儀禮注疏, in *Classics*.
"I-yang"	"Hu-nan I-yang Chan-kuo Han mu", 湖南益陽戰國漢墓, in *Kaogu xuebao* 1981/4, pp. 519–548.
Jung Chao-tsu	Jung Chao-tsu, "Yüeh-ling ti lai-yüan k'ao," 容肇祖, 月令的來源考 in *Yen-ching hsüeh-pao* 18 (1935), pp. 97–105.
Kamada	Kamada Shigeo, *Shin Kan seiji seido no kenkyü*, 鎌田重雄, 秦漢政治制度の研究 (Tokyo, Nihon Gakujutsu shinkōkai, 1962).
Kao Heng	Kao Heng, "Ch'in lü chung ti yao-shu wen-t'i—tu Yün-meng Ch'in chien cha-chi", 高桓, 秦律中的徭戍問題—讀雲夢秦簡扎記, in *Kaogu* 1980/6, pp. 530–535.
Kao Heng, "Chih-kuan"	———, "Ch'in chien chung yü chih-kuan yu-kuan ti wen-t'i", 秦簡中與職官有關的問題, in *YMYC*, pp. 207–225.
Kao Heng, "Li ch'en ch'ieh"	———, "Ch'in lü chung 'li ch'en ch'ieh' wen-t'i ti t'an-t'ao", 秦律中「隸臣妾」問題的探討, in *Wenwu* 1977/7, pp. 43–50.
Kao Heng, "Nu-pi"	———, "Ch'in chien chung ti ssu-jen nu-pi wen-t'i", 秦簡中的私人奴婢問題, in *YMYC*, pp. 140–151.
Kao Min, *Ch'u t'an*	Kao Min, *Yün-meng Ch'in chien ch'u t'an*, 高敏, 雲夢秦簡初探 (Honan, Jen-min ch'u-pan-she, 1979).
Kao Min, "Se-fu"	———, "Lun Ch'in lü chung ti 'se-fu' i kuan", 論秦律中的嗇夫一官, in *She-hui k'e-hsüeh chan-hsien* 社會科學戰線 1979/1, pp. 135–141.
Kao Min, "T'ing"	———, "Ch'in Han shih ti t'ing", 秦漢時的亭, in *YMYC*, pp. 302–315.
Kao Min, "Yu-ch'ih"	———, "Yu-ch'ih fei se-fu pien", 有秩非嗇夫辨, in *Wenwu* 1979/3, pp. 70–72.
Karlgren, "Documents"	Bernhard Karlgren, "The Book of Documents", in *BMFEA* 22 (1950), pp. 1–81.
Karlgren, "Glosses Documents I, II"	———, "Glosses on the Book of Documents I", in *BMFEA* 20 (1948), and *idem* II in *BMFEA* 21 (1949).
Karlgren, "Gleanings"	———, "Gleanings for a lexicon of classical Chinese", in *BMFEA* 44 (1972), pp. 1–74.
Karlgren, "Glosses Kuo-feng"	———, "Glosses to the Kuo-feng", in *BMFEA* 14 (1942), pp. 71–247.
Karlgren, "Glosses Li-ki"	———, "Glosses on the Li-ki", in *BMFEA* 43 (1971), pp. 1–66.
Karlgren, "Glosses Siao ya"	———, "Glosses on the Siao ya Odes", in *BMFEA* 16 (1944), pp. 25–170.
Karlgren, "Glosses Ta Ya and Sung"	———, "Glosses to the Ta Ya and Sung Odes", in *BMFEA* 18 (1946), pp. 1–198.
Karlgren, "Loan chracters"	———, "Loan characters in Pre-Han texts". I in *BMFEA* 35 (1963), pp. 1–128; II in *idem* 36 (1964), pp. 1–106; III in *idem* 37 (1965), pp. 1–136; IV in *idem* 38 (1966), pp. 1–82; V in *idem* 39 (1967). pp. 1–40.
Karlgren, *Odes*	———, *The Book of Odes* (Göteborg, Elander, 1950).
Karlgren	see GSR.
Kierman	Frank A. Kierman Jr., *Ssu-ma Ch'ien's historiographical attitude as reflected in four late Warring States biographies* (Wiesbaden, Harras-

	sowitz, 1962).
Koga, *Chōan*	Koga Noboru, *Kan Chōan-jō to senpaku ken ri tei seido*, 古賀登, 漢長安城と阡陌縣里亭制度 (Tokyo, Yūsankaku 雄山閣, 1980).
"Ku ch'ien"	"Ku ch'ien", 古錢, in *Wenwu* 1981/9, p. 88.
Kuan and Sung, "Li ch'en ch'ieh"	Kuan Ch'ang-wei and Sung Min, "'Li ch'en ch'ieh'shih Ch'in kuan nu-pi", 官長爲, 宋敏, 「隷臣妾」是秦官奴婢, in *Chung-kuo shih yen-chiu* 1982/1, pp. 120–126.
Kudō, "Naishi"	Kudō Motoo, "Shin no naishi—shu to shite Suikochi Shin bo chikkan ni yoru", 工藤元男, 秦の內史—主として睡虎地秦墓竹簡による, in *Shigaku zasshi* 90 (1981), pp. 275–307.
Kudō, "Shōnai"	———, "Suikochi Shin bo chikkan ni mieru dainai to shōnai—Shin no shōfu no seiritsu wo megutte", 睡虎地秦墓竹簡に見える大內と小內—秦少府の成立をめぐって, in *Shikan* 105 (1981), pp. 19–34.
Kudō, "Tokan"	———, "Sengoku Shin no tokan—shu to shite Suikochi Shin bo chikkan ni yoru", 戰國秦の都官—主として睡虎地秦墓竹簡による, in *Tōhōgaku* 63 (1982), pp. 1–14.
Ku Liang chuan	*Ku Liang chuan chu-su* 穀梁傳注疏, in *Classics*.
Kuan-tzu	Tai Wang, *Kuan-tzu chiao cheng*, 戴望, 管子校正, in *CTCC*, vol. 5.
Kung Yang chuan	*Kung Yang chuan chu-su* 公羊傳注疏, in *Classics*.
Kuo-yü	*Kuo-yü* 國語. Kuo-hsüeh chi-pen ts'ung-shu ed. (Shanghai, Commercial Press, 1935; reprinted 1958).
Kurihara	Kurihara Tomonobu, *Shin Kan shi no kenkyū*, 栗原朋信, 秦漢史の研究 (Tokyo, Yoshikawa Kōbunkan, 1960).
Lao Kan, *K'ao-shih k'ao-cheng*	Lao Kan, *Chü-yen Han chien k'ao-shih chih pu* (with *k'ao-cheng*), 勞榦, 居延漢簡考釋之部 (考證) (Taipei, Academia Sinica, 1960).
Lao Kan, "Ping chih"	———, "Han tai ping chih chi Han chien chung ti ping chih", 漢代兵制及漢簡中的兵制, in *CYYY* 10 (1948), pp. 23–55, now included in *Lao Kan hsüeh-shu lun-wen chi* 勞榦學術論文集 (Taipei, I-wen 藝文 Publishers, 1976), pp. 204–241.
Lao Kan, "T'ing-chang"	———, "Shih Han tai chih t'ing-chang yü feng-sui", 釋漢代之亭鄣與烽燧, in *CYYY* 19 (1948), pp. 501–522, now included in *Lao Kan hsüeh-shu lun-wen chi*, pp. 699–720.
Legge, *Chuang-tzu* 39 & 40	James Legge, *The writings of Kwang-tze*, in *Sacred Books of the East*, vols. 39 and 40 (Oxford, 1891, reprinted by Dover Publications, New York, 1962).
Legge, *Li-chi* 27 & 28	———, *The Lî Kî*, in *Sacred Books of the East*, vols. 27 and 28 (Oxford, 1885).
Legge, *Yi-king*	———, *The Yi-king*, in *Sacred Books of the East*, vol. 16 (Oxford, 1899, reprinted by Dover Publications, New York, 1963).
Li Chao-ho, "Ch'ing-ch'uan"	Li Chao-ho, "Ch'ing-ch'uan ch'u t'u mu tu wen-tzu chien k'ao", 李昭和, 青川出土木牘文字簡考, in *Wenwu* 1982/1, pp. 24–27.
Li-chi chu-su	*Li-chi chu-su* 禮記注疏 in *Classics*.
Li Chien-nung	Li Chien-nung, *Hsien Ch'in liang Han ching-chi shih kao*, 李劍農, 先秦兩漢經濟史稿 (Peking, Chung-hua shu-chü, 1962).
Li Hsüeh-ch'in, "Ch'in-kuo wen-wu"	Li Hsüeh-ch'in, "Ch'in-kuo wen-wu ti hsin jen-shih", 李學勤, 秦國文物的新認識, in *Wenwu* 1980/9, pp. 25–31.
Li Hsüeh-ch'in, "Ch'ing-ch'uan"	———, "Ch'ing-ch'uan Hao-chia-p'ing mu-tu yen-chiu, 青川郝家坪木牘研究, in *Wenwu* 1982/10, pp. 68–72.
Li Hsüeh-ch'in, "Ku wen"	———, "Ch'in chien ku-wen-tzu-hsüeh k'ao-ch'a", 秦簡古文字學考察, in *YMYC*, pp. 336–345.
Li Hsüeh-ch'in "Mo-tzu"	———, "Ch'in chien yü 'Mo-tzu' ch'eng shou ko p'ien", 秦簡與「墨子」城守各篇, in *YMYC*, p. 324–335.
Li shih	Hung Kua (1117–1184), *Li shih*, 洪适, 隷釋 (Ssu-pu ts'ung-k'an edition).
"Liang ts'ang"	Lo-yang Museum, "Lo-yang Chan-kuo liang ts'ang shih chüeh chi lüeh", 洛陽戰國粮倉試掘紀略, in *Wenwu* 1981/11, pp. 55–65.
Liao	W.K. Liao, *The Complete Works of Han Fei Tzu*, 2 vols. (London, Probsthain, 1939 and 1959).

Lin Chien-ming — Lin Chien-ming, "Li ch'en ch'ieh pien", 林劍鳴, 隷臣妾辨, in *Chung-kuo shih yen-chiu* 1980/2, pp. 91–99.

Lin Chien-ming, "T'e-tien" — ———, "Ch'in-kuo nu-li-chih she-hui hsing-t'ai ti t'e tien", 秦國奴隷制社會形態的特點, in *CHSLT*, pp. 3–26.

"Lin-t'ung" — Ch'in yung-k'eng k'ao-ku-tui, "Lin-t'ung Cheng-chuang Ch'in shih-liao chia-kung-ch'ang i-chih tiao-ch'a chien-pao", 秦俑坑考古隊, 臨潼鄭莊秦石料加工場遺址調查簡報, in *Kaogu yü wenwu* 1981/1, pp. 39–43.

Liu Chan-ch'eng, "T'ung p'i" — Liu Chan-ch'eng, "Ch'in yung k'eng ch'u t'u ti t'ung p'i", 劉占城, 秦俑坑出土的銅鈹, in *Wenwu* 1982/3, pp. 12–14.

Liu Chih-yüan — Liu Chih-yüan, "Han tai shih-ching k'ao", 劉志遠, 漢代市井考, in *Wenwu* 1973/3, pp. 52–57.

Liu Hai-nien — Liu Hai-nien, "Ch'in Han 'shih-wu' ti shen-fen yü chieh-chi ti-wei", 劉海年, 秦漢「士伍」的身分與階級地位, in *Wenwu* 1978/2, pp. 58–62.

Liu Hai-nien, "Hsing-fa" — ———, "Ch'in lü hsing-fa k'ao-hsi", 秦律刑罰考析, in *YMYC*, pp. 171–206.

Liu Pao-nan — Liu Pao-nan, *Lun-yü cheng-i*, 劉寶楠, 論語正義, in *CTCC*, vol. 1.

Lo K'ai-yü "Shih-wu" — Lo K'ai-yü, "Ch'in kuo 'shih-wu', 'wu-jen' k'ao", 羅開玉, 秦國「什伍」「伍人」考, in *Ssu-ch'uan ta-hsüeh hsüeh-pao* 2 (1981), pp. 85–88.

Loewe, "Manuscripts" — Michael Loewe, "Manuscripts found recently in China, a preliminary survey", in *T'oung Pao* 63 (1977), pp. 99–136.

Loewe, "Measurement" — ———, "The measurement of grain during the Han period", in *T'oung Pao* 49 (1961), pp. 64–95.

Loewe, "Rank" — ———, "The orders of aristocratic rank in Han China", in *T'oung Pao* 48 (1960), pp. 97–174.

Loewe — see also *RHA*.

van der Loon — P. van der Loon, "On the transmission of Kuan-tzu", in *T'oung Pao* 41 (1952), pp. 357–393.

LSCC — Lu Pu-wei, *Lü-shih ch'un-ch'iu*, 呂不韋, 呂氏春秋, in *CTCC* vol. 6.

Lu Ch'i, "Ta-pao-ta'i" — Lu Ch'i, "Shih t'an Ta-pao-t'ai Hsi Han mu ti tzu-kung, pien-fang, huang-ch'ang t'i-ts'ou" 魯琪, 試談大葆台西漢墓的梓宮便房黃腸題湊, in *Wenwu* 1977/6, pp. 30–33.

Lu Ch'i, "T'ung tse" — ———, "Pei-ching-shih fa-hsien Chin-tai t'ung-tse", 北京市發現金代銅則, in *Wenwu* 1979/9, p. 94.

Lun-heng — Wang Ch'ung (A.D. 27–100?), *Lun-heng*, 王充, 論衡; references are to Huang Hui, *Lun-heng chiao-shih*, 黃暉, 論衡校釋 (Taiwan Commercial Press, 1946 reprint of the 1935 edition).

Lun yü — *Lun-yü chu-su* 論語注疏, in *Classics*.

Ma Tsung-huo — Ma Tsung-huo, *Shuo-wen chieh-tzu yin ch'ün shu k'ao*, 馬宗霍, 說文解字引羣書考 (Peking, K'e-hsüeh ch'u-pan-she, 1959).

Makino — Makino Tatsumi, "Sei-Kan no hōken sōzokuhō", 牧野巽, 西漢の封建相續法, in *Tōhōgakuhō* 3 (Tokyo, 1932), pp. 255–329.

Maspero — Henri Maspero, *La Chine antique* (Paris, 1955[2]).

Maspero, "Serment" — ———, "Le serment dans la procédure judiciaire de la Chine antique", in *Mélanges chinois et bouddhiques* 3 (1935).

Maspero, *Stein* — ———, *Les documents de la troisième expédition de Sir Aurel Stein en Asie Centrale* (London, British Museum, 1953).

Matsuzaki — Matsuzaki Tsuneko, "Suikochi juichi-gō Shin bo chikkan 'Hen-nen ki' yori mita bo-shu 'Ki' ni tsuite, 松崎つね子, 睡虎地十一號秦墓竹簡「編年紀」よりみた墓主「喜」について, in *Tōyō gakuhō* 61 (1980), p. 255–284.

Ma-wang tui — *Ch'ang-sha Ma-wang tui i hao Han mu* 長沙馬王堆一號漢墓, 2 vols. (Peking, Wen-wu ch'u-pan-she, 1973).

Mayer — K.P. Mayer, "Variations in the shapes of the components of the Chinese *nu-chi* (crossbow latch)", in *T'oung Pao* 52 (1965/1966), pp. 1–7.

McKnight — Brian E. McKnight, *The quality of mercy. Amnesties and traditional Chinese justice* (Honolulu, The University Press of Hawaii, 1981).

Meng-tzu chu-su — *Meng-tzu chu-su* 孟子注疏, in *Classics.*

Mh — Edouard Chavannes, *Les mémoires historiques de Se-ma Ts'ien*, 6 vols. (reprint Paris, 1967–1969).

Miyazaki — Miyazaki Ichisada (宮崎市定), "Les villes en Chine à l'époque des Han", in *T'oung Pao* 48 (1960), pp. 376–392.

Momiyama, "Hōka" — Momiyama Akira, "Hōka izen", 籾山明, 法家以前, in *Tōyōshi kenkyū* 39 (1980), pp. 249–285.

Momiyama, "Reishinshō" — ———, "Shin no reizoku mibun to sono kigen; reishinshō mondai ni yosete", 秦の隷屬身分とその起源—隷臣妾問題に寄せて, in *Shirin* 65 (1982), pp. 795–828.

Mori, "Kan kan" — Mori Shikazō, *Tōyōgaku kenkyū, Kyoën Kan kan hen*, 森鹿三, 東洋學研究, 居延漢簡篇 (Kyoto, Dōhō sha 同朋社, 1975).

Moriya, "Furō" — Moriya Mitsuo, "Furō", 守屋美都雄, 父老, in *Tōyōshi kenkyū* 14 (1955), pp. 43–60.

Morohashi — Morohashi Tetsuji, *Dai Kan Wa jiten*, 諸橋轍次, 大漢和辭典 (Tokyo, 1960; Formosan reprint, no place, no date).

Mo-tzu — Sun I-jang, *Mo-tzu hsien ku*, 孫詒讓, 墨子間詁, in *CTCC* vol. 4.

Niida, "Saiken" — Niida Noboru, "Kan, Gi, Rikuchō ni okeru saiken no tanpō", 仁井田陞, 漢魏六朝に於ける債權の擔保, in *Tōyō gakuhō* 21 (1933), pp. 91–103; included in Niida Noboru, *Chūgoku hōseishi no kenkyū, Tochi-hō, torihiki-hō*, 中國法制史の研究—土地法, 取引法 (Tōkyō Daigaku, Tōyō Bunka Kenkyūjo, 1960), pp. 477–498.

Niida, *Tō-rei* — ———, *Tō rei shū i* 唐令拾遺 (Tokyo, Tōhō bunka gakuin, 1933)

Nishijima — Nishijima Sadao, *Chūgoku keizai shi kenkyū*, 西嶋定生, 中國經濟史研究 (Tokyo, Tokyo University Press, 1965).

Ōba, "Dōko-fu" — Ōba Osamu, "Kan no dōko-fu to chikushi-fu", 大庭脩, 漢の銅虎符と竹使符", in *Kamada hakushi kanreki kinen rekishi-gaku ronsō* 鎌田博士還暦記年歴史學論叢 (1970), pp. 43–54; included in Ōba, *Shin Kan*, pp. 263–275.

Ōba, "Ensho kō" — ———, "Ensho kō", 爰書考, in *Seishin Joshi Daigaku Ronsō* 13 (1958); included in Ōba, *Shin Kan*, pp. 636–647.

Ōba, *Mokkan* — ———, *Mokkan*, 木簡 (Tokyo, Gakusei-sha, 1979).

Ōba, "Pasupōto" — ———, "Kan dai no kanjo to pasupōto", 漢代の關所とパスポート, in *Kansai Daigaku Tō-Sei gakujutsu kenkyū ronshū* 16 (1954), included in Oba, *Shin Kan*, pp. 593–625.

Ōba, *Shin Kan* — ———, *Shin Kan hōseishi no kenkyū*, 秦漢法制史の研究 (Tokyo, Sōbunsha 創文社, 1982), 680 pp.

Ōba, "Shisen-kei" — ———, "Kan no shisen-kei ni tsuite", 漢の徙遷刑について, in *Shisen* 史泉 6 (1957), pp. 7–28; included in Ōba, *Shin Kan*, pp. 165–198.

Ōda — Ōda Yoshio, "Kohoku Suikochi shutsudo Shin ritsu no sō-ritsu wo megutte; sone ichi, 太田幸男, 湖北睡虎地出土秦律の倉律をめぐって, その一, in *Tōkyō Gakugei Daigaku kiyō* III/31 (1980), pp. 143–155; sono ni その二 in *idem* 32 (1980), pp. 165–182.

"P'i chia chou" — "Hu-pei Sui-hsien Lei-ku-tun i hao mu p'i chia chou ti ch'ing-li ho fu-yüan", 湖北隨縣擂鼓墩一號墓皮甲冑的清理和復原, in *Kaogu* 1979/6, pp. 542–553.

P'ien — P'ien Yü-ch'ien, "Ch'in 'tao' k'ao", 駢宇騫, 秦「道」考, in *Wen shih* 文史 9 (1980), pp. 229–230.

Průšek, — Jaroslav Průšek, *Chinese statelets and the northern barbarians*, 1400–300 *B.C.* (Dordrecht, Holland, D. Reidel, 1971).

Pulleyblank — E.G. Pulleyblank, "Emphatic negatives in classical Chinese", in D. Roy and T. Tsien, eds., *Ancient China; studies in early civilization* (Hong-kong, The Chinese University Press, 1978), pp. 115–135.

RHA — Michael Loewe, *Records of Han administration.* 2 vols. (Cambridge, Cambridge University Press, 1967).

RHL — A.F.P. Hulsewé, *Remnants of Han law* I (Leiden, Brill, 1955).

Rickett — W. Allyn Rickett, "An early Chinese calendar chart: *Kuan-tzu* II.8 (*Yu-kuan* 幼官)", in *T'oung Pao* 48 (1960), pp. 195–251.

San fu — *Chiao-cheng San fu huang t'u* 校正三輔黃圖 (Shanghai, Ku-tien wen-hsüeh ch'u-pan-she, 1958).

Satake, "Kazoku" — Satake Yasuhiko, "Shin-koku no kazoku to Shō Yō no bun'i-rei", 佐竹靖彥, 秦國の家族と商鞅の分異令, in *Shirin* 63 (1980), pp. 1–29.

Satō — Satō Takeshige, *Chūgoku kodai kōgyō-shi no kenkyū*, 佐藤武敏, 中國古代工業史の研究 (Tokyo, Yoshikawa Kōbunkan, 1962)

SC — Ssu-ma Ch'ien, *Shih chi*, 司馬遷, 史記; references are to Takigawa Kametarō, *Shiki kaichū kōshō*, 瀧川龜太郎, 史記會注考證 (Tokyo, 1934; reprinted in Taipei).

Shang-chün shu — Chu Shih-ch'e, *Shang chün shu chieh ku ting pen*, 朱師轍, 商君書解詁定本 (Peking, Ku-chi ch'u-pan-she, 1956).

Shen Chia-pen, *Hsing-chü k'ao* — Shen Chia-pen (1840–1913), *Hsing-chü k'ao*, 沈家本, 刑具考 (anastatic reprint in *Jen-jen wen-k'u* 人人文庫, vol. 2272, Commercial Press, Taipei, 1976).

Shen Chia-pen — see *HLCI*.

Shen chien — Hsün Yüeh, *Shen chien*, 荀悅, 申鑑, in *CTCC*, vol. 8.

Shen Chih-yü — Shen Chih-yü, "Shuo 'chih' ", 沈之瑜, 說「至」, in *Wenwu* 1979/11, p. 69.

Shen Chung-ch'ang — Shen Chung-ch'ang, " 'Kao tai t'u' hua-hsiang chuan chih i", 沈仲常, 「告貸圖」畫像磚質疑, in *Kaogu* 1979/6, pp. 525–527.

Shih-ching — *Mao Shih cheng-i* 毛詩正義 in *Classics*.

Shin-kan kōdoku-kai — see Hori.

Shu Chih-mei — Shu Chih-mei, "Chen-kuei ti Yün-meng Ch'in chien", 舒之梅, 珍貴的雲夢秦簡, in *YMYC*, pp. 1–13.

Shu-ching — *Shang-shu cheng-i* 尙書正義 in *Classics*.

Steele — John Steele, *The I-li*, 2 vols. (London, Probsthain, 1917; reprinted in Formosa in one volume).

Stein, *Report* — Sir Aurel Stein, *Serindia*; *detailed report on explorations in Central Asia and westernmost China* (Oxford, Clarendon Press, 1921).

Stein, *Tracks* — ——, *On ancient Central Asian tracks*; *brief narrative of three expeditions in innermost Asia and westernmost China* (London, 1933).

"Sui-hsien" — "Hu-pei Sui-hsien Tseng hou I mu fa-chüeh chien-pao", 湖北隨縣曾侯乙墓發掘簡報, in *Wenwu* 1979/7, pp. 1–24.

Sun Chi, "Ch'e-chih" — Sun Chi, "Ts'ung hsiung-shih hsi-chia-fa tao an-t'ao-shih hsi-chia-fa — wo kuo ku-tai ch'e-chih lüeh-shuo", 孫機, 從胸式係駕法到鞍套式係駕法—我國古代車制略說, in *Kaogu* 1980/5, pp. 448–460.

Sun Pin — *Yin-ch'iao-shan Han mu chu-chien Sun Pin ping fa* 銀雀山漢墓竹簡孫臏兵法 (Peking, Wen-wu ch'u-pan-she, 1975).

Sun-tzu — *Sun-tzu shih chia chu* 孫子十家注, in *CTCC*, vol. 6.

Sun-tzu ping-fa — *Yin-ch'iao-shan Han mu chu-chien Sun-tzu ping fa* 銀雀山漢墓竹簡孫子兵法 (Peking, Wen-wu ch'u-pan-she, 1976).

Sung Chao-lin — Sung Chao-lin, "Chan-kuo i-she t'u chi i-she su-yüan", 宋兆麟, 戰國弋射圖及弋射溯源, in *Wenwu* 1981/6, pp. 75–77.

Sung Chih-min — Sung Chih-min, "Han-tai ming-k'o so-chien chih-kuan hsiao chi", 宋治民, 漢代銘刻所見職官小記, in *Kaogu* 1979/5, pp. 459–460.

SW — Hsü Shen (A.D. 30–124), *Shuo-wen chieh-tzu*, 許愼, 說文解字.

Swann — Nancy Lee Swann, *Food and money in ancient China* (Princeton, N.J., Princeton University Press, 1950).

SWKL — Ting Fu-pao, *Shuo-wen chieh-tzu ku-lin*, 丁福保, 說文解字詁林 (1st ed. 1931; reprinted in 17 vols. by the Taiwan Commercial Press, 1976).

SWTHTS — Chu Chün-sheng, *Shuo-wen t'ung hsün ting sheng*, 朱駿聲, 說文通訓定聲, included in *SWKL*.

Tai Chen — Tai Chen (1724–1777), *K'ao-kung chi t'u*, 戴震, 考工記圖 (Shanghai Commercial Press, 1955).

T'ang Tsan-kung, "Nu-li" — T'ang Tsan-kung, "Yün-meng Ch'in chien kuan ssu nu-li wen-t'i shih-t'an", 唐贊功, 雲夢秦簡官私奴隸問題試探, in *Chung-hua wen shih lun-ts'ung* 中華文史論叢 3 (1981), pp. 143–165.

T'ang Tsan-kung, "So-yu-chih.' — ——, "Yün-meng Ch'in chien so-she-chi t'u-ti so-yu-chih hsing-shih wen-t'i ch'u t'an", 雲夢秦簡所涉及土地所有制形式問題初探, in

YMYC, pp. 53–66.

TCTC — Ssu-ma Kuang, *Tzu-chih t'ung-chien*, 司馬光, 資治通鑑, 10 vols. (Peking, Ku-chi ch'u-pan-she, 1956).

Teng Ssu-yü — Teng- Ssu-yü (鄧嗣禹), *Family instructions for the Yen clan* Yen-shih chia-hsün 顏氏家訓. Monographies du T'oung Pao, vol. IV (Leiden, Brill, 1968).

Thorpe "Marxist perspective" — Robert Thorpe, "The Chinese bronze age from a Marxist perspective", in *Early China* 6 (1980–1981), pp. 97–102

T'ien and Liu — T'ien I-ch'ao and Liu Chao, "Ch'in t'ien lü k'ao shih", 田宜超, 劉釗, 秦田律考釋, in *Kaogu* 1983/6, pp. 545–548.

T'ien-shih — T'ien-shih, "Hsi-Han tu-liang-heng lüeh shuo", 天石, 西漢度量衡略說, in *Wenwu* 1975/12, pp. 79–89.

Tjan, *Po-hu t'ung* — Tjan Tjoe Som, *Po-hu t'ung* 白虎通, *The Comprehensive Discussions in the White Tiger Hall*. Sinica leidensia VI; 2 vols. (Leiden, Brill, 1949 and 1952).

"Ts'ang Chieh p'ien" — "Fu-yang Han chien 'Ts'ang Chieh p'ien' ", 阜陽漢簡「蒼頡篇」, in *Wenwu* 1983/2, pp. 24–34.

Tsien — Tsien Tsuen-hsuin, *Written on bamboo and silk; the beginnings of Chinese books and inscriptions* (Chicago, The University of Chicago Press, 1962).

Tso chuan — *Ch'un-ch'iu Tso chuan cheng-i*, 春秋左傳正義, in *Classics*.

Tsou Chieh-cheng — Tsou Chieh-cheng, "Wo kuo hsiang ma wai hsing hsüeh fa-chan shih lüeh", 鄒介正, 我國相馬外形學發展史略, in *Nung shih yen-chiu chi-k'an* 農史研究集刊, vol. 1 (Peking, K'o-hsüeh ch'u-pan-she, 1959), pp. 37–53.

Tsou Shu-wen — Tsou Shu-wen, "Li-chi Yüeh-ling pien wei", 鄒樹文, 禮記月令辨僞, in *Nung-yeh i-ch'an yen-chiu chi-k'an* 農業遺產研究集刊 1 (1958), pp. 183–214.

TLSI — *T'ang lü su i* 唐律疏義 (Shanghai, Commercial Press, 1929; Wan-yu wen-k'u, no. 0248).

TLT — *T'ang liu-tien* 唐六典 (anastatic reprint of the Konoe 近衛 edition of 1724 by Kyoto Imperial University, 1934; Taiwan reprint).

T'ung tien — *T'ung tien* 通典 (Chekiang shu-chü ed. of 1896).

Tz'u t'ung — Chu Ch'i-feng, *Tz'u-t'ung*, 朱起鳳, 辭通 (Shanghai, K'ai-ming shu-tien, 1934).

Uchida — Uchida Tomoo, *Yakujū Chūgoku rekidai keihō-shi*, 內田智雄, 譯注中國歷代刑法志 (Tokyo, Sōbunsha, 1964).

Vandermeersch — Léon Vandermeersch, *La formation du légisme; recherche sur la constitution d'une philosophie politique dans la Chine ancienne*. Publication de l'Ecole française d'Extrême Orient, vol. LVI (Paris, 1965).

Vandermeersch, "Procédure" — ———, "Le développement de la procédure écrite dans l'administration chinoise à l'époque ancienne", in D. Eikemeier and H. Franke, eds., *State and law in East Asia; Festschrift Karl Bünger* (Wiesbaden, Harrassowitz, 1981), pp. 1–24.

Vogel — Kurt Vogel, *Neun Bücher arithmetischer Technik*. Ostwalds Klassiker der exakten Wissenschaften, Neue Folge, Band 4 (Braunschweig, F. Vieweg & Sohn, 1968).

von Dewall, *Pferd und Wagen* — Magdalena von Dewall, *Pferd und Wagen im frühen China* (Bonn, Habelt, 1964).

Wang Jen-chün — Wang Jen-chün, "*Shuo-wen chieh-tzu yin Han lü ling k'ao*," 王仁俊, 說文解字引漢律令考, in *Kuo hsüeh* 國學, *Sinologists' Monthly* I/i and 2 (Shanghai, Ta-tung shu-chü, 1926; reprinted Taipei, Chin hsüeh 進學 shu-chü, 1970); separate paging for each article).

Wang Kuang-yung — Wang Kuang-yung, "Feng-hsiang-hsien fa-hsien Yü-yang-kung t'ung ting", 王光永, 鳳翔縣發現羽陽宮銅鼎, in *Kaogu yü wenwu* 1981/1, pp. 44–47.

Wang Kuo-wei — Wang Kuo-wei, *Liu sha chui chien*, 王國維, 流沙墜簡 (Kyoto, Tōzan Gakusha 東山學社, 1914).

Wang Li-ch'i — Wang Li-ch'i, *Yen-t'ieh lun chiao chu*, 王利器, 鹽鐵論校注 (Shanghai,

	Ku-tien wen-hsüeh ch'u-pan-she, 1958).
Wang Yü-ch'üan	Wang Yü-ch'üan 王毓銓, "An outline of the central government of the Former Han Dynasty", in John L. Bishop, ed., *Studies in governmental institutions in Chinese history* (Cambridge, Mass., Harvard University Press, 1968), pp. 2–56.
Wang Zhongshu, *Han civilization*	Wang Zhongshu, *Han civilization, translated by K.C. Chang and others* (New Haven and London, Yale University Press, 1982).
Watson, *Courtier*	Burton Watson, *Courtier and commoner in ancient China. Selections from the History of the Former Han by Pan Ku* (New York and London, Columbia University Press, 1974).
Watson, *Records*	———, *Records of the Grand Historian of China, translated from the* Shih-chi *of Ssu-ma Ch'ien* (New York and London, Columbia University Press, 1961; 1962), 2 vols.
Wen-hsüan	*Wen-hsüan Li Shan chu* 文選李善注 (Shanghai, Wen-hua 文化 shu-chü, c. 1925, a lithographic reproduction of the Hu K'o-chia 胡克家 edition of 1809).
Wilbur	Martin C. Wilbur, *Slavery in China during the Former Han Dynasty, 206 B.C.-A.D. 25* (Chicago, Field Museum of Natural History, Anthropological Series vol. 34. Publication 525, 1943; reprinted in Formosa)
Wilhelm, *Frühling*	Richard Wilhelm, *Frühling und Herbst des Lü Bu We* (Düsseldorf, Diedrichs, 1971; reprint of the 1st edition, Jena, 1928).
Wu Jung-tseng	Wu Jung-tseng, "Han hsing-t'u chuan-chih tsa shih", 吳榮曾, 漢刑徒磚志雜釋, in *Kaogu* 1977/3, pp. 193–196.
Wu Jung-tseng, "Ho-lin-ko-erh"	———, "Ho-lin-ko-erh Han mu pi-hua chung so fan-ying Tung Han she-hui sheng-huo", 和林格爾漢墓壁畫中所反映東漢社會生活, in *Wenwu* 1974/1, pp. 24–30.
Wu Jung-tseng, "Shou kung-yeh"	———, "Ch'in ti kuan-fu shou kung-yeh", 秦的官府手工業, in *YMYC*, pp. 38–52.
"Wu-k'u"	"Han Ch'ang-an-ch'eng wu-k'u i-chih fa-chüeh ti ch'u-pu shou-huo", 漢長安城武庫遺址發掘的初步收獲, in *Kaogu* 1978/4, pp. 261–270.
Wu Shu-p'ing, "Chieh-chi"	Wu Shu-p'ing, "Yün-meng Ch'in chien so fan-ying ti Ch'in tai she-hui chieh-chi chuang-k'uang", 吳樹平, 雲夢秦簡所反映的秦代社會階級狀況, in *YMYC*, pp. 79–130.
Yang Hung, "Chia-chou"	Yang Hung, "Chung-kuo ku-tai ti chia-chou", 楊泓, 中國古代的甲冑, in *Kaogu xuebao* 1976/1, pp. 19–46.
Yang Hung, "Chia ho k'ai"	———, "Chia ho k'ai", 甲和鎧, in *Wenwu* 1978/5, pp. 77–83.
Yang Hung, "Chan-chü"	———, "Chan-chü yü chü-chan", 戰車與車戰, in *Wenwu* 1977/5, pp. 82–90.
Yang K'uan, *Chan-kuo shih*	Yang K'uan, *Chan-kuo shih*, 楊寬, 戰國史 (Shanghai, Jen-min ch'u-pan-she, 1955).
Yang K'uan, "Ch'ing-ch'uan"	———, "Shih Ch'ing-ch'uan Ch'in tu ti t'ien-mu chih-tu", 釋青川秦牘的田畝制度, in *Wenwu* 1982/7, pp. 83–85.
Yang Lien-sheng	Yang Lien-sheng 楊聯陞, *Studies in Chinese institutional history* (Cambridge, Mass., Harvard University Press, 1961).
Yang Shu-ta	Yang Shu-ta, *Han shu k'uei-kuan*, 楊樹達, 漢書窺管 (Peking, K'o-hsüeh ch'u-pan-she, 1955).
Yates	Robin D.S. Yates and Katrina C.D. McLeod, "Forms of Ch'in law: an annotated translation of the *Feng-chen shih*", in *HJAS* 41 (1981), pp. 111–163.
Yeh Hsiao-yen	Yeh Hsiao-yen, "Ch'in mu ch'u t'an", 葉小燕, 秦墓初探, in *Kaogu* 1982/1, pp. 65–73.
Yen Keng-wang	Yen Keng-wang, *Ch'in Han ti-fang hsing-cheng chih-tu*, 嚴耕望, 秦漢地方行政制度, 2 vols. (Taipei, Academia sinica, 1961).
Yen Keng-wang, "Lang li"	———, "Ch'in Han lang li chih-tu k'ao", 秦漢郎吏制度考, in *CYYY* 23 (1951), pp. 89–143.
Yen K'o-chün	Yen K'o-chün, *Ch'üan shang-ku san-tai Ch'in Han San-kuo liu-ch'ao*

wen, 嚴可均, 全上古三代秦漢三國六朝文, 4 vols. Peking, Chung-hua shu-chü, 1958; reduced reprint of the Kuang-ya shu-chü edition of 1893).

YMYC — Chung-hua shu-chü pien-chi-pu, *Yün-meng Ch'in chien yen-chiu*, 中華書局編輯部, 雲夢秦簡研究 (Peking, Chung-hua shu-chü, 1981).

Yoneda — Yoneda Kenjirō, "Chōfu yori mitaru Kan-dai kanryō soshiki ni tsuite", 米田賢次郎, 帳簿より見たる漢代官僚組織について, in *Tōyōshi kenkyū* 14 (1955), pp. 81–102.

Yoshida — Yoshida Torao, *Ryō Kan sozei no kenkyū*, 吉田虎雄, 兩漢租稅の研究 (1st ed. 1942; anastatic reprint Tokyo, Dai'an 大安, 1966).

YTCC — *Yen-tzu ch'un-ch'iu* 晏子春秋, in CTCC, vol. 4.

YTL — *Yen-t'ieh lun* 鹽鐵論, in CTCC, vol. 7.

Yü Hao-liang, "Chih-kuan" — Yü Hao-liang, "Yün-meng Ch'in chien so chien chih-kuan shu-lüeh", 于豪亮, 雲夢秦簡所見職官述略", in *Wenshih* 文史 8 (1980), pp. 5–25.

Yü Hao-liang, "Ch'ing-ch'uan" — ———, "Shih Ch'ing-ch'uan Ch'in mu mu tu", 釋青川秦墓木牘, in *Wenwu* 1982/1, pp. 22–24.

Yü Hao-liang, "Nu-li" — ———, "Ch'in chien chung ti nu-li", 秦簡中的奴隸, in *YMYC*, pp. 131–139.

Yü and Li — Yü Hao-liang and Li Chün-ming, "Ch'in chien so fan-ying ti chün-shih chih-tu", 于豪亮, 李均明, 秦簡所反映的軍事制度, in *YMYC*, pp. 152–170.

INDEX OF SUBJECTS AND CHINESE TERMS

INDEX OF LOAN CHARACTERS

Index of loan characters used in the texts translated in the present volume

This list contains usual loans, but also quite a number that are not attested elsewhere, as far as I am aware. Some of these loans had already been suggested in different contexts by commentators to classical literature. I am unable to judge, whether these loans were in general use; I suspect that quite a few of the present cases may be due to the scribes' ignorance, leading them unconsciously to write a homophone for the correct character in the text they were copying. Not being an epigraphist, I cannot vouch for the correctness of the editors' decipherment.

chan 斬 used for *ch'ien* 塹 A 64, n. 15.
chan 毚 used for *ts'ai* 纔 D 11.
che 者 used for *chu* 諸 D 19.
chen 貞 used for *chen* 楨 A 73.
chi 迹 used for *chi* 跡 E. 1.
chi 幾 used for chi 譏 E 3.
chi 及 used for *chi* 急 A 64, n. 5.
chi 耤 used for *chieh* 藉 D 176.
chi 籍 used for *chieh* 藉 A 68.
chi 羈 used for *chi* 寄 A 98.
ch'i 毄 used for *chi* 繫 A 65, n. 3.
chia 叚 used for *chia* 假 A 8.
chia 賈 used for *chia* 價 A 46.
chia 駕 used for *chia* 加 D 1.
ch'iang 彊 used for *chiang* 疆 G.
ch'iao 闕 used for *ch'üeh* 闋 D 21, n. 3.
chieh 節 used for *chi* 即 A 82.
chieh 介 used for *kai* 匃 D 186.
chieh 結 used for *chi* 髻 D 69.
chieh 戒 used for *hsieh* 械 D 105.
chien 堅 used for *ch'ien* 掔 D 106.
ch'ien 千 used for *ch'ien* 阡 D 136.
chih 止 used for *chih* 趾 D 1.
chih 治 used for *ch'ih* 笞 A 70.
chih 直 used for *chih* 値 A 40.
chih 致 used for *chih* 質 A 5, n. 4.
chih 智 used for *chih* 知 A 57.
chih 紩 used for *li* 盭 A 74, n. 9.
chih 支 used for *chih* 肢 D 21.
"*chin*"* 釿 used for *chin* 近 A 68 * *recte chiu.*
ch'in 欽 used for *hsien* 咸 B 6 .
ch'ing 請 used for *ch'ing* 情 E 1.
chiu 久 used for *chiu* 灸 E 20.
chiu 久 used for *chi* 記 D 124.
cho 斲 used for *tou* 鬭 D53.
chou 州 used for *chou* 周 D 84.
chu 朱 used for *chu* 株 E 3.
chu 朱 used for *shu* 銖 B 4.
ch'u 出 used for *ch'u* 屈 C 23b.
ch'u 出 used for *cho* 頔 E 20.
ch'ui 炊 used for *chui* 箠 ? C 17, n. 6.
chün 均 used for *hsün* 徇 D 166.
fa 灋 used for *fei* 廢 A 90, n. 5.
*feng** 尌 used for *shu* 尌 A 1, n. 2. * obviously a mistake.
feng 紂 used for *pang* 綁 or *feng* 奉 A 37, n. 11
fu 膚 used for *lu* 臚 ? A 7, n. 1.
fu 負 used for *fu* 復 B 22, n. 4.
fu 傅 used for *fu* 附 A 64, n. 20.
fu 福 used for *fu* 幅 A 43.
fu 復 used for *fu* 腹 E 23.
*fu** 饅 used for *fu* 負 B 9. * for the additional element see *tsu.*
ho 河 used for *ho* 呵 A 2, n. 10.
hou 矦 used for *hou* 候 A 103.
hsi 棲 used for *ch'ih* 遲 C 22.
hsi 析 used for *hsi* 晳 E 20.
hsiang 襄 used for *hsiang* 穰 A 25, n. 7.
hsing 刑 used for *hsing* 邢 E 13.
hsiao 削 used for *hsiao* 絜 D 15, n. 1.
*hsien** 鮮 used for *su* 穌 G, n. 23. * obviously a mistake.
*hu** 壺 used for *i* 壹 A 10, n. 6. * obviously a mistake.
hui 毀 used for *hui* 毀 A 29. n. 8.
hung 紅 used for *kung* 功 A 35, n. 5.
jo 弱 used for *niao* 溺 E 21.
juan 耎 used for *ju* 濡 E 20.
jung 容 used for *jung* 鎔 E 9.
ken 艮 used for *ken* 根 E 19.
k'en 豤 used for *shan* 犍 or *chien* 艱 A 37, n. 10.
k'en 豤 used for *k'en* 墾 A 1, 3.
k'o 可 used for *ho* 何 D 1.
ku 結 used for *ku* 嫴 A 64.
ku 結 used for *chü* 裾 E 22.
ku 胋 used for *ku* 枯 D 62.
*ku** 醢 used for *ku* 酤 A 6. * unknown.
k'u 秙 used for *hu* 黏 A 25, n. 5.
kuai 夬 used for *ch'üeh* 缺 A 79.
kuai 夬 used for *chüeh* 決 C 4.
le 捋 used for *le* 埒 G.
lei 羸 used for *lei* 絫 A 54.
lei 羸 used for *lei* 累 B 1.
li 離 used for *lai* 萊 ? G, n. 23.
li 立 used for *wei* 位 D 141.
li 藶 used for *li* 曆 or *ti* 藡 or *ti* 荻 A 3, n. 5.
li 荔 used for *chia* 甲 ? A 2, n. 5.
liang 量 used for *liang* 糧 D 174.
lieh 列 used for *lieh* 裂 A 74.
lin 粼 used for *ling* 齡 A 35.

SIMPLIFIED FINDING LIST

Simplified finding list to the pages in SS (the 1978 paperback edition of *Shui-hu-ti Ch'in mu chu chien*) and the corresponding articles in the present work.

SS, page	article	SS, page	article
24–35	A 1–9	171	D 37
35–47	A 19–33	171	D 93
47–53	A 10–18	172	D 34
53	A 35	173–178	D 40–51
54	A 34	178	D 136
55–57	A 42–46	179–183	D 52–59
58–63	A 36–41	183	D 62
64–79	A 47–64	183	D 153
80–83	A 73–77	184	D 60–61
(omitted)	A 78	184–190	D 63–76
84	A 68	190	D 137
87	A 65	191–199	D 77–92
88	A 66–67	200–218	D 94–135
89–91	A 69–72	218–221	D 138–144
92–93	A 90–91	221	D 175
94–101	A 79–89	222–225	D 145–152
101–104	A 92–97	225–235	D 154–174
105	A 107	235	D 176
105–108	A 98–104	236	D 179
108	A 106	237	D 177–178
109	A 105	238–242	D 180–190
109–110	A 108–110	245–246	E 1–2
113–126	B 1–29	247	E 4
127–148	C 1–26	249	E 3
150–168	D 1–33	250	E 5
169	D 35–36	251–278	E 7–25
170	D 38–39	278	E 6

ADDENDA ET CORRIGENDA

p. 35, **A 19**, note 2, add: *Chung-kuo hua-pao* 中国畫報 1983/11, p. 39, contains a brief illustrated article on the excavation of the vast ruins of the Capital Granary, *ching-shih ts'ang* 京師倉 East of Hsi-an; this granary is mentioned in *HSPC* 99C.25b and 28b, *HFHD* III, pp. 460 and 467.

p. 38, line 8 from above, after August A.D. 30 add: (*HHSCC* Ann. 1B.2a).

p. 51, **A 51**, note 13, add:

1 *Kuan fu* is not a general term for government buildings, for that seems to be *kung she* 公舍, as in A 64 the two terms are mentioned side by side.
2 *Kuan fu* is contrasted with an official's private household, *chia shih* 家室 in the essay "How to be a good official", SS, p. 284.
3 *Kuan fu* engaged in commercial dealings and had money at their disposal (A 42, 45, 51).
4 *Kuan fu* loaned official carriages to officials (A 74).
5 *Kuan fu* stored hides (B 18).
6 *Kuan fu* were guarded, *shou* 守 (A 71; D 111).
7 Certain persons, who "worked off" various debts to the government, or holders of aristocratic rank who had let the prisoners they were supposed to guard escape, were made to work in *kuan fu* (A 68; D 51, 106), whereas others were not allowed to do so (A 101).
8 Officials also worked in *kuan fu* (D 136), as did workmen (A 41).

Morohashi, vol. 3, p. 971, under *kuan fu*, has collected a number of examples from traditional texts. In the *Chou li*, *kuan fu* clearly means "government offices" (*Chou li* 1/2, pp. 41–42; *Chou-li chu-su* 2.1a–b (55–56); Biot I, p. 21: "officiers de tout grade"). In the *Tso chuan*, Duke Chao 16 (*Tso-chuan* 47.9b (1924); Couvreur, *Tch'ouen-ts'ieou*, vol. 3, p. 265) a jade ring is said to be "not an object preserved in a *kuan fu*", which Couvreur renders by "magasin public". According to *HSPC* 24B.13a in c. 117 B.C. *kuan fu* were established in connection with the iron and salt monopoly. Miss Swann here translates the term by "administrative offices" (Swann, p. 278), but when *HSPC* 91.2a writes that artisans discussed their technical skills in the *kuan fu*, she renders it by "government buildings" (Swann, p. 416). In the *Mo-tzu*, ch. 70, p. 347, prominent persons are lodged in *kuan fu* during a siege (not in Forke, *Mê Ti*).

From all this I find it hard to reach a definite conclusion; as a temporary solution I suggest "government storehouses", although I am well aware that A 105 mentions *tsang fu* 臧府, "storehouses", and *shu-fu* 書府, "archives". But it seems after all more logical that carriages or hides should be kept in a storehouse than that such things would be available in an office; that these places were guarded and that they had money in their care is another indication. Huang Sheng-chang, "San Chin", p. 39, adds that *fu, k'u, ts'ang* and *lin* 府庫倉廩 were not only storehouses, but also workshops, i.a. for the manufacture of tools.

pp. 52, 53, **A 42** and **45**. Professor J.L. Kroll (Leningrad) has kindly drawn my attention to another instance of the use of the "cloth" in trading. This is to be found in ch. 47 of the *Mo-tzu* (p. 268), where we find "When a merchant uses a "cloth" in his deals, he does not haphazardly buy (things) by means of it; he will surely select a good one". Sun I-jang correctly explains *pu* as a medium of exchange, although he seems to consider it to be a coin. The translators, however, wrongly assume that it is a bale of cloth (Forke, *Mê Ti*, p. 557; Y.P. Mei, *The ethical and philosophical works of Mo-tse* [London Probsthain, 1929], p. 225).

p. 170, **D 154** add:

3 cf. D 62 above.
4 Both the tattooing and the leaving intact imply a hard-labour punishment.
5 *Tang* 當, "to match; to be equal to; to be adequate to"; cf. *RHL* I, pp. 80 and 403, note 268.